Race, Ethnicity, and Education:
What is Taught in School

**A Volume in: International
Perspectives on Curriculum**

Race, Ethnicity, and Education: What is Taught in School

by

Theresa R. Richardson
Ball State University
and
Erwin V. Johanningmeir
University of South Florida

INFORMATION AGE
PUBLISHING

80 Mason Street
Greenwich, Connecticut 06830

Library of Congress Cataloging-in-Publication Data

Richardson, Theresa R., 1945-
  Race, ethnicity, and education in the United States : what is taught
in school / by Theresa R. Richardson and Erwin V. Johanningmeir.
      p. cm. – (International perspectives on curriculum)
  Includes bibliographical references and index.
    ISBN 1-59311-080-4 (paperback) – ISBN 1-59311-081-2 (hardcover)
  1. Multicultural education–Curricula–United States. 2. United
States–Race relations–History. 3. United States–Ethnic
relations–History. 4. Pluralism (Social sciences)–Study and
teaching–United States. I. Johanningmeir, Erwin V. II. Title. III.
Series.
  LC1099.3.R53 2003
  305.8'0071'173–dc22
                                   2003021161

Printed in the United States of America

CONTENTS

SERIES FOREWORD

David Scott, *Series Editor*

The purpose of the series *International Perspectives on Curriculum* is to provide scholarly and authoritative debate about current curriculum issues. The series includes overviews of research in this area, examination of theoretical models and principles, discussion of the work of key curriculum theorists, and the reporting of new empirical research. Contributors to the various volumes in the series are not asked to provide definitive answers to questions that theorists and practitioners working in this field are asking. What they have been asked to do is to critically assess ways of thinking, influential models, and current policy initiatives that relate to the curriculum.

The curriculum is defined in its widest sense, and refers to programs of teaching and learning that take place in formal settings. Examples of formal settings are schools, colleges, and universities. A curriculum may refer to a system, as in a national curriculum, an institution, as in the school curriculum, or even to an individual school, as in the school geography curriculum. The four dimensions of curriculum are:

1. aims and objectives,
2. content or subject matter,
3. methods or procedures, and
4. evaluation or assessment.

Race, Ethnicity, and Education: What is Taught in School, pages vii–viii.
A Volume in: International Perspectives on Curriculum
Copyright © 2003 by Information Age Publishing, Inc.
All rights of reproduction in any form reserved.
ISBN: 1-59311-080-4 (paper), 1-59311-081-2 (cloth)

The first refers to the reasons for including specific items in the curriculum and excluding others. The second refers to the knowledge, skills, or dispositions, that are implicit in the choice of items, and the way that they are arranged. Objectives may be understood as broad general justifications for including particular items and particular pedagogical processes in the curriculum; or as clearly defined and closely delineated outcomes or behaviors; or as a set of appropriate procedures or experiences. The third dimension is methods or procedures, this refers to pedagogy and is determined by choices made about the first two dimensions. The fourth dimension is assessment or evaluation and refers to the means for determining whether the curriculum has been successfully implemented. A range of issues have surfaced and been debated in relation to these four dimensions.

The series focuses on these issues and debates. This volume, *Race, Ethnicity and Education: What is Taught in Schools*, examines the historical origins and significance of race and ethnicity in the United States, in order to develop curricula and pedagogy to address issues of diversity. This series is timely as administrators and policy-makers in different parts of the world have taken an increased interest in education, and as moves to centralize curriculum provision have gathered pace. This has, in some cases, driven a wedge between curriculum theory and curriculum practice, as policy-makers developed and implemented proposals without referring to academic debates about these issues. It therefore seems to be an important task to reassert the need to discuss and debate the curriculum in a critical manner before implementation occurs. This series will attempt this difficult, but much needed, task.

INTRODUCTION

This book addresses the historical origins and significance of the ideas of race and ethnicity in the United States from the colonial period to the present. It is written for future teachers, other professionals who will serve a diverse clientele, and for those who will have children in school in the coming years. Today's schools are different from those we and our readers attended. Every indication is that they will continue to be different. The students are more diverse than they were a generation ago, and that diversity promises to continue to grow. It is also designed to provide an overview of the history of diversity in the United States for those who are interested in seeking a better understanding of how Americans have conceptualized and dealt with race and ethnicity. It is argued that the lack of access to a readable comprehensive history of race and ethnicity in the United States contributes to the hegemonic and reproductive role schools traditionally play in reproducing social class, racial, ethnic, and gender relationships.

Advanced western societies are currently undergoing rapid demographic change. The domain assumptions of the past have been challenged. In spite of significant breakthroughs in science and the development of new technologies, the long held assumption that unequivocal solutions to local, national, and global economic and political problems can be found is increasingly questioned. There is a need to learn to live with and provide for the multiplicity of beliefs and values that charac-

Race, Ethnicity, and Education: What is Taught in School, pages ix–xii.
A Volume in: International Perspectives on Curriculum
Copyright © 2003 by Information Age Publishing, Inc.
All rights of reproduction in any form reserved.
ISBN: 1-59311-080-4 (paper), 1-59311-081-2 (cloth)

terize modern post-industrial societies. This is a challenge and an opportunity for the United States. The nation faces perplexing contradictions between its professed ideals and values on the one hand and its practices on the other—practices that include a history of racial oppression and persistent patterns of class and ethnic inequality. Schools are located at the crossroad of these issues. Other important sites include the workplace as employers and personnel officers address these issues, as do other public service professionals. Finding answers is a practical necessity, especially for professionals in education who face increasingly heterogeneous student bodies. This means pressure to develop curricula and pedagogy to address issues of diversity. In spite of efforts to expand multicultural components in teacher certification requirements and other certification programs, few novice teachers come prepared with even a basic understanding about race or ethnic relations and their implications for teaching.

While there are many texts for courses on diversity and while there is a growing body of work in social history that addresses race and ethnicity, the purpose of this book is to use the specialized works in order to integrate the history of African Americans and other minorities into the mainstream of American history. To a significant extent, it was not until the Civil Rights Era in the 1960s and 1970s that historically subordinated groups received attention. Recent significant historical works such as Theodore Allen's *The Invention of the White Race, Volumes I and II* and legal studies such as *Critical Race Theory* edited by Richard Delgado have not for the most part made it out of their own spheres and into interdisciplinary forums.[1] Many works on multicultural education either ignore history or treat subordinated groups as though they have no history in the United States.

THE NEED FOR HISTORY—
THE STATE OF MULTICULTURAL EDUCATION

In the 1970s and 1980s, multicultural education emerged as an educational solution to demographic and social change and the stubborn inequities entrenched in U.S. society. Multicultural education was supposed to reduce interracial, inter-ethnic, and religious tensions through the reduction of intolerance and prejudice through the exchange of knowledge about other people's lifestyles and beliefs. When Michael Olneck reviewed the status of multicultural education at the end of the 1980s, he declared it a failure in that the curriculum never moved beyond the cultural artifacts approach of intercultural education that originated in the 1930s and 1940s.[2] Multicultural educators who tried to introduce fundamental change in the curriculum and develop new pedagogical strategies were attacked by several prominent traditionalist academics such as E. D. Hirsch, Jr., and historians, Arthur Schlesinger, Jr., and Diane Ravitch.[3] A popular backlash, aided by conservative politicians, felt "family values" and other "American" traditions were violated by the reorientation of school and community toward a pluralistic vision of solidarity. Multiculturalism was argued to be an attack on traditional Anglo-Saxon, Protestant, middle class, male dominated society, and fundamentally subversive to the "American" way. A backlash against legislation from the Civil Rights Era, which continues, has the potential to undo gains in dismantling *de jure* inequality and to cripple efforts to attack *de facto* inequality.[4] Demographic shifts in the 1990s, however, continued to put pressure on policy makers and educators to address cultural diversity in society and in schools in the twenty-first century. Efforts to convince the public that racial oppression was no longer an issue and that colorblindness and a tolerance for subcultures were the answers to differences, it is argued, hinged on the transformation of race into an ethnic category. As the differences between the richest and poorest Americans increases, it again becomes clear that concerns about caste-like minorities persist not just in textbooks. Those differences are social facts.[5]

Current texts do not offer an approach that integrates social and educational issues in order to develop a comprehensive analysis of persistent inequalities, inequalities that are so often associated with race and ethnicity. A commitment to a critical approach that includes a historical perspective that examines privilege and oppression as products of human interaction over times is required. Multicultural education in the United States is commonly taught as an isolated, superficial exercise lacking historical context for both the subject and the object of study.[6] The dominant culture remains the subject and minority cultures remain silent objects.[7] At its best this constitutes a relatively safe exercise in reconstruction; at its at worst it is fundamentally reproductive of inequality. Social reconstructionists are increasingly demanding courses that teach social justice in active opposition to racism, sexism, and class bias.[8] These critical approaches to cultural studies use but do not necessarily emphasize in practice history/genealogy as a vital aspect of the knowledge necessary if students are to acquire tools for critical social analysis that offer the possibility of establishing an integrative and equitable form of social solidarity. Critical race theory and the recent emphasis on white ethnicity and privilege that often do use history, need to be integrated into multicultural education.[9]

An analysis of racial and ethnic discourse as an ever-present factor in the social organization in the United States is essential. Legislation and court decisions may have rendered discrimination on the basis of race, ethnicity, religion, or gender illegal but discrimination and oppression continue. The politics of residential segregation further divide and isolate minorities into cultural and linguistic enclaves away from mainstream society.[10] More significantly, institutional forms of bias and discrimination limit the potential children have to succeed. The dialogue surrounding diversity should fundamentally extend and elaborate the sociopolitical discourse that began with the American Enlightenment on the nature of reason and progress and how societies and states are organized politically by law, custom, and arrangement of power as well as economically and socially. Enlightenment concepts underlying modernity are under fire and in the process of adapting to the needs of a post-modern economy, society, and technology. A global discourse is necessary to address commonality and diversity. This opens the possibility of the construction of classrooms and workplaces that affirm human rights as well as diversity in self-determined communities.

NOTES

1. Theodore Allen, *The Invention of the White Race, Volumes I: The Origin of Racial Oppression and Social Control* (New York, Verso, 1994, reprint 2000; Theodore Allen *The Invention of the White Race, Volumes I: The Origin of Racial Oppression in Anglo-America* (New York, Verso 1997); Richard Delgado, ed., *Critical Race Theory: The Cutting Edge* (Philadelphia: Temple University Press, 1997, 1999).

2. Michael Olneck, "The Recurring Dream: Symbolism and Ideology in Intercultural and Multicultural Education," *American Journal of Education* 98, 2 (1990): 147-174.

3. Arthur Schlessinger Jr., *The Disuniting of America* (New York: Norton, 1992); Arthur Schlessinger Jr., "The Disuniting of America: What we All Stand to Lose if Multicultural Education Takes a Wrong Approach." *American Educator* 15, 3 (1991): 14, 21-33.

4. Gary Orfield with Carole Ashkinaze, *The Closing Door: Conservative Policy and Black Opportunity* (Chicago: University of Chicago, 1991); Gary Orfield et. al. *Dismantling Desegregation: The Quiet Reversal of Brown v the Board of Education* (New York: New Press dist. W.W. Norton & Co. 1996).

5. William Julius Wilson, *When Work Disappears: The World of the Urban Poor* (New York: Knopf, 1996); John Ogbu, *Minority Status and Schooling: A Comparative Study of Immigrant and Involuntary Minorities,* 1991); Douglas S. Massey and Nancy Denton, *American Apartheid: Segregation and the Making of the Underclass* (Cambridge, MA: Harvard University Press, 1993); Jean Anyon, *Ghetto Schooling* (New York: Teachers College Columbia, 1997); Lois Weiss and Maxine Seller, *Beyond Black and White: New Faces and New Voices in U.S. Schools* (Albany, NY: State University of New York Press, 1997); Henry Giroux and Peter McLaren *Between Borders: The Politics of Cultural Studies* (New York: Routledge, 1994).

6. Olneck, "The Recurring Dream;" Christine E. Sleeter, *Multicultural Education as Social Activism* (New York: State University of New York Press, 1996).

7. Lisa Delpit, "The Silenced Dialogue: Power and Pedagogy in Educating Other People's Children," in Lois Weiss and Michelle Fine, eds., *Beyond Silenced Voices: Class, Race and Gender in United States Schools* (Albany, NY: State University of New York Press, 1993).

8. Sleeter, *Multicultural Education;* Giroux and McLaren, *Between Borders;* Noel Ignatiev and John Garvey, eds., *Race Traitor* (New York: Routledge, 1996).

9. Noel Ignatiev, *How the Irish Became White* (New York: Routledge, 1995); Richard Delgado, *Critical Race Theory;* Karen Brodkin, *How the Jews Became White Folks & What That Says About Race in America* (New Brunswick, NJ: Rutgers University Press, 1994)

10. Massey and Denton, *American Apartheid.*

CHAPTER 1

MYTHS AND HISTORY IN THE MAKING OF RACE AND ETHNICITY

United States' history is commonly portrayed in a series of founding myths about Protestant Anglo-Saxon heroes and expanding frontiers.[1] Frederick Jackson Turner in his classic work, *The Frontier in American History* portrayed the main characters as white males. The frontier, in this view, was a place where white men conquered the wilderness, transformed it into fertile and productive farmland, and achieved their "masculine identity."[2] President Theodore Roosevelt, the Rough Rider, at the beginning of the twentieth century, described the frontier in terms similar to Turner but he added a new component. For Roosevelt, American history was "the history of a series of battles pitched against both native inhabitants and European countries such as England, France, and Spain over the possession of the American continent." The series of battles tested Americans and created "the distinct, exceptional, masculine American character."[3]

Historian Merle Curti reported that the United States was often portrayed as an instrument of history, destined to lead other peoples and nations to a better future.[4] Frontier life was part of this progress, to "civilize" the continent with "plain [white] folk secure in their political free-

Race, Ethnicity, and Education: What is Taught in School, pages 1–23.
A Volume in: International Perspectives on Curriculum
Copyright © 2003 by Information Age Publishing, Inc.
All rights of reproduction in any form reserved.
ISBN: 1-59311-080-4 (paper), 1-59311-081-2 (cloth)

dom and economic opportunity."[5] As early as 1848, Senator Thomas Hart Benton argued for westward expansion into Indian and Mexican territory and on to the Pacific and North to Canada.[6] This expansion is depicted as pure, as untarnished by the corruption of the old world.[7] American exceptionalism manifested its destiny from "sea to shining sea" and bound its restless regions into one nation by the end of its first one hundred years.[8] By the end of the nineteenth century, Benton's defense of domestic expansion was extended, and the nation's interests and vision was beginning to extend beyond its shores. In the nation's second one hundred years the United States expanded its destiny beyond the American continent. As the British Empire's "white man's burden" devolved in the twentieth century, the mantle was assumed by the United States. The idea of the "white man's burden" was popularized in Kipling's poem published by *McClure's Magazine* in 1900. Kipling reflected England's belief in the superiority of its institutions and administrative ability as well as its disdain for the abilities of the cultures and institutions of native peoples in its far-flung empire. The British assumed that the non-British would never overcome their inferiority nor ever gain the capacity for self-governance in a way that would match the accomplishments of the English crown.[9] Curti noted: "white man in taking up the burden of governing darker people, could hardly hope to do the subject races much good." [...Senator Benton] felt "nevertheless obligated to assume the task as a token of his manly athleticism."[10] The image of the United States that was then projected was one of a nation that was young, male, and strong. It was also overwhelmingly white. The American revolutionary heritage as an improvement of the Anglo-Saxon tradition authorized the United States to champion and advance the old world's political potential and to move other nations toward freedom and republican government. This reflected a faith in individualistic democracy as not only good for the United States but also a good to be carried to others.

The problem with these stories is that they are not only untrue but also are not harmless.[11] Yet, most Americans do not think twice about either these stories or the messages embodied in them. What consequences do these beliefs have on our views of the United States as a nation and a people? What consequences do these stories and their messages have for the future of children who are taught overtly or covertly that white male dominance is normal and good; that white folks civilized the continent and that it properly belongs to them exclusively? Historical writing can omit part of the past, distort or transform it. For example, the Civil War has been portrayed in different ways for different regions of the country. Even the early *McGuffey Readers* produced one version for the South and another for the North. After the Supreme Court ruled that racially segregated public schools were unequal and therefore unconstitutional and when desegregation of public education began, textbooks prepared for schools in the North contained pictures of African American and white children in the same setting while textbooks prepared for schools in the South contained only pictures of white children."[12]

At its best, history can bring a people together by reminding them of their common and shared experiences. It can heal. At its worst, history can teach "truths" that privilege some groups and justify demeaning others. It can reproduce and maintain wounds. Distortions and omissions in history at its most damaging can also justify discriminatory actions in the present and insure a future for bigotry. The use of history is addressed in this chapter as well as the questions that are asked throughout this work: Who is an American? How does a person become an American in the United States of America? What is American culture? Who participates fully in American culture? How are these questions and their answers connected to the social constructs of race and ethnicity in relationship to gender, social class, and status?

CULTURAL MYTHS, WHITE IDENTITY, AND THE USES OF HISTORY

In a positive sense myths are "images, or collections of them charged with values, aspirations, ideals, and meaning." In a negative sense myths are what is false about another person's beliefs. One noted American historian observed that: "false historical beliefs are so essential to our culture that if they did not exist...they would have to be invented."[13] Myths are a window on historical reality in that if people believe myths and act on them, they take on their own reality. As W. I. Thomas noted in what Robert K. Merton calls the "Thomas Theorem," what people "believe to be real, is real in its consequences."[14] Myth and reality are often confused in cultural fictions, legends, and stories that permeate all human societies.[15] All human beings live in some way according to norms, social customs, and rules of behavior that are at least partly drawn from oral and other traditions past and present.[16] These mechanisms are essential to the establishment of social continuity, collective identity, and self-understanding.

Collective myths as cultural fictions must be examined seriously because even if they are factually wrong, they are embedded in legal canons, legislation, and public policy as well as norms, mores, cultural traditions, and attitudes. Examining the origins, debates, and rhetoric as well as the historical contexts that create and are created by these myths provides the tools for human beings consciously to control continuing social and political realities. The stakes are very high because even the most pernicious and absurd myths are not easy to dislodge socially or psychologically. While historical claims may be factually false, they may be psychologically true. The psychological truth takes on more significance than the illegitimacy of the claim. The creation of the historical fiction of the biological reality of subspecies of human races along with the idea of white racial supremacy is a case in point. Simply proving that these are contrary to scientific fact, as the human genome project has successfully done in the late 1990s and early 2000s, does not eliminate the racist practices embedded in the social structure of the United States. Disproving stereotypes about people of different cultural, linguistic, or religious backgrounds does not automatically transform social, political, and economic structures that discriminate even if such discrimination is recognized as offensive and is against the law. Examining transformations in the debates over race, and more recently ethnicity, provides insight into the longevity of these ideas and practices as psychological, behavioral, and institutional realities. It also offers choices and avenues for change.

AN OVERVIEW OF AMERICAN NATIONHOOD: THREE ERAS

It is useful to examine an overview of the trajectory of American history and changing concepts of nationhood and citizenship. Michael Lind argued that American history can be divided into three eras, which he described as republics that were: Anglo American, Euro-American, and Multicultural. The first Anglo American Republic began at the end of the American Revolution and took off in 1789 with the framing of the Constitution. It ended with the beginning of the Civil War in 1861. After the Civil War and the failure of Reconstruction, the second era began in 1875 as a Euro American Republic, which ended at the onset of the Civil Rights Era in 1957. After the Civil Rights Movement, or second Reconstruction in the 1960s, a Multicultural era began in the early 1970s and this is the era in which Americans now live. In each of these era's race, culture, and citizenship—what Lind called the "basic building blocks of the nation-state"—have been configured in different ways.[17] In each of these republics Americans, as the nation grew and immigration increased, had to decide who would be considered eligible to become an American and thus participate fully in American society.

The Anglocentric Concept of America

In the *Anglocentric* era to be eligible to be a "real American" one had to be of Anglo-Saxon or of Anglo-Germanic heritage. Those whose heritage was either Anglo-Saxon or Anglo-Germanic were acceptable because it was believed that the Anglo-Saxons had descended from Teutonic tribes in Germany. It was expected and assumed that Americans were Christians, but it was Protestant Christianity that dominated. Catholics, especially Irish

Catholics, Jews, and anyone of African descent, and members of the indigenous Indian tribes of the Americas were excluded. They were in America but were not considered by the dominant group to be truly American. Other Europeans such as the French, Spanish, and Dutch were also excluded. "Americans" eligible to participate in the political creed of federal republicanism that bound the former colonies were limited to a select group. Those outside the group could never really qualify as a legitimate member of the body politic. This may have been what was meant by the term "white person" in the 1790 Naturalization Act passed by the nation's founders. The framers of the Constitution saw themselves as the model for the ideal American citizen. To be an American was to be a wealthy male and a landowner. This ideal has persisted in that those individuals and families who are dominant in the United States tend to be Anglo-European, middle to upper class, Protestant, and male. This configuration can be seen in the boardrooms of corporations, on the floor of the stock market, in the halls of Congress, and on the streets of upper class gated communities, as well as in the ideal-typical structure of the "best" families. The policy-making hierarchies of social and political elites who currently control most of the wealth in the wealthiest nation of the world largely conform to ideals of the Anglo-Saxon republic. The closer a person comes to this ideal the more likely he or she will fare well in American society whether child health, success in school, adult income, or longevity is considered. A person's father's income and social status best predict his or her educational attainment and social status as an adult.

The latter part of the *Anglocentric* era was the period during which race as a scientific theory based on polygenesis was constructed and popularized. It was widely circulated that there were multiple origins of human beings, that the white or Caucasian race was superior and that the other non-white, " red, black, and yellow," races were inferior. In the Antebellum Era (1830-1860) planter class elites and "pseudo-scientists" used claims of the racial inferiority of Africans to argue that slavery was good for inferior peoples, that it should not be abolished, and that slaves should not be freed.

After the Civil War the status and the standing of African Americans, Mexican Americans, Asian Americans, and American Indians were defined and redefined, negatively, positively, then negatively. The process of definition and redefinition, of assigning status and denying status, was a process that developed throughout the nineteenth century and continued into the twentieth. The white population was not exempt. The Irish in the early nineteenth century came to the United States with great sympathy for the plight of African American slaves. Fleeing the Potato Famine, they found themselves impoverished and in a position similar to that of freed blacks in the north. Anglo-Protestants considered the Irish Catholics to be inferior and treated them accordingly. The poor Catholic Irish served as wageworkers, often in conditions equal to and sometimes worse than the conditions slaves endured. However, as the racial politics and curious notions of racial superiority and inferiority developed in the nineteenth century, the Irish were moved from a caste nearly identical to that of the blacks and were assigned a white racial identity.[18]

The Eurocentric Concept of America

The second period, as *Eurocentric*, favored all Europeans, even those formerly considered suspicious such as Catholics or immigrants from southern or eastern Europe. All Europeans were included into an expanded notion of what it meant to be an American. The Anglo-European American consensus emerged after the Civil War and Reconstruction. Concern turned from the Thirteenth, Fourteenth, and Fifteenth Amendments and the establishment of rights for African Americans to the integration of the post-Civil War South into the Union. Northern business elites, philanthropists, and southern leaders sought to construct a sound economic basis for the South, to provide common public education, and to elevate in journalist Walter Hines Page's words, the "forgotten man" of the South, the poor white. During this period new European groups were distinguished from former slaves and non-European populations. The expanded notion of what an American was still emphasized that Americans were white persons. Individuals whose origin was outside of Europe, noticeably Africa, Asia, the Middle East, the Far East, the Pacific Islands, the Caribbean, Latin and South America and indigenous peoples of all continents were all clearly excluded. Reconstruction failed. African Americans' civil rights were not institutionalized and were systematically denied. Segregation was legalized. African Americans were more likely to be excluded than any other identifiable group, but so were others.

As the nation's power and influence expanded through economic development and even through imperialistic expansionism in this period, arguments against including groups from areas of the world outside of Europe as well as people who were seen as Christian (that usually meant some form of Protestantism) grew. The Anglo- European Republic period included the invention and implementation of what has been described as an "overtly racist regime" that began with the enactment of Jim Crow legislation in the South.[19] While African Americans, Asian Americans, and Mexican Americans and other Hispanics were disenfranchised by various direct and indirect means, most white males achieved suffrage. Women finally achieved suffrage when the Nineteenth Amendment was enacted August 26, 1920. Civil rights were also extended to most white persons on a national basis. To be a "genuine American" in this period a person had to be of European extraction and a Christian. This expanded the civic religion to include both Protestants and Catholics. This version of a civic religion was nominally identified as "Judeo-Christian," but, as Lind observed, "in practice [this was] a polite euphemism for pan-Christian" and only reluctantly included Jews after the Second World War. The Anglo-European Republic ended with the beginning of the Civil Rights Movement in the mid-1950s.[20]

The Multicultural Concept of America

The current Multicultural era originated out of the Civil Rights era in the 1950s and 1960s when attempts were made to dismantle white only restrictions, and to end racial inequality, racial segregation, and disadvantages according to race, class, and gender. Lind has argued that the goal of creating a truly colorblind society failed: "A revolution that began as an attempt to purge law and politics of racial classifications and to enlarge the middle-class to include the disadvantaged ended, ironically, with a renaissance of race-conscious government and the political triumph of economic conservatism."[21] Part of the problem with implementing a conception of an ideal America that is more inclusive than it previously has been is the failure to transform conflicting versions of history into an inclusive past that can develop into a common future. Consequently, "culture wars" over multicultural education continue today.[22]

Movements to limit American history to its traditional Anglo-Saxon or Anglo-European version emerged during debates that sought to bring about historical revisions and changes in social attitudes in the still emergent third Republic of Multicultural America. Writing in the midst of the Civil Rights era at the end of the 1960s, diplomatic historian and Stanford University scholar, Thomas Bailey, is a good example. As a respected historian even as he denounced cultural fictions as distortions of fact in American diplomatic history as dangerous and unnecessary, he also expressed doubts about acknowledging a past that he feared might relegate "white man's achievements . . . [to a] subsidiary treatment." Bailey was not alone in his reluctance to open America and to include those excluded from the melting pot into the nation's history. Truly implementing a pluralistic vision of the United States as a nation with many cultures where citizenship is inclusive rather than exclusive remains a subject of debate even if diversity in the population is a fact.

THE MYTH OF RACE AND THE QUESTION OF ETHNICITY

In order to join forces in the struggle for social justice and fairness in society it is necessary to examine the origins and trajectory of the major divisions in American society as formed along what has become a color line, as it is effectively enforced in a land of "freedom." Race and ethnicity are not the same concepts even though they are often used interchangeably. Modern science and DNA technology have demonstrated conclusively that there is one human race. Human beings are so closely related as a species that they are in point of fact of one family. Extraneous differences such as features, hair, skin, eye color are insignificant from a biological standpoint but not so in a social, political, or economic sense.[23]

The aspect of the American dream that is "white" is problematic. The myth of six "races" or "ethnicities" required by all Federal Agencies as of January 1, 2003—American Indian or Alaska Native; Asian; Native Hawaiian or Pacific Islander; Hispanic or Latino/a; White; and Black[24]—are, in fact, neither races nor ethnic groups that share a significant cultural heritage. They are inventions or social constructions. In many ways they are inconsistent with the values of freedom and equity espoused in the nation's originating documents.

The Idea of Race

The imposition of the belief that there are races and the sorting of human populations into categories of difference take on a reality only as they are imposed and enforced by dominant groups over subordinated groups. Noel Ignatiev and John Garvey point out that race and ethnicity do not "occupy the same analytic space and do not exist on a continuum." Race, they point out, is assigned and ethnicity has to do, "at least symbolically," with culture.[25] The concepts do not have a common origin. Race in its modern form originated in the nineteenth century, and ethnicity is a twentieth century formation. Both are relatively new. Oppression is not new; neither is the attempt to create and monitor just institutions through the rule of law.

Theodore Allen used race in another sense. For Allen, it is connected with certain forms of absolute oppression that place one group over another into a caste-like division where the lowest member of the dominant group is above the highest member of the subordinate group.[26] Race in the United States, as practiced with racial slavery in the eighteenth and nineteenth centuries and segregation in the twentieth century, was based on the elevation of "whiteness" into a position of privilege. Thus, the poorest of the whites were led to believe that they were superior to the highest member of the lower group in a caste-like division of whites privileged regardless of their status over black slaves or former slaves. Hence, the formation of perceived white skin as privilege and the ubiquitous black-white division of the social structure in the United States are based on the social and political enforcement of what Allen has described as "racial" oppression.

Racial oppression, as in racial slavery, predated the idea of modern races and modern racism. Racial oppression is not necessarily based on phenotypic differences. In Northern Ireland, the domination of Irish Catholics by English Protestants is not based on skin privilege but can be argued to be a form of racial oppression that has powerful and ancient origins.[27] The Middle East conflict between Israel and Palestine is also drawn along the lines of religion and power differentials based on territorial conflicts. Race in this sense is not a biological term but a political one manifested in social behavior.

The Idea of Ethnicity

Ethnicity, the more recent term, can be self-assigned or imposed as a fluid form of identity that can be manipulated over time by an individual or group. Cultures can and do survive oppression. They can even be created by oppression. As based on culture, ethnicity has to do with both material and non-material aspects of how people live and problem solve. Material culture has to do with things, the objects, artifacts, dress, tools, shelters, technologies, belongings, art, architecture, and property associated with a group or particular identity that is manifested in an objective reality. Non-material culture includes beliefs, what is held to be true; values, what is held to be good or bad; attitudes, what is important and not important; biases, what one is predisposed to like or dislike; and norms, what is considered to be socially acceptable behavior.

Everyone has a culture and participates most often in multiple cultures in a single day from family, to work, to recreation, and places of worship. Institutions such as schools also have dominant and subordinate cultures as well as subcultures. Societies also have multiple cultures and subcultures that are to various degrees coherent and homogeneous or heterogeneous depending on the diversity and shared experiences of the people involved.

All human societies are very much alike in that they serve common basic needs. However, these needs are met in different ways depending on the climate and terrain; availability of materials for building, making tools and clothing; and opportunities for skill building and learning from others. Culture includes one's language, religion, social class or status category, age and gender, mutual history and shared experiences including rituals, ceremonies, and traditions. All cultures have ways to transmit the culture to others either informally by oral traditions and experience or formally such as schooling. Education is the broad category of socialization for life; and schooling is the formal aspect for the teaching of formal skills through specific curricula, pedagogy, and assessment exchanged between a special person or teacher and student.

The Intersection of Race, Class, and Culture

Race, class, and culture are confusing in the United States because while the categories are neither analytically the same nor continuous, they can be imposed in complex ways and complicate each other. Ignatiev and Garvey illustrated this well in the following observation on the bizarre complexity of race and ethnicity as practiced in the United States:

> Black people and traditional southern "whites" share a common speech, religion, music, cuisine, and even ancestry, and probably resemble each other culturally more than any other two groups in this country; ethnically they are one, yet they are divided along "race" lines. At the same time two of the most distinctive ethnic groups in the country are the Hasidic Jews of New York and the Amish of Lancaster County, Pennsylvania; yet in neither case has their insistence on maintaining their unique cultures prevented them from enjoying the rights and immunities of "whites."[28]

What is the relationship between race and ethnicity? All societies have ways to identify and distinguish among different human social groups on the basis of what is taken to be common knowledge or some formal criteria accepted by a significant portion of the society.[29] The practice of distinguishing groups from one another by "race," that is, identifying them by some perceived innate and immutable characteristic such as skin color, is not practiced in most societies. However, the concept of race in the United States and Great Britain is "important to the extent that [it] informs people's actions."[30] Actions based on the belief that personality or psychological characteristics can be explained by one's "race" constitute racism. While the belief that there are races and that there are real and significant differences among them has no scientific basis and thus has no reality, at least for those committed to the traditional canons of scientific inquiry and the kinds of evidence required to satisfy those cannons, it does have a reality as a social construction with the consequence of producing a belief system and pattern of actions that elevate certain groups and discriminate against others. Thus, the study of race or "race relations" by social scientists, especially in the United States and Great Britain, is the study of the consequences of race as social phenomena that determine how people are treated.

Anthropologist Thomas Hylland Ericksen pointed out that: the "ideas of 'race' may or may not form part of ethnic ideologies, and their presence or absence does not seem a decisive factor in ethnic relations." That view is based on the observation that "ethnicity can assume many forms" related to culture, whereas beliefs in race tend to be framed as mutually exclusive categories. However, "ethnic ideologies [also] tend to stress common descent among members," heritage in a family lineage for example. This is similar to rigid classifications of innate racial categories. "The distinction between race and ethnicity is a problematic one."[31] Race especially in the latter half of the twentieth century is confounded with and "studied as part of local discourses on ethnicity."[32]

Education and the Discourse on Ethnicity

In the United States in the field of education, race is indeed part of the discourse on ethnicity. For example, in a text for future teachers Young Pai and Susan A. Adler explain that "ethnicity is not a single trait or a rigid category." For them, "it is a complex of interrelated factors such as nationality, language, cultural tradition and values, racial characteristics (e.g. skin color), religion, socioeconomic status, and educational level."[33] In many current texts, discussions or mentions of ethnicity invariably include or turn out to be discussions of either race or of African-Americans. Robert Miles argued "that race was not a scientific concept and therefore it was a methodological error to treat it as a sociological reality of the same kind as class." Social scientists appeared to have "a choice of using ethnicity and ethnic relations or 'race' and 'race' relations for their field of inquiry." "To some extent, social scientists and policy makers were making a transition from 'race' to 'ethnicity' and from 'race' relations to ethnic relations." That race and racial characteristics are still linked to ethnicity in much of the literature shows that that transition has not been completed. Indeed, there is no reason to believe that it may ever be completed. Even though "race" lost its legitimacy as a scientific concept, its use has persisted in academic, political, and popular discourses, especially in the United States.[34] Indeed, our history reveals that race has been used in many ways by historians, social scientists, and governments and that the practice of moving a people from one racial category to another is not a new social practice.

Race and Citizenship

Race early became entwined with citizenship rights. Most people acquire citizenship as a birthright, but as a land of immigrants, naturalization became a privilege accorded to "white persons." The first states to restrict citizenship to "white persons" were Virginia in 1779, South Carolina in 1784, and Georgia in 1785. In 1790, shortly after the Constitution was ratified, Congress limited naturalization to "any alien, being a free white person who shall reside within the limits and under the jurisdiction of the United States for a term of two years." How is one to determine whether a person is white? Who is to make that determination? The courts made those determinations on a case-by-case basis. The decisions and the criteria employed were certainly not consistent. They changed from time to time or were different from one jurisdiction to another. The criteria were sometimes grounded on naturalistic studies and common beliefs and at other times they were based on what was taken to be "scientific evidence," on false concepts of biology. The determination for any given group was unstable. Individuals from India, Syria, and Arabia have been legally white and not white.[35] Stereotypes of Chinese in California were initially based on stereotypes of African Americans.[36] The court argued that the Chinese were ineligible for citizenship because their heritage was similar to that of the American Indians, who had descended from people from Asia. In 1878, the courts described the Chinese as "Mongolian," and determined that this was a "not-white" category. The Chinese gained the right to naturalization in 1943 before the white only restriction was lifted from the naturalization laws. Individuals of African descent were allowed to become naturalized citizens in 1870 even though the naturalization law still specified "white-persons" only. Mexicans were early identified with the Spanish and were thus a white nationality. Mexican identity went from being a national identity to a racial identity.[37] As Ian F. Haney López noted: "we live race through class, religion, nationality, gender, [and] sexual identity."[38] As concepts of race are dismantled as false and unstable, ethnic identities and the concept of ethnicity come into play as a social category used, in some instances, as a way to subordinate some groups and to assign privilege to others.

The Politics of Ethnic Groups and Ethnicity

Clearly, ethnic and ethnicity are related, but social scientists seem not able to say exactly how they are related. There is no universal agreement about the definition of either ethnic or ethnicity. For example, Ross McCormack reported that sociologists frequently cite the observation that Vilfredo Pareto made over fifty years ago that the term "ethnic" is one of the most vague used in sociology. "We use it merely to designate a state or fact, going in no sense into the question of explaining the fact." Apparently there has been little change in the intervening half century. Certainly, the present debate has not produced a theoretical consensus. In a recent article Manyoni warns: "We do not yet have a reliable definition of ethnicity from which generalizations about ethnic groups can be made."[39]

That the original meaning of ethnic was heathen is, however, suggestive. Dominant, invading, and colonizing peoples typically saw indigenous groups as heathens or savages who needed to be converted, conquered, or expelled. For example, as Robert Hughes has observed, the notion that the indigenous peoples of the Americas had a right to their homeland was not even considered by European invaders.[40] If native peoples were not immediately expelled, they had to be controlled either through force or through conversion. Typically, heathens were not acceptable as they were. More often than not the visitors or the colonizers viewed indigenous peoples as people who either did not dress and needed to or did not dress properly and people who did not study Scripture. For example, "The early explorers in the south painted the portraits of the Southeast Indians as royalty and nobles, placing upon their impressive physiognomy the mark of European aristocracy and dressing them in the clothing of the courts."[41] However, how indigenous peoples are portrayed often depends on the space they occupy or their proximity to those of the dominant class. For example, the settlers of New Zealand tended to view the Maori in romantic terms while they were "away on their reservations" and considered them as "bearers of a poetic cosmology equaled only by the Greeks" However, once the Maori were close by in town, "they sank to the position of colored proletariat, carrying all the stigmata that Europeans accord people who have lost their relationship to their previous tribal status and differ in physique from the European colonizers,"[42] In a curious but very important way the modern (nineteenth and twentieth century, especially twentieth century) use of "ethnic" retains some of its original meaning.

Social scientists and historians have acted as agents of the dominant class and clearly distinguished who did and who did not belong to the dominant class and those who did not belong to the nation.[43] Until relatively recently, indices of texts provided no reference to "ethnicity" but did contain references to "ethnic groups." Often, those references instructed the user to see also one or more of the following: 'Negroes,' immigrants, Indians.[44] Ethnic groups were different, peculiar, not full participants in mainstream society. They were assigned minority or inferior status in society. Ethnic groups were those who were not yet assimilated into the mainstream, those who had not yet been transformed in the "melting pot."[45]

When an ethnic group is the object of one's inquiry," ethnic" is an adjective. "Ethnicity," like "ethnics,"[46] however, is a noun. While not denying the vast literature on ethnic groups and its importance, here the focus is on the noun "ethnicity" and the significance of its relatively recent appearance and use in Western nations, especially as it relates to African-Americans who up until a half-century ago, were described as members in a non-white color-caste identity. While so assigned to a caste defined by the color line, African Americans were commonly identified as "Negroes" or as "colored." In the 1950s during the Civil Rights and the Black Power Movements Americans of African heritage for the first time designated their own collective identity as African American, Afro-American, or "black."[47] It is no longer appropriate to use the terms "colored" or "Negro" except in a historical sense. The designation of black counters the ubiquitous "white" Anglo-European identity that formerly was privileged as eligible for citizenship as specified in the 1790 Naturalization Law. "African-American" an ethnic-like title of origin and culture has been the most appropriate designation since the 1970s. This is significant in that a population that was formally assigned a caste or caste-like status acquired the right to self-identify within the framework of an ethnic category. It is also significant that since the 1970s, African American Studies began to appear in American colleges and universities as a field recognizing the long history and significance of America's African heritage.[48]

Then What is White? And Other Questions

Scholars began to question the other side of the binary division of black and white in the 1990s and to ask: What is whiteness? Cornell West has questioned the political processes where designations of race and ethnicity enter daily discourse. He describes "whiteness" as "a politically constructed category parasitic on 'Blackness.'"[49] White has been legally constructed on the basis of a double negative, not being constructed as not white.[50] "Whites" are people who are "not-black," that is "not people of color." Dean MacCannell in his study of language explored the way that groups in power are able to define themselves in terms that avoid being identified as ethnic.[51] They are "less ethnic" than those over whom they exercise power. To be a white ethnic has historically been a negative identity, an obstacle on the path to becoming "normal," meaning just "white." The traits and values of white culture are seen to be valid, correct, and universal while the traits and values of other cultures are seen as alien, only "others" have "ethnic" qualities.[52]

The ascendance and use of "ethnicity" and the new meaning assigned to it constitute a transvaluation of values and ideas. Its ascendance and use are intricately related to the attempts to solve, especially in the United States but also in Great Britain, what has been typically viewed as the "race relations" problem in the social sciences and public policy. The prominence of ethnicity in social scientific literature and in literature designed to educate and train social service workers of all sorts, especially public school teachers, can be viewed as the abandonment of one question or problem in favor of another. As John Dewey observed long ago, "We do not solve them [old questions]: we get over them."[53] New questions take the place of old questions and perhaps, with some qualified success, new questions present new alternatives. In this instance "ethnicity" has been put in the place of the "race relations" problem.

According to Dewey, the belief "that all the questions that the human mind has asked are questions that can be answered in terms of the alternatives that the questions themselves present" is but a "hallucination." The fact of the matter, he argued, was that "intellectual progress usually occurs through sheer abandonment of questions together with both of the alternatives they assume—an abandonment that results from their decreasing vitality and a change of urgent interest." New questions present not only new alternatives or new answers but also indicate a "changed attitude of endeavor and preference."[54] The increased attention given to "ethnicity" since the post-World-War-II era, when it grew in "political importance in the world,"[55] is indicative of a realization that earlier conceived and proposed solutions to the "race relations" problem did not and could not work. A new question and a new "preference," a new conception of how American society functioned, were urgently needed. Consequently, melting pot and assimilationist constructions gave way to multiculturalism, cultural pluralism, and countless discussions of "ethnicity."

CHANGING BOUNDARIES OVER TIME

That, "in every day language," as Eriksen has related, "ethnicity still has a ring of 'minority issues' and 'race relations' requires a consideration of the scientific basis for attaching importance to race and to race as a social construction. Modern geneticists recognize that the alleged differences among the "five races" are false, "for it would be meaningless to talk of fixed boundaries between races" because "there has always been so much interbreeding between human populations" and "the distribution of hereditary physical traits does not follow clear boundaries."[56] That is to say that variation within a given group is invariably greater than the variation between groups.[57]

While ethnicity and race are related and associated, ethnicity as a construction can be distinguished from that other construction—race. The ascendance of ethnicity in the literature and its popularization are subsequent to, if not contemporaneous with, movements that emphasized that black was beautiful, the need for black pride, and black power. Indeed, ethnicity may be seen as a substitute for race. For example, when Glazer and Moynihan examined those ethnic groups who had not been successfully amalgamated in the "melting pot," they included "Negroes" along with "Puerto Ricans," "Jews," "Italians," and the "Irish."[58] African Americans were then not seen as members of a caste or caste-like group. Ethnicity legitimates the creation of African-Americans as an ethnic group with status equal to that of other ethnic groups. While this development may be viewed as an endorsement of pluralism or multiculturalism, it may be just another way to draw the line between the dominant group on one side and the subordinated groups on the other.

The concept of ethnicity began to change in the 1970s and by the end of the 1990s "ethnicity" did not necessarily imply any sense of limitation, though the earlier sense of it as a barrier was there at a tacit, if not sometimes an explicit, level. But that is a one-way transaction. Ethnicity may be assigned or ascribed by others but it is also created by those who have it;

and those who have it, or belong to an ethnic group can say who does and does not have it, or who does or does not belong. Indeed, it had a new and favorable connotation, certainly not necessarily a pejorative connotation. It was used to convey "a sense of peoplehood," something with which people could identify and something in which they could take pride. The transformation of its meaning and its attachment to multicultural education signify that somehow racial groups or people of color were being transformed into ethnic groups. Writing at the end of the 1970s, Maurice Craft and Alma Craft observed:

> It may be significant that what we began the decade by calling 'multi-racial' education is now known as 'multicultural' (or 'multi-ethnic') education. The rise of ethnicity, a sense of peoplehood, is a world-wide phenomenon, fuelling social and political movements in the way that nationalism did in the past.[59]

Significantly, it was a rapid transformation. The Crafts reported that there was no "mention of multicultural education" in "the three-volume review of British research in education by Butcher and Pont published between 1968-73." However, by 1981 "multicultural education ha[d] come to attract a good deal of attention professionally, academically and politically." Journals were devoting entire issues to multicultural education and in 1981 *The World Yearbook of Education* was devoted to multicultural education. Yet, as has been observed as late as 1999, "race and ethnicity appear conflated, if not confused, in many discussions which are not entirely free from the earlier legacy of writing on race and culture."[60] The legacy of race as invented and reified in the past shapes the present, but the mythologies of the past do not have to shape the future. Americans can shape their future. It is not determined.

The configuration of race and culture, ethnic relations, and the changing meanings of ethnicity today have ancient origins in the history of western civil society and particularly in European colonialism in the Americas. How did an Anglo-Saxon, patriarchal, Protestant heritage and middle to upper class ideology became the dominant ideal for the United States? This configuration is perpetually contested and defended in the politics of white identity. American concepts of exceptionalism and privilege extend back into English history. English travails are a source of our ideology and governance system as well as the ethnic and racial divisions both within the dominant culture and between the dominant culture and traditional subordinate cultures. The early conquest of the Americas by Europeans who were not of Anglo-Saxon heritage, as most Americans today are not, created ethnic and cultural divisions that, at various times were racialized, meaning that they were configured as immutable innate categories of superiority and inferiority.

STRUGGLING FOR SOLUTIONS:
WHO WE ARE NOT, PRETENDING WE ARE

American exceptionalism, as it projects itself as idealized white history, also has a solution that follows from a version of white privilege along the line of race and ethnic identity. It is the myth of colorblindness as the perfect solution to diversity. If the all-white myths of American history are problematic because they leave some people out and distort the character of others, then simply admitting everyone into the myth as an honorary "white person" resolves the contradiction. Colorblindness, as a solution to the all-white version of American history, contends that if white people ignore or cease to see "color," racism and discrimination will disappear. This reverses the observation that myths become reality because they are believed. The logic is that if no one believes the myth, it will lose its power.

The problem is that the myth of race became real because it was acted on. The effect of the myth is embedded in behavior. Refusing to acknowledge the behavior does not dislodge its effect. It entrenches it by hiding it from view. It makes it autonomous in that racial discrimination continues without its supposed cause, racism. It removes the sword from the wound but does not provide a healing process. Unconscious racism wields its own sword. The advantage of this solution for white people is that they are not the victims in the first place and can easily do what is in the very nature of white supremacy, hide behind white privilege. There would be no need to address civil rights issues or recognize diversity either positively or negatively since the problem is dismissed.

Colorblindness is a double-edged sword in a racist society. It demands a kind of uniformity from people designated as "white." It misrecognizes white identity by denying that the white experience is also a lived reality with a great deal of variation. Advocating the dismissal of the reality of collective cultural experiences, identities, and social processes robs all people of their personal histories and it mythologizes the collective American experience in ways that advantage only those who have been accorded high status and are economically secure. White self-interest created the myth of race and made it a lived reality through discrimination and the pervasive racism that was early embedded in American institutional life. It has not always been recognized that these patterns of behavior embedded in American institutions have generally limited rather than advantaged the majority of white people. The immigrants' need to become "white" upon their arrival meant that millions had to lose or deny their culture.

The United States is often portrayed as made up of atomistic individuals who operate independent of larger cultural contexts. Such views make it difficult to recognize myths such as the fiction that there are inferior and superior groups of human beings and that each group has its proper place in society. In spite of beliefs in the viability of a radical version of competitive individualism as driving society, racial subdivisions (group identities) were believed and implemented in policies that ensured a subpopulation below poor whites for over one hundred and fifty years. Policies of discrimination against working and poor populations, women, children, and people of color, evolved from the origins of the colonial settlement of British North America. They are embedded in social policies and practices. They are domain assumptions in existing law. Ignoring their existence does not make discrimination go away for people on either side of the color line.

The heightened consciousness of the lack of equal opportunity and social justice issues also affected white society. In this way colorblindness has assumed a covert racist form when whites perceive their own inequality in the system and blame the attention given minorities and object to what they believe is reverse discrimination. Many whites believe that the Civil Rights movement solved the problem of white skin privilege. They believe and argue that they did not do anything to create civil rights violations in the first place and resent any "advantages" given to minorities. They too struggle to achieve the American dream and they are not always as successful as they would like. Rather than understand inequalities and limits to opportunity as endemic problems associated with social class stratification and other forms of cultural reproduction that skew distribution as issues of mutual concern that need to be solved collectively, minorities are blamed. Racist ideas persist in new forms. Whiteness is a problematic aspect of American exceptionalism. It is not natural. It is taught and learned.

Colorblindness would work in a society where the constructed concept of race was not a part of the historic past and did not have a practiced present in ongoing relationships. If racial bias and discrimination were not historic facts, colorblindness would automatically be part of the social configuration. Colorblindness was a goal of the Civil Rights movement—a goal that was shared by whites as well as African Americans. It provided an escape route. Unfortunately, it also has the potential for a circular return to that from which it seeks to escape. The solution of colorblindness seems to convey the notion that the problems of inequality, racism, and white skin privilege have been solved. Sometimes this is extended to the claim that now the problem is reverse discrimination. The social and institutionalized aspects of white supremacy are reborn and old myths in new forms appear. These issues remain central to the myth and historical reality of what it means to be an American and are taken up in the following chapters.

OF PATRIOTS

American exceptionalism has sometimes been confused with patriotism but it does not really have anything to do with loving one's country and believing in the United States as a homeland. To the extent that "white" exceptionalism has been used to conquer, limit, and divide citizens of the United States it follows a trajectory that violates the constitutional rights and freedoms upheld by patriots. During various historical eras, such as the Progressive Era at the turn of the nineteenth to twentieth century, nativist ideas about protecting American ideals included exceptionalist principles in the determination of who was a "good" American. Nativists asserted the claim that earlier "true" Americans were morally and intellectually superior as compared to the newer immigrants. The superior immigrants, it was argued, should have the power to act within the authority of the state to regulate internal conformity to establish supposedly "better" lifestyles and beliefs. Those who have subscribed to American exceptionalism have usually but not always viewed being different as a threat to their own well being. Those who appear to be different are often, but incorrectly, seen as un-American.

In the twenty-first century, as global communication and easy, rapid travel have become increasingly commonplace, issues of diversity have become not only national issues but also universal issues. New technologies that provide earthbound human beings views from space remind them that all live together on a small planet called Earth in a vast universe. Yet, human conflicts imperil innocent bystanders as well as those consciously involved in promoting their own self-interests by violent means whether organized by nation states, radical political groups, religious sects, or individual acts. Violence is not only overt but also covert and symbolic. Incredible disparities exist between individuals and groups in the United States as the richest country in the world much less between rich and poor nations. As new colonization, imperialism, and international markets draw everyone closer and show to all what post-industrial technologies can accomplish, they also divide peoples, for the vastly uneven distribution of goods and services from luxuries to basic necessities becomes ever more apparent. Proximity and access to the various media that communicate what others do and have also underscore differences in beliefs, tastes and values that can appear insurmountable if people are not educated about one another and do not learn to listen to one another's stories.

The United States, from its origins, has served as an experiment in the integration of multiple peoples, ideas, values, and cultures from around the world. As a world leader and economic power, the attitudes of the American people as well as government policy are critical forces in the determination of how political, social, and economic opportunities are distributed. The question arises: How do we learn to address and benefit from the rich and textured landscape and culture of the people of the United States as reflecting universal human values? Education must play a central role in this endeavor.

Much of what is discussed in the following chapters is about the formation and significance of race and ethnicity as it is played out in the diverse society of the United States. The role of schooling and educators in furthering the harmful effects of often unconscious views of American exceptionalism built into curriculum, pedagogy, and assessment is of vital concern. American schools have, in the last quarter of the twentieth century, finally legally attempted to educate all children regardless of any category of ability or exceptionality that they may fall under whether physical, mental, social, economic, or political. This has produced the most diverse student population ever witnessed by educators, complicated by new immigrant populations that do not match the American exceptionalist ideal. It is a great challenge.

Some would rather privatize and dismantle public education rather than meet this challenge. The question is whether or not American exceptionalism will divide and segregate children with rationales embedded in the past. If educators recognize the arguments of the past and the solutions that have not been solutions but roadblocks to fulfilling American ideals, we can learn to problem solve together to serve the needs of all children. By doing so we join the ultimate human struggle for the right to pursue lives well-lived under one's own standards. It is possible to live with peace and good will toward others by acknowledging the right to self-determination and mutual cooperation in a democratic community.

The origin of the fascination with and use of racial divisions coincide with the earliest colonial beginnings of the United States of America. They are the historical and thus social creations of our forefathers. The next chapter turns to these beginnings and the Hispanic, Anglo-Saxon, African, and Indigenous American roots of British North America.

NOTES

1.   James Baldwin, "A Talk to Teachers," from an article, "The Negro Child-His Self Image," published in the *Saturday Evening Post*, December 21, 1963. The original was delivered as a lecture on October 16, 1963. On the origins of American Racial Anglo-Saxonism see Reginald Horsman, *Race and Manifest Destiny* (Cambridge, MA.: Harvard University Press, 1981).

2.   Michael K. Johnson, *Black Masculinity and the Frontier Myth in American Literature* (Norman, OK, University of Oklahoma Press, 2002), p. 4.

3.   Ibid., p. 51.

4.   Merle Curti, *The Growth of American Thought*, 3rd Edition (New York: Harper and Row, 1964, original 1943, 1964), p. 642.

5.   Ibid.

6.   Paul Johnson, *A History of the American People*. New York: Harper Collins, 1997, p. 292

7.   Curti, *The Growth of American Thought*.

8.   Frederick Jackson Turner, *The Frontier in American History* (New York: Holt, Rinehart & Winston, 1920, 1940).

9. Curti, *The Growth of American Thought*, 3rd ed. (New York: Harper and Row, 1964, original 1943, 1964) p. 654; Alfred T. Mahan, *The Interest of America in Sea Power* (Providence, RI: Little Brown & Co., 1897), p. 21; John Willinsky, *Learning to Divide the World: Education At Empire's End* (Minneapolis, MN: University of Minnesota, 1998).

10. Curti, *The Growth of American Thought*.

11. Baldwin, "A Talk to Teachers."

12. Nicolas Cords and Patrick Gerster, eds., *Myth and the American Experience* (New York: Glencoe, 1973), see the Introduction.

13. Thomas A. Bailey, "The Mythmakers of American History," *Journal of American History*, LV (June 1968), pp. 5-21.

14. W. I. Thomas, *The Child in America* (New York: Knopf, 1928; New York: Johnson Reprint, 1970). Thomas' observation was cited as the Thomas Theorem by sociologist Robert K. Merton, "The Self-Fulfilling Prophecy," in Lewis Coser, *The Pleasures of Sociology* (New York: American Library, 1980), pp. 29-47.

15. Stephen John Hartnett, *Democratic Dissent and The Cultural Fictions of Antebellum America* (Urbana-Champaign, IL. University of Illinois, 2002), see the Introduction, pp. 1-9.

16. William Graham Sumner, *Folkways: A Study of the Sociological Importance of Usages, Manners, Customs, and Mores, and Morals*. Intro. William Lyon Phelps. (Boston: Ginn & Co. 1940, original 1907).

17. Lind, *The Next American Nation*, p. 11.

18. Noel Ignatiev, *How the Irish Became White* (New York: Routledge, 1996).

19. George M. Fredrickson, *Racism: A Short History* (Princeton, NJ: Princeton, 2002), p. 100.

20. Lind, *The Next American Nation*, p. 89.

21. Ibid.

22. Maurice R. Berube, "The School Culture Wars," in *American School Reform: Progressive, Equity, and Excellence Movements 1883-1993* (Westport, CN: Praeger, 1994), pp. 112-129.

23. The Human Genome Project has proven through microcondial DNA that human populations around the world are so closely related as to genetically be siblings. Only a handful of lineages originating in Africa survived the 150,000 years of modern human existence. As small a group as 20,000 human beings left Africa and spread out across the globe over the past 70,000 or so years. Nicolas Wade, "The Human Family Tree, 10 Adams and 18 Eves, Tracing Human History Through Genetic Mutation," *New York Times*, May 2, 2000, pp D 1, D5; also see "Science Times," *New York Times*, Tuesday, November 12, 2002, p. D1.

24. *Federal Register*, (July 9, 1997), Part II, pp. 36873-36946, available <http://www.whitehouse.gov/omb/fedreg/directive15.html>

25. John Garvey and Ignatiev Noel, *Race Traitor* (London: Routledge, 1996).

26. Theodore Allen, *The Invention of the White Race: The Origin of Racial Oppression in Anglo-America*, Vol. 2 (New York: Verso, 1997).

27. Genevieve Richardson, "Divided Societies: Northern Ireland's Religious Struggles and Racial Struggles in the United States," *International Journal of Educational Policy, Research & Practice* 1, 4 (Winter 2000): 509-529.

28. John Garvey and Noel Ignatiev, "The Editors Reply," *Race Traitor*, 6 (Summer 1996): 37.

29.   In the U.S. the legal construction of race through the courts has also waffled between common knowledge and "scientific" explanations. Neither approach has proved stable and each is based on false premises. Ian F. Haney López, *White By Law: The Legal Construction of Race* (New York: New York University Press, 1996).

30.   Thomas Hylland Ericksen, *Ethnicity and Nationalism: Anthropological Perspectives.* (London: Pluto Press, 1993), p. 4.

31.   Ibid.

32.   Ibid., p. 5.

33.   Young Pai and Susan A. Adler, *Cultural Foundations of Education.* 2nd. ed. (Upper Saddle River, New Jersey: Merrill, 1997), p. 181.

34.   R. Barot, H. Bradley and S. Fenton, "Rethinking Ethnicity and Gender," pp. 3-4 in R. Barot, H. Bradley, and S. Fenton. eds., *Ethnicity, Gender and Social Change* (London: Macmillan Press Ltd. 1969), pp. 1-26

35.   López, *White by Law,* pp. 2-5.

36.   Ronald Takaki, *Iron Cages: Race and Culture in the Nineteenth Century: Race and Culture in the Nineteenth Century America* (New York: Random House, 1979. 1990), p. 101; Dan Caldwell, "The Negroization of the Chinese Stereotype in California," *Southern California Quarterly.* 53 (June 1971): 128.

37.   Richard Delgado and Vicky Palacious, "Mexican American s as a Legally Cognizable Class Under Rule 23 and the Equal Protection Clause," *Notre Dame Law Review* 20 (1975): 393; Gary A. Greenfield and Don B. Kates, Jr., "Mexican Americans, Racial discrimination, and the Civil Rights Act of 1866," *California Law Review* 63, (1975): 662; López, *White By Law,* pp 125-126.

38.   López, *White By Law,* p. xiii.

39.   Ross McCormack, "Cloth Caps and Jobs: The Ethnicity of English Immigrants in Canada 1900-1914," in Jorgen Dahlie and Tissa Fernando, eds., *Ethnicity Power and Politics in Canada* (Toronto: Methuen Publications, 1981), p. 38; Joseph R. Manyoni, *Ethnics and Non-Ethnics: Facts and Fads in the Study of Intergroup Relations* in Martin L. Kovacs, ed., *Ethnic Canadians: Culture and Education* (Regina: University of Saskatchewan, 1978), p. 31.

40.   Robert Hughes. *American Visions: The Epic History of Art in America* (New York: Alfred A. Knopf, 1997), p. 23.

41.   Margaret Mead. *Ethnicity and Anthropology in America* in Lola Romanucci-Ross and George De Vos, eds., *Ethnic Identity: Creation, Conflict, and Accommodation* (Palo Alto, California: Mayfield Publishing Co, 1975), p. 175.

42.   Ibid., p. 176.

43.   It should be noted "nationalism and social science. . . grew out of the same historical circumstances of modernisation, industrialisation and the growth of individualism in the nineteenth century." See: Ericksen. *Ethnicity and Nationalism,* p. 13.

44.   The practice of either equating ethnic groups or linking them to immigrants may have been set by the 1950s if not earlier, by Oscar Handlin, *Harvard Guide to American History.* (Cambridge: Belknap Press of Harvard University, 1954). The index contains no reference to "ethnicity" but there is a reference to "ethnic groups" that instructs the user to "*See also* Immigrants; Indians, Negroes," p. 587.

45.   The first use of "melting pot" in the sense of an experience that assimilated all into one mold may have been Israel Zangwill's play *The Melting Pot,* first performed in 1908. The notion, however, is, as pointed out by Daniel P. Moynihan, "as old as the Republic," for it was J. Hector St. John de Crèvecoeur who wrote in 1782: "I could point out to you a family whose grandfather was an Englishman, whose

wife was Dutch, whose son married a French woman, and whose present four sons have now four wives of different nations. *He* is an American, who, leaving behind him all his ancient prejudices and manners, received new ones from the new mode of life he has embraced . . ... Here individuals of all nations are melted into a new race of men . . .." See: Nathan Glazer and D. P. Moynihan. *Beyond the Melting Pot: The Negroes, Puerto Ricans, Jews, Italians, and Irish of New York City* (Cambridge, Massachusetts: The M.I.T. Press and Harvard University Press, 1963), p. 288.

46.   "In the United States," according to Ericksen, "ethnics' came to be used around the Second World War as a polite term referring to Jews, Italians, Irish and other people considered inferior to the dominant group of largely British descent." See: *Ethnicity and Nationalism* (London: Pluto Press, 1993), p. 5.

47.   At the end of the 1960s, Norman E. Whitten, Jr. and John F. Szwed explained that "Afro-American" is once again being used to refer to a cultural stream, sometimes to an idealized, non-existent, or newly created stream; it also refers to communities of American Negroes involved in cultural revitalization." See: *Afro-American Anthropology: Contemporary Perspectives* (New York: Free Press, 1970), p. 19.

48.   See: Perry A. Hall. *In the Vineyard: Working in African American Studies.* (Knoxville, Tn: University of Tennessee Press, 1999).

49.   Cornel West, *Race Matters.* (New York: Vintage, 1990, 2001), p. 29.

50.   López, *White By Law.*

51.   Dean MacCannell, *Empty Meeting Grounds: The Tourist Papers* (London, New York: Routledge, 1992).

52.   Ibid.

53.   John Dewey, *The Influence of Darwinism on Philosophy* in John Dewey. *The Influence of Darwinism on Philosophy And Other Essays in Contemporary Thought* (New York: Peter Smith, 1910), p. 19.

54.   Ibid.

55.   Eriksen, *Ethnicity and Nationalism*, p. 4.

56.   Ibid.

57.   Nicolas Wade, "The Human Family Tree."

58.   Nathan Glazer and Daniel P. Moynihan, *Introduction in* Nathan Glazer and Daniel P. Moynihan. eds. *Ethnicity: Theory and Experience* (Cambridge, Massachusetts: Harvard University Press, 1975), p. 1. *Ethnicity: Theory and Experience* was based on a conference held in October 1972 at the American Academy of Arts and Sciences in Brookline, Massachusetts supported by the Ford Foundation.

59.   Maurice Craft and Alma Craft, *Multicultural Education* in Louis Cohen, John Thomas and Lawrence Manion, eds., *Educational Research and Development in Britain 1970-1980* (NFER—Nelson Publishing Company Ltd., 1982), pp. 445-446.

60.   Barot, Bradley and Fenton, *Rethinking Ethnicity and Gender*, p. 5.

CHAPTER 2

WHAT IS NOT TAUGHT IN SCHOOL
The Origin of British North America and Racial Slavery

"In fourteen hundred and ninety-two Columbus sailed the ocean blue..."

Christopher Columbus (1451-1506), we are told, discovered America in his tiny fleet of tall ships the Niña, Pinta, and Santa Maria, which led to the founding of the "New World" and the United States of America. Until recently most descendants from immigrants from Europe, Asia, or Africa have given little thought to the validity of the claim that America was "discovered" by Europeans even if it is acknowledged that the discoverers were greeted by representatives of well-established civilizations when they arrived.[1] The dismissal of the first nations of the Americas in founding stories teaches acceptance of European superiority and dominance. Whether the "discovery" should be viewed from the point of view of those who were "discovered"[2] is a question only recently asked. The view to the east, the view of those "discovered," is quite different from the view to the west, the view of the "discovers."

Race, Ethnicity, and Education: What is Taught in School, pages 25–52.
A Volume in: International Perspectives on Curriculum
Copyright © 2003 by Information Age Publishing, Inc.
All rights of reproduction in any form reserved.
ISBN: 1-59311-080-4 (paper), 1-59311-081-2 (cloth)

European colonialism did irrevocably change the world and its people. Columbus' voyage signaled a turning point that was matched in importance six years later by Vasci de Gama's voyage around the African continent in 1498 and his discovery of ocean currents that effectively connected Europe with the African slave trade and the Americas. Columbus set forth from Palos, Spain in behalf of the Spanish monarchy on August 3, 1492. His charter from the Spanish Crown was to discover a shorter trade route to spice-rich India and the "land of the Great Khan" in Southeast Asia and the Orient. However, he landed on a small island in the Bahamas, which he called San Salvador, or the Holy Savior, October 12, 1492. Thinking he had landed in *las indias* [India], Columbus called the Arawak and Carib peoples who greeted him *indios* [Indians].[3] Columbus continued his journey and landed on what is now Cuba, which he mistakenly thought was *cipon* [Japan]. Columbus did not claim to find a new world when he returned to Europe. He died believing he had found a route to Asia. That he had found a landmass entirely new and unexpected in the worldview of Europeans was soon recognized and named.[4]

THE AMERICAS AND THE AMERICANS

The Americas took their European name from Amerigo Vespucci, whose 1501 voyage of discovery was supported by the Portuguese Crown. After landing in South America and returning to Portugal, Vespucci wrote to Lorenzo de'Medici, a wealthy merchant from Florence who was his patron on an earlier voyage. In the letter Vespucci claimed that he discovered a new world. The name, *Amerigo*—America—became associated with all of the continental landmass between Europe and the Far East. Over the next two hundred years educated people who migrated from Europe and settled anywhere from the tip of South America to the forests of North American "began calling themselves Americans to distinguish themselves from their colonial motherlands."[5] The habit by which citizens of the United States call themselves "Americans" and use "America" as synonymous with the United States is not always well received by "other Americans"—from Canada to Chili—who are unwilling to surrender their continental identity.

Canadians, for example, as citizens of North America are "Americans." Citizens of countries that were once part of the colonial empires of Spain and Portugal sometimes refer to their territory as "*nuestra America*, our America, to distinguish themselves from English-speaking America."[6] Identity terms create a complex lexicon. For example: "Latino/a, Spanish speaking, white persons of Spanish surname, Latin American, Hispanic, Hispano, Chicano, Tejano, Mexican-American, Puerto Rican American, Boricua, and Cuban-American" bear witness to the evolution of a complex and often conflicting terminology used in the United States. These terms are often used interchangeably. However, they have specific meanings for particular groups, and no one term accurately defines the diverse populations either in the United States or in the other Americas.[7]

Even identifying general terms and recognized boundaries between the English speaking and non-English speaking Americas is difficult. England uses the term "South America" for territory south of the Rio Grande, the southern border of the United States. This ignores Mexico's North American latitude as well as Central America. British North America included Canada and the United States. Spain prefers the term *Hispano America* with the notion of Hispanism or Hispanismo, as encompassing both Spanish and Portuguese cultures anywhere in the Americas. The concept of hispanism holds that there is something special about Hispanic people that transcends race and gives them a unique culture. At one time Spain preferred "New Spain" for Mexico and *Spanish America* for their Empire. France introduced the concept of *Latinidad* in an effort to gain recognition for Quebec and New France as well as exert more influence over the new nations of the Americas. The concept of Latin is broader than Hispanic referring to countries with a Romance language, which includes France, Spain, Portugal, Italy, Belgium, and Romania. Latin America or Latino/a is the most popular term today but it leaves out indigenous nations, cultures, and languages such as Nahuatl, Maya, and Zapotec.

Iberian or Hispanic Power in the New World

In 1694 Spain and Portugal signed the Treaty of Tordesillas that divided the New World between them. These nations of the Iberian Peninsula, whose languages can be subsumed under "Hispanic" or "Hispano," are often cited as the leaders of the European exploration and conquest of the Americas between the fifteenth and nineteenth centuries. The hegemony of the Iberians is misleading, however, since the English, Dutch, French, Polish and Italians contributed ships, manpower, and finances even when they sailed under the flag of Spain or Portugal. Iberian monarchs, however, were quick to claim sovereignty over the "New World." They did so a century before the French and Dutch came to North America and before the English Crown became an active participant in the Caribbean and on the North American continent. Between 1492 and 1550 Spain claimed the empires of the Maya and Aztecs in Mexico, the Inca Empire in Peru, and what is now Florida, the Gulf Coast Region, Texas, Oklahoma, Kansas, New Mexico, California and Oregon. New Spain spread from North America south through Mexico, Central America and South America. Portugal claimed Brazil and the vast Amazon River basin in East Central South

America. Ponce de León searched for the "fountain of youth" in Florida as early as 1513. Invaders such as Hernando de Soto between 1539 and 1541 and Tristán de Luna between 1559 and 1561, consciously and unconsciously, spread destruction and death from European diseases among the native peoples.

New Spain

Neither Spain nor Portugal was in a position to populate the vast territory they claimed. There were great manpower shortages in the fields and growing urban centers in Europe. Contagious diseases devastated urban populations. Men who survived to become soldiers were immunized against the disease but they became carriers of deadly diseases to the vulnerable populations of the New World. In the sixteenth century wars involved nearly every country in self-defense over land acquired by conquest. The Portuguese, for example, numbered less than 1.4 million and were involved in protecting a world empire from both Moslem and Christian rivals. A total of only 200,000 Spaniards migrated to all of the vast territories of the Spanish Empire. The few individuals who migrated from Europe had no intention of becoming menial laborers on plantations or in gold mines thousands of miles from home.

Spain had the good fortune to land among wealthy advanced civilizations with sophisticated stratified societies of royalty, priests, commoners, peasant and laboring servant classes. The infrastructures for food production, manufacture and distribution of goods; urban centers; temples; codified laws; and the means to accumulate and maintain wealth were already in place. A relatively few Spaniards could take over the reigns of governance in the name of the king and continue to use and adapt the system to their own purposes.[8] Through grants the king bestowed a few chosen Spaniards with legal authority to enforce their rule over large tracts of agricultural land. Laborers were guaranteed through the practice of *encomienda*, which gave the Spanish elite not only the territory but also the right to the labor of the people in the villages within their territory.

Spanish law and Roman Catholic doctrine opposed brutality and advocated the spread of Christianity so that all souls could be saved. This meant that the Spanish language, customs, and faith were enforced and dominated in spite of resistance. The predominance of single male immigrants encouraged sexual laisions and intermarriage with the native population. To various degrees the cultures and peoples blended. A unique cultural heritage from both Europe and the indigenous cultures of the Americas emerged in places such as Central Mexico. A hierarchy of status and power reflected an individual's heritage. Those able to claim direct birth ties to Spain had high status while those with an indigenous heritage were at the bottom of the social ladder.[9]

In other places such as the Caribbean the indigenous population was driven to extinction or near extinction by forced work and the introduction of European diseases. Bartolomé de las Casas, a Catholic Bishop, was horrified at the population decrease among the indigenous peoples of the Caribbean and the barbarity of their treatment under the Spanish regime. He campaigned vigorously against the practice of *encomienda* as well as slave raiding and the trading of the Indian populations among the Spanish authorities. He claimed these populations for the church and placed them under the protection of the clergy. His campaign against the *encomienda* and the enslavement of the indigenous peoples of the Americas was successful. A Papal Bull in 1542 declared that American Indians were human beings. The Indians, as human but heathen, were properly the wards of the Church. The *encomienda* and the enslavement of the indigenous peoples of the Americas was outlawed by Spain in 1542. This had great consequences for Mexico, for its large indigenous population was a valuable labor source. There were significant variations in other regions of the Iberian Empire. Forced migration from Africa added a significant third factor in the population mix of Iberians and Indians.[10]

The campaign against the enslavement of Indians was not a campaign against slavery. Spain authorized a slave trade to New Spain in 1501. Unable to supply their own labor, labor needs intensified in Spanish and Portuguese territories. Consequently, the slave trade grew. In the slave trade and African Diaspora approximately fifteen million people from West Africa became part of a chain of involuntary migration to the Americas. This slave labor population would have been inadequate and unstable without renewed supplies of slave labor. The hardships of slavery ensured that the demand for slaves was continuously renewed.

As the population of enslaved Africans increased so did the population of free Africans. If slaves survived, they could marry, have a family life, and purchase their own freedom. Access to self-determination varied widely. A growing free African population countered racialized classifications of free and unfree, citizen and non-citizen. Slave populations, free populations and mixed heritages of European, indigenous, and African presented an array of statuses. A rigid caste or caste-like system did not develop. Portraits of families show indigenous and African women, with European men and their children, representing the acceptance of ethnic mixing. "By the middle of the seventeenth century, *castas*—all free men and women of mixed ancestry—were the largest population sector in most urban centers and mining camps in Iberian colonial society."[11]

The Spanish and Portuguese empires in America were multicultural, multiracial, and multiethnic from their origin. The concept of race, *la raza,* was not ever considered an absolute biological classification and did not have any distinct biological markers. Their populations remained diverse and did not represent one language group, religion, social class, or ethnic affiliation but included indigenous populations, Europeans, Africans, Asians, and, to various degrees depending on the region and nation mixes of these groups. While Roman Catholicism was the dominant religion, many of the immigrants after independence in the early 1800s were Protestant, Jewish, or Muslim.[12]

ENGLISH EXCEPTIONAISM AND THE REPRESSION OF THE IRISH

English colonialism differed greatly from the efforts of other European powers largely because of the special demographic position England enjoyed by the sixteenth century. It had a surplus population instead of a shortage of possible colonist-laborers. In part, this came about because of England's unique history of colonialism. England's oppression of Ireland began one hundred years after William the Conqueror, a Norman from what is now France, conquered the Angles and Saxons in the eleventh century. The Normans, like the later Spaniards, could not populate "Angle-land" with their own people. Like the Spanish, they adapted to the indigenous populations while maintaining their own position of superiority.

The Normans did not impose a French culture on the Anglo-Saxons but were assimilated into the language and customs of the people they defeated. They took a similar tactic in Ireland. Norman noblemen and their progeny took over the crown of the Anglo-Saxon kings and formed a hierarchy of power that descended from the nobles of Norman heritage to the lowest Anglo-Saxon peasant. The elite of this hybrid system of conquest pacified its motley constituency through an innovative use of structured governance institutions and power sharing. The nobles established a number of institutions that became the basis for modern republican governments:

1. The authority of English Common Law was established and is the basis for the legal systems of Canada, Australia and the United States.
2. They wrote the Doomsday Book, which set rules for the taxation of property in order to pay for the cost of governance.
3. They chartered civil rights in the Magna Carta, though they limited such rights to the upper classes.
4. Finally, they created royal courts to settle disputes and the parliament to make laws.

These institutions formed the foundation for the belief in the superiority of Anglo-Saxons as a civilized people ruled by law and destined to rule others. The Irish were the first to feel the ethnocentrism built into this perspective. The Normans sent envoys to Ireland to conquer the Celts in the twelfth century. The envoys from England largely assimilated into Irish Celtic culture while they maintained themselves as a caste above the Celtic Irish chiefs.

Given that the English prized their civil institutions as superior to the "savage" Celts, the repression of the Irish was harsh and unrelenting. The Irish were considered inferior. Consequently, they were not allowed to be citizens. The English prohibited marriage between the Irish and the English. The Irish could not bear arms on pain of death. They could not own land, hold office, or bear witness in a court of law:

> . . . every Irishman shall be forbidden to wear English apparel of weapon upon pain of death. That no Irishman, born of Irish race and brought up Irish, shall purchase land, bear office, be chosen of any jury or admitted witness in any real personal action.[13]

In 1327 the Irish chieftains led by Donal O'Neill, King of Tyrone, produced a manifesto that the kings of England and Anglo-Norman "middle nation" enacted "for the extermination of our race most pernicious laws."[14] The trials of the Irish, who were converted to Roman Catholicism before the English, were not to lessen but to increase with the English Reformation two hundred years later.

English Exceptionality: Surplus Labor

A century before England founded its first colonies in North America a wholesale change took place that transformed England from a feudal agrarian society to one based on the cloth making industry and merchant capitalism.[15] England's move toward capitalism was fostered by the rise of a strong monarchy and central control over a naturally protected territory. England's relative isolation as an island protected it from the wars and diseases that decimated European populations at this time. Crowding in England, on the other hand, put a premium on land use. The population of the British Isles was growing so labor was plentiful. Technological developments contributed to improved means of navigation and improved waterpower to run textile mills. Another growth factor was the placement of the cloth making mills in rural settings away from the strong urban guilds that protected workers.[16] The need for wool to run the mills made pasture land for sheep more valuable than cropland. As the land devoted to pasture was increased, peasants who once worked the land were cast adrift. The growing surplus population grew even greater due to the years of plenty that supported a population that increased from 1.3 million to 4.1 million in the last six decades of the sixteenth century. Peasant uprisings grew more violent. As English historian R. H. Tawney noted:

> Reduced to its elements their complaint [was] a very simple one, very ancient and very modern...[the peasants'] property [was] being taken away from them... [and] to them it seem[ed] that all the trouble arose because the rich [were] stealing the property of the poor.[17]

The English Reformation

The English Reformation set off by King Henry VIII in the mid sixteenth century shaped the trajectory of British colonialism in Ireland as well as in the New World. King Henry VIII petitioned the Catholic Pope in Rome to annul his marriage. The Pope refused. On the advice of his associates, Henry proceeded to defy the Roman Catholic Church. Henry established the Anglican Church with himself as its head and declared it heresy to belong to any other church. This began the English Protestant Reformation that resulted in bloodshed and repression over religious diversity that eventually sent the Pilgrims and Puritans on their way to North America. It also gave Henry VIII access to the rich holdings of the Roman Catholic Church in England and Ireland.

The break with Roman Catholicism had three consequences. The first was that it was an economic bonus to the English crown in that it gave the monarchy access to the substantial wealth of the Church. Between one sixth and one third of the land in England was owned by Roman Catholic enterprises such as monasteries, nunneries, and abbeys. The Catholic Church also controlled land occupied by a large peasant population. The second consequence was that it released another wave of peasants from their traditional ties to the land and Church. Third, the Irish who had been Christianized by St. Patrick before St. Augustine in England, embraced the Catholic Church and refused the Anglican alternative. Henry was determined to confiscate the property of the Irish Roman Catholic Church as well as England's. This required exercising greater centralized control over Ireland and the imposition of English law and practices, including Protestantism. The Irish were to rebel and lose.

When Henry VIII died he left the throne to Edward I, who was ineffective in pushing through his father's unwieldy religious and political changes. Edward I was succeeded by his sister Queen Mary I, a Tudor who was estranged from her father. She was called Bloody Mary due to her efforts to undo her father's Protestant Reformation and return England to Roman Catholicism by eliminating the Heresy Acts. In 1558, Elizabeth I, the so called Virgin Queen because she never married, took the throne and the Elizabethan Age began. Elizabeth abolished allegiance to the pope once again. Pope Pius V excommunicated her in 1570. Civil unrest grew in England, but Ireland took the brunt of Elizabeth's considerable will in this Golden Age of the English monarchy.

From Henry II to Henry VIII, the Irish were considered beyond the English "Pale." Queen Elizabeth took up the task of forcing Irish submission to English ways. She moved to subdue Ulster by force in Northern Ireland in the mid 1560s, but the Irish struck back in Shane O'Neill's Rebellion in 1573 and Desmond's Rebellion in 1579.[18] Elizabeth's response to resistance to her will was overwhelming and the brutality was deliberately monumental. Villages and crops were burned. The Irish were put on "reservations" and no "man, women or child" was spared. Heads of the beheaded became trophies and were impaled on the walls of Dublin. Sir Humphrey Gilbert ordered that the severed heads of the Irish be "laid out upon the ground" before the tents of the families so that the mothers, fathers, and siblings of the victims would have to pass by the horrific sight so that they would be terrorized into compliance.[19] One Englishman described the effects of the slaughter on those that survived in ghastly terms. In their defeat the Irish came "out of every corner of the woods and glens. . . creeping forth upon their hands, for their legs would not bear them. They looked the anatomies of death; they spake like ghosts crying out of their graves."[20] The English claimed that "nothing but fear and force can teach duty and obedience" to the rebellious "savage" Irish. Contrary to the common lore of tribal savagery, the English were the perpetrators of the atrocities they attributed to their victims.[21] The lessons were learned and passed along. The men who gave the orders against the Irish in the name of the English Crown included the first explorers and colonizers of British North America, including Sir Humphrey Gilbert, Lord De La Warr, Sir Francis Drake, and Sir Walter Raleigh.[22]

Queen Elizabeth I drove the Irish chieftains out of Ireland in the Tyrone War (1594-1603) just before Jamestown was settled in North America. Non-racial co-existence ended and the Irish became an unwanted stigmatized population in their homeland. English Protestants who ascended to power in Ireland regarded the Irish as "enemies to God and man and indeed as a race of savages who were a disgrace to human nature."[23] The Irish were not formally slaves. However, when the English tried to establish the first plantation society in Ulster, Northern Ireland, consideration was given to enacting slave laws between 1571 and 1575. England looked elsewhere to make use of its unwanted populations. A precedent was set that differed from the experience of the Spanish and Portuguese whose colonies exploited but also, to various degrees, assimilated indigenous peoples. The English refused assimilation and were prepared to annihilate those who were not compliant especially since they did not require their labor.[24]

FOUNDING BRITISH NORTH AMERICA

The English Crown was late in the competition to claim the Americas. In the late sixteenth century it was still unknown if there was a passage to the North that would provide access to the riches of Asia. Leading up to the founding of Jamestown, the first permanent settlement in North America, the English Crown under Elizabeth I sent Sir Humphrey Gilbert on a mission to find a Northwest Passage and to indulge his dream of colonizing North America. In 1578 he was granted a patent. He was to occupy "barbarous and heathen land" and share any profits from his trade with the English Crown, should he reach the Orient. The settlers of Gilbert's colony were to retain their rights as English citizens. Sir Gilbert disappeared in the North Atlantic in 1583 and was never to be heard of again.

In 1584, Gilbert's half brother, Sir Walter Raleigh, was given a patent named after the "Virgin Queen" to follow his brother's path and establish a colony called Virginia in North America. Raleigh landed on the North Carolina coast and surveyed Roanoke Island. Raleigh returned a year later with 600 men, many of whom were veterans of the wars against the Irish. They raided Spanish colonies for supplies and headed north to find the Northwest Passage. Governor Ralph Lane remained in Roanoke with 107 would-be settlers. There they came into contact with the Roanoke and Croatoan tribes whose land they were occupying. The Roanokes and Croatoans were described as friendly until they started becoming ill. The English unwittingly introduced European diseases, much like the Spanish had in the Caribbean. Chief Wingina in an attempt to save his people scurried to move his group inland away from the English. Lane followed them, attacked and murdered the chief. Sir Francis Drake, the English explorer, arrived at the colony shortly thereafter. Fearing an Indian counterattack, the English party elected to return to England with Drake.

In July 1587, Raleigh sent another party of 114 settlers with the same patent under the governorship of John White. A month later, White's daughter gave birth to the first English subject born in North America, Virginia Dare. White shortly thereafter left to acquire supplies in England but was prevented from returning as planned when war broke out between England and Spain. When he was able to return in 1590, the colony had disappeared. The only sign was an inscription "Croatoan." It is not known whether Virginia Dare and the other settlers died of starvation, were killed by the Croatoans, or were absorbed into the tribe. Raleigh decided that the settlement was too dangerous to continue and gave up the Virginia patent.

The Virginia Company: Inventing White Slavery in America

The next attempts to colonize North America were conducted by merchant capitalists in the name of the English crown, now held by King James I, who hoped to profit from chartering a company as a capital investment paid for by stockholders. This strategy was also used in Ulster, Ireland.[25] Chartered in 1606, the Virginia Company was awarded Raleigh's patent and the name Virginia. The company was given first claim to all land between Cape Fear River in present-day southern North Carolina to northern Maine. The investors were the West Country Merchants of Plymouth, England and the London Merchants. The settlers were called "Adventurers" and their enterprise was adventure or merchant capitalism.

The West Country Merchants were granted land between the mouth of the Potomac River and northern Maine, which overlapped with the London Merchant's land that extended from present day Cape Fear River in North Carolina to New York City. There was an understanding that the two groups would settle at least one hundred miles from one another. The West Country Merchants set sail in 1607 with forty-four colonists. They landed in Sagadahoc, Maine. The few that survived the winter returned to England in 1608. None returned to North America and their patent expired.

In December 1607, one hundred forty-four subjects funded by the Virginia Company's London Merchants set sail under Captain Christopher Newport. Thirty-nine passengers died on the voyage, an omen of the difficulties to follow. They arrived on an island in Chesapeake Bay. The land was not unoccupied.

The Powhatan Confederacy

The English landed in the territory of Algonquian tribes that originally settled in the tidewater area sometime between 3500 B.C. and 1000 B.C. The various tribes built permanent village settlements, cultivated maize (corn), beans, squash, and tobacco, hunted and took advantage of the abundant supply of seafood. They lived in a stratified society with chiefs, nobles, and religious leaders who acquired their status through heredity but had to secure a consensus to retain their leadership. The leadership strata conducted the business of governance, engaged in warfare when necessary, and performed religious rituals. The Powhatan were familiar with crafts and constructed sophisticated pottery and basketry. They traded with neighboring tribes. When the English arrived, the tribes were confederated under the leadership of Chief Powhatan into a polity they called Tsenacommacah, meaning heavily populated land. It is speculated that the confederation of the tribes came about as a response to a Spanish incursion into their territory forty years earlier.

In the early 1560s, Spanish soldiers abducted a young chief as an experiment by Luis de Velasco, the viceroy of New Spain, to introduce the people of Ajacán (the Spanish term for North America) to "civilization" by converting them to Roman Catholicism. The boy was renamed Don Luis de Velasco after his sponsor. The child was converted to Catholicism. Every attempt was made to educate Don Luis as a Spanish gentleman and religious leader. He was sent to live in Mexico and then Havana. He studied for at least two years in Spain in the court of Prince Philip II. Don Luis was returned to his homeland with Juan Baptista de Segura, S. J., vice-provincial of Florida, and eight other Jesuit fathers and lay catechists. They landed near the James River in September 1570 and established a mission post with the intention to proselytize the Indians.[26]

Almost as soon as the expedition landed Don Luis left the Jesuits and returned to his own people. He took up his hereditary leadership position in the community. He returned to the mission two years later with a group of warriors who proceeded to kill all the Jesuits except a young boy named Alonso. The story of the priests' death, as told by Alonso, is described by Juan Rogel in a letter to Francis Borgia written on August 28, 1572:

> He [Alonso] said that when Don Luis arrived [at the mission] with his tribe armed with clubs and lances, he greeted Father Baptista who was as we describe ["in bed, sick and praying...on the eve of Our Lady's Purification"]. Raising his club and giving his greeting were really one gesture, and so in wishing him well, he killed him. All the rest were murdered also. Then going out to search for Brother Sancho de Zaballos, who at that time had gone to the forest to get firewood, they slew him there...After the Indians were sated, Don Luis summoned Alonso and told him to show the Indians how to bury the bodies of the Fathers as was the custom of the Christians.[27]

When the Spanish returned to Powhatan territory in the summer of 1572, they sought revenge. They demanded the return of Don Luis. When the Powhatan refused, the Spanish took hostages, conducted a hasty tribunal, executed several captives and freed the remainder. Alonso, who had nearly forgotten Spanish, returned with them to Spain.

The indigenous tribes of the Americas through trade and word of mouth were aware of the European incursions. The events of the 1560s and 1570s likely shaped the Powhatan perception of Europeans' strengths and abilities as well as the dangers of contact. The English were apparently unaware of the failed Jesuit mission. Chief Powhatan and later Chief Opechancanough, who greeted the merchant Adventurers from the Virginia Company, were both born before the demise of the Jesuit mission and could have witnessed or participated in the events. Several writers have suggested that one or the other of these leaders may have been Don Luis.[28] The Virginia Company settlers took up residence thirty miles up from the James River not far from the failed Jesuit site. They named the settlement after their patron, King James. Jamestown became the first permanent English settlement in North America.

Jamestown

The first English adventurers to arrive in Virginia in 1607 were divided into two distinct groups with different roles. The first group was comprised of mercantile capitalist Adventurers and representatives of the monarchy, who were privileged by being given large tracts of land and authority as managers of the company. Many of these men were the second or third born sons of English noblemen whose elder brother would inherit all of the family's wealth under the principle of primogeniture (first born male inheritance). They came as a leisure class.

The second group of vagrants, former peasants, and commoners was designated as a working class of skilled and unskilled craftsmen, laborers, and fieldworkers. The working classes were composed of free English citizens and indentured servants hoping to rise above their station, acquire property, and social position at the end of their bondage. The laborers did not arrive in family groups. Women and children comprised only twenty percent of the group. The intention of both the ruling class and laboring class was to acquire land and wealth.[29] At first labor class settlers were given free passage and the promise of tools and land to work in exchange for half of their crops. This plan faltered at an early stage due to a high mortality rate. Nearly half of the settlers died in the first three years.

The Jamestown settlers remained in spite of the "starving time." The Powhatan saved the colony from starvation by trading food. They introduced maize (corn) as staple food crop in 1608. The Indians also introduced what became the primary source of income for the colony, tobacco. The Powhatan were apparently willing to cooperate from their position of strength or as equal trade partners with the relatively weak English colonists. The English leadership was aware of their vulnerability but refused to treat the Powhatan peoples as equals even though they depended on their largess.

There is some reason to believe that from an early date the Company leadership was also wary of a conspiracy between the servant classes and the Indians. Proclamations from the governor attempted to restrict contact between the settlers and native traders. They were especially concerned that the Powhatans would gain access to guns. The governor of the colony, Sir Samuel Argall declared "no trade w [with] ye [the] perfideous savages nor familiarity lest they discover our weekness [weakness]."[30] Decrees were issued "ags [against] private trucking with savages," and "ags teaching Indians to shoot with guns on pain of death to learner and teacher."[31]

The colonists felt justified in taking the Powhatans' land and restricting interaction. The company leadership cited the Spanish experience. It showed, the leadership maintained, that when the Spaniards arrived in the New World they tried to educate the Indians to see their errors and to confess their sins. The result of their efforts were so problematic that they were forced to conclude that the Indians could only safely be treated as barbarians and "natural slaves:"

> For when at first discouery of these partes, ye Spaniard did subject ye consideration of yt to casuists and confessors, it became so indeterminable, yr he wore forced to resolue roundly vpon ye worst way, least he should have none, to prosecute ye Indians as Barbar's, and therby Naturally Slaues.[32]

Unlike the Spanish, the Powhatan did not have great obvious wealth to offer the English. The wealth was hidden. Tobacco was a ritual commodity to the Indians but it became a commercial commodity to the English. Initially planted in 1612, the first tobacco to arrive in London in 1613 was an unexpected sensation and financial success. The Powhatan were not rewarded for their contribution. As demand for tobacco increased in England so did the demand for field workers in Virginia to cultivate the labor-intensive crop. The company leadership attempted to force the Powhatans to become servant workers. This strategy was unsuccessful. The Powhatan did not consider themselves inferior to the English and did not recognize English authority. The Indians remained an elusive and contentious source of labor when captured.[33]

The only solution was for the Company leadership to force more work out of the working class settlers. In the two years of his reign Governor Argall began to sentence English and Irish laborers to extended forced labor, or "slavery," as a punishment for infractions against his proclamations. On May 10, 1618, he declared that all persons in the company's employment must "go to church Sundays and holidays or lye [lie] neck and heels on the Corp du Guard [a punishment device] ye night following and be a slave ye week following." Similarly, "no man to shoot but in defense of himself ag [against] enemies till a new supply of ammunition comes on pain of a years slavery."[34]

In spite of the population surplus in England and Ireland the Virginia Company leadership faced a constant labor shortage. Not enough workers could be recruited and transported fast enough to overcome the high mortality rates. The planters were faced with high costs of transportation, inadequate supplies, and pressure to produce profit. They systematically extended the use of the available labor in the colony wherever possible.

What independence non-leisure class settlers enjoyed was undermined. Tenants-at-half and independent yeoman farmers, who paid half of their annual crops to the company, took up valuable cleared land and did not produce enough tobacco, it was argued. More servants, individuals bonded to work without pay for a specified period, were needed, not more would be settlers. The poor populations of England, Scotland, and Ireland became the source for bonded servants. Propaganda about opportunities in the New World increased. Popular ignorance of the true conditions of settlement fed fantasies of wealth and prosperity. Dreams acted as incentives for impoverished and vagrant men and women to place themselves in servitude voluntarily.

There was enormous pressure from the crown and other shareholders for the Virginia Company to realize a profit. To this end, more laborers were needed to boost production. At first potential workers were lured with guarantees of "freedom," full citizenship rights, and land ownership, which would be impossible to achieve in England. As the Company struggled to make money and extract ever more output from workers, these promises were often ignored. Workers were increasingly subjected to the complete domination of their master over the course of their servitude. As a result of hard labor, disease, and abuse few lived to experience freedom.

Voluntary migration was matched by involuntary migration. Beggars and vagrants were kidnapped off the streets of London; jails and poor houses were emptied of inmates. Impoverished girls and women were "bought" from their families and shipped to the colony to be sold as maids or as marriage partners. In "A Notice of Shipping Men and Provisions Sent to Virginia," in 1619 the treasurer of the company lists workers for the governor, for the company, for colleges (a charity that was supposed to educate the Indians), for the clergy, and finally the public: "Tennants for gouernours land, 80; Tennants for Companies land, 130; Tennants for Colledges land, 100; Tennants for Ministers gleve, 50; Young maids to make wives for so many former tennants, 90; Boyes to make apprentices, 100; Seruvants for the publicke, 50."[35] The latter two categories indicate that merchants in the business of supplying labor took advantage of the weak position of women and children. "Young maids," women usually acquired from their fathers, were sold for 120 pounds of tobacco to settlers who could marry them or use them as servants. The "boys" were children taken off the streets of London and sold involuntarily into apprenticeships. In 1627 the London managers of the Virginia Colony shipped 1500 "kidnapped" children to the colony.[36] The device of limited term, individually contracted bondage, was created to ensure that as many immigrants as possible spent as long a period of time as possible in unpaid labor. The labor needs of the Governor and Virginia Company elite were favored over the Company's interests as responsible to shareholders. Small independent farmers were seen as a detriment to the success of those in power. Servant laborers were required to work for three years without pay. Men, women, and children, landless and powerless in their poverty in England, took another step down in Virginia. Their labor was literally transformed into a commodity bought and sold by others without their will. The first involuntary chattel workers, "slaves," were white, Anglo-Saxons, Irish. and German, who like those "spirited" off the streets of London were spirited off the banks of the Rhine River.

The first transfer of indentured servants and tenants without their consent, a characteristic of chattel bondage, occurred in 1618. Eager to maximize the production of each worker, company managers and planters adopted the practice of "hiring out laborers" by "assigning" them to other planters. This assured that no field would lie fallow due to the shortage of laborers. Servants and tenants found themselves laboring continuously under conditions of depravation without free time to tend to their own crops. This established a chattel status without basic rights or guarantees to life's necessities. Instead of discouraging this trend, stockholders encouraged it as facilitating profits. In February 1619, planters were formally given absolute authority over their servants.[37]

It is important to note that this chattel indenture system was in place before the arrival of the first Africans. It was not based on cultural or phenotypical differences since it applied to poor working class English and Irish. In August of 1619, a Dutch warship traded twenty African men and women for supplies. They were placed in a position of contracted bondage undifferentiated from other servants as indicated in a census five years later.[38] It is important to note that African servant laborers were an insignificant portion of the labor force throughout the seventeenth century. Slavery in the southern British North American mainland colonies in Virginia was established with the exploitation of powerless white, not black, unfree workers.

The Powhatan Confederacy and the "Massacre of 1622"

The first systematic differentiation of English and non-English groups in British North America occurred in connection with the resistance of the Powhatan to English imperialism.[39] In 1622, the Powhatan Confederacy under Opechancanough retaliated for the loss of their land and unfair treatment. The Opechancanough raid reduced the colony by one-third. Four hundred colonists were murdered, and precious tobacco and food supplies were destroyed. Planters used the threat of Indian attacks to consolidate control over servants and tenants by limiting their freedom and restricting them to the plantation on the pretext that the Powhatan would kill them. American Indians were viewed as dangerous enemies similar to the savage Irish Celtic tribes. To the extent that they were not "usable" as forced labor, they were viewed as expendable. Indian culture was defined as inferior, barbaric, and heathen.[40] The oppression of the Irish Celtic tribes foreshadowed these attitudes and reflects the discrimination tribal peoples still experience in their interaction with Anglo-European culture.[41]

The famine and hardship that followed the so-called Massacre of 1622 did not lead to the abandonment of tobacco, in spite of the severe shortage of workers and supplies. Unable to recover the losses fast enough, the Virginia Company was on the road to bankruptcy. When James I died in 1624, the charter of the struggling company was revoked and the group was reorganized as a colony under the direct control of the Crown. George Yardley was installed as governor and as the king's representative. A general assembly was formed under the rule of a small group of former Virginia Company leadership. Even later in the century as the colony population expanded into the tens of thousands this ruling elite never numbered more than two hundred to four hundred individuals. The upper class consolidated its powers by limiting, when possible, a settler's chances of rising to landed status. Food crops were outlawed in favor of tobacco production, making tobacco an equivalent of gold currency. The settlement became completely dependent on goods and food shipped from England. Servants, without land to raise tobacco to trade for food, were even more dependent on their masters. This strongly favored the development of an aristocracy whose wealth and power was supported by a tobacco monoculture. This outcome was not inevitable. Had the colony leadership stabilized food production before expanding tobacco production and encouraged free labor, Virginia may have prospered through small farms.[42]

The Headright Privilege and Christian Status as a Precursor to White Privilege

A political, economic, and social gap grew between the wealthy landowners of high status and the increasingly impoverished mass of commoners caught in very oppressive conditions of bonded servitude. Unstable markets for tobacco in England and pressure from the English Crown to increase production further encouraged the exploitation of all available workers. Servants' contracts were violated and the length of bondage extended for a variety of offences including fornication, pregnancy, insubordination, petty crimes, and running away. Planters had to justify their authority over chattels and at the same time attract volunteers into servitude with the guarantee of rights. Statutes in Virginia (1642-1643) and Maryland (1638-1639) cleverly justified the status of bonded servitude in terms of privilege. Contracted, voluntary, limited term bondage was justified as the "head right privilege" of Protestants. The cost of transportation to the colony was transferred to the servant who was then contracted to work off this debt through limited term bonded servitude. This distinguished between limited term chattels holding a head right contract and those potentially subject to long term and life term bondage such as involuntary immigrants, all non-Protestant Christians, Irish Catholics among them, and not baptized Indians and Africans.[43]

A Protestant's right to a contract was based on the premise that Christians could not put each other into "perpetual servitude." It was, however, possible in the case of non-Christian enemies and criminals. The first case of "life-long bondage" was handed down as a punishment in an unprecedented bench decision in 1640. John Punch, a non-Christian of African descent and two Protestant indentured servants plotted an escape from their master. When captured, they were brought before the Virginia General Court for the serious crime of running away. One of the Europeans was sentenced to 30 years of bondage, the equivalent of a life sentence in that he was unlikely to live long enough to be freed. The other received a lighter sentence with a limited term. Punch, "being a Negro," in the court words, was singled out in his sentence to be a "servant-for-life." Punch's African heritage was not likely to be the legal source of his ill luck even though his origin is mentioned as a descriptor. As an African non-Christian, his status as unbaptized and unprotected from the head right privilege left him uniquely vulnerable to the court's action.[44] The cooperation of Europeans and Africans indicate mutual interests among individuals of low status in resistance to the dominant class rather than an early formation of color consciousness.[45]

Slavery and Matrilineal Descent: The Case of Elizabeth Key

The principle of Christian status and birthright as a barrier to perpetual bondage was tested in 1656 when Elizabeth Key petitioned the court for her freedom. The child of a free landed Englishman and his African servant, Key was indentured to her godfather who also owned three African servants, four English servants, and one Irish servant. Her indenture contract stipulated that she be freed in nine years; be returned to her father if her godfather decided to return to England before that time; or freed immediately in the case of her godfather's death. The executor of her godfather's estate, however, refused to release her. She sued for her right to manumission. The General Assembly of Virginia granted her petition on two grounds. First, she was to be freed, as the daughter of a free Englishman on the basis of the principle of patrilineal descent, where she inherited her father's not her mother's status. Second, she was to be freed as a Christian since she was baptized as a Protestant. The court further ruled that she had been illegally indentured and should be compensated for her services. Her godfather's estate again refused to release her and Governor Berkeley upheld the court's decision. Key's name does not, however, appear in the final settlement of the estate apparently because she married her lawyer, William Greenstead, a free Englishman and acquired his free status. The Assembly's affirmation of Key's civil rights did not set a precedent for other children of free and unfree parents. Key's petition and the court's decision were on the basis of the inheritance of status, not race. If the court decision in Key's case had been acted on and upheld, inherited slavery would have been blocked on the basis of patrilineal descent and Christian heritage. Skin color would not have become a signifier of inherited slave status.[46]

The First Slave Law, 1661

Five years after the Key case the first statutory recognition of slavery in North America as life long bondage, or "perpetual servitude," was enacted in Virginia. The law changed the definition of servitude and did away with bonds, indentures, and contracts in cases where servants held the status of "servants-for-life." The slave law consolidated the trend toward lengthening the terms of servitude and eliminated the possibility that servants retained in perpetuity could sue for their freedom as in the case of Elizabeth Key. The trend toward lengthening servitude was not unique to Virginia. In 1658, English law extended indentured servitude from three to four years, and it was extended to five years in 1662. Irish indentured servants served six years for a brief period.[47] Even so, the system in the North American colonies was an aberration in comparison with English domestic policy,[48] and with policy elsewhere in the colonial world.

The legalization of slavery anticipated an increase in racial oppression but, as legislated, it did not specify race. Up to at least 1666, African Americans who survived bonded servitude were actually more successful than their English and European counterparts in terms of their record of attaining the status of landholders and owners of servants and slaves.[49] This is evidence that *racial* oppression did not exist up to that time even as the general oppression of workers as a class escalated. The slave law was part of a sequence of restrictive statutes undermining the rights of all low status individuals. Gender oppression, which was closely aligned with class status, set up conditions of inherited servitude. In 1664, the English common law tradition of patrilineal descent was reversed in the case of the offspring of indentured servants and slaves. Children in the position of Elizabeth Key, from this time, inherited their mother's status.[50] Matrilineal descent made it possible to establish an identifiable stratum of unpaid workers with an inheritable caste status below other unpaid workers. It placed the reproductive capacity of women in the hands of their masters, who were free to exploit them with impunity. The provision for the manumission of the spouses of free citizens was also reversed. The right of servants to redress grievances through the courts was restricted. By 1670, to be baptized as a Protestant was eliminated as a path to civil liberties for Irish Catholics, Africans, and American Indians. Gender oppression continued and began to overlap with race as the final conditions for racial oppression came into place. African women were singled out first; in 1668 they were declared tithable. Even legally free African American women were denied the "exemptions and impunities of English [women]."[51] This presaged the trend toward the creation of a color-caste, the identification of low status servants by skin color.

Bacon's Rebellion

Bacon's Rebellion in 1676 is typically argued in history books to be an Indian War that was a precursor for the American Revolution and overthrow of British rule in the British North American Colonies. Historian, Theodore Allen argued that Bacon's Rebellion was a watershed leading to racial oppression and the institutionalization of white supremacy as a reaction to civil war.[52] There was widespread resistance to the oppressive policies of the planters in the first six decades of the colony. This was exacerbated by pressure from the English nobility to maximize profits. The English Civil War, 1639-1660 and Dutch Wars in the 1660s and 1670s depleted the crown's wealth. A navigation tax designed to give the crown a larger share in tobacco profits was passed during this period. The burden was onerous but possible to manage for the numerically tiny group of landowners with large holdings who took advantage of bankrupt small landowners to confiscate their land. The tax devastated small landowners and caused widespread discontent. The crown, in its own interest, also sent new planters to the colony to expand tobacco production on the edges of the earlier settlement. The older large-scale plantation elite resented the competition. A breach in the solidarity of the upper classes occurred between old and new planters. The establishment of an elected House of Burgess of Virginia in 1663, as a separate part of a bicameral assembly, was an attempt to redress the balance of power among the planter elite. The tenants, small landowners, and yeoman farmers were further isolated and were closer in their interests to the servant population than the planter elite. The masses at the bottom were increasingly rebellious. Only one out of fifteen property owners controlled over 1000 acres and only ten percent of the tobacco growers had the money to purchase labor outside of their own family. The interests of the powerless numerical majority of the colony opposed the interests of the minority ruling classes.

A significant crisis among the elite occurred, set off by frontier plantation owners led by Nathanial Bacon, a cousin of Governor Berkeley by marriage and a member of the Virginia Council. Bacon and the frontier planters wanted to increase the land available for cultivation by forcibly evicting the Susquehannock Indians. Berkeley, a representative of the older planter class, disagreed with this tactic. He wanted to use friendly "buffer" tribes against unfriendly tribes. He also, it ends up correctly, feared Bacon's plan to create a militia made up of the lower classes of the colony. Bacon, however, gained favor with the members of the House of Burgess. In September 1675, he recruited a militia of one thousand men in order to attack the tribes in the path of plantation expansion. The raid rapidly deteriorated into a civil war against the planter elite as the militia grew out of control. Commoners, small farmers, tenants, bonded servants, and slaves formed an army two-thirds Anglo-European and one-third African American. Bacon attempted to regain control of his motley corps by declaring all participants free citizens. He led the charge on Berkeley and the planter representatives of the crown. Berkeley fled and Jamestown was set on fire. Bacon did not live to see victory. He died of an unknown, but apparently unrelated, cause. Governor Berkeley returned to put down the rebellion. Control by the planter upper class was reestablished in January 1677. Just as in the case of the Massacre of 1622, the planter class used the opportunity to consolidate their authority. They sought repressive measures to eliminate the possibility of a future coalition of the lower strata into a rebellious army.[53]

The problem was not to control African or African-American workers but to control the majority of the servant population, which remained of English, Irish, and German origin. Two out of three of the 92,000 Anglo-Europeans, who immigrated to Virginia between 1607 and 1692, arrived as chattels. The labor problem was one of control over Anglo-European small landowners and indentured servants. Due to the long history of Irish Catholic resistance to English rule, the Irish were the most feared as troublemakers and up to this time were consistently excluded from Anglo-Saxon privileges. The inclusion of the Irish in oppressive legislation retarded the creation of "white supremacy" and even prevented its formation in the West Indies.[54] One member of the House of Burgess illustrates attitudes toward the Irish as "the worser sort of people of Europe...such numbers of Irish [are in the colony]...that we can hardly govern them...If they are armed...we have just feare that they may rise vpon us."[55]

SLAVES IN SPIRIT: THE IRISH IN IRELAND

Conditions for the Celtic Tribes of Great Britain also deteriorated. The Celtic Irish and sometimes the Celtic Scots were captured and made into human cargo, not unlike the Africans, where they were bartered like goods in a profitable slave trade. The English also sold Scottish "servants" for profit. Irish men were sold in Sweden and looked on as a human "commodity in trade." It is estimated that between 35,000 and 40,000 Irish soldiers defeated by Cromwell in the period of the English Civil War 1630 to

1660 were involuntarily sold to foreign nations in order to rid England of the threat of their resistance. Priests, women, and children were shipped with the soldiers in forced transportation into servitude.[56] The English distaste for the Irish and their resistance to English rule made them available to be used to populate British North America. The Irish served as the unfree labor force for English colonies before England gained access to the African slave trade in the 1660s after the English Revolution. The defeat of the Dutch in the Dutch Wars that followed the restoration of the English monarchy gave the lucrative *asciento de negro* contract to England as the sole supplier of African labor to the colonies of the Americas. It is said that the rise of industrialization in England was funded by the slave trade.

The export of the Irish had unforeseen outcomes. The Irish population became so large in the Caribbean that even with the importation of African labor, when the English tried to establish laws privileging "whites," the Irish refused to be identified with the English. That served to protect the population of indigenous peoples and people of African descent from the formation of a color line based on skin color privilege as happened in the United States.[57] The repression of the Irish on a caste basis, as a group that was below the lowest English vagrant, was not on the basis of phenotype or the way people look since the English and Irish cannot be distinguished by their complexion, hair or eye color, or physical features. The English claim to superiority was on the basis of their claim to a superior culture and religion. Edmund Burke observed that Irish Roman Catholics under repressive Penal Laws were obliged to submit to "daily and hourly insulting and vexatious [demonstrations] of superiority" on the part of Protestant poor and working peoples who lived much like the Irish Catholics except for the fact that they were Protestant and English.[58] In the late seventeenth century when racial slavery and white privilege were being legally consolidated in colonial North America, the Protestant Parliament in Ireland enacted laws that privileged Protestants and acted against the Irish Catholic population. Burke observed that the legal ascendancy of Protestantism over Catholicism was a deliberate political "contrivance" of the state designed "for the oppression, impoverishment and degradation of [the Irish] people." The Penal Laws were parallel to the legalization of white supremacy in racial slave laws in that they excluded members of the subordinated population from participation in the state and elevated the dominant group to positions of permanent superiority in power, status, and access to wealth.

WHITE SUPREMACY AND THE PECULIAR INSTITUTION

Colonial planters preferred an English or Anglo-Saxon bonded-labor force as late as 1695, when a tax was levied on "the importation of Negro slaves and such white servants as were not a native of England or Wales [a reference to the Irish]." The resolution cited the danger of insurrections from "Catholic Irish and Negro" servants and slaves.[59] To counter this, a demographic shift in the servant population occurred at this time due to the establishment of the English slave trade. The number of Africans in the colony began to rise dramatically. The English acquired monopoly rights over the slave trade after winning a series of deliberately provoked wars with the Dutch in the 1660s and 1670s. The charter of the Royal African Company in 1672, an offshoot of the original Merchant Adventures who settled the Virginia Company, made Africa a major source of workers, as well as a source of income through the lucrative sale of chattels. England dominated the slave trade from 1672 to 1712. Of the fifteen million people of African heritage distributed around the world in the African Diaspora between the sixteenth and nineteenth century, only three percent landed in the southern colonies of the mainland. In all between 400,000 and 500,000 Africans came to North America between 1618 and the end of the slave trade in 1807.[60]

After Bacon's Rebellion racial oppression increased. That led to the formation of racial slavery. Complexion was not a dominant issue, yet the Anglo-European group was elevated by legal privileges, along the line of the "head right" protections denied others. Protestants over twenty-one years of age were barred from life long slavery in 1686. The term of the bondage of Protestants was also limited to five years, still excluding "infidels" such as African-Americans, Indians, and the Irish.[61] A regulation forbidding mixed marriages of African Americans to Anglo-Europeans became law in 1691. Between 1691 and 1698 fourteen women were punished under the statute. Four of these women bore children with African fathers. The children were confiscated and placed in bondage for 30 years. This ruling constituted the first precedent that a child of Anglo-European and African heritage inherited the status of their African parent regardless of their status as free or unfree. This made it easier to identify children subject to hereditary servitude as the number of Africans in the British North American colonies increased. It also contributed to the use of complexion as a marker to identify those individuals subject to economic exploitation as perpetual unpaid labor.[62]

The African population, as vulnerable to extended servitude, numerically outnumbered European chattel indentured servants by the early decades of the eighteenth century. Free workers or those likely to be freed from apprentice and bond contracts were Anglo-European. Even the lower classes of impoverished whites including the Irish, given these practices, gradually acquired a social status not available to even free and landholding non-whites. Anglo-Saxon European privilege protected them from slave status even though their exploitation as unpaid contracted labor continued. The position of Anglo-Europeans was justified on the basis of the superiority of the English/European heritage of non-tribal, "civilized"

Protestant institutions. Positions of privilege and oppression emerged in practice as associated with skin color.

The rights of English and European servants were consolidated in 1705 by a complete revision of the colony's legal codes. Anglo-Saxon Europeans were given legal protections against becoming chattels through the transfer or sale of their contract. Anglo-Saxon European bonded servants were also protected by contract from abusive punishment, unless a written order allowed an exception. Disobedient or runaway bonded servants and slaves of non-Anglo-European heritage were unprotected from abuse. As slavery was racialized, the rights of non-whites were directly reduced. The right to personal property was denied slaves. Their livestock and other belongings could legally be confiscated.

The permanence of slave status was increased in 1691 with the elimination of the right of masters to free their slaves, which was strengthened in the legal codes of 1705. If freed, slaves were required to leave the colony, but this did not necessarily occur. The right to free an African American slave was not reinstituted until 1770, just prior to the American Revolution. Anti-manumission was not enforced until 1723 when a slave's right to self-defense, access to the courts, and to trial were explicitly denied.

The caste status of racial slavery was solidified in the denial of the right to vote for *free* African Americans. Richard West, the Attorney General and advisor to the Board of Trade, questioned the law as unfair and as being contrary to English Common law and practice. However, Governor Cooch argued that the provision was necessary in order to eliminate the sense of pride accorded a manumitted slave who would forget his inferior status. It would also, argued Cooch, reduce the potential of rebellion by separating "whites" and "blacks," and to "make the free Negroes sensible that a distinction ought to be made between their offspring and the descendants of English-men." This is a clear policy statement of deliberate racial division for the purposes of social control.[63] The Board of Trade, the regulating body over the slave trade, made no further objections. Deliberate policies of racial oppression followed Bacon's Rebellion in the effort to maintain social control over laborers without a standing army. Racial slavery as opposed to racial oppression became a reality in the revised legal codes of 1705 and 1723.

NOTES

1.   Columbus Day is celebrated the second Monday in October each year. Civil rights activists representing the indigenous peoples of the Americas protest the celebration of Columbus Day and refer to a more appropriate title as Indigenous Peoples Day to mourn those lost in the European invasion of their homeland.

2. Gordon S. Wood, "Founding a Nation," in Arthur M. Schlesinger, Jr., gen. ed., *The Almanac of American History* (New York: Barnes & Noble, 1993), pp. 16-23.

3. The indigenous people of the Americas have adopted the term American Indian to refer to their collective presence and common experiences in the face of European imperialism. The American Indian Movement (AIM) is a civil rights organization that has operated since the Civil Rights Movement. The term Indies in reference to the Caribbean persisted for several centuries and is common today with the modification of West Indies.

4. Samuel Eliot Morison, ed., *Journals and Other Documents on the Life and Voyages of Christopher Columbus* (New York, Heritage Press, 1963), pp. 26-30; Samuel Eliot Morison, *Admiral of the Ocean Sea: A Life of Christopher Columbus* (Boston: Northeastern University Press, 1982, 1970, 1942), pp. 138-45.

5. California Senate Concurrent Resolution SRC 43, Fall 1987, David Pierpont Gardner, Chair, Taskforce: The Challenge: Latinos in a Changing California, see the "Executive Summary," and "America and Its People: A Mosaic in the Making," October 17, 1995. Also see "Defining the Latino Population: Policy Implications," by James Kirby Martin, Randy Roberts, Steven Mintz, Linda O. McMurry, James H. Jones, available <http://clnet.ucr.edu/challenge/polim.htm>.

6. Ibid.

7. Ibid.

8. Mark A. Burkholder and Lyman L. Johnson, *Colonial Latin America*, 4th ed. (New York: Oxford, 2001), Ch. 2 and 3.

9. Burkholder and Johnson, *Colonial Latin America*, p. 204-209.

10. Ibid, p. 107, see Ch. 4.

11. Ibid, p. 205; (reproductions of family portraits), pp. 204-215.

12. Martin, et al. "America and Its People."

13. James Muldoon, "The Indian as Irishman," *Essex Institute Historical Collections*, Vol 111, October 1975, p. 269; quoted in Ronald Takaki, *A Different Mirror: A History of Multicultural America* (Boston: Little, Brown & Co. 1993), p. 27. Also see David B. Quinn, *The Elizabethans and the Irish.* (Ithaca: Cornell University Press, 1966,) p. 76.

14. Edmund Curtis and R. B. McDowell, eds., "Remonstrance of the Irish Princes to Pope John XXII, 1317," in *Irish Historical Documents* (London, n.p., 1943), p. 41.

15. Richard H. Tawney, *The Agrarian Problem in the Sixteenth Century* (New York: B. Franklin, 1912); George M. Trevelyan, *A Shortened History of England* (New York: Longman, Green and Co., 1942).

16. Theodore Allen, *The Invention of the White Race: The Origin of Racial Oppression in Anglo-America*, Vol 2, (New York: Verso, 1997), p. 10.

17. Tawney, *The Agrarian Problem*, p. 333.

18. John Frederick Fausz, "The Powhatan Uprising of 1622: A Historical Study of Ethnocentrism and Cultural Conflict," Ph.D Dissertation, 1977, The William and Mary College, p. 182, fn 207.

19. Ronald Takaki, *A Different Mirror: A History of Multicultural America*, (Boston: Little, Brown & Co. 1993), pp. 27-28. Francis Jennings, *The Invasion of America: Indian, Colonialism, and the Cant of Conquest* (New York: Norton, 1976), p. 153; 312. Nicholas P. Canny, "The Ideology of English Colonization: From Ireland to America," *William and Mary Quarterly*, 3rd series, Vol. 30, No. 4, (October 1973): 598.

20.   Nicholas P. Canny, "The Ideology of English Colonization," p. 593; George M. Frederickson, *White Supremacy: A Comprehensive Study in American & South African History* (New York, Oxford University Press, 1971), p. 15.

21.   It has been noted that the genocidal treatment of the Irish served as a model for the English response to resistance to English rule that they encountered in tribal societies they found in British North America and the Caribbean. Historian George Fredrickson describes the conquest and repression of the Irish as a "rehearsal" for the English treatment of the indigenous peoples of America as well as Africa. George M. Fredrickson, *White Supremacy,* p. 13.

22.   Ronald Takaki, *A Different Mirror: A History of Multicultural America* (Boston: Little, Brown & Co. 1993), pp. 27-28; Jennings, *The Invasion of America: Indian, Colonialism,* pp. 153, 312.

23.   Theodore Allen, *The Invention of the White Race: The Origin of Racial Oppression and Social Control* Vol. 1, (New York: Verso, 1994, 2000), pp. 31-32.

24.   The precedent continued well into the twentieth century. The Associated Press in London reported that the British government considered "ethnic cleansing" as a solution to sectarian conflicts between Catholic and Protestant factions in the 1970s by removing Irish Catholics from Northern Ireland. A "top secret contingency plan—dated July 23, 1972—rejected" the idea for fear that it would not work and would provoke outrage. *The Star Press,* [Muncie, IN.] Wednesday, January 1, 2003, p. 3A.

25.   Eric Williams, *The British West Indies at Westminister, 1789-1823* (Westport, CT: Negro Universities Press, 1970, reprint 1954); Eric Williams, *Capitalism and Slavery* (New York: Russell and Russell, 1961); Allen, *The Invention,* Vol II, Chs. (New York: Verso, 1997), pp. 1, 12.

26.   John Fredeick Fausz, The Powhatan Uprising of 1622, p. 52, fn 26. Other explorations include: Estéban Gómez in 1525, Nunez Cabeca de Vaca and Luis Vasquez de Ayllón in 1526 and Pánfilo de Narveáez in 1528. Hernando de Soto's conducted a more extended expedition between 1539 and 1541, as did Tristán de Luna between 1559 and 1561. Pedro Menéndez de Avilés arrived in 1565 and Juan Pardo led a party in 1566 and 1567.

27.   Juan Rogel, "Letter of Juan Rogel to Francis Borgia, From the Bay of the Mother of God, August 28, 1572," in *The Spanish Jesuit Mission in Virginia, 1570-1572,* trans. and ed. Clifford M. Lewis, S. J. and Albert J. Loomie. S.J. (Chapel Hill: University of North Carolina, 1953), pp. 119-20; also reprinted in Frederick W. Gleach, *Powhatan's World and Colonial Virginia: A Conflict of Cultures* (Lincoln: University of Nebraska), 1997, p. 92.

28.   Gleach, *Powhatan's,* p. 97.

29.   Allen, *The Invention,* Vol. II., See ch. 4, and pp. 173-176.

30.   Governor Argall, "Proclamation, 10 May 1618, 18 May 1618," Ref. No XXIII, List No. 75, Library of Congress, *The Records of the Virginia Company of London,* ed. Susan Myra Kingsbury, Vol. II. (Washington D.C.: U.S. Government Printing office), 1933, p. 93.

31.   Ibid.

32.   Library of Congress, *The Records of the Virginia Company of London,* ed. Susan Myra Kingsbury, Vol. II. (Washington D.C.: U.S. Government Printing, 1933), pp. 2-3.

33.   Allen, *The Invention, Vol I.,* pp. 51-59.

34.   Argall, "Proclamation," p. 93.

35.   Virginia Company of London, "A Notice of Shipping Men and Provisions Sent to Virginia by the treasurer and Co. in the Yeare 1619," XLIX, *The Records of the Virginia Company of London* (Washington: Government Printing Office, 1906-1935), p. 115.

36.   Gordon S. Wood, "Founding a New Nation," in Arthur Schlesinger, Jr., *The Almanac of American History*, p. 41.

37.   Fearful of the distance from London and the threat of insubordination, planters were authorized by the crown to write "orders, ordinances and constitutions for better ordering and dyrectinge of their servants." Allen, *The Invention*, Vol II, p. 59.

38.   Ibid, pp. 64-69, 56-59. Africans were listed among the servant classes in the censuses of 1623 and 1624; John Hope Franklin, *From Slavery to Freedom: A History of Negro Americans*, 3rd ed., (New York: Alfred A. Knopf, 1967), p. 71.

39.   Allen, *The Invention, Vol I;* Genevieve Richardson, "Divided Societies: Northern Ireland's Religious Struggles and Racial Struggles in the United States," *International Journal of Educational Policy, Research and Practice* Vol 1, No. 4 (2000): 509-528.

40.   See J. Leitch Wright, Jr., *Creeks and Seminoles* (Lincoln: University of Nebraska, 1986); Robert Williams, Jr., "Documents of Barbarism: The Contemporary Legacy of European Racism, Colonialism, Narrative Traditions of Federal Indian Law," in Richard Delgado, ed., *Critical Race Theory: The Cutting Edge* (Philadelphia: Temple University Press, 1995), pp. 98-109; Takaki, *A Different Mirror*, chs. 2 and 6; Horsman, *Race and Manifest Destiny*, ch. 10. The oppression of the Irish Celtic tribes was similarly justified as the capture of enemies who were heathen, uncivilized and savage. The prejudice here on the part of Anglo-Saxons is the superiority of their institutions as more civilized and free than the institutions of other people with a special disdain for tribal societies.

41.   Thirty-two tribes under the leadership of Opechancanough joined together in a surprise attack. While the attack was destructive, the strategy did not work in that the English colony remained and adapted in even more pernicious ways. See Allen, *The Invention, Vol II*, pp. 59 fn 65 on p. 299, 84-93; Helen C. Roundtree, *Pocahontas's People: The Powhatan Indians of Virginia Through Four Centuries* (Norman, Ok.: University of Oklahoma, 1990), p. 89.

42.   Allen, *The Invention of the White Race*, Vol II.

43.   Oscar Handlin, *Race and Nationality in American Life*, (Boston: Little and Brown, 1957), p. 7, 11; Loren Schweninger, *Black Property Owners in the South, 1790-1915* (Urbana, Il.: University of Illinois, 1990), p. 12.

44.   Allen, *The Invention*, Vol. II, p. 178.

45.   The English invasion of Celtic Ireland forced them to become Catholic. When Henry VIII established the Church of England, Catholicism was considered to be inferior and heathen, a corruption of the more perfect Anglo-Saxon heritage. See Horsman, *Race and Manifest Destiny*, pp. 4, 9-12; Handlin, *Race and Nationality*, pp. 12-13.

46.   Ibid., Handlin, *Race and Nationality*, pp. 194-196.

47.   Ibid., p. 179. The law extending Irish servitude was repealed in 1660 when Cromwell was removed from office by Charles II (1660-1685).

48.   Gordon S. Wood, *The Radicalism of the American Revolution* (New York: Vintage Books, 1993), pp. 52-55.

49.   Carter G. Woodson, *Free Negro Owners of Slaves in the United States in 1830* (New York: Negro Universities Press, 1924, reprint 1968); Schweninger, *Black Property Owners*, p. 17; Allen, *The Invention*, Vol.. 2, p. 181-194.

50.   Ibid., p. 14.

51.   Allen, *The Invention*, Vol. II, p. 187.

52.   Ibid.

53.   Allen, *The Invention*, Vol II, ch. 11.

54.   Ibid., ch. 12.

55.   Phillips, *Life and Labor in the Old South*, p. 29, fn. 1, reference to Henry Read McIlwaine, ed., *Legislative Journals of the Council of Colonial Virginia* (Richmond: Virginia State Library, 1979), p. 188.

56.   Phillips, *Life and Labor,* pp. 73-4 see also footnotes 12, 16, 17, 19.

57.   Theodore Allen, *The Invention of the White Race*, Vol. II, pp. 230-238.

58.   Edmund Burke, "letter to Hercules Langrishe, 3 January 1792," in *The Works of the Right Honorable Edmund Burke*, 6th ed. (Boston: Little, Brown & Co., 1880), 4: 241-306, 4: 249-52, 4:305 cited in Theodore Allen, *The Invention of the White Race*, Vol 1, p. 71, see fn. 2.

59.   Ibid., p. 148.

60.   Franklin, *From Slavery,* pp. 42-59. North America received approximately 400 thousand slaves (some estimate half a million) out of 15 million. This is approximately 3% of the total trade. However, by 1860 at the brink of the Civil War, the African American population was 4 million in the U.S. The growth as a natural population increase was the only slave society in the Americas to reproduce itself and not to require fresh supplies of laborers on a yearly basis. Comparative discussions of the slave trade tend not to identify the unique qualities of slavery in the southern states and there is also a tendency to elevate the numbers using the larger figure and descriptions of the passage, which distorts the experience and trajectory of the evolution of free, not free, and slave. John R. Spears's, for example, *The American Slave Trade: The Facts About the Overcrowded Ships and Brutal Masters in the Odious Traffic in African Slaves* (New York: Ballantine, 1960) is sensationalist history. See UNESCO, *The African Slave Trade From the Fifteenth to the Nineteenth Century: The General History of Africa Studies and Documents* (Paris: United Nations, 1979).

61.   Even in the Portuguese colony of Brazil, which established the closest form of slavery to the United States, baptism remained a means of escape from servitude.

62.   Offspring of slave and free parents placed the child in a confusing status. The courts sought to clarify this problem. The Colonial Assembly wanted to eliminate court manumissions brought by slaves in such cases as Elizabeth Key, a servant of mixed parentage who successfully gained freedom in 1656 when her master died and she fought the inheritors of his estate. Allen, *The Invention,* Vol II, pp. 194-199.

63.   Ibid., pp. 241-242, 250-251.

CHAPTER 3

" CITTY UPON A HILL"
The Contradictions of Humanism and Exceptionalism on the Road to Revolution

We hold these truths to be self evident, that all men are created equal, that they are endowed by their creator with certain unalienable Rights, That to secure these rights, Governments are instituted among Men, deriving their powers from the consent of the governed. That whenever any Form of government becomes destructive of these ends, it is the right of the People to alter or abolish it, and to institute new Government, laying the foundation on such principles and organizing its powers in such form, as to them shall seem most likely to effect their Safety and Happiness.[1]

The Puritans more than the other colonists in British North America carried the dream of freedom and exceptionalism in their quarrel with the English Reformation and the crown's religious leadership. Their arrival on

Race, Ethnicity, and Education: What is Taught in School, pages 53–83.
A Volume in: International Perspectives on Curriculum
Copyright © 2003 by Information Age Publishing, Inc.
All rights of reproduction in any form reserved.
ISBN: 1-59311-080-4 (paper), 1-59311-081-2 (cloth)

the American continent coincided with the English Civil War and the ascent of Oliver Cromwell, a Puritan, who ruled England from 1640 until the monarchy was restored in 1660. The Puritans who left for the "New World" did not believe that England could be reformed. Instead, as John Winthrop proclaimed in a sermon given aboard the *Arabela*, the Puritans intended to serve "as a Citty upon a Hill." It was to be a community that lived by and observed the Creator's laws and thus serve as a beacon for all others, for as Winthrop indicated, "the eies [eyes] of all people are upon us." They believed that England was so corrupt that it could only be saved from the outside, not from within.[2] The Puritans believed they were a special people for whom the Creator had saved the land they settled. The notion that the land belonged to the Native Americans as Robert Hughes observed, "would have seemed as absurd to the Puritans as it would to any other seventeenth century Englishman, and was hardly even raised by them." The Puritans viewed New England as "*terra nullus*, noman's land; it was *vaccuum domicilium*, empty of settlement; in one expressive phase, it was 'the Lord's Waste' not full of imaginary gold like Spanish New Mexico but ready to be made fruitful by English farming."[3]

ENGLISH COLONIAL WORLD VIEWS

English colonists came for different reasons but not always so different as one might suppose. James Baldwin points out that part of the overlooked truth in the mythology of America's early colonists is that they would not have come if they were "making it" where they were.[4] Colonists came with ulterior motives just as the governments that sponsored them had ulterior motives. In England plantations were developed to use and to control surplus and troublesome populations, to create wealth through capital investment, and to secure land and power. Three plantations were organized by the London Company with the English crown's blessing in the early seventeenth century. One was in Ireland and the other two in the United States. The Ulster plantation settled by vagrants from London was imposed on the Irish in what is now Northern Ireland. The Virginia Company plantation in Jamestown established Virginia as the first colony in British North America. Pilgrims who landed in Plymouth, Massachusetts to form the second colony in British North America, initially populated the third plantation. King James I issued patents in 1620 to four other plantation colonies including Massachusetts, New Hampshire, Maine, and Connecticut.

The Pilgrims perhaps provide the most vivid visual images that depict the early colonists. In November 1620, thirteen years after the founding of Jamestown, they landed off course in the cold late fall in Plymouth, Massachusetts. They developed and signed the Mayflower Compact. The Compact was necessary because the charter given to them from the King was invalidated when they landed far north of their destination. It was as if God had intervened in their destiny and blown the Mayflower off course. The formal agreement among the group avoided a mutiny and made them responsible to the community and God. All forty-one free adult males aboard the ship signed the Compact and agreed to "covenant and combine ourselves together into a civil body politic . . . and by virtue hereof to enact, constitute, and frame such just laws, ordinances, acts, constitutions, and offices, from time to time, as shall be thought most meet and convenient for the general good of the Colony unto which we promise all due submission and obedience."

In 1623 additional settlers arrived in Plymouth. Some were "particulars," settlers who had paid their own passage. Because they had paid their own passage, they had no obligation to the Virginia Company and no reason to assume the economic obligations of the other settlers. Their presence challenged the then well-integrated community. Before their arrival, the entire community shared political and economic motivations and, in some measure, religious beliefs. The "particulars" had to agree to obey the laws of the settlement, to pay taxes annually, and not to take part in the profitable trade with the Indians. The agreement with the "particulars" constituted a formal recognition of different classes of citizenship. It also illustrates how little interest the early settlers had in extending freedom to others.

During the first years of the Plymouth settlement, the Pilgrims participated in a communal system. Profits, harvests, or developed assets were divided equally. In 1623, the year the "particulars" arrived, the settlers asked Governor Bradford to abandon the communal system so that each household head would work for himself and then pay taxes to the settlement. The taxes were necessary because the settlers still had to pay the Company. Bradford agreed to the change, and each family was assigned a plot of land. Bradford later wrote that the new system was more effective than the original communal system.

The precedent of independent rule was set for the other groups. The Massachusetts Bay Colony, founded in 1630, created an assembly with representatives from each town in 1634. Lord Baltimore's charter for the founding of Maryland in 1635 stipulated that he would secure consent for his actions from the "free men" of the colony. Connecticut's Fundamental Orders of Connecticut, framed in 1639 included a general assembly, governor, courts to represent towns, and elected magistrates under one commonwealth. Long Island and New Haven established representative legislatures in 1643.

CONFLICTING GOVERNANCE POLICIES IN BRITISH NORTH AMERICA

While Enlightenment ideas about freedom and governments built on a consensus of the people slowly circulated, colonial governments were ruled by an oligarchy of elites at home and by an increasingly absolutist English monarchy from abroad. From the first colony in Jamestown to the American Revolution there were two opposing governance trends in British North American colonies. First, there was a tendency to allow self-rule that encouraged independence and supported Enlightenment ideologies. Second, as the English monarchy attempted to consolidate its power at home, there was also an attempt to strengthen the central authority of the crown in the colonies. Unlike Spanish and French colonialism where there was strong central control from the beginning of the colony, the English experimented with self-governance. This partly had to do with vastly different conditions of settlement as well as the English Civil War in the mid-seventeenth century. When the monarchy was disbanded, the English colonies were left for the most part to their own devices in the early stages of settlement. Patents and charters from the King authorized local control and even representatives of the King often nominally shared power with their fellow settlers in the northern and middle colonies.

Two major issues dominated the debates over the tension between Enlightenment ideas about the power of the people with a preference for loose governance as they clashed with ideas derived from the English Monarchy about the need for ordered central governance and hierarchal social relations based on a prescribed order of privilege and power. The first collection of specific issues around Enlightenment ideas were concerned with self-determination as an individual in relationship to the state. A central theme in this early civil rights debate was over which criteria determined a person's right to exercise citizenship privileges through the vote and or representation. The second set of issues concerned territorial expansion, on the one hand; and the maintenance of traditional power, on the other hand. Whoever had the power and authority to control the acquisition of land and its use monopolized the political as well as the economic spheres. The issues were whether the answers were to be determined by the rule of laws as impartial and potentially equalitarian or if they would be imposed by traditional elites based on social hierarchies and inherited rights. The power to impose taxes crossed both of these issues. Voting rights awarded to full citizens offered a solution to the distribution of property as determined by laws, whereas central absolutist powers could impose taxes without regard to representation, thereby limiting access to property, power, and status in ways that maintain traditional elites.

These seventeenth-century debates are important because the issues became embedded in compromises in the government and the structure of the United States. The tensions around the right to claim citizenship and suffrage as well as power over territory and personal property were at the heart of the tension between the monarchy and republican government with its emphasis on individual rights. In England, civil rights followed inherited social status. The majority of the disenfranchised in the middle and northern colonies were similarly of a low status as servants or laborers. The property owning merchants acquired rights. The turning point was whether a middle class with rights would emerge as free and relatively independent of the upper classes.

Political, Religious, and Economic Differences Among the Colonies

Political, religious, and economic differences distinguished status and access to rights in the colonies. The Virginians in the southern colonies openly sought status and wealth. The Pilgrims in the northern colonies needed to escape religious persecution in England and had tried Holland prior to making arrangements to serve the London Company. Fundamentally, the colonists were indentured to the company who paid the cost of their passage. They intended to stay and to survive. The Puritans who landed in Massachusetts after the Pilgrims did not come to amass great wealth. They came as families and as a community. They wanted to live a life based on Scripture. They worked small farms and practiced skilled trades that lent themselves to mercantile capitalism and later to industrialization.

The southern colonies pursued agrarian capitalism and developed plantations and plantation societies. The plantation society consisted of a small number of rich landowners who controlled large numbers of impoverished laborers. Oppressive servitude, predominantly but not exclusively in the southern colonies, took precedence over the English tradition of civil rights. Oppression was also fostered by the economies of the northern colonies that profited from its participation in the slave trade. Boston became part of the triangular slave trade from Liverpool, England to Africa and then to the Americas. The solution for reducing the potential of servant revolts and civil rebellion required elevating the rights of Christians and the privileges of Anglo-Saxons or those of European Christian status. The devaluation of the status of those not so privileged formed the "American dilemma," a society divided by slavery as the English directed slave trade with Africa increased.[5] Slavery, as a system of labor, cannot be separated, especially in the colonial period, from discussions of property, labor, and the accumulation of wealth.

THE CAROLINA CONSTITUTION: JOHN LOCKE'S DEFENSE OF SLAVERY

The political philosophy of John Locke (1632-1704) had a great impact on popular eighteenth century social and political thought leading up to the

French and American Revolutions. Locke was a significant contributor to Thomas Jefferson's thought. Locke's essays were still read and were relatively widely available in the eighteenth century.[6] A common interpretation of Locke emphasizes his concept of individualism, natural rights, the ultimate sovereignty of the people, and the right to redress injustice.[7] Locke was also interested in the economic issues of his day. He observed that there were two ways to grow rich: "either conquest or commerce." He maintained that the "defense of imperialism and commerce, therefore is the only way left to us [the English], either for riches, or subsistence." And further, the "…industry and inclination of our people…do naturally fit us" for this role. While Locke made the assertion that "private men's interests ought not thus be neglected, nor sacrificed to anything, but the manifest interest of the public," the public was fundamentally represented by the wealth of the nation and its proprietors. Locke in his defense of the pursuit of money explained: "by gold and silver in the world, I must be understood to mean not what lies hidden in the earth but what is already out of the mine in the hands and possessions of men." The pursuit of such wealth was a path to prosperity and progress as an encouragement to trade.[8]

The Plantation System and Civil Government in the Constitution for Carolina

This idea of progress was early evident in Locke's ideas of civil government, which were practically illustrated in his construction of the ideal entrepreneurial plantation as illustrated in the constitution he wrote for Carolina. Locke's relationship with Lord Ashley, Earl of Shaftesbury, put him in a position to write a constitution for Carolina in 1668. Ashley was a member of the Royal African Society that acquired the right to the slave trade and the ability to control the worldwide slave market. Ashley and an elite group of nobles and early capitalist entrepreneurs envisioned not only the lucrative sale of chattels to others but also the use of slave labor in a new British North American colony. Locke agreed to prepare the "Fundamental Constitution of Carolina," in March 1668. It was adopted as the law of the land by the eight reigning proprietors of the colony on March 1, 1669. The eight proprietors were designated as "the people" and democracy was explicitly not part of either the political or the economic organization:

> Our sovereign lord the king having, out of his royal grace and bounty, granted us the province of Carolina…establishing the interests of the lords proprietors with equality, and without confusion avoid erecting a numerous democracy; we the lords and proprietors of the province aforesaid [Carolina], have agreed to this following form of government to be perpetually

established among us, unto which we do oblige ourselves, our heirs, and successors, in the most binding ways that can be devised.[9]

Conflicting Views of Freedom and Slavery

Locke created a constitution that assured the privilege of the original entrepreneurs and their heirs along the male line. The territory was subdivided into eight signatories and within them were eight baronies divided into four precincts with six colonies in each. There was to be no freedom of movement, habitation, production, or commerce among the servant and slave classes. Another provision required that there would be "no freemen" who did not "acknowledge a GOD, and that GOD is publicly and solemnly to be worshipped." The "Church of England [was designated as the] only true orthodox" church. In this way all members of American Indian Tribes, Africans, Catholics and other non-Church of England members were excluded from the free, semi-free, or wage work force.[10] The provisions of the Carolina Constitution appeared to follow Sir Robert Filmer's rationale for absolutist government expressed in *Patriarcha* (1680). Filmer argued: "all government is absolute monarchy," and "that no man is born free...we are all born slaves and we must continue to do so."[11] Locke, to the contrary, previously argued that:

> . . . slavery as so vile and miserable an estate for man, and so directly opposite to his generous temper and courage of the nation, that it is hardly to be conceived that an Englishman, much less a gentleman should plead for it.[12]

In the chapter on slavery in the *Second Treatise on Civil Government*, Locke argued that the natural liberty of man was to be free from any superior power on earth, not to be under the will or legislative authority of man, but to have only the law of nature for his rule.[13] The condition of slavery existed as a "state of war continued between a lawful conquer and a captive." Yet, this did not give the captive the collective right of rebellion, to wage war. Since man was by nature free, he could not consent to slavery, an unnatural state. The act of capture became an:

> act of forfeiting his own life, by some act that deserves death; he, to whom one has forfeited it, may (when he has it in his power) delay to take it, and make use of him to his own service, and he does him no injury by it: for whenever he finds the hardship of his slavery outweigh the value of his life; it is in his power, by resisting the will of the master, to draw on himself the death he desires.[14]

Locke used his version of natural law and the equality of humanity to place slaves in a state of limbo. They constituted a workforce of not literally but virtually dead people at the unconditional mercy of their masters. No other colonial power employed this argument. The Carolinas, even armed with this harsh template, did not live up to its potential for human suffering. Slavery, even when rigidly imagined, in practice was a human institution composed of human actors.

SLAVERY IN THE OLD REGIME

The practice of slavery grew slowly in the eighteenth century. As a practice or institution, it developed in different ways in different places. There were large plantations worked by large numbers of slaves and there were small family farms where only a few slaves were to be found. Fraternization between the black and white populations, common in the seventeenth century continued even after the color line of racial slavery became a legal reality. Black and white unions produced enough mulatto children in Carolina by 1717 that laws were passed against such relationships, but they were not particularly effective. Masters commonly preyed on slave and servant women producing children that were most often not acknowledged but sometimes were looked on with favor. John Custis, for example, preferred his son, Jack, born to a slave woman "young Alice" over his legitimate son and provided for his manumission and "handsome" maintenance. He even threatened to disinherit his legitimate son in favor of Jack, but apparently deferred to public opinion and did not.[15]

Human Relations Between Anglo-Europeans and Slaves of African Heritage

There were also incidents of interracial cohabitation and marriage in spite of laws and general public disapproval. Thomas Wright, a white man, owned a 390-acre plantation in the piedmont area of Virginia where he lived with a slave, Sylvia, to whom he was "much attached." She bore him a son and three additional children between 1784 and 1793. He freed her, and they lived openly as man and wife. He also freed his son Robert, whom he called "Robin," who rode his horse to school where he was befriended and was apparently treated the same as a white child. When Thomas died in 1805 his son inherited the plantation and six slaves. Robert married a white woman. The marriage was illegal but apparently did not arouse controversy. He was looked upon favorably by his white neighbors. The story of the Wright family suggests that the black–white division was permeable in the eighteenth century and that there was a "level of openness in interracial sexual relationships, and a degree of white acceptance of miscegenation that challenge historical generalizations and traditional stereotypes" of the naturalness of white-black prejudice.[16]

Thomas Jefferson's life is a good example of the complexity and relative openness of intergenerational relationships between blacks and whites, slave and free. When Jefferson's father-in-law, John Wayles, became a widower, he took in Elizabeth Hemming, the daughter of a sea captain and an African woman. They had six children between 1762 and 1773. Jefferson never defended himself against accusations concerning this relationship since the Wayles-Hemming family included his wife's half brothers and sisters. Sally Hemming, the last child born in 1773, became the mistress of either Jefferson or, as others argue, Jefferson's favorite nephew Peter Carr. Sally bore five children and repudiated Carr's paternity in her lifetime. Her progeny today claim they are direct descendents of Thomas Jefferson. Jefferson's legitimate children deny this allegation. Regardless, Jefferson was not only a slave owner who did not manumit his slaves but also headed a family where interracial sex was commonplace.[17] More recently, descendents of slave holding families have acknowledged their historical and often intimate relationships with the descendents of the slaves held by the family.[18] The sexual exploitation of black women stemmed from the prevalence of male supremacy and sexism combined with the central problem of slavery in the first place, the authority of white men to treat other human beings as property, as things to be used.

The aristocracy of the South was in a position to exploit both slaves and the poor white population. Philip Morgan described the relationship between masters and slaves as not bilateral but trilateral; it consisted of planter/patriarchs, slaves, and "plain white folks." Planter patriarchs presided over women, slaves, servants, and free whites. The great chain of being of the Enlightenment thinkers demanded in the view of planters subordination of lower orders, not on the basis of permanent differences but permanently different statuses. Planters spoke of slaves abstractly in terms of property in the language of the market economy. There was also a patriarchal ideology that held that the labor of the slave should be "rewarded" with protection and guardianship. As the eighteenth century progressed, masters began to speak of individual rights and duties where slaves and whites were differentiated not on the basis of biology but on the basis of those who had rights and those who did not. Slaves were defined as "people without rights." The denial of rights placed slaves outside of society and justified absolute authority over them. The close contact with masters and similar experiences between the poor white "plain folk" of the southern colonies paralleled the experience of the black slave population. White servants lived similarly and shared the same experiences but this gradually differentiated along the color line. As the eighteenth century progressed and the numbers of slaves increased, living quarters, work situations, and other opportunities for interaction decreased on large plantations.

The Demographics and Life Style of Slaves

While Carolina was deliberately established as a slave-intensive colony, Virginia had twice as many African slaves as the area that became South Carolina. Large landowners with one thousand or more slaves were rare even if this group dominated in terms of status, politics, and local economics even in Virginia. In order to make a profit it was necessary to cultivate hundreds of acres and to employ thousands of workers. Yet, it was possible to set up a tobacco plantation without slaves and with little capital since tobacco crops lent themselves well to small operations. Small farmers diversified their crops and produced corn and other staples. They also raised livestock. By 1780 fewer than sixty percent of the landowners owned slaves. Slave owning was a symbol of being a gentleman, a luxury most could not afford. "Plain white folk" worked their own fields.

In Virginia in the 1730s and 1740s the majority of slaves lived along the peninsula. The relatively small-scale agriculture that dominated the area operated with a limited labor force that consisted of landowning family members who worked the fields with their servants or slaves. An average workforce consisted of eleven such workers in addition to family. Often the servants or slaves also consisted of intergenerational adults and their children.[19] In this way, the slave population grew naturally. Stable families clearly produce more children than disrupted ones. Recognized two parent households existed in approximately one sixth of the slave population.[20]

Housing

Living conditions varied greatly, but in general slaves lived in poor dwellings, were inadequately clothed and had inadequate diets. Living conditions tended to be somewhat better on the larger plantations. There is archeological evidence that slave dwellings improved over the eighteenth century. There was some privacy and autonomy as plantation size increased. The size of slave quarters was incredibly small. Separate dwellings were often only 150 to 250 square feet. Slaves often were able to cook their own food. In some cases they were given padlocks to protect their belongings. However, the evidence is that they possessed little of value. Often laws did not allow them to own anything. Nonetheless, human ingenuity prevailed. Some planters allowed slaves to build their own houses in a designated location. Some records show that occasionally they took on the shape and character of an African village. Slaves grew small plots of crops consistent with African culture. Gourds served as a utensil for storage and carrying water. While some dwellings went without any furniture, others had a few pieces of basic furniture and, sometimes, family heirlooms of flatware or dishware. In some cases chickens were raised and could be bartered for other necessities.[21]

Clothing

Depending on the wealth and predisposition of the slave owner, a specified amount of cloth, usually a coarse German made linen or British wool, was given to each slave on a yearly basis to make clothes, but the amount varied greatly. In 1732, William Hugh Grove traveled through Virginia and reported that each slave was given a pair of shoes and brown linen enough to make two pairs of pants and two shirts. In some cases slaves were provided with shoes, stockings and two outfits, which included a jacket, waistcoat, and two shirts for men, and a jacket, petticoat, and two shifts in the case of women. Shipments of material, the actual sewing of the garments, and their distribution were by no means uniform or even forthcoming. It was more common for children to go without clothes and for slaves to suffer cold and depravation for the lack of protection against the elements.[22]

Food

Food was similarly rationed. Clearly, when times were good, there were better provisions. Portions of corn, unsellable rice, and other products of the land were distributed in specified amounts. Slaves ate chickpeas, yams, corn, and potatoes. While meat was occasionally specified as an item on the distribution list for a plantation, there is little evidence that slaves were given any kind of domestic meat with any regularity. Archeological finds indicate that the protein consumed came from hunting and fishing, from the forethought of slaves in providing for their own survival. Deer, squirrels, rabbits, and possums were sources of meat protein. Slaves also fished for pickerel, gar, and bluegill. It is clear that slaves fared more poorly than the free poor given that they had little control over their time so that they could hunt, fish, and grow crops.[23]

Labor

The work was often hard and tedious. Over the course of the eighteenth century the opportunities arose for learning skills. Fieldwork dominated ninety-eight percent of the work in the early eighteenth century but was reduced by twenty percent by the time of the Revolution as more slaves learned trades and served as skilled laborers. Slaves were taught trades necessary for maintaining large plantations. They became master carpenters, coopers, and sawyers or semi skilled carters and watermen, managing the boats on the waterways. Slave artisans made baskets and ceramics. Domestic servants managed the main house, conducting all the necessary work of cleaning, cooking, washing clothes, sewing, nursing children, waiting on the masters, serving in jobs of various statuses from butlers to stable hands. Large plantations were not necessarily contiguous and drivers or overseers, who were sometimes also slaves, often managed fields at a distance from the main house.

Tobacco, Indigo, and Rice Production

The image of the dominance of tobacco in slave colonies is in some ways a myth. Rice and the production of indigo dominated in South Carolina. Each crop had its advantages and disadvantages. Building the necessary irrigation ditches for rice production provided an opportunity to learn skills in engineering but it was also hard work. Rice required a tedious planting process, difficult hoeing in terrible conditions, and the torturous process of beating out the grain by hand with a mortar and pestle. Runaways were more common in times of hard work, bad weather, and stress. Gradually, machines contributed to easing the more onerous aspects of rice production. Indigo production was in some ways worse than rice. Indigo became popular in 1740. It had the advantage of having a shorter growing season. However, the plants, once harvested, had to ferment, a process that produced a terrible stench as the leaves rotted and attracted flies and other disease carrying insects. Workers often became ill and some died. Tobacco, as has been noted, was planted for almost a century without slave labor in Virginia, but in intense large production on large plantations tobacco became identified with slavery. In fact, tobacco could have become a small farm crop. Rice on the other hand was only possible with the help of a large labor pool.[24]

Tasks versus Gangs

The forms of labor varied between tasks and gangs. Task labor resulted in an unending conflict between taskmasters and workers over the size of the task and the amount of time it took to be accomplished. The advantage was that it allowed slaves to have some control over their work and allotment of time. Gang labor offered less choice and therefore less respite for works on one's own garden plot and other necessary tasks required for survival. Luckily, sometimes work was impossible and a holiday would be declared. Frozen ground, for example, could not be worked. There was only so much repair and preparation that could be done waiting for a new season to begin.[25]

Age, Gender, and Health

Age, gender, and poor health did not provide ways out of the demands of slave existence. White women were less likely to work the fields but black women were often treated callously. Death was the only excuse Thomas Jefferson offered as a legitimate excuse for staying out of the field on a given day. Children were sent to work the fields at age six or seven, sometimes earlier for domestic work. Between the ages of nine and fifteen youths were considered a "half-slave."[26] Young slave children worked at chores such as hoeing potatoes, feeding chickens and scaring birds away from the crops. Families and children survived due to the struggle of individuals and extreme commitment of individuals who fought to stay together and to find one another when torn apart under the most wrenching and of circumstances.[27]

Attitudes Toward Slavery on the Part of Southern Elites

The patriarchs of southern society did not expect their slaves to be either content or submissive. As Philip Morgan points out, "the myth of the happy and docile slave was not an eighteenth century invention."[28] Slavery was dehumanizing. The callousness with which slaves were treated set it apart from all other kinds of labor. The denial of individual or collective rights meant a loss of self-determination. The horror of human bondage as chattels and the lack of control over maintaining family unity constitute a primary aspect of the evolution of chattel bondage. Human beings fell victim to economic considerations and even more cruel forms of exploitation. Brutality was common in the Old Regime due to the "nakedness of the exploitation to which they [slaves] were subject."[29] Old Regime slavery was riddled with complexity and contradictions. Slaves were property and their lives were totally contingent on their master's whim. "An act about the casuall killling of slaves" passed in 1669 in Virginia declared that masters were not responsible for beating their slaves to death "since it cannot be presumed that prepensed malace should induce any man to destroy his owne estate."[30] In point of fact, slaves were human beings and "masters implicitly, if not always explicitly, recognized the humanity of their slaves. "The slave could never become the thing he or she was supposed to be."[31]

CIVIL UNREST: RESISTANCE TO SLAVERY

Carolina, as noted, was organized according to the provisions of Locke's Constitution. It created a plantation system to be worked by European artisans and servants with masses of African slaves. Rigorous controls were implemented to reduce the possibility for insurrection. The harshness of the order seemed to invite insurrection. The planter class became increasingly wary as the slave population grew. In 1708, the white and the black populations were approximately equal. By 1724, the African population was three times that of the white population. Beginning in 1686, the colonial legislature had enacted laws that guaranteed the domination of masters over slaves as Locke's Constitution specified. However, it was unclear if sheer numbers could offset the intentions of the laws. Africans could not engage in any kind of trade, were to be confined between sunset and sunrise, and could not carry weapons. Patrols had the authority to search slaves and punish offenders. Serious crimes such as murder or robbery were capital offenses. Branding punished stealing a chicken.

As the population of slaves grew, the actual occurrence of rebellion increased. There were three uprisings in 1739. The most serious uprising, known as the Cato conspiracy, involved slaves on a plantation west of Charleston. Two guards were killed. Some fled to freedom in Florida and others joined them. They repelled or killed any whites that attempted to interfere with their escape. The rebels were eventually engaged in battle during which forty-four blacks and thirty whites died. However, ten slaves succeeded and found freedom. Fear among whites escalated. In 1740, a conspiracy by 200 blacks was suspected and supposedly uncovered by whites. The planters rounded up 150 unarmed Africans. Fifty were hanged in a public spectacle of ten hangings a day for five days. When a fire swept through Charleston, slaves were suspected and at least two blacks were executed. Laws were enacted to restrict importation of slaves, especially from other colonies, through the imposition of duties. The importation of white servants was to the contrary rewarded with a bounty in order to maintain a balance of whites and blacks.

Practices perceived as leading to insurrections, such as selling liquor to slaves, were outlawed. Undue cruelty was outlawed. Depending on the season, masters were restricted from working their slaves over fourteen or sixteen hours a day. Another solution was to Christianize and educate the slaves so that their personality would become more docile and spiritual. The Society for the Propagation of the Gospel in Foreign Parts (SPG) wanted slaves to be given time to learn to read. They started schools for blacks in Charleston where the teachers were African slaves owned by the society. The planters were led to believe that slavery was a truly benevolent institution favored by God. The SPG improved conditions for Indians and Africans in both Carolinas as they set an example of benevolent leadership for planters to emulate.

COMPARING CAROLINA, VIRGINIA, MARYLAND, AND GEORGIA

Carolina becomes the Carolinas

As early as 1700, the northern portion of Carolina was evolving in significantly different ways from the southern portion. The Cape Fear region attracted poor white Virginians—Irish, Germans and Scots—who came to settle. The African population was small, especially in the early years. When the Carolinas split in 1729, the differences became more apparent even though the two shared the same slave codes. North Carolina passed "An Act Concerning Servants and Slaves" in 1741, that specified the procedures for the trial of slaves accused of crimes. Even though blacks could not own property, carry arms, move about without permission, and could be punished for being "insolent," thievery, or transacting business with whites, they were entitled to a trial.

The presence of Quakers also mediated conditions in the northern colony. The Quakers urged regular religious services for blacks and by the mid-eighteenth century began to discourage slave ownership among Quakers. In 1770 they disparaged the slave trade as immoral and encouraged its prohibition. Interestingly, North Carolina did not experience any slave insurrections and was relatively calm in the period before the War for Independence.

Virginia and Maryland

Slavery evolved in the Virginia colony over a period of one hundred years. The population of Africans was limited until after Bacon's Rebellion. In Maryland there was no statutory recognition of slavery until 1663, two years after Virginia, but the African population was not large enough to draw attention to racial slavery. In 1681, a law was passed that the child of a white servant and an African was free. As the free African population increased, the status of the children of African descent increased as well. The population of Africans increased slowly. In 1708 it was reported that six or seven hundred had been imported in the last ten months. By mid-century, John Hope Franklin reported that there were approximately 40,000 Africans and 100,000 whites. By 1790 the white population had doubled and was approximately twice as large as the black population.[32] Franklin noted that while the slave codes in Maryland were very strict and followed from the experiences of Virginia where the possibility of revolt was demonstrated, the laws were often mediated by lenient interpretation. In 1766 a slave was reprieved from a conviction of stealing after a confession and his master's plea for a pardon. Franklin also reported that the Africans in Maryland were also implicated in the religious strife that pervaded the colony between the Catholics, favored by the ruling Calverts, and the Protestants. It was feared that Catholics, Indians, and Africans would conspire with an international clique such as the French to overthrow English rule.[33]

Georgia, the Frontier

Georgia is the most unique of the southern colonies in that three restrictions were placed on settlers: there were no free land titles, no alcohol, and no African slaves. The trustees were determined to keep slavery out of the colony. It was to be settled by convicts released from prison in England as a social experiment in rehabilitation. Hardly had the experiment begun that there was discontent. The first petition to import slaves in 1738 was rejected. When the 1741 petition was rejected, settlers began to hire slaves from South Carolina on a 100-year lease. The prohibition on slavery was lifted in 1750 along with the prohibition against land titles and alcohol. A ratio of four African slaves to one white servant was introduced as a way to regulate the slave trade. Slaves were to be inspected for purposes of health; marriage between slaves was sanctioned; and slaves were given certain rights in a court of law. Slave holding families from South Carolina started relocating to Georgia. By 1760 there were six thousand whites in the colony and three thousand slaves. Within six years there were ten thousand whites and eight thousand slaves. In the last count before the Revolutionary War, in 1773, the white population had increased to eighteen thousand and the slave population to fifteen thousand. Georgia laws reflected the experiences of South Carolina and the fear of insurrection. Yet, slaves were pressed into military service. That made possible the ironic practice of using slaves to fight as militiamen in the colonial period. The rights given on the repeal of the anti-slave prohibition were nonetheless weakened by restrictions on slave activity. Slaves could not gather in groups of more than seven from Saturday to Monday morning. They could not possess horses, canoes, or cattle. They could not possess weapons. They could not be taught to read or write. The planters often provided the means to learn the skills of survival. However, the proximity of Spanish Florida left open a corridor for escape. The Indian population of Georgia, the Cherokees, Creeks, and Seminoles helped slaves to escape to Florida.

Georgia remained largely a frontier society in the colonial period. The planter class master held absolute power within his own realm and tended not to pay much attention to either the colonial legislature or the laws of England. Planters created their own slave codes. John Hope Franklin reported that the planter made the institution of slavery what he wanted it to be and "the wastefulness which characterized his treatment of the land was likely to characterize his treatment of the slaves. With no discernable threat to the supply of land or the use of slaves, he was likely to be ruthless, reckless, and extravagant in the use of both."[34]

THE LIMITED RIGHT TO CITIZENSHIP, SUFFRAGE, AND REPRESENTATION

The right to citizenship, suffrage, and representation was essential to a free society. Slaves were a caste beneath these privileges but it was not guaranteed that the Anglo-European population automatically gained access to rights. Who was actually able to vote, be a representative, or be represented varied from colony to colony. All men who had civic rights could vote, but usually only landowners had civic rights. Often the amount of land a person had to own was specified. For example, in Pennsylvania free men had to own at least fifty acres; in New York the property had to be worth more than forty English pounds to gain voting rights. Even in New England and in the middle colonies the vast majority of men were denied the franchise. In Pennsylvania only ten percent of the population had the right to vote, and in Philadelphia only two percent actually did so. In Massachusetts and Connecticut sixteen percent were eligible for suffrage, again only two percent actually voted. In the southern colonies with large slave populations less than two hundred individuals dominated populations in the tens of thousands. This grew even more lopsided as the slave trade increased the African slave population throughout the eighteenth century.

Citizenship Rights Restricted

Those citizens entitled to vote and to participate in the legislature supposedly had the power to create laws that assured control over life, property, and the liberty of inhabitants. However, the governor, as the king's representative, had veto powers. Between 1624 and 1752 what little popular control there was over the actions of the local governance systems deteriorated rather than expanded. The original broad charters for companies were dissolved, and the colonies were made into proprietary territories under the crown. The strongest form of control was as a royal province modeled after Virginia. In this case, a governor appointed by the king ruled the government with absolute authority over the colonists. Virginia was the first royal province established in 1624, others followed: 1679, New Hampshire; 1685, New York; 1691, Massachusetts; 1702, New Jersey; 1729, North and South Carolina; 1752, Georgia. Eight of the thirteen colonies became royal provinces. Maryland, Pennsylvania, and Delaware remained as proprietary colonies. Only two were allowed to retain an assembly of voters, Connecticut and Rhode Island. England's actions slowly alienated wide portions of the colonial populations, North and South. The people who had the most to lose were the ascendant landlords and merchants who lived on the coasts and depended on urban ports. The frontier in the uplands tended to be composed of small farmers where local government persisted, but the crown's increasingly tight control hit all groups enough to flame the fires of revolution at a time when British territory was expanding.

The English View: Kings Over People

God bless the squire and his relations,
And keep us all in our proper stations.[35]

The American revolutionary spirit chafed against efforts of the English crown to impose its will on the colonies. The diverse colonies drew together in their own defense against the English belief in the legitimacy of a monopoly of power held by the king for the common good. The crown used its monopoly of power for its own benefit. It believed, or argued, that what benefited the crown benefited all. To the colonists the imposition of will for the benefit of the mother country was tyranny. The colonists invoked what they believed was their right to free themselves from tyranny. The English crown saw that as rebellion. To the crown the southern colonies of British North America were wayward children.

The English held to their conviction that "true-born Britons" were a superior people. The colonists as English citizens, it was argued, had a duty to the crown. However, because they had not been born on English soil, because they were not "native-born" they were not considered to be as "good" as the native-born, no matter what their heritage, no matter how great their wealth, or no matter how useful they were or could be. The colonists were automatically beneath their British benefactors, and like children were required to obey the authority of England as their "mother country." Patriotism demanded submission to the paternal authority of the crown. Dr. Samuel Johnson observed in regard to the colonies that "we do not put a calf into the plow, we wait until he is an ox."[36]

THE DEBATES OVER REVOLUTION AND ABOLITION

The American Revolution was a time of great upheaval and political debate that foretold future controversy. Slavery was part of the discourse over natural rights, civil liberty, and independence. Holding human beings in bondage was an issue as the colonies debated their right to free themselves from the English Monarchy. Those who favored the abolition of slavery grew more vocal. Abolitionists argued that slavery was incompatible with Christian theology. The northern colonists were more predisposed than the southern colonists to join abolitionists and criticize the slave trade. In the northern and middle colonies, slavery was inefficient and more expensive than wage labor given their climate, landscape, and their industrializing economies. The practice of holding slaves was limited and less essential to their stability and the direction of their advancement toward modern social classes in a capitalist society with a non-agricultural base. The movement toward industrialization in the North early created tensions with England that differed from the situation in the South. The English crown did not welcome the competition in textiles or interference in international commerce including the slave trade. A colony was expected to supply raw materials and produce wealth that would revert to the mother country.

The southern colonies' plantation system coincided with the needs of England to a greater degree than the northern economy. The oligarchy of wealthy landowners, as the government, was also more compatible with the monarchy of England. The pre-Revolutionary South with its concentration of power and assets in the hands of the few was wealthier than the North. The owners of large plantations in the South were often descendents of the original colonists, whose power and right to land had been granted by the crown. They were a leisure class determined to maintain their independent position and power.

Northern colonists carried, as part of their ethos, the heritage of the Puritans and the Protestant ethic of independence, hard work, austerity, religious piety and competition that clashed with the crown's interests. They had developed the tradition of local governance in which many participated. Small farms, early textile manufacturing, and commerce in urban centers diversified the northern economy. This dispersed wealth to a greater degree than in the South even though the number of free white males who qualified for full citizenship rights was extremely limited.

In spite of their identification with the English elites, southern upper class society was also influenced by Enlightenment ideas about freedom and independence. The English Civil War in the middle of the seventeenth century was a conflict between England's traditional royal elite and the growing new capitalist classes similar to the South's upper class. Interest in the rights of wealthy commoners to control their resources contributed to the southern elites' indignation at the efforts of George III to exercise absolute power over the colonies.

John Locke tried to balance these interests in his *Treatises on Government.* Locke justified the right of southern elites to rule and justified their right to throw off unjust governments. The concentrated wealth in the South produced educated planter-gentlemen, who like Thomas Jefferson, had the time to study Locke's ideas and to contribute their own perspectives. Even though they ruled as an oligarchy, controlled the land, the economy, held slaves, and held the poor white underclass hostage to a system of inequality, the southern planter class attended to the meaning of liberty. The planters' lifestyle was founded on the plantation economy. Their position and leisure depended on the inequality they created and enforced. However, in their intellectual life they pursued the important questions of the day. They were to dominate the Continental Congress and later in the Constitutional Convention. Southern men such as Thomas Jefferson articulated the ideals of liberty and rights that were expressed in the *Declaration of Independence*, the *United States Constitution*, and its *Bill of Rights*.

Property Rights, Taxation, and Representation

Territory and property issues rose as the primary contentious concerns that led up to the American Revolution. By 1754, England established a permanent settlement above the French colony of Quebec along the Hudson Bay. Newfoundland and parts of what would become the maritime provinces of Canada became part of British North America. France still controlled a segment of North America, including Quebec, the American West, the land around and south of the Great Lakes including the central plains and land defined by the Ohio and Mississippi River Valleys all the way to the Gulf Coast. The Seven Year's War with France, 1756-1763, spurred changes in British policy toward the colonies from New England southward. This prolonged and expensive war was resolved with an English victory in 1763. England then acquired all of New France, consolidating British dominance across what are now Canada and the central United States. Spain controlled the West, Mexico, Latin, and South America.

The king decided that the American colonies should pay for the protection afforded them and replenish the Crown's coffers. The king's right to fix prices on American goods and to restrain American merchants and shippers was exercised. The colonies were directed to limit their own manufacturing and to concentrate on the production of raw materials, grain, and lumber for English markets. The colonies were required to purchase British finished products. British capitalists gained advantages in investing in land. They also benefited from virtually all trade or commerce conducted in the colony. English mercantilism pursued policies with direct advantages to itself and limited the growth and independence of the colonies. Colonies were to be producers of raw materials and consumers of finished products produced in England. They were to supply England with any emergent form of wealth including minerals or other natural resources. England reserved the right to monopolize the commerce of the colonies according to its own rules. Dutch and French goods were banned, and the colonies were not allowed to sell their tobacco, grain, rice, iron, lumber, fur and hides, and other commodities to any other country except Great Britain. New legislation by the British Parliament built on former repressive Navigation Acts, Trade Acts, and the Molasses Act in 1733, which taxed goods from the French West Indies, but was not enforced. British soldiers were sent to enforce policies and practices that were directly counter to the interests of the colonies.

King George III came to power in 1760. In 1763 he rescinded the right of the colonists to acquire land from the Indians, reserving for himself all rights to the western frontiers. A year later a Sugar Act taxed imports. That same year the right of the colony to issue its own currency was withdrawn. The colonies were unable to repay debts or borrow money. In 1765, Parliament passed the most pernicious legislation of all that touched the lives of the most common citizen of the colonies. The Stamp Tax required that in order to obtain any paper related documents such as deeds, mortgages, licenses to practice law or medicine, sell liquor, obtain college diplomas, play cards or dice, buy almanacs, or calendars a person had to buy a stamp issued by the king. An additional law required the colonies to quarter the soldiers sent to enforce such laws. The general outcry began the familiar "no taxation without representation" slogan.

The situation deteriorated and the first shots rang out on April 19, 1775. The Second Continental Congress met the following month. Britain captured Boston that June, and the city was under a siege that lasted until the British were pushed back in March 1776. The widely distributed pamphlet, *Common Sense,* which had a distribution of 100,000, raised popular support with its cry for independence not just the redress of grievances. The colonies decided to form their own sovereign governments. South Carolina formed an independent government that month and proposed to frame a constitution by 1778. Virginia also declared itself to be a free state.

THE PEOPLE OVER KINGS

Let us dare to read, think, speak and write.[37]

The pending birth of the United States of America was announced on July 4, 1776 when the Continental Congress ratified the *Declaration of Independence*. The Congress assigned the task of drafting the *Declaration* to a committee of three—John Adams, Benjamin Franklin and Thomas Jefferson. Jefferson was the one who organized the ideas Franklin edited the work. The *Declaration of Independence*, to this day, is a powerful document. It not only argues that "all men" are naturally free and have certain rights but also argues that those rights can not be rightfully denied by any earthly power, for those rights are "endowed" by the "creator." It gives "the people" the sole right to form a government. From Voltaire the committee borrowed the idea of progress and thereby rejected the idea that life on earth was to be spent in misery and servitude to others. From Locke the committee took the doctrine of natural rights that held that all people had the right to life, liberty, and the pursuit of happiness.

While the colonists were loyal to England, ideas about self-determination, freedom to pursue ones goals, freedom to secure possessions and to enjoy life as one defined it attracted an increasingly large audience, especially in the middle and northern colonies. Given that the literacy rate among the colonists was relatively high, it is not surprising that many were aware of and participating in the intellectual movement, known as the Enlightenment, that spanned across several nations. The Enlightenment, as Peter Gay recorded, was "a loose, informal, wholly unorganized coalition of cultural critics, religious skeptics, and political reformers from Edinburgh to Naples, Paris to Berlin, Boston to Philadelphia." Those who participated in the Enlightenment were "united on a vastly ambitious program of secularism, humanity, cosmopolitanism, and freedom, above all freedom in its many forms—freedom from arbitrary power, freedom of speech, freedom of trade, freedom to realize one's talents, freedom of aesthetic response, freedom in a word, of moral man to make his own way in the world."[38] Those who were part of that coalition in a variety of ways argued for freedom and for protection of the people's rights. John Locke's *Treatise on Government* described governments as compacts or contracts among the people designed to protect life and property. When contracts were broken, when government failed and became tyrannical, the people, Locke argued, had the right to revolt. Revolutionary social thought circulating in France before the American and French Revolutions also found its way to England and the colonies. Montesquieu's *Esprit des Lois* (*The Spirit of the Laws*) published in 1748, was made available in English and reinforced ideas of freedom where the legitimacy of the state and stability are enforced by the rule of law rather than royal decree or divine intervention. Adam Ferguson's *An Essay on the History of Civil Society* depicted humans as active, creative, and capable of making progress toward their own happiness.

Enlightenment concepts of science and religion opened the possibility of human intervention into the physical and spiritual order. Sir Isaac Newton's rationalism challenged old superstitions and notions of astrology that placed the Creator at the center of the physical universe. The universal God of the New Testament replaced Jehovah, the God of the Old Testament. Human life and civilization were now seen as progressive rather than circular or apocalyptic. The Creator's design and will was made manifest in human initiative that improved material existence through technological innovation as well as the search for truth through the application of systematic scientific methods of inquiry. Human beings could find God's order through science, through the law, and through the struggle to overthrow tyranny.

Loyalists and Dissenters

Not all colonists disagreed with England's claims. Loyalists to the monarchy and England chose to leave the rebellious new nation and headed north to what are now the Maritime Provinces of Canada. The northernmost English colonies in what is now the Dominion of Canada did not participate in rebellion. Even former New France, whose people resented the imposition of English ways, chose loyalty to the monarchy over the disorder the prospect of a civil war promised. Even in the Continental Congress there was fear of the disorder and uncertainty that would likely accompany revolution. Where would the right to self-determination lead? There was disagreement over language used in the *Declaration of Independence*. The use of "the people" and "all men" was unsettling to some. Charles Beard and Mary Beard, in their *Basic History of the United States*, reported that: "Americans who, though they were disposed toward independence, were afraid that "the people" might set up governments destructive of the privileges hitherto enjoyed by particular classes in the colonies."[39] This fear persisted as the work to create a stable government began.

The Constitution and Nationhood

A treaty was signed between the United States of America and England on September 3, 1783. The Continental Congress ratified it in January 1784. From the early 1780s the colonies were bound together by *The Articles of Confederation*, but by the mid 1780s it was becoming clear that the *Articles* were not capable of dealing with the issues and problems the new nation faced. Consequently, a constitutional convention met in the spring of 1787 in Philadelphia to revise the *Articles*. The result of the convention's revision was the *United States Constitution*. The *Constitution* had to mediate among the interests of powerful groups fearful of losing privilege to "the people," the differences in the economies of the North and the South and the varying sizes of the populations in the former colonies. The *Constitution* was written as an agreement between the government and the people, but the people were to participate not directly but through representatives. The framers of the *Constitution* distrusted the common man and democratic rule. True democracy, they feared, would lead to the redistribution of property.[40] Following from the *Declaration of Independence*, it deals with individuals not states as part of a compromise. The states were to retain their autonomy. The role of the federal government and the role of the state governments, which were supposed to be quite powerful, were separated. The division of Congress into a Senate and a House of Representatives was a compromise. Each house was an agency of republican, not democratic government. The House would consist of representatives of people, and states with greater populations than others would have more representatives. However, in the Senate each state, no matter how large or small its population, would have two senators, and through that specification each state was equal to every other state in the Senate.

"The People" Qualified

The House of Representatives represented population and was intended as the vehicle of "the people." The people, however, consisted of "free persons," a designation that excluded those who were not free and explicitly excluded "Indians." To be one of "the people" one had to be a male and one had to own property. Since the southern white population of propertied people was quite small, slaves were counted as "three-fifths of all other persons." This was a compromise with the South, which otherwise would have had far fewer representatives in the House of Representatives. That compromise gave southern planters considerable power in the House of Representatives. Gender was not mentioned but it is clear that the idea that women had rights was not considered at any point. "People" clearly meant males. The House of Representatives as the "voice of the people" referred to free, landed, males. Other citizenship criteria were left up to the states but not for long. Explicit reference limiting citizenship to "white persons" was made clear in the Naturalization Act passed on March 26, 1790. By 1790, all the states had agreed to the *Constitution*, and the new nation had agreed on the ways it would govern and be governed.[41]

SLAVERY AND THE AMERICAN REVOLUTION

Allan Kulikoff observed that the American Revolution could have occurred without the presence of southern plantation slavery. Theodore Allan also emphasized that the choices that were made in the seventeenth century formation of large plantations with slave labor in the South could have been played out differently in the seventeenth century with the result that the "white race" based on skin privilege and concepts of white supremacy would not have been "invented."

The English crown and its colonial representatives in the South were correct in their belief that their pursuit of capital gain was enhanced by the concentration of wealth and power in their own hands at the expense of the common people. Had the South not been so successful in agrarian capitalism with the use of unpaid labor, it would have been in the same position as New England—a potential competitor with England. It would have been in a position to industrialize, build its own mills and would not have found use for slave labor. The colonies of the "Chesapeake planters . . . would have been as racially homogeneous as New England's"[42] without the slave trade or a need for it. The American Revolution would have taken place in a nation not divided by the color line of racial slavery and the dilemma it presented the new nation.

The Enlightenment's challenge to traditional views of human nature and Christian perceptions of history was a major ideological impetus for revolution that was felt worldwide. It also produced a major critique of slavery that demanded its abolition. By the 1750s the justifications for slavery sounded hollow, and critiques were widely distributed. Locke's defense was thoroughly discredited by Enlightenment thinkers such as Montesquieu in the 1730s. Montesquieu flatly stated in *The Spirit of the Laws*, that: "Slavery, properly so called, is the establishment of a right which gives to one man such a power over another as renders him absolute master over his life and fortune. The state of slavery is in its own nature bad." He maintained that "it is neither useful to the master nor to the slave; not to the slave because he can do nothing through a motive of virtue; nor to the master, because by having an unlimited authority over his slaves he insensibly accustoms himself to the want of all moral virtues, and thence becomes . . . cruel." Slavery was especially pernicious in democracies according to Montesquieu since "democracies . . . are all upon equality . . . Slavery is contrary to the constitution; it only contributes to give a power and luxury to citizens which they ought not to have."[43] Secular arguments in favor of slavery were further undermined by philosophes such as Jean Jacques Rousseau, Diderot, as well as David Hume and Benjamin Franklin. John Locke was the last major thinker to justify enslaving captives on a permanent basis. Locke's argument for liberty was found in the *Declaration of Independence*, not his defense of slavery.

Comparison with Ancient Slavery

It is important to note that other secular and religious defenses of slavery in the eighteenth century were not racially based. Slavery was defended on the grounds that it was a practice found in Greece, Rome, and even among early Christians. However, slavery in those eras and in those places was not based on any rationale that employed anything like a nineteenth century notion of race. One's eligibility for slavery depended on the nature of the society to which he belonged. Those who belonged to societies considered barbarous as opposed to civilized by those who invaded and conquered them were eligible for slavery. A person's or group's degree of civilization was not considered inborn by the either the Greeks or the Romans. Athens and Rome distinguished between being civilized and uncivilized according to one's citizenship and participation in a city-state with a political life.[44] In Athens and Rome some slaves had extensive rights and a variety of statuses. Some were highly respected and educated. Others had few rights and low status. Being a slave was not a permanent status. Having been a slave carried no stigma. Rome enslaved individuals from all the frontiers of its empire. Early Christians emphasized the spiritual equality of humanity and made no distinctions on the basis of phenotype.[45] Montesquieu criticized the arguments that justify slavery on the basis of its ancient origins as specious, ill conceived and self-serving. That included justifications based on:

1. the capture of prisoners in war;
2. as a right to enslave oneself when threatened with capital punishment, or benevolently to save another person's life by becoming his master;

3. to enslave people to save them in the name of religion; or
4. that people deserve to be enslaved on the basis their physical appearance or disagreements about their judgments.

Montesquieu emphasized the dangers of using slaves as a work force or for military purposes where their "multitudes" may well join with other so-called free and abused populations.[46]

The campaign to abolish slavery in the United States was carried on by the various Christian sects. Christian opposition to slavery developed before the War of Independence. The Quakers, also called the Society of Friends, moved to expel slaveholders and buyers at a meeting in Philadelphia in 1758. The ban was to exclude those who trafficked in slavery from their business meetings. This was extended to expulsion from the congregation in 1761. To enforce these edicts committees visited slaveholders and worked to convince them to free their slaves. David Brion Davis argued that the challenge of social change forced American Calvinists to resolve contradictions in their views. They perceived the contradictions between creating a society based on conscience and the "higher laws" of nature that transcended human laws that justified revolution based on individual rights of self-determination and the presence of slave labor that nullified free will. Abolitionists rejected the notion that black slavery could be rationalized by Christian love and mutual obligation.[47] In their view, treating the human as an object or commodity was a serious transgression. Slavery was an evil that revealed the infinite depravity of the human heart. The Abolition movement in both England and in the American colonies campaigned for manumission. Closing the door to the unlimited power wielded by the master was a precursor to closing the door of evil to all forbidden desires and unimaginable transgressions against God. Quakers and evangelical abolitionists concluded that the power to do evil was evil itself.[48]

Slavery Did Not Cause Racism

A persistent humanism influenced by the Enlightenment pervaded social thought leading up to the American Declaration of Independence. While slaves were of inferior status and treated as such, they were not considered a different species, nor was their enslavement justified on these grounds. Divisions in social standing were taken, in the terms of John Locke, as caused by differences in experience. It was assumed that Africans were in a transition from tribalism to civilization. Slavery for African Americans, in this view, was good as a transition. The elevation of the privileges of Anglo-Saxon Europeans as bonded-servants and wage labors, and the relegation of African Americans to hereditary racial slavery, justified the elite position of a plantation aristocracy as representatives of the superior

English way of life. Regardless of the contorted ideology, the political use of racial division was to offset the potential for mass rebellion in the tumultuous years leading to the American Revolution.

Common social thought and historical scholarship often reverse the causal relationships among oppression, slavery, and racism. Racism did not cause slavery and oppression. Racial slavery was not founded on ideological differences with African Americans but rather circumstantial decisions that allowed elites to maintain and extend their wealth and power by repressing the freedom and civil rights of the weakest group in order to establish a large unpaid labor force.[49] Similar tactics were used to oppress the Irish both in Ireland and in the colonies as well as the American Indians almost as soon as the English encountered them. African Americans were not able to protect their civil rights from the encroachment of plantation owners; and elites successfully established white supremacy and racial slavery as an antidote to the potential for lower class Anglo-European, Irish rebellion. White supremacy, racial oppression, and racial slavery depended on the elaboration of the Anglo-Saxon view of their right to conquer and subjugate others. Their belief in the privileges of social class and the superior quality of their institutions (legal and religious) was used to justify war, genocide, acts of cruelty, and barbarism against groups they stripped of their power to retaliate.[50] The paternalistic system of subordination in the colonial South was sufficient to maintain Anglo-Saxon supremacy as the guiding legal principle for nearly a century. Explanations for physical differences and differential treatment were described and justified in environmental, not innate, terms.[51]

Western European colonialism, as the origin of the settlement of all of the Americas including the United States, was premised on the expansion of trade and on the right of superior civilizations and conquerors to usurp the land, wealth, property, and persons of "lesser" peoples and nations. The multiple European origins of the colonies as African, Spanish, Portuguese, French, and Dutch as well as English did not become part of the origin myths of the United States any more than the perspectives of the original indigenous tribes and high civilization of pre-Columbian America. The English version of the nature and origin of the United States shaped the dominant image and projected preferred practices even though the actual origin of the colonies was much more diverse. English institutions and peculiar problems also took on a new life in the colonies of British North America.

The Anglo-American Republic Confirmed

The vision of a nation "for the people," made assumptions about who Americans were to be. They were narrowly seen to be of Anglo-Saxon origin and of Christian faith with specifically Protestant values. The 1790 Naturalization Act limited the right to naturalized citizenship to land owning "white persons" without specifying gender, but male dominance was understood and unquestioned. Citizenship, leadership, inheritance, and ideal family structure retained a typical English patriarchal format. Women were assigned the status of the dominant males in their lives and were not included in governance. The founders were educated and of middle to upper class standing as landowners and persons of power in their communities. The self-chosen dominant group projected not only an Anglo-Saxon outlook but also the English language as the dominant means of communication. The nation did not exclude but did not recognize the languages spoken by colonists from other countries or the languages of the American Indian nations. Groups or individuals that differed from themselves did not have equal claim to their own language, culture, religion, or lifestyle.

The establishment of English as the dominant language and the Americanization of the population through a break with classical traditions in education can be attributed to Benjamin Franklin and Noah Webster. Franklin was the promoter, organizer, and designer of the Philadelphia Academy, which opened in 1751.[52] The Academy emphasized the English language and de-emphasized Latin and Greek. The school was to be an "English school" where children in a sequence of six classes would learn reading, speaking, letter writing, and composition in English to the exclusion of other languages. The texts were also to be of contemporary English authors or English translations of the classics.[53] Webster carried the English emphasis even further with his speller published in 1783. Webster argued that: "as an independent nation, our honor requires us to have a system of our own, in language as well as in government." A common American English was to unify the people. He sought to standardize not only the spelling and "purity of the American tongue," but to standardize the purity of the American people as English speaking.[54]

Anglo-Saxon supremacy of civil society was translated into an amorphous "white" male dominated, Protestant, middle to upper class ideal family and social structure. What it meant to be an American was conceptually and legally defined by criteria that excluded many and included only a few. It became necessary for established residents and new comers to try to prove that they matched the ideal. As immigrants struggled to do so the historical fixation on classifying human beings became a part of American social, political, and economic structure.

FORESHADOWED CONVENTIONS OF RACE AND ETHNICITY

Slavery was early justified by Europeans on the basis of a religious mission to Christianize heathens. That argument was not dominant in the slow development of slavery in the United States although the presence of slavery failed in the Middle Colonies and New England in part because of religious opposition as well as the advance of industry, urbanization, wage labor, and the predominance of small farms that made slavery inefficient. The Virginia Assembly demonstrated its indifference to the mission of evangelizing individuals being subjected to repressive laws leading to racial slavery and white privilege: "Baptisme doth not alter the condition of the person as to his bondage or freedom . . ."[55] The change in the attitude toward Christianity as distinct from a doctrine of freedom, which originally protected white chattel servants from becoming perpetual slaves gave way to the use or misuse of scripture to justify enslaving Africans as heathens. The other more pernicious development was a follow through on the idea of the savage and wild aspects of tribal peoples. Servants came from Christian lands and Africans came from lands of barbarians. They were separate from the civilizing influence of European culture. The cultural prejudices of the English somehow allowed them to believe that Africans were a separate race, by nature, by temperament, by skin color, by ability. This belief, like slavery in British North America, was slow to evolve but, its use as a defense of slavery was devastating for free and enslaved African Americans in the years leading up to and even long after the American Revolution.

NOTES

1. Thomas Jefferson, Benjamin Franklin, and John Adams, *Declaration of Independence*, Ratified July 4, 1776.
2. Quoted in Robert Hughes. *American Visions: The Epic History of Art in America* (New York: Alfred A. Knopf, 1997), p. 23.
3. Ibid.
4. James Baldwin, "A Talk to Teachers," from an article, "The Negro Child-His Self Image," published in the *Saturday Evening Post*, December 21, 1963. The original was delivered as a lecture on October 16, 1963.
5. Gunnar Myrdal, *An American Dilemma: The Negro Problem and Modern Democracy* (New York: Harper and Brothers, 1944); Alexis de Tocqueville, *Democracy in America*, Garvey C. Mansfield and Delba Winthrop, trans., eds., (Chicago: University of Chicago, 2000), pp. 302-400.
6. John Locke, *The Works of John Locke, in Ten Volumes* (St. John's Square, Clerkenwell, England: J. Johnson et. al.1801).
7. Ivan Hannaford, *Race: The History of an Idea in the West* (Baltimore: Johns Hopkins University Press, 1996).
8. John Locke, "Some Considerations on the Consequences of lowering the Interest, and raising the Value of Money, a letter sent to Parliament in 1691," pp. 2-116; "Short Observations on a printed paper, a letter to Sir John Sommers, knt., Lord Keeper of the seal of England, and one of his Majesty's most Honorable Privy Council," pp. 117-130; and "Further Considerations concerning raising the Value of Money," pp. 131-207, in *The Works of John Locke*, Vol. V.

9. John Locke, "The Fundamental Constitution of Carolina," in the *Works of John Locke*, Vol. X, pp. 175-199.

10. Ibid, see sections XCV, XCVI, XCVII.

11. John Locke, "Two Treatises of Government, Book I," in *The Works of John Locke, Vol. V*, pp 285-409.

12. Ibid., § 2, p. 212.

13. Ibid., Book II, § 22, p. 351.

14. Ibid., p. 352.

15. Josephine Zuppan, "The John Custis Letterbook, 1724 to 1734," Masters Thesis, College of William and Mary, 1978, pp. 34-35.

16. Thomas E. Buckely, S. J. "Unfixing Race: Class, Power and Identity in an Interracial Family," *Virginia Magazine of History and Biography*, CII (1994, pp. 340-380, see 350, 355, 363).

17. Douglass Adair, Jefferson Scandals, in Douglas Adair, ed., *Fame and the Founding Fathers: Essays by Douglass Adair* (New York: Trevor Colbourn, 1974), pp. 160-191; Lucia Stanton, "Those Who Labor for My Happiness: Thomas Jefferson and his Slaves," in Peter S Onuf, ed. *Jeffersonian Legacies* (Charlottesville: University of Virginia, 1993), p. 147-180.

18. Edward Ball, *Slaves in the Family* (New York: Ballantine Books, 1999); Henry Wiencek, *The Hairstons: An American Family in Black and White*. (New York: St. Martin's Press, 1999).

19. Philip D. Morgan, *Slave Counterpoint: Black Culture in the Eighteenth Century Chesapeake and Low Country* (Chapel Hill: University of North Carolina, 1998), p. 61.

20. Ibid., p. 94.

21. Ibid., pp. 125-127, 130, 132-133.

22. Ibid., pp. 125-127.

23. Ibid., pp. 134-142.

24. Ibid., pp. 147, 159, 164.

25. Ibid., pp. 19, 191, 195.

26. Ibid., pp. 197.

27. Wilma King, *Stolen Childhood: Slave Youth in Nineteenth Century America*. (Bloomington: Indiana University, 1995); Deborah Gray White, *Ar'n't I a Woman? Female Slaves in the Plantation South*. (New York: W. W. Norton, 1999); Morgan, *Slave Counterpoint, pp.* 498-519.

28. Morgan, *Slave Counterpoint*, p. 262.

29. Ibid., p. 261.

30. William Waller Hening, *The Statutes at Large: Being a Collection of All the Laws of Virginia . . .*" 13 Volumes. (Richmond: State Library of Virginia, 1809-1823), Vol 2, p. 270.

31. Morgan, *Slave Counterpoint*, p. 262; see also, Igor Kopytoff, "Slavery," *Annual Review of Anthropology*, XI, 1982): 207-230; Moses I. Finley, *Ancient Slavery and Modern Ideology* (Harmondsworth, England, 1983; expanded ed. Princeton, N.J.: Markus Wiener, 1998), pp. 73-75; David Brion Davis, *The Problem of Slavery in Western Culture* (Ithaca, NY: Cornell University, 1966).

32. John Hope Franklin, *From Slavery to Freedom*, 3rd ed. (New York: Knopf, 1967), p. 76.

33. Ibid., pp. 77-8.

34. Ibid., p. 88.

35. This is an old English couplet cited in Charles Beard and Mary Beard, *A Basic History of the United States* (New York: Doubleday, Doran & Co. 1944,) pp. 55-56.

36. Beard and Beard, *Basic History of the United States*, p. 87.

37. This quotation is from John Adams in 1765.

38. Peter Gay. *The Enlightenment: The Rise of Modern Paganism* (New York: Alfred A. Knopf, 1966), p. 1.

39. Ibid., p. 108.

40. Richard Hofstadter, *The American Political Tradition and the Men Who Made It* (New York: Vintage Books, 1976), p. 15.

41. Ian F. Haney Lopez, "Then What is White?" in Richard Delgado, *Critical Race Theory*, ch. 47, pp. 542-550. The second act on citizenship, 26 March 1795, ch 3., 1 Stat 103, became the Immigration and Nationality Act § 1101 (a) (23) (1952).

42. Allan Kulikoff, "The Colonial Chesapeake: Seedbed of Antebellum Southern Culture?" *Journal of Southern History*, 45, (1975): 525-526; Theodore Allen, *The Invention of the White Race*, Vol 2.

43. Baron de Montesquieu, Trans. Thomas Nugent, Intro. Franz Neumann, *The Spirit of the Laws*, Book XV (London: Collier MacMillan, 1949, first published in France 1731), p. 235.

44. George M. Fredrickson, *Racism: A Short History* (Princeton: Princeton University Press, 2002), p. 17.

45. Ibid.

46. Montesquieu, *The Spirit of the Laws*, pp. 235-250.

47. David Brion Davis, *Slavery and Progress* (New York: Oxford, 1984), p. 146

48. Ibid., p. 147.

49. U.B. Phillips, *Life and Labor in the Old South*, (Boston: Little, Brown and Co., 1929), p. 160.

50. See Reginald Horsman, *Race and Manifest Destiny: The Origins of American Racial Anglo-Saxonism* (Cambridge, MA.: Harvard University Press, 1981), chs.1 and 2 on the Anglo-Saxon tradition; and ch. 5 on its impact in the United States.

51. Oscar Handlin, *Race and Nationality in the United States* (Boston: Little and Brown, 1957), p.19.

52. Benjamin Franklin, "Proposals Relating to the Education of Youth in Pennsylvania," in Thomas Woody, ed., *Educational Views of Benjamin Franklin* (New York: McGraw-Hill, 1931), p. 150.

53. Benjamin Franklin, "Idea of the English School," in Woody, *Educational Views of Benjamin Franklin*, p. 129; Erwin V. Johanningmeier, *Americans and their Schools* (Dallas, TX: Houghton Mifflin Co., 1980), pp.40-41.

54. Noah Webster, *Dissertations of the English Language: With Notes, Historical and Critical* (Boston: Isaiah Thomas and Co. 1839), p. 20; Henry Steele Commanger, ed., *Noah Webster's American Spelling Book* (New York: Teacher's College Press, 1962), pp. 61-63; Johanningmeier, *Americans*, pp. 62-63.

55. Statement by the Virginia Assembly, 1667, quoted in Franklin, *From Slavery*, p. 86.

CHAPTER 4

THE AMERICAN REVOLUTION TO THE CIVIL WAR
Abolition, and the Invention of Racism

No Matter how many years may pass, the stigma of slavery will remain ineradicably imprinted on our country. It was an established fact long before our birth as a nation; it caused our greatest war; it has shadowed every struggle, defeat, and victory of our land. Whites still apologize for it; blacks still resent it; and we are all oppressed by its legacy.[1]

LET MY PEOPLE GO

The abolitionists' optimism and their campaign for manumission and the end of slavery met with some success in the Revolutionary period. Many African Americans were emancipated during and after the War for Independence. Hundreds of thousands of slaves were emancipated or won free-

Race, Ethnicity, and Education: What is Taught in School, pages 85–118.
A Volume in: International Perspectives on Curriculum
Copyright © 2003 by Information Age Publishing, Inc.
All rights of reproduction in any form reserved.
ISBN: 1-59311-080-4 (paper), 1-59311-081-2 (cloth)

dom through revolt, military service, or escape. In colonies, such as Virginia, religious and humanitarian values undermined traditional support for bondage. Revolutionary ideology, reward for service and fear of reprisals encouraged widespread manumission in the southern colonies. The impact of the American Revolution also sanctioned the manumission of African slaves throughout the Caribbean and Spanish America.[2]

The Constitution allowed slavery to continue as states had the right to determine patterns of immigration and the importation of labor. However, the demand for human rights as self-evident truths heightened awareness of the contradictions in a society composed of free men and slaves. The slave trade seen as incompatible with the political ideology of freedom came under great fire and was prohibited state by state, first in Delaware in 1776, Virginia in 1778, Maryland in 1783, South Carolina in 1787, North Carolina in 1794, and Georgia in 1798. It was briefly opened again in South Carolina in 1803, and finally closed completely by federal legislation in 1807.

The position that slavery was anti-Christian seemed to be winning. According to popular opinion, the end of slavery was inevitable. The War for Independence and the end of the slave trade encouraged some to free their slaves. Freed slaves moved to Savannah and Charleston in the South and to New York, Boston, and Philadelphia in the North. The numbers of free African Americans increased in both rural areas and the growing urban centers of commerce, transportation, and manufacturing between 1776 and 1812. The number of free African-Americans in 1790 was 60,000. This number doubled in the next ten years; and tripled in the next twenty. The free African-American population stood at 300,000 in 1830 just as the abolitionist movement and its opponents both gathered strength.

The assumption that slavery would end a natural death proved false. It did not. The abolitionist movement rose in response to the recognition that slavery was becoming more entrenched in response to economic changes and political decisions of those who stood to lose power and who wanted to maintain their ideology, traditional status, and life styles.

King Cotton and Slavery

A new crop emerged to take the place of tobacco, and it had a dire effect on the future of slavery and the fate of the nation. The invention of the cotton gin in 1794 made raw cotton production profitable and raised the price of slaves as a valuable source of labor. The rise of the cotton monoculture in the antebellum period was similar to the rise of the tobacco monoculture in the early colonial era. The division of labor in the southern colonial plantation economy, however, established contradictions that hampered a transition from agrarian capitalism to industrial capitalism in the Nationalist Period. When the North industrialized, urbanized, and expanded, immigrants provided the needed labor. The dependence on cotton and the rejection of industrial manufacturing in the textile industry continued and reinforced the inequalities of earlier times. Cotton rejuvenated agricultural mercantile capitalism and with it the Southern aristocracy. However, the South was dependent on the industrial North where the textile mills in the United States were first located or they had to rely on England's mills.

The South's commitment to monoculture, unstable markets, and competition favored large plantations and weakened small farmers. Small farmers were more vulnerable to cycles of over production and falling prices than were the holders of large plantations. New slave states and the expansion of the Cotton Belt challenged the older cotton economies to increase their production in order to stay competitive. The small minority of southern landowners with plantations over two thousand acres and more than one plantation were the only ones capable of managing the political and economic pressures, but it was becoming increasingly difficult. In the antebellum period, the fixed capital of the plantation elite was tied up in property—land, slaves, and equipment; and their liquid capital was drained away by the cost of shipping raw cotton. Tariffs, commissions, interest, and freight costs drastically reduced profits. To plant crops and buy equipment money had to be borrowed. The planter class also faced competition from northern capitalist adventurers as well as a growing class of bourgeois urban Southerners who were attracted by entrepreneurial opportunities and were pushing for industrialization, which could have ended slavery and diversified production.[3] The entrepreneurial classes were unable to develop mills without wage labor, and the plantation elite believed they could not maintain their lifestyle with wage labor. Plantation elites were reluctant to allow industrialization if it undermined their power and way of life, even if allowing and developing industry solved the problem of their dependence on the industrialized economies in the north. The planter elites remained at odds with the urban bourgeoisie. They had to choose between dependency on the British textile industry or the mills of New England. To choose New England would have disadvantaged the plantation aristocrats and risked pressure from abolitionists to emancipate slaves. They chose to retain traditional colonial class relations, the colonial political power and status hierarchy, and the plantation economy, including slavery. The South did not industrialize and develop textile mills until a coalition of southern elites and northern philanthropists emerged after Reconstruction in the Progressive Era.[4]

INVENTING SCIENTIFIC RACISM IN THE ANTEBELLUM PERIOD

Understanding the experience of African Americans in the United States is important because the colorline also shaped the experience of other groups, especially in the antebellum period when racism was legitimated. Racism also affected the experience of the Irish as they fled the potato famine and came to the United States in the mid-nineteenth century. American Indian nations were adversely affected as the nation expanded across the plains and converted the ancestral homes of the first nations into United States territory where Indians were not wanted. The Spanish and Mexican populations of the West stood in the way of the expansion of the United States in its press toward the Pacific.

Up to 1812, elites in both the North and South rejected the idea of immutable divisions between groups of human beings, but this was rapidly changing.[5] Racial taxonomies directed toward the differentiation of human beings into subcategories did not predate the invention of the taxonomies based on "scientific evidence" and their questionable application to human populations. Up to this time there was virtually no conception of racial divisions among humans, free or not free as innate, unchangeable, and biological. There was little reason to make such a distinction. John Locke justified the use of not free and unpaid labor in racial slavery as a legitimate outcome of acts of war in the capture and use of prisoners whose lives had been spared. The right of planters and those in power to use labor as they saw fit was not generally questioned and certainly did not need justification on the basis of a theory of racial superiority. Class superiority and power to enforce the legality of bondage was sufficient.

The persistence of humanism in popular thought as an outgrowth of the Enlightenment was paralleled by Enlightenment insistence on science and objective investigation based on the observation of natural phenomena, rational thought, deliberate action, and the rule of law. The earliest use of the term "race" was in the late sixteenth century and referred to divisions in living creatures that spoke of the "human race or the races of mankind." Shakespeare used it in this sense in 1607, as did Milton in 1667.[6] Race was used as a synonym for " a people" or "a nation." Racist ideas that suggested innate biological differences among races of humanity were expressed in the eighteenth century without systematic follow through. Carolus Linnaeus in *Systema naturae*, mixed character and physical attributes in 1758.[7] These ideas were refuted in Samuel Stanhope Smith's, *Essay on the Causes of the Variety of Complexion and Figure in the Human Species*, originally published in 1787, and republished after his death in 1810. A Presbyterian minister, he argued for monogenesis, the common lineage of human beings as one species. The Bible supported his argument for the divine origin of humankind created in the image of

God. Smith attracted widespread public support for his environmentalist position.[8]

Debates over Polygenesis and the Formation of Racism

The doctrine of Anglo-Saxon, "white" supremacy was a useful way to defend politically racial slavery and the status of the plantation elite in the southern economy, but it had to be brought up to date and made immutable. The myth of the superior, free, and noble institutions of Anglo-Saxon, Protestant, patriarchal tradition was carried to its logical extreme by replacing the claim of superior institutions with the claim of a group of people with inborn superior attributes, a superior race. The next step was to establish a scientific argument for multiple, unequal races of human beings. Enlightenment thought pressed human beings toward self-determination. It also was adapted to justify oppression. The first taxonomies of human races were based on pre-scientific ideas about observation and evidence.[9]

Intellectuals and would-be scientists were the first to support racism. Early theories that held that there were multiple human races were based on arguments rather than results of scientific investigations. Charles Caldwell, a doctor in North Carolina, began to criticize Smith as early as 1811 in *Thoughts on the Original Unity of the Human Race.* He employed a biblical argument for polygenesis and the separate origin of Africans, dating from Noah's ark.[10] George Cuvier, a founder of the fields of geology and comparative anatomy in France wrote about "degraded" human races in 1812.[11] Racist theories and claims of human biological differences among races were politically useful. Richard H. Colfax employed race to counter the abolition movement.[12] Probably the first scientific arguments heard in the United States were from French immigrant, J. J. Virey, a proponent of polygenesis whose 1801 book was translated and presented at the Charleston Literary and Philosophical Society in 1837.[13] His thesis became the doctrine that supported the American "school of ethnology" that embraced the idea that the races of mankind were biologically distinct and unequal. Ethnology was integrated into the early disciplines of physical anthropology and the social sciences that combined eugenics and racist ideology. By the late eighteenth century, these views were a significant part of scientific dogma and were included in encyclopedias and texts as fact.[14] The explanations or justifications for slavery in the late eighteenth century somehow overlooked that chattel servitude and racial slavery began as institutions that solved the practical needs of elite planters for cheap labor in their quest for power and profit.

Measuring Heads: Samuel Morton and Josaih Nott

Samuel George Morton of Philadelphia, a student of ethnology, published *Crania Americana* (1839), a study of head circumferences. He measured white, "Negro," and Indian skulls. A second book was published in 1844 with a supply of Egyptian skulls from Egyptologist, George R. Gliddon. Morton concluded that American Indians and "Negroes" were inferior to Anglo-Saxons and that Egyptians were Anglo-Saxon.[15] Josiah C. Nott of Alabama, who conducted research trying to prove that mixed races were weaker and less fertile than pure races, joined Morton and Glidden as researcher and spokesperson. When Morton died in 1851, R.W. Gibbs wrote in an obituary published in the *Charleston Medical Journal* of his appreciation for Morton's contribution to the planters' argument that Africans should remain slaves. "We of the South should consider him as our benefactor, for aiding most materially in giving to the Negro his true position as an inferior race."[16]

Josiah Nott took Morton's place as a leader in the polygenesis debate. He published articles on the significance of race for culture. He lobbied for slavery, claiming the inferiority of African Americans. He gave addresses to the Southern Rights Association in Mobile and anti-abolition lectures on, "The Natural History of Mankind." In 1856, he edited the classic racial text by French Count Joseph Arthur de Gobineau, *Essae sur l'iné-galité des races humaines,* for an American audience.[17] When Swiss biologist, Louis Agassiz, joined the Harvard faculty in 1848, he was drawn into the race debate. Agassiz concluded that since differences in the plant and animal kingdom could be attributed to environmental differences, human difference must similarly indicate the permanence of race characteristics and that race theory could be subsumed under an accepted scientific chronology of life on earth.[18]

The Use of Stereotypes to Foster Racist Beliefs

With increased manumission and sharper criticism of slavery, the general public became more aware of the issues. Two perspectives developed over the validity of slavery and its defense on the basis of race. In popular histories the concept of race is often depicted as a debate between the North and the South. However, in both the North and the South racist propaganda was not confined to the halls of science. Stereotypes and propaganda that defended slavery and advertised the problem of the "Negroes" to people in the North were actively discussed in the living rooms and society clubs of the educated upper class as well as in the popular media. Few northerners or pioneers in the western movement had personal experience with African Americans and they were vulnerable to negative stereo-types.

The stereotypical figures of slaves on plantations were depicted in female "Mammy" figures and the male "Uncle Tom" figures in the 1820s.[19] Minstrel shows, the first form of popular mass musical entertainment, car-ried the images of blacks to millions of northerners. The most popular fig-ures were anti-African American and successful nearly overnight. The "Jim Crow" figure of the dancing slave became the popular title of the legisla-tion that segregated the South half a century later.[20] It is not accidental that the Irish, the lowest rung of the Anglo-European bonded servant group, became the first black face minstrels. Ridicule encouraged accep-tance of race as a category and it popularized racist thinking.[21] This was not done without protest from the African American community but to lit-tle avail. At the Colored National Convention, held in Rochester New York in 1853, participants loudly condemned the "Jim Crow branding of the Negro citizen . . . with prejudice and prosecution."[22]

Propaganda against African Americans grew more vicious in the North. Free African Americans were depicted as indolent vagrants, vicious, and an economic burden to whites as well as a threat to civilization. The white press and popular mythology suggested that the social exclusion of free African Americans made them discontent, and with this sense of grievance they would plot the overthrow of whites. The imagery of the idleness and shiftlessness of free blacks resulted in the negative urban stereotypic char-acters of "Zip Coon" and "Jim Dandy" who mocked the ability of African Americans to handle freedom and responsibility. African Americans regardless of their social, economic, or political status were subjected to inescapable discrimination on the basis of their skin color.[23]

Modern Racism

The use of pseudo-science to defend slavery was the beginning of mod-ern racism. This was translated into social policy. Ending the slave trade did not end slavery. It continued to expand throughout the antebellum period. The ordinance of 1787 prohibited slavery north of the Ohio River but not south of it. With Western expansion, the slave state and free state line grew until 1845 to include Kentucky, Tennessee, Mississippi, Alabama, Louisiana, Missouri, Arkansas, and Florida. The Missouri Compromise in 1850 opened Utah and New Mexico as potential slave states and potential cotton monocultures with the help of slave labor. The *Scott v Sanford,* case better known as the Dred Scott decision, was handed down by the Supreme Court in 1857. It declared slaves to be personal property and non-citizens who could not sue in court. Even free blacks were barred from citizenship according to the court because they did not have any rights that a "white man is bound to respect."[24]

ANTEBELLUM SLAVERY: SLAVE NARRATIVES

One way to examine the black experience is from the perspective of those who lived within its grasp. From 1619 to the death of the last person to be born into slavery in the 1970s, six thousand American slaves wrote their stories or told them to others who recorded them. Perhaps, as consistent with the tendency to pay little or no attention to the actual experiences of subordinated groups, these narratives have been questioned, ignored, and even dismissed as false. They often have not been considered legitimate sources of information in spite of the fact that they are direct records of what individuals experienced often with considerable details of their daily life. Only recently have these voices of the past found an audience and been heard. Slavery was such a contentious issue that descriptions of it still often carry considerable emotional content.

Slave narratives served many purposes, as propaganda, as stories, as records. They are a witness to the strength, fortitude, and intelligence of the African people who became Americans. The earliest narratives from 1770 to 1820, such as Olaudah Equiano's, tend to be adventure stories and tell of journeys of spiritual awakening. Olaudah's narrative was the second to be published and is among the three in which the subject was not born a slave. Olaudah's narrative is also among three that achieved the status of legitimate classic literature. Other famous narratives include Frederick Douglass' *Narrative of the Life of Frederick Douglas: An American Slave, Written by Himself*, and Harriet Jacob's *Incidents in the Life of a Slave Girl, Written by Herself*. The classic narratives are complemented by less formal narratives told to researchers or other individuals. At Fisk University, the Social Science Institute's, *The American Slave: A Composite Autobiography*, fills nineteen volumes. The stories and records of individuals from North and South Carolina, Texas, Alabama, Indiana, Oklahoma, Mississippi, Arkansas, Georgia, Kansas, Kentucky, Maryland, Ohio, Virginia, Tennessee, and Florida are included.

"I Speak with My Own Voice. In My Own Words."

Olaudah Equiano, a Guinean by birth published his autobiography in 1789. He told the story of his childhood in West Africa, his capture and enslavement by African raiders and his subsequent abduction and journey to the West Indies. Olaudah's story describes the expected cruelty of slavery but also its bizarre fluidity and instability. Olaudah at various times experienced life both as a slave and as a free person in the Caribbean, in the mainland colonies of North America and England. Intelligent, innovative, and educated, Olaudah experienced the extremes of slavery and freedom. He suffered the discomfort and pain of the total loss of control over his life as a slave but managed to find ways to mediate his situation. He gained freedom not once but several times and eventually achieved independence in a safe environment. His life demonstrates the dangers of being an African in the times of the slave trade. Acquiring freedom legitimately through manumission or buying his own freedom did not protect him from being recaptured by traders legitimate and illegitimate. His masters were sometimes cruel and unreasonable and at other times reasonable and intelligent. Others were stupid and capable of being tricked. His original forced exodus from Africa took him on an involuntary journey, but he was also able to choose voluntary adventures and traveled throughout much of the New World. Olaudah's story demonstrates that slavery took a number of forms depending on the time and location. Being subject to individual masters in urban settings and as a mariner rather than born on a large plantation in the southern colonies made a significant difference in that travel offered considerable opportunity for education, training, and ultimately self-expression. Urban dwelling provided opportunities to be hired out or to engage independently in wage labor. The ability to acquire personal property and freedom varied enormously. Olaudah eventually died in England after creating a sensation with his expose of slavery. His obvious wit and scholarly ability belied the illegitimacy of racial inferiority.[25] As he noted: "The abolition of slavery would in reality be a universal good. Tortures, murder, and every other imaginable barbarity and iniquity, are practiced upon the poor slaves with impunity."[26]

Narratives are the unwritten history of slavery. They expose the inhumanity of an impersonal institution that operated with real people. The creation of an ideology of racial differences and rationalizations for forced servitude simply fall apart in light of what the narratives reveal. The narratives also reveal an incredible capacity for human understanding and resistance to injustice. The legal system of slavery was simply cruel, but it was either made worse or mediated by the actions and decision of individuals. Individuals tell narratives, but they represent patterns shared by others.

The Attitudes of "White Folk"

What masters thought about slaves and what white people learned to believe about people of African or Indian heritage, created ironies and pathos. As Kenneth M. Stampp noted: "to understand the South is to feel the pathos in its history . . . they know, better than most other Americans, that little ironies fill the history of mankind and that large disasters from time to time unexpectedly shape its course."[27] The common humanity of master and slave is evident in the narratives. Former slaves sometimes note: "there are some good white folks." However, the institution that allowed human beings to be treated as things assured that "mighty few," whites of any class could rise above the social norms.[28] White people, especially in the South, were taught directly and indirectly to disregard the humanity of those held in bondage as property. Charles Bell described the callous behavior of one of his masters:

> He never spoke to us in words of either pity or hatred; and never spoke of us, except to order us to be fed or watered, as he would have directed the same offices to be performed for so many horses, or to inquire where the best prices could be obtained for us. He regarded us only as objects of traffic and the materials of his commerce . . .[29]

Most often slaves referred to the cruel and arbitrary behavior of "white folks" when given the opportunity to recount their experiences with impunity: "My ole master's son was mean and his wife was mean"[30] is a simple statement of observation. J. David Knottnerus argued that relationships on plantations were both hierarchical and highly ritualized. Much has been made of a "slave personality," that was docile, and dependent on their masters. It benefited whites to project these images. However, draconian laws and outrageous punishments for small infractions are evidence that whites only half believed, if they believed at all, their own myths. Their actions to insulate themselves from their critics and protect themselves from the victims of an unjust system tell otherwise.[31]

Poor blacks and poor whites had much in common. Sometimes blacks had the upper hand and reached out to help whites. "When I had a restaurant I never turned a [white] hobo down. If they would come in hungry I would give them something to eat. I always had a big table full..." Occasionally their acts of kindness were recognized: "I remember one day a white man come up to me and shook me...and said "You don't know me do you?" She had no recollection of the person, who continued: "Well if you don't know me, you will know me. This is the old hobo."[32] He returned to recognize and reward her when his fortune changed. Much to her surprise "he threw three silver dollars in my lap." Just dessert occasionally surfaced.

Family Life in a Regime of Coercion, Discipline, and Punishment

Discipline was at the heart of the power struggle that defined master-slave relations. Most slaves had witnessed terrible beatings and were themselves beaten. Some witnessed lynchings: " I do remember when they hung a man up there at the jail." The description does not stress the horror or helplessness of being powerless in the face of injustice. Instead the bravery, pride, and dignity of the victim is recalled: "And he walked out just as unconcerned and stood up on his own coffin, with a cigar in his mouth and his cap tilted back on his head . . . He told them they was doing wrong."[33] Another description of a lynching is factually descriptive, yet personal: "they hung two men by the neck right where I was living."[34] Physical threat was real, palpable, and ever present in ways that controlled the lives of slaves and masters, the oppressed and the oppressor.

Families did all they could to protect themselves and each other but that was not always possible. Poor whites also had the power to abuse black women and children. Children were well aware of their white lineage: "My grandfather was an Irishman and he was a foreman." This fact did not necessarily mean that this father and grandfather spared his offspring. "He had to whip his children and his grandchildren just like the others."[35]

As Wilma King emphasized, black family loyalty was a prominent feature of the slaves' struggle to survive. Families worked hard to maintain connections. "My father belonged to another set of white people. When my mother was living, he come most every week to see her. Then after she died he comes every two weeks to see me and my brother."[36] Others, after years of separation, still sought out their kin. Some were successful. "In 1890 I found my mother; and I was gone from her for 33 years before I knew anything about her. She was no further than Springfield, Kentucky. I went to get her, and she wanted to come, but she belonged to the Catholic Church, and they wouldn't let me have her. She was 73 years old then and earning wages . . . They drove me out of there when they found out I was a Protestant. . . She died two years later."[37]

Personal lives, families, and sexual relationships, black and white, were voluntary and involuntarily intertwined. White dominance over black was unquestioned in the institution of slavery, but lived reality was more complex. The South's own political and moral superstructure circumscribed the conduct of slaves and masters but it did not always work out in an orderly or disciplined manner. One woman commented on the bizarre blended families that resulted from the power of white masters over slave women: "You know when a man would marry, his father would give him a woman for a cook and she would have children right in the house by him, and his wife would have children too."[38] Due to the uneven power structure the slave was the one to suffer the folly of white conduct. Vindictive behavior placed black families and children at risk of being separated. A former slave noted: "Sometimes the [slave] cook's children [offspring of the master] favored him [the master liked them better] so much that the wife would be mean to them [the children] and make him sell them."[39] Other children fared better. "I used to play with the white children all the time when we was at mistress' house . . .they say my mother was half Spanish and half Indian." She goes on to say what she considered obvious: "My father was a white man of course."[40]

The horror of the circumstance of being treated as property was made worse in the antebellum period after the slave trade was closed. Since new slaves could not be brought into the country except illegally, the only way to increase one's slave holdings was through natural reproduction. The condition of allowing human beings to be a form of wealth opened the door to extreme forms of sexual exploitation. One girl noted a lucky escape from such a fate: "I was stout and they were saving me for a breeding woman but by the time I was big enough I was free."[41] Even when the exploitation was not deliberate, it encouraged overlooking sexual liaisons. Others were rightfully indignant and angry about their inability to prevent these occurrences and found the masters who abused black women beneath contempt: "I got no mercy on nobody who bring up their children like dogs. How could any father treat their children like that?"[42]

The irony of the status of blacks was that they often were descendents of wealthy, prominent white males. The family relations of Thomas Jefferson have recently been the subject of scholarship and public attention, but he was clearly not an aberration either for his time or thereafter as long as slavery continued. One man born in 1843 claimed to be a descendent from Abraham Lincoln. After explaining that he had been "sold four times in my life," he explained his heritage. The "first time [I was sold was] by my half brother." His half brother, who presumably was white "carried me [took him] away from Springfield when I was 7 years old." It was not uncommon for children of slaveholders to be given a servant who was the offspring of one of the family's slaves. He continued, "When I had come to the age of 12, my half brother sold me. I was mighty near like Joseph; my own half-brother sold me." Their common father was a first cousin to Abraham Lincoln: "His father and my father and Abe Lincoln was first cousins."[43]

Black parents had to protect their children as best they could from the horrors of separation. One woman commented on watching processions of slaves being taken to market but not imagining what was going on: "We children didn't know the grief of it then, but they would sell them apart ... The meanest thing they did was to selling babies from their mother's breast, but not all of them didn't do that."[44] Children were taken from their parents when they were approximately seven years old. This was also the traditional age when children were apprenticed. Parental bonds were strong, but slave mothers and fathers had little power to protect their children. Harriet Jacobs noted that her childhood ended at six on her mother's death. She began her narrative with the poignant words: "I was born a slave, but I never knew it till six years of happy childhood had passed away."[45]

Slavery and Wage Labor: Hiring Out

As a system of labor, a peculiarity of slavery was that when slaves were not needed they were used in other ways to provide an income for masters. The practice of hiring out slaves literally involved keeping title to the individual but "renting" their services to someone else for a profit. "I was taken away from my mother when I was seven . . . I belonged to a girl but she wasn't old enough and she had to have a guardian for me. I was hired out to make money for that child . . . I was never mistreated. They got $100 a year for me and they had to pay my doctor's bill and feed and clothe me."[46] Harriet Jacobs noted a similar practice whereby slave owners charged the slave for his cost of living and deducted that cost from her father's earnings.

> My father was a carpenter, and considered so intelligent and skilful in his trade, that, when buildings out of the common line were to be erected, he was sent for from long distances to be head workman. On condition of paying his mistress two hundred dollars a year, and supporting himself, he was allowed to work at his trade.[47]

Slaves were sometimes able to hire themselves out and to live fairly independently. It was even possible to acquire enough money to buy their own and their family's freedom even though this often went against the law.

Resistance and the Civil War

Before and after the Civil War blacks resisted. The most obvious way to resist was to run away. That was risky as was helping others to escape, but it also had its rewards. A sister described her brother's escape: "Well, On Monday morning my old master got up and found my brother's work wasn't finished, and I was out there cooking breakfast and he come up and asked me, "Isn't Dave come to the house yet?" I said, "New, I isn't seen him." I told that story and I was scared too." The thought of escape was thrilling and frightening: ". . .Well I was so tickled that I couldn't hardly get breakfast." Later the master learned from an outsider that his slave had disappeared: " . . . and then while they was talking to a man—he was a friend of me and my brother—from the next farm, and he come up in the yard and said, "Uncle Bob, Dave's gone."[48]

The pretense of being ignorant was also a way to avoid overt confrontation while getting one's own way when possible. Free blacks lived in the South from the seventeenth century. In the antebellum period this was also true. Not standing out and having a mentor seemed essential if a free black was not to be kidnapped and enslaved. "There was some free Negroes;

nobody bothered them if they had some white man to stand up for them. Some of them was carpenters, dig cisterns and things like that. They would go from place to place working."[49]

Blacks were eager to control their lives after emancipation and intended to fight back as they had never done before when confronted by arrogant whites: "I am one of the first voters of Montgomery County. They told me at one time that I was not to come to the polls or 600 men on horses would meet me. So about six or eight of us armed and went to the polls with our bayonets . . . So we voted, and voted for whom we wanted. They were also eager for an education and sought it out whenever or wherever they could. The ones that had access to schools were lucky. "When I first came here we had no teachers here but white teachers. They would call the roll same as calling the roll for soldiers . . . They taught school in the churches before they had school houses."[50]

Many African Americans joined the war effort.[51] "A heap of colored people would run away to the Yankees; after they had so many they got them up a company of soldiers. See masters was 'fraid to meet their slaves after freedom 'cause some of them was so mean."[52] It is interesting in this case that the young man returned to say hello to his former mistress, but his choices were made with a clear conscience. "When I went to the War I was turning seventeen. I was in the battle of Nashville, when we whipped old hood. I went to see my mistress on my furlough, and she was glad to see me. She said 'you remember when you were sick and I had to bring you into the house and nurse you?' And I told her, 'yes'm, I remember.' And she said, 'and now you are fighting me!' I said, 'No'm, I ain't fighting you, I 'm fighting to get free.'[53]

The Struggle for an Education

Kentucky was the only state that did not enact laws against the education of slaves. While a few slaves were illegally taught to read and write or were able to teach themselves, as the published slave narratives illustrate, more often slaves were unable to read. They also had no access to calendars or clocks. Few knew when they were born or their age. While slaveholders often kept precise records, they apparently were reluctant to share this information.[54] Slaveholders desired a factory like efficiency in the operation of large plantations, but the agrarian character of the operation lent it to natural rhythms based on seasonal patterns. Events and rituals that integrated a religious worldview compatible with West African traditions were used to measure the time. The equatorial balance of the twelve-hour day was not as standard in North America but the sun and moon could similarly be used to measure the rhythm of daily intercourse. The contradiction of the standardization of western clock time in the nineteenth century and its particular irrelevance to plantation culture is indicative of the way that slavery shaped the southern experience and slowed its progress in relation to the northern economy. It was, so to speak, caught in time. Lack of information and lack of power did not mean slaves were necessarily unaware of current events beyond the plantation fields. External events were used as markers of time. In the reference to the militant white abolitionist John Brown one former slave placed himself and his experience in time: "I was a slave way back in [1856], John Brown's time." He added, "They were mighty hard on colored people [back then]."[55]

Dignity, Courage, and Defiance:
A Daughter Remembers Her Mother's
Life and Death

Some stories are the stuff of legend and show humanity at its fiercest, as a defiant spirit that could be neither tamed nor broken. The heroes were remembered:

> My mother was the smartest black woman in Eden. She was as quick as a flash of lightning and whatever she did could not be done better...She had her faults as a slave...She was a demon. She said that she wouldn't be whipped...she was loud and boisterous..." I will kill you gal if you don't stand up for yourself and she would say: 'Fight and if you can't fight, kick, if you can't kick, then bite.' Ma was generally willing to work, but if she didn't feel like doing something none could make her do it. At least the Jennings couldn't make, or didn't make her.... I was the oldest child. My mother had three other children by the time I was 6 years old.

Her mother bore five children as a slave in the Jennings household.

> One day my mother's temper ran wild. For some reason mistress Jennings struck her with a stick. Ma struck back and a fight followed. . . . Ma was mad for two days, "Why I will kill her if she ever strikes me again." . . . Two mornings afterward two men came to the gate.

By law a slave was supposed to be whipped because she had struck a white person. Instead she fought the men and luckily her master, Mr. Jennings, was home and saved her by sending her to her cabin and driving the men off with his rifle. He concluded that she would have to be sent away.

> 'You won't be whipped and I am afraid you'll get killed... You can't take the baby Fannie.' ... "Ma and Pa sat up late... Pa loved ma and I heard him say, 'I'm going too, Fannie.' About a week later she called me in to say they were going to leave for Memphis and she didn't know how long . . .The next day I

saw ma walking around with the baby under her arm . . . Pa came up to the
cabin with an old mare for ma to ride and an old mule for himself. Mr. Jennings was with him. 'Fannie, leave the baby with Aunt Mary,' said Mr. Jennings very quietly. At this, ma took the baby by its feet, a foot in each hand,
and with the baby's head swinging downward, she vowed to smash its brains
out before she'd leave it. Tears were streaming down her face. It was seldom
that ma cried, and everyone knew that she meant every word. Ma took her
baby with her . . .

Both her mother and father were hired out to another family living in Tennessee leaving the other children behind.

My sorrow knew no bound. My very soul seemed to cry out. My mother was
right. Slavery was cruel, so very cruel... Things were not the same . . . One day
sitting by the roadside in a kind of trance . . . thinking about ma and pa.

After a year without her beloved parents one day, they unexpectedly
returned.

[Suddenly] they were standing over me. I thought it was a dream. Ma was
speaking to me. 'Puss we've come back, me and pa, and we've come to stay...'

Her mother's fierce personality and will power in the face of the bizarre
twists of fate that had been dealt her, came to bear fruit at her death. At last
she could choose. Mr. Jennings bows to her will as she will soon be beyond
his control.

On the day my mother died, she called pa and said, 'Bob what time is it?' Pa
went to the window and pushed it back and looked up at the sun. 'It's four
o'clock, Fannie.' 'Well I'm going to leave you at eight o'clock. Go tell master
Jennings to come in, and get all the slaves too.'

Mr. Jennings asked if there was anything he could do. She replied:

'But I would like for you to take Puss [the daughter telling the story] and hire
her out among ladies, so she can be raised right. She will never be any good
around here.' A funny look came over master Jennings face and he bowed
his head up and down.

Her passage is noted as is due someone with great fortitude.

All the hands had come in and were standing around with him [Mr. Jen-
nings]. My mother died [just as she said] at just about eight o'clock.[56]

CHAMPION OF THE PEOPLE? JACKSONIAN DEMOCRACY

Except for two four-year periods the Democratic Party controlled the federal government from 1828 to 1861. The era is named for Andrew Jackson who was elected to the presidency in 1828. Jackson, not born into the upper classes, was hailed as a champion of the "common man."[57] He had a vision for the nation's destiny and a ruthless insistence on his own views. He did not stand up for the aristocracy but he did champion the common "white person" of the middle and working classes and their privilege over those who would not conform to relatively constricted views of what it meant to be a "white" American.

THE BLACK IRISH BECOME WHITE

The Irish who had participated in the origin of chattel servitude and the harsh hand of English prejudice had a great deal of sympathy with the abolitionist movement in the United States in the antebellum period. Daniel O'Connell, known as the "Liberator" in Ireland, was the first to sign an 1841 petition from Ireland with sixty thousand names that called for Irish Americans to join the abolition movement. This solidarity was not to last. It fell victim to rising racial rhetoric and intense labor competition as industrialization and territorial expansion proceeded.[58]

Between 1750 and 1810 the British brought Ireland and the Irish into their ideal of a plantation colony. Irish exports increased from two million to six million pounds, and that was a significant benefit for the crown. Instead of providing a living for the Irish, British colonization reduced the Irish people to extreme poverty. Between 1815 and 1920, five and a half million Irish migrated to the United States in order to survive and to escape British oppression. Noel Ignatiev noted: "contrary to the popular stereotype not all [Irish] were poor, and not all were Catholic." Part of the early nineteenth century migration was of the "Scotch-Irish" who were Presbyterian and Ulster Protestants, who were English but had married Irish wives and considered themselves Irish. Even though they had a privileged position due to their closer affiliation with the English, they had many of the same grievances with the English as the Catholics concerning discriminatory commercial interests and landholding practices imposed by the English. Ignatiev made note of the odd position of the the Scotch-Irish in the Irish Diaspora as a portion of the group that "became known as "the Irish" a racial (but not ethnic) line invented in Ireland [that] was recreated as an ethnic (but not racial) line in America."[59] Between 1845 and 1855 the number of poor Irish immigrants increased. The victims of the Great Famine of 1846 often spoke Gaelic not English and attended Catholic Masses that were said in Gaelic. This group lamented their forced emigration with the typical Irish use of poetry:

I would not live in Ireland now, for she's a fallen land
And the tyrant's heel is on her neck, with her reeking
blood stained hand.
There's not a foot of Irish ground, but's trodden
down by slaves,
Who die unwept, and then are flung, like dogs,
into their graves.[60]

The Potato Famine: Driven from Beloved Ireland

By the early 1840s, the Irish could not survive on the land. Those who refused to leave Ireland became migratory workers, leaving their homes for work in the spring and returning with small sums of money for necessities in the fall. Their diet consisted largely of potatoes since one year's supply of the root vegetable could be grown on an acre and it kept well in storage. This sorry pattern was broken in 1840 when a little known fungus attacked the potato plants and killed nearly forty percent of the crop. The deadly disease persisted and returned year after year until by 1855 when the blight ended, a million Irish had died of starvation and illness caused by malnutrition. The English did not respond to the Great Famine and desperation of the people but rather continued to export grain and livestock to England. Ronald Takaki noted that half the people of Ireland could have been fed with the livestock exported in 1846. The Potato Famine generated a mass migration. One and a half million fled to the United States. Poor and unskilled, they arrived to bend their backs to manual labor building waterways, railroads, and roadways for poor pay. They were exploited as workers and pitted against other low caste laborers including the Chinese on the West Coast and the African Americans who fled the South for northern cities on the East Coast. Just as African Americans were portrayed in unfavorable and objectionable ways and as members of some other race, so were the Irish racialized and depicted as "a race of savages" with apelike features and with an intelligence equal to the blacks. The Reverend Theodore Parker of Boston preached that "the inferior people of the world . . . were inferior in nature, some perhaps only behind us [whites] in development [but others are] a lower form in the great school of Providence—Negroes, Indians, Mexicans, Irish, and the like."[61]

Being Black in America

While the Irish in Ireland and in the early days of their existence in the British North American colonies lived parallel to the African American population, shared their grief, and joined them in rebellion, the new wave of immigrants in the face of the growing bigotry in the United States fought back not by joining the fight against the growing racism but by adjusting to the pecking order. The Irish were able to take the jobs of the free black population as waiters and longshoremen, hackney coachmen, draymen, and stevedores. The Irish were a cheap labor supply. In Alabama officials in a stevedoring company hired the Irish over slaves because if they died "nobody loses anything." Similarly, when a road was to be built across the swamps of southwest Louisiana, the landowner refused to risk his slaves in the marsh.[62] A song commemorated those who died of cholera while building the New Basin Canal in New Orleans in 1831:

> Ten thousand Micks, they swung their picks
> To dig the New Canal
> But the choleray was stronger'n they.
> An twice it killed them awl.[63]

Choosing Whiteness: The Immigrant's Tale

That the Irish chose to become white is a development that is an example of David Roediger's argument in the *Wages of Whiteness* that managers and owners stand to benefit if their work force is divided and therefore does not cooperate in protests against low pay and poor working conditions. White privilege and white supremacy became the dividing line.[64] Labor did not act in its own collective interests. The competition that already existed among white workers and the disastrous competition with skilled and unskilled black labor in the South led the Irish to empathize with anti-black sentiment. John Finch, a traveler from England in the early 1840s noticed: "It is a curious fact that the democratic party, and particularly the poorer classes of Irish Immigrants in America, are greater enemies to the negro population, and greater advocates for the continuance of negro slavery, than any portion of the population in the free States."[65] The labor movement supported Andrew Jackson's anti-aristocracy stand and it denounced the abolitionists as turning their back on the laboring peoples. Seth Luther in an "Address to Mechanics and Workers," described the abolitionists as "philanthropists moaning over the fate of the Southern slave when there are *thousands* of children in this State as truly slaves as the blacks in the South."[66] The labor movement did not argue for support and solidarity with fellow workers in chains; they did the opposite.

The Irish were made into the pawns of racism; they paradoxically were the first minstrels in black face in the first forms of popular entertainment. When African Americans came to the minstrel shows as actors, they not only had to apply black face makeup on their already dark complexions but also had to take Irish names to be acceptable on the billboards.[67] A minstrel joke that appeared in the *New York Irish American* on January 6, 1850 puts down both groups. In the repartee a black man denounced his master as "a great tyrant," because he "treats me as badly as if I was a *common Irishman.*"[68]

The Irish displaced blacks as house servants. In the 1830s the majority of servants in New York were black but by 1850 the majority were Irish women. Daughters of impoverished farmers in Ireland became the maids of the middle and upper classes of America. More women than men immigrated because there were more opportunities for employment for women. In 1860 half of the Irish immigrants were women as opposed to twenty one percent of the Italians and four percent of the Greeks.[69] While Irish women came to dominate the domestic servant niche in America, they gradually turned to factory work in the mills of New England in the garment industry and sewing trades.

The Irish as "white" were gradually able to achieve some economic and social mobility. The fact that they settled in urban areas allowed them the opportunity to acquire an education and better opportunities for employment. In 1850 one in three Irish lived in one of fifteen cities. There were 134,000 Irish in New York, 72,000 in Philadelphia, and 32,000 in Boston. Irish Catholic children outnumbered Protestant children in 1885 where the population constituted one third of the population of New York. The concentration in urban areas in such large numbers provided the opportunity to acquire political influence. As the Irish came to be regarded as "white persons," they were eligible for citizenship. As citizens they had the right to vote, and the franchise was important in cities. By the end of the nineteenth century the transformation of the Irish into white was complete. They occupied a portion of the labor market in the blue color and the skilled trades. Through leadership in union work, exemplified by such legendary figures as Mary Harris, "Mother Jones," the Irish wielded political power through the Knights of Labor and American Federation of Labor. The Irish transition to whiteness and relative prosperity exacted a price.

TRAIL OF TEARS/TRAIL OF DEATH AND RESISTANCE

The roots of the English disrespect for tribal societies and the concept of their cultural superiority can be traced to their dealings with the Celtic Irish in the twelfth century. Those beliefs and the practices they supported were transferred to British North America and defined the relations between the English colonists and the indigenous American tribes. The confusion between trying to "civilize" the "wild Irish" or to eliminate them through genocidal policies was transferred to official United States policy against the "wild Indian." The balance often tipped toward genocide after the War of Independence. The rising tide of scientific racism exacerbated the perception that the Indians were in the way of the American God given mission of manifest destiny in the name of human progress. The concept of white supremacy was used to justify the confiscation of Indian lands and to support the claim that the solution to the "Indian problem" was to make them disappear. After defeating the Cheyenne in 1867, General Philip Sheridan's comment "The only good Indians I ever saw were dead" was reported and spread. It was translated into the vicious popular saying "the only good Indian is a dead Indian."[70]

Jackson and the Anti-Indian Campaigns of the Antebellum Period

Plunder of the ancient lands, culture, and physical well being of the indigenous peoples continued throughout the nineteenth century. In 1803, President Thomas Jefferson wrote future president Andrew Jackson, then a young politician in Tennessee, that he should urge Indians to sell their "useless forests" and become farmers.[71] Jackson learned how to brutalize Indians at a young age as a military leader in campaigns against the Creeks. He purposefully enflamed anti-Indian sentiment with his accounts of alleged Indian savagery—murdering settlers and raping women. Jackson was not beneath self-aggrandizement. He used his Indian raids to gain favorable publicity and personally acquired some of the Indian lands he "freed."

Jackson practiced the savagery he attributed to the Indians, bragging: "I have on all occasions preserved the scalps of my killed." At the Battle of Horseshoe Bend in March 1814, Jackson and his armed troops surrounded eight hundred Creeks and killed almost all, including the old, defenseless, women, children, and infants. He bragged to Major General Thomas Pinckney of the murders calling the victims "savage dogs . . . doomed to destruction by their own restless and savage conduct." His troops used the flesh of the dead to make bridles for their horses and cut off noses to keep a count of the conquests.[72] As president, Jackson engineered the Indian Removal Act of 1830 that authorized the president to create an Indian Territory west of the Mississippi River in exchange for the acquisition of Indian lands east of the Mississippi River. The president was authorized to assist in this migration and resettlement. The act allowed the involuntary removal of seventy thousand Cherokee and Choctaw from their homeland. They were driven through severe weather with poor provisions across the Mississippi River to Indian Territory, now Oklahoma in 1830.

The Five Civilized Tribes:
The Struggle of the Cherokee and Choctaw

The experience of the Cherokee and Choctaw is informative. It shows that no matter what the efforts of the tribes, Americans insisted on carrying out the policies that had their origins with the earliest English colonists. Both the Choctaw of Mississippi and the Cherokee of the southern Appalachia region and northern Georgia were members of the Five Civilized Tribes also including the Creek, Chickasaw, and the Seminoles who in their treaties with the United States government insisted on the right to an education in exchange for the sale of their land. The Cherokee prized their language, were eager to maintain their culture, and successfully establish equity with the encroachment of white settlers. A written Cherokee language was created by a tribal member of the Cherokee Nation named Sequoyah in 1821. Sequoyah worked on the alphabet for twelve years. He created eighty-six symbolic characters that represent sounds in the Cherokee language. The genius of his phonic alphabet was that once a native speaker mastered the relationship between the characters and the sounds he or she could become literate in a week. The Cherokee quickly had a higher literacy rate than the Euro-Americans who thought them uncivilized. To deal with the United States government the Cherokee established a government that was based on the United States Constitution. It called for the establishment of schools to ensure the continuing literacy of Cherokee children so they could master their own culture as well as gain the skills to work successfully with the dominant society. This was to no avail. In spite of prolonged negotiations the Cherokee were forced off their land at gunpoint and sent on in what is now known as the "Trail of Tears."

The Choctaw in Mississippi were originally horticulturalists who also hunted and shared common grain reserves. They lived in towns and chiefdoms where they emphasized reciprocity for all basic needs and cared for all tribal members on an equal basis. In the early nineteenth century they became property owners and producers but that was not enough to ward off having their land seized. In 1830 the state of Mississippi abolished the Choctaw sovereignty of the Choctaw Nation. A treaty was forced upon the Choctaw with the threat of federal forces. They seceded 10,423,130 acres to the federal government and were forced to migrate west of the Mississippi River. An agreement that families could choose to stay and be governed under the laws of Mississippi was broken as Indians were cheated out of their property. The total cost of abolishing the Choctaw was slightly over five million dollars. The government sold the land to white settlers for over eight million dollars. Since the Treaty of Dancing Rabbit Creek specified that the government was not to profit from the migration, the Choctaw sued and won a three million dollar settlement but, unfairly, most of the funds went to pay the court costs.

It was not necessarily an honor to be included as part of the Five Civilized Tribes in that the promises of the government were rarely kept. Treaties were broken whenever it advantaged the government or local settlers. Thomas McKenney, the first head of the Office of Indian Affairs 1824-1830, targeted the Five Civilized Tribes for what Joel Spring called "deculturalization" and what McKenney thought of as civilizing savages through education. McKenney was a Quaker who brought his religious values to his work originally as superintendent of Indian Trade before heading the Office of Indian Affairs. McKenney shifted from trade as a means of civilizing the tribes to education, the kind that David Adams identifies as "education for extinction" either culturally or physically. Missionary Christians with little understanding or even an attempt to understand the people they chose to destroy assumed their own superiority and would settle for nothing less than having Indians renounce their tribal affiliations. The Five Civilized Tribes acquired citizenship in 1901 after prolonged court battles and petitions. The remainder of the tribes remained "foreign nationals" until 1924 when all Native Americans were granted United States citizenship.

Perseverance: Survival in the Face of Genocide

In 1891 D. M. Riordan, who spent twenty years as an Indian agent for the United States, presented a paper before the Sunset Club of Chicago in which he described his experience. His candid account showed that the indigenous peoples were oppressed and mistreated. The tribes tried to accommodate to the ways of those who were occupying their lands while holding on to their traditional values, but the overwhelming presence of the Europeans made the possibility of their enjoying any success virtually impossible. In the opinion of the "Five Civilized Tribes" and apparently Riordan's as well the ways the federal government attempted to convert or civilize Indians were all unsuccessful. While the tribes suffered diseases introduced by Euro-Americans as well as attempts at deliberate genocide, they somehow survived. Riordan pointed out: "We may as well make up our minds to the fact that the Indians are not disappearing and will not disappear from natural causes, even in the face of our advanced civilization." He explained: "We may exterminate them partially, as we did the heroic band who were led by Nez Pierce, Joseph; who lost fifty percent of their number from sheer homesickness after their removal to the Indian Territory. Or we may inveigle them into a surrender by fraud as Crook did Geronimo, and send them to die in the swamps of Florida." Riordan acknowledged what was consistently ignored by the white culture going as far back as the English response to the Celtic Irish and their resistance to Anglo-Saxon rule: even when people are ignored and brutalized, they can and will endure. As Riordan observed: "They are a vital living fact with which we have to deal; and the most vital so far as our national honor is concerned. And we can only cause them to disappear by extermination or absorption." Riordan bravely expressed the most obvious but difficult point: "I sometimes feel that if it could be arranged that this big, awkward and unjust machine that we call the Government, could be prevailed upon to take its hands off the Indians and let them alone, *that [sic]* would be one step in the right direction. In my twenty-years of life in Indian country, I have seen a great many cases of controversy between Indians and white men; and *I have never known of a single case in which the Indian was not right. Not a single one* (authors' emphasis)."[73]

AMERICAN IMPERIALISM AND RESISTANCE: POR LA RAZA Y PARA LA RAZA

It was inevitable that the westward thrust of the United States would come into competition with Spanish colonial territory. The United States as a small to medium sized agrarian republic had yet to acquire its imperial form. The acquisition of New Orleans by Spain and its return to France prompted the ambition for empire. Spain acquired the Mississippi Delta including New Orleans when France lost its North American territory to Britain in 1763. In 1802 Spain transferred Spanish Louisiana back to the French, then ruled by Emperor Napoleon Bonaparte, the dictator who ended the French Revolution with his ambition for empire. President Thomas Jefferson was alarmed by the presence of Imperial France on the American continent. Control over New Orleans and the mouth of the Mississippi was vital, for it served as a port through which sizable amounts of produce had to pass to market. Jefferson negotiated with France, and Bonaparte's government offered the whole of Louisiana and Mississippi Valley for $15 million. The deal was concluded and announced on July 4, 1803. American expansion bloomed. A giant step had been taken away from the idea that the United States did not have is own ambitions for empire.

There was some question whether the Constitution allowed such a purchase of foreign land. Many believed that it did not. However, Jefferson used an ends-justifies-the means argument. The purchase proceeded and the Constitution questions were dismissed as "metaphysical subtleties" as indicated by a letter to John Breckenridge written on August 2, 1803:

> I would not give one inch of the Mississippi to any nation, because I see in a light very important to our peace the exclusive right to its navigation...the Constitution has made no provision for our holding foreign territory, still less for incorporating foreign nations into our Union. The Executive, in seizing the fugitive occurrence, which so much advances the good of their country,

have done an act beyond the Constitution. The Legislature, in casting behind them metaphysical subtleties, and showing themselves like faithful servants, must ratify and pay for it, and throw themselves on their country in doing for them unauthorized what we know they would have done for themselves had they been in a situation to do it.[74]

The First Texans: Ordeal of the People of the Northern Territories of Spain and Mexico

The Spanish Mexican territory of Texas was the next goal. In 1812 a group of Mexicans and Americans marched from Louisiana to San Antonio, Texas with the intention of taking it over. The Spanish soundly repulsed them. The latent idea of expanding ever westward had been unleashed. The term "Manifest Destiny" was used in 1845 by John L. O'Sullivan in the *Democratic Review* when he lashed out at foreigners whose actions were aimed at "limiting our greatness and checking the fulfillment of our Manifest Destiny to over spread the continent allotted by Providence for the free development of our yearly multiplying millions."[75]

Mexicans and Spaniards occupied Texas as a Spanish territory devoted to ranching, especially in West Texas. East Texas in the San Antonio area was settled with a series of missions. There were also transplants from the American South who were cultivating cotton with slave labor. The Spanish rule in Mexico and hence Texas was not stable, and Mexican General Santa Ana, who became dictator, succeeded in throwing off the Spanish and in 1829 founded an Independent Mexico that included Texas, New Mexico, Arizona, lower Colorado, and California. The new Mexican government was also unstable but it moved to consolidate its territory. Slavery was outlawed in 1824 and immigration from the United States into East Texas was halted in 1830. Texas was divided into three territories, and military forts were built.

People like Stephen Austin, who had colonized a large area and was joined by 5,000 Americans including illegally imported slaves, were unhappy. Austin and the others considered themselves Americans and wanted the United States to annex Texas. On February 26, 1836 a band of 187 explorers and "desperados" including Davy Crockett and James Bowie, vowed to fight for Texas at the mission in San Antonio known as the Alamo. Greatly outnumbered, they lost the battle in a heroic fight to the death, so the legend goes. Santa Ana's forces defended Mexican territory and left no survivors. The continuing battle over Texas lasted seven weeks. The ultimate outcome was a victory for the U.S. Americans. Annexing Texas was problematic in that it raised the issue of the spread of slavery. Consequently, Texas became independent. The border with Mexico remained disputed, the United States claiming the Rio Grande as a border, which was not recognized by Mexico. Mexican nationals now lived in an ill-defined Texas. Annexation awaited a war with Mexico that was brewing as the United States looked beyond Texas to California.

The Californios

Hernán Cortéz sent a mission to California in 1542 after the conquest of Mexico. Other explorers including Sir Francis Drake had ventured along the California coast. Given the problem Spain had with populating its vast territories with Spaniards and its emphasis on using the indigenous population, Spanish colonization took a long time and did not begin until 1769 when Father Junipero Serra founded the mission of San Diego de Alcala, the first of a series of twenty-one missions that stretched five hundred miles up the coast to Sonoma. With the pretense of converting the indigenous peoples, the missions settled what became the major cities of Los Angeles, Santa Barbara, Monterey, San Jose, and San Francisco. The result was disastrous for the Indians who were forced into servitude and often death. A few settlers from Spain were given large land grants, called rancheros, from the Spanish crown. Most settlers were from Mexico. The forty-six settlers sent to Los Angeles with the promise of land, herds of cattle, food, and equipment in the eighteenth century were described as *mestizo*, a mixture of people indigenous to Spain, Mexico, and West African or African-European.[76] The numbers did not swell. Even with the rich land and resources there was little draw from Mexico, which also had rich land and a sophisticated society. The unrest in Mexico did not create refugees. By 1781 the population of Californios was only around six hundred. By 1821 this had grown to three thousand mostly by natural reproduction rather than new settlement. The families that received royal Spanish or Mexican land grants were a special elite. Don Vallejo's ranchero covered 175,000 acres. Some who made it into the elite were soldiers or officers who received land as a reward for their services.

Californian society, like Mexican society, was socially stratified. The elite as closer to a Spanish heritage were of high status and composed an educated leisure class. They were *gente de razon*, people of reason, who spoke Castilian Spanish. The male head of the family's name was prefaced by "Don," a term of respect and status. His wife's title was Doña. They saw themselves and were described as a gracious elite, not unlike the plantation elites of the South. For example, Don Juan Bandini was described as "a slight and elegant figure, who moved gracefully, danced and waltzed beautifully, spoke good Castilian, with a pleasant and refined voice and accent, and had, throughout, the bearing of a man of birth and figure."[77]

Many dependent servants worked the cattle and fields and waited on the elite who lived in the hacienda. The laboring classes below them were also stratified. Mexicans whose heritage was mostly Spanish had a higher status than those whose heritage was mostly indigenous. Mexicans of indigenous heritage and the indigenous people of California had little or no status. John March, a visitor in 1836, noticed that the Indians did all the work. They were "kept" poor, constantly in debt, and paid little. Doña Vallejo, a mother of sixteen children, reported that each of her children had a servant to care for them and she had two. Servants were assigned to grind corn, prepare food, entertain guests, wash clothes, herd the cattle, and tend fields. They were not paid but supposedly cared for "like members of the family."[78] The patriarchal tradition placed the elites as benefactors of those who served them. This was extended to guests who at first were welcomed to the aristocratic life style with abundant food and drink in a ritualized social intercourse characterized by many holidays and gatherings that occurred in spite of the distances between the rancheros with their local missions and villages.

Invaders from the East: View from the Other Side

The California lifestyle began to change rapidly with the growth of the eastern seaboard, immigration, and the expansionist mentality. American settlers began to arrive as early as 1828, and stories of California and Oregon became popular in the 1840s. Ronald Takaki reported that as the United States deliberately set out to acquire the continent in the 1840s, the Irish became part of the push westward. Many Irish joined the army. As they became white Americans, they joined the campaign to make the continent one people, one language, under the same laws, with one flag. The "Lone Star Republic," Texas, was annexed by the United States in 1845. Mexico broke off relations with the United States. Congressman Abraham Lincoln argued that President Polk started the war because he wanted California and because of his desire for "military glory."[79]

President Polk's long awaited chance to start a war with Mexico began when Mexican forces attacked an American army unit on May 11, 1846. The United States claimed that the Mexicans had crossed into U.S. territory north of the Rio Grande, which was of course disputed and not recognized by Mexico who claimed the Texas border to be one hundred fifty miles farther north. A brutal war followed. Little consideration was given to civilians who were murdered along with soldiers. In some ways the Mexican War was a "rehearsal for the Civil War."[80] Women were raped. Murder and robbery were not uncommon. Ulysses S. Grant, then a young officer, as if in preparation for the blood bath of the Civil War wrote: "Some of the volunteers and about all the Texans seem to think it perfectly right to impose on the people of a conquered city to any extent, and even to murder them where the act can be covered by dark. And how much they seem to enjoy acts of violence too." General Winfield Scott wrote that the American "soldiers committed atrocities to make Heaven weep and every American of Christian morals blush for his country. Murder, robbery, and rape of mothers and daughters in the presence of tied-up males of the families have been common all along the Rio Grande." Mexican papers denounced the Americans as "the horde of banditti, of drunkards, of fornicators . . . bad-smelling, long-bearded men with hats turned up at the brim, thirsty with the desire to appropriate our riches and our beautiful damsels."[81] These were not the brave pioneers of lore.

The showdown in California began June 6, 1846, when a group of thirty rebel American's seized General Mariano Vallejo in his Sonoma hacienda in northern California. The Californios had little power to resist even a small band of an armed militia who intended to set up the "Bear Flag Republic," taking California out of the hands of Mexico. Their homemade flag boasted a star and a bear, a resemblance to the Texas flag. To the Californios the bear was a predator of their cattle, a thief and plunderer. They called the uneducated, violent, intruders, los Osos, the bears. Vallejo was jailed. When he was released, he found his home vandalized and his pastoral and aristocratic lifestyle gone. The battle over California was not without bloodshed. The oppressed Mexican peasants and Indians revolted. Peace was not restored until January 1847. A treaty was not signed with Mexico until February 1848, barely a month after gold was discovered at Fort Sutter Mill, January 24, 1848. That discovery attracted the "Forty-Niners," and masses from around the world flocked to California's golden hills.

The Treaty of Guadalupe de Hildago

The Treaty of Guadalupe de Hildago settled the Rio Grande as the border between Mexico and Texas. California, New Mexico, Nevada, and parts of Colorado, Arizona, and Utah were seceded to the United States for an indemnity of $15 million. This totaled over one million square miles. In 1853, the Gadsden Purchase from Mexico added Arizona and New Mexico, another 29,640 square miles for $10 million. The acquisition fulfilled the doctrine of manifest destiny; it appeared, perhaps not ironically, as a "masculine," "white" victory. While the treaty contained protections for the Spanish and Mexican populations that now lived in the United States through no desire on their part, the protection of citizenship and rights to property and civil rights were hardly considered worthy of notice. Soldiers bragged about their prowess on the battlefield and in bed. The excuse was that the "senoritas of California [and Mexico] ...invariably preferred" Anglo-Saxon men.[82] Ashbel Smith, former secretary of state for the Texas Republic proclaimed white supremacy:

> The two races, the Americans distinctively so called, and the Spanish Americans or Mexicans, are now brought by the war into inseparable contact. No treaties can henceforth dissever them; and the inferior must give way before the superior race.[83]

Mexicans who had settled the land and lived for generations on their own property were allowed to leave or supposedly were guaranteed the citizenship rights of white persons. By law they acquired the right to "the enjoyment of all of the rights of citizens of the United States according to the principles of the Constitution."[84] However, Mexicans in California found that suffrage was in name only. While at first Mexicans outnumbered Americans, the gold rush quickly changed that. Mexican Americans became a racialized category in California. By 1849, the population jumped to one hundred thousand, and only thirteen thousand were Mexicans. An anti-vagrancy act called the "Greaser Act" defined the vagrant as "all persons . . .commonly known as "Greasers" or the issue of Spanish or Indian blood . . . and who [are] armed and not peaceable and quiet persons." A tax of twenty dollars a month was imposed on mining. Spanish speaking miners, including American citizens of Mexican descent were included, as if they were foreign nationals. Anglo-European Americans claimed that they had a right to the gold even though the Mexicans had perfected gold mining, and even the names, such as "bonanza" for ore and "placer" as deposits of ore, are of Spanish extraction. Anglos invaded the mines of Mexicans and forced them to flee for their lives. It was easy to identify and discriminate against Mexican citizens if they spoke their language, Spanish, or practiced their Catholic religion.

In Texas, Mexicans similarly were granted suffrage in name only. White primaries or poll taxes were established to disenfranchise African Americans and Mexicans. It was increasingly impossible to retain their rights as citizens and as landowners. Article X of the Treaty of Guadalupe de Hidalgo stated that "all prior and pending titles to property of every description" would be protected. The United States, however, omitted this article and instead promised not to annul grants of lands made by Mexico in ceded territories. The courts did not uphold titles. Congress established a commission to review the validity of land grants and their boundaries. With the excuse that the land grants were not precise as to boundaries or that there was insufficient proof of title, many land grants were not recognized. In California squatters settled on the rancheros and the authorities rarely intervened in behalf of the landowners who were hampered by their language and customs as well as lack of familiarity with the Americans' manipulations of the legal process. Mexicans were systematically robbed of their land and resources whenever possible.[85]

Manifest Destiny

The market system of the United States not only appropriated the land and resources of the landowners but also the labor of the Mexican middle and working classes. The injustices of the Spanish and Mexican system of paternalism were not corrected but rather adapted for the purposes of a new elite. The population was reduced to poverty. This was facilitated by the growing belief in inferior races and the conviction that the Spanish speaking peoples were all of inferior talent but adaptable for labor. The cattle ranching vaqueros, the original models for the legendary American cowboy, became field hands in the cotton growing areas of Texas and the orchards and field of California. They were forced to join the labor gangs who built the railroads that increasingly transported American culture westward. This migrant work pattern, moving as the rails needed to be laid, disrupted family life and portended the future patterns of migrant labor and poverty. Mexicans continued to mine, but the nature of the industry changed from independent workers to large mines and a hierarchy of labor. A racial hierarchy followed from the white wealthy mine owners to a dual system of pay and privilege on the bottom. White American miners received higher pay than "Mexican labor." Mexicans were especially vulnerable to peonage debt in company towns and worked as free labor in name only. The tremendous population expansion in California swept the Mexican population from power. In 1848 the population was 14,000 not including the indigenous population. By 1852 there were a quarter of a million people in the state. Between 1848 and 1858 over half a million people settled in California. California produced forty-five percent of the world's gold between 1851 and 1855. The population count in Nevada County in 1852 is cited as 12,500 white males, 900 females, 4,000 Chinese cooks, laundry men and camp workers and 3,000 Indian coolies."[86]

As the United States of America completed its western extension, the very future of the nation was increasingly at risk. On the other side of the country events were swirling out of control. Who had the power to decide issues of labor, citizenship, and territory was being contested.

NOTES

1.   Yuval Taylor, ed., *I Was Born a Slave: An Anthology of Classic Slave Narratives, Vol. I, 1770-1849* (Chicago: Lawrence Hill Books, 1999), p. xv.

2.   David Brion Davis, *Slavery and Human Progress* (New York: Oxford, 1984), p. 78.

3.   Joseph W. Newman, "Antebellum School Reform in the Port Cities of the Deep South," in David N. Plank and Rick Ginsberg, *Southern Cities, Southern Schools Public Education in the Urban South* (Westport, CT: Greenwood, 1990), ch. 2, p. 17; George Novack, "The Rise and Fall of the Cotton Kingdom," in George Novack, *America's Revolutionary Heritage* (New York: Pathfinder, 1976), pp. 181-220.

4.   Textile Mills were successfully established in the 1880s in North Carolina, South Carolina, Georgia, and Alabama using women (40%) children (25%) as labor. Southern mills fared well since the hours were longer and wages lower than northern mills, which were experiencing labor problems and the beginning of labor unions. The workweek was 74 hours with $2.50 the average wage in 1885, which actually decreased in 1895. Victoria Byerly, *Hard Times Cotton Mill Girls: Per-*

sonal Histories of Womanhood and Poverty in the South (Ithaca, NY: ILR Press, 1986); Mitchell Broadus, *The Rise of the Cotton Mills in the South* (Baltimore: Johns Hopkins Press, 1921); Eric Foner, *Reconstruction, America's Unfinished Revolution, 1863-1877* (New York: Harper & Row, 1988), pp. 24-25; Edward L. Ayers, *The Promise of the New South: Life After Reconstruction* (New York: Oxford, 1992); Dewey W. Grantham, *The South in Modern America: A Region at Odds* (New York: Harper Perennial, 1994).

5.   Oscar Handlin, *Race and Nationalism in American Life* (Boston: Little and Brown, 1957), p. 24-25; Fredrickson, *The Black Image*, pp. 1-2; Thomas Jefferson, "Notes on Virginia," in Adrienne Koch and William Peden, eds., *The Life and Selected Writings of Thomas Jefferson* (New York: The Modern Library, 1944), pp. 256-262; Winthrop D. Jordan, *White Over Black: Attitudes Toward the Negro, 1550-1812* (Chapel Hill: University of North Carolina Press, 1968), Parts 4 and 5, Chapters XI and CV, p. 455, pp. 533-538.

6.   *Oxford English Dictionary,* condensed version, p. 2400 (text p. 87).

7.   Carolus Linnaeus, *Systema naturae*, (Stockholm: Rediviva, 1977, original 1758).

8.   Samuel Stanhope Smith, *An Essay on the Causes of the Variety of Complexion and Figure in the Human Species*, ed., Winthrop D. Jordan (Cambridge: Belknap Press of Harvard University, 1965).

9.   German anatomist, Johann Friedrich Blumenbach, divided the human races into five: Caucasian, Mongolian, Ethiopian, American, and Malaysian in 1861. See John Willinsky, *Learning to Divide the World: Education at Empire's End* (Minneapolis: University of Minnesota, 1998), see pp. 161-188 on the role of academics and science in the formation of a science of race and race theory.

10.   Charles, Caldwell, *Thoughts on the Original Unity of the Human Race* 2nd ed. (Cincinnati: J.A. & U.P. James, 1852, original New York: 1830).

11.   George Cuvier, *Recherches sur les ossemens fossiles*, Vol. 1, (Paris: Deterville, 1812).

12.   Richard H. Colfax, *Evidence Against the Views of the Abolitionists, consisting of physical and moral proofs of the inferiority of the negroes* (New York: J.T.M. Bleakley, 1833).

13.   Julien Joseph Virey, *Historie Naturel du Genre Humane* (Paris: Crochard, 1824, 1810), J. H. Guenbault, *Natural History of the Negro Race* (Charleston, S.C.: D. J. Dowling, 1837, 1833) was an American translation of extractions from Virey used as propaganda against "the Negro."

14.   "Ethnography and Ethnology," *Encyclopedia Britannica*, 9th ed, (Chicago: R. S.Peale, 1891), pp. 613-626.

15.   Samuel George Morton, *Crania Americana; or a Comparative Views of the Skulls of Various Aboriginal Nations of North and South America* (Philadelphia: J. Dobson, 1839); Morton, *Crania Aegyptiaca, or Observations on Egyptian Ethnography, Derived from Anatomy, History and the Monuments* (Philadelphia: J. Penington, 1844).

16.   R.W. Gibbs: "We of the South should consider him as our benefactor, for aiding most materially in giving to the Negro his true position as an inferior race," in "Obituary for Morton," *Charleston Medical Journal* 1851, cited in Stephen Jay Gould, *Mismeasure of Man* (New York: Norton, 1981, 1996).

17.   Josiah C. Nott, *Two Lectures on the Connexion between the Biblical and Physical History of Man* (New York: J. B. Lippincott, 1849); J.C. Nott with Samuel G. Morton, H.S. Patterson, George R. Gliddon, *Types of Mankind or Ethological Researches . . .* (Philadelphia: Grambo, 1854; reprint Miami, FL.: Mnemosyne Publishing Co.,

1969); Count Joseph Arthur de Gobineau, *The Moral and Intellectual Diversity of Races, with Particular Reference to Their Respective Influence in the Civil and Political History of Mankind* (Philadelphia: J. B. Lippincott, 1856); William Sumner Jenkins, *Pro-Slavery Thought in the Old South* (Chapel Hill: University of North Carolina, 1935), pp. 256, 259-260; Fredrickson, *The Black Image*, ch. 3, p. 78, fn. 10, 11 on letters between James Henry Hammon and Josiah C. Nott; William R. Stanton, *The Leopard's Spots: Scientific Attitudes Toward Race in America, 1815-1859* (Chicago: University of Chicago, 1960).

18.   Edward Lurie, *Louis Agassiz: A Life in Science* (Chicago: University of Chicago, 1960).

19.   Patricia A. Turner, *Ceramic Uncles and Celluloid Mammies: Black Images and Their Influence on Culture* (New York: Anchor, 1994).

20.   William L. Van Deburg, *Slavery and Race in American Popular Culture.* (Madison: University of Wisconsin Press, 1984), pp. 18, 22, 39-46,47-48, 111-15, 117-18.

21.   Alexander Saxton, *The Rise and Fall of the White Republic: Class, Politics, and Mass Culture in Nineteenth Century America* (New York: Verso, 1990), Ch. 7; David Roediger, *The Wages of Whiteness: Race and the Making of the American Working Class* (New York: Verso, 1991), Ch. 6; Eric Lott, *Love and Theft: Blackface Minstrelsy and the American Working Class* (New York: Oxford, 1993); Marlon Riggs, dir., *Ethnic Notions: Black People in White Minds* (Oakland, CA: California Newsreel Video, 1986).

22.   Turner, *Ceramic Uncles and Celluloid Mammies*; Roi Ottley and William J. Weatherby, *The Negro in New York: An Informal Social History, 1626- 1940* (New York: Praeger, 1967), p. 129.

23.   Ibid., p. 171, see fn 1.

24.   Franklin, *Up From Slavery*, p. 269.

25.   Olaudah Equiano, *The African: The Interesting Narrative of the Life of Olaudah Equiano.* (London: The X Press, 1998, first published in 1789).

26.   Ibid., p. 215.

27.   Kenneth M. Stamp, *The Peculiar Institution: Slavery in the Ante-Bellum South.* (New York: Vintage Books, 1956), p. 3.

28.   Anonymous, "Massa's Slave Son," in George P. Rawick, gen ed., *The American Slave: A Composite Autobiography*, Vol. 18, *Unwritten History of Slavery* (Fisk University), Contributions in Afro-American and African Studies Number 11 (Westport, CT: Greenwood Publishing Co. 1972, original 1941), p. 84.

29.   Charles Ball, *Slavery in the United States: A Narrative of the Life and Adventures of Charles Ball, A Black Man* (Lewistown: John W. Shugert, 1836. Reprint Yuval Taylor ed., Vol I. Chicago: Lawrence Hill Books, 1999), pp. 260-486. See pp. 299-300.

30.   Anonymous, "From Ole Virginny," in Rawick, *The American Slave: A Composite Autobiography*, p. 112.

31.   J. David Knottnerus, "Status Structures and Ritualized Relations in the Slave Plantation System," in Thomas J.Durant Jr. and J. David Knottnerus, *Plantation Society and Race Relations: The Origins of Inequality* (New York: Praeger, 1999), pp. 137-147; John W. Blassingame, *The Slave Community: Plantation Life in the Antebellum South*, Revised and Enlarged (New York: Oxford, 1979); Eugene Genovese, *Roll Jordan Roll: The World the Slaves Made* (New York: Vintage, 1974).

32.   Anonymous, "Fed more white folks than anybody," in Rawick, *The American Slave: A Compositet Autobiography*, p. 154.

33.   Anonymous, "Sold From the Block at Four Years Old," in Rawick, *The American Slave: A Composite Autobiography*, p. 70.

34.   Anonymous, " One of the First Voters in Montgomery County," in Rawick, *The American Slave: A Composite Autobiography*, p. 121.

35.   Anonymous, "One of Dr. Gale's 'Free Niggers,'" in Rawick, *The American Slave: A Composite Autobiography*.

36.   Ibid.

37.   Anonymous, "Knew Lincoln's Cousin, in Rawick, *The American Slave: A Composite Autobiography*, p. 88.

38.   Anonymous, "One of Dr. Gale's 'Free Niggers,'" in Rawick, *The American Slave: A Composite Autobiography*, pp. 1-15.

39.   Ibid.

40.   Anonymous, "Mulatto Whom Owners Treated like Family Member," in Rawick, *The American Slave: A Composite Autobiography*, p. 199

41.   Anonymous, "One of Dr. Gale's 'Free Niggers,'" in Rawick, *The American Slave: A Composite Autobiography*, pp. 1-15.

42.   Anonymous, "White fathers slave children," in Rawick, *The American Slave: A Composite Autobiography*, p. 84.

43.   Anonymous, "Knew Lincoln's Cousin," in Rawick, *The American Slave: A Composite Autobiography*, p. 85.

44.   Anonymous, "One of Dr. Gale's 'Free Niggers,'" in Rawick, *The American Slave: A Composite Autobiography*, pp. 1-15.

45.   Harriet A. Jacobs, *Incidents in the Life of a Slave Girl, Written by Herself* (Cambridge: Harvard University Press, 1987, first ed.1861). p. 5.

46.   Anonymous, "Sold From the Block at Four Years Old," in Rawick, *The American Slave: A Composite Autobiography*, p. 61.

47.   Jacobs, *Incidents in the Life of a Slave Girl*, p. 5.

48.   Anonymous, "Sold From the Block at Four Years Old," in Rawick, *The American Slave: A Composite Autobiography*, p. 6.

49.   Ibid, p. 83.

50.   Anonymous, "One of the First Voters in Montgomery County," in Rawick, *The American Slave: A Composite Autobiography*, p. 124.

51.   Anonymous, "My father Belonged to Uncle Sam. He Fought with the Yankees," in Rawick, *The American Slave: A Composite Autobiography*, p. 169.

52.   Anonymous, "Sold From the Block at Four Years Old," in Rawick, *The American Slave: A Composite Autobiography*, p. 61.

53.   Anonymous, "All my Bosses were Nigger Traders," in Rawick, *The American Slave: A Composite Autobiography*, p. 253.

54.   Genovese, *Roll Jordan Roll*, p. 293.

55.   Anonymous, "One of the First Voters in Montgomery County, in Rawick, *The American Slave: A Composite Autobiography*, p. 121.

56.   Anonymous "My Mother was the Smartest Black Woman in Eden born in 1844," in Rawick, *The American Slave: A Composite Autobiography*, p. 283.

57.   Beard and Beard, *A Basic History of the United States*, pp. 249-250.

58.   Noel Ignatiev, *How the Irish Became White* (London: Routledge, 1995), p. 6.

59.   Ibid., p. 38

60.   Kirby A. Miller, Bruce Boling, and David Doyle, "Emigrants and Exiles: Irish Cultures and Irish Emigration to North America, 1790-1922," *Irish Historical Studies*, 40, (1980): 100, 99.

61.   Ronald Takaki, *A Different Mirror: A History of Multicultural America* (Boston: Little Brown and Co., 1993), pp. 148-149.

62.   Ignatiev, *How the Irish Became White*, p. 109.

63.   Cited in Ignatiev, *How the Irish Became White*, p. 109

64.   David R. Roediger, *The Wages of Whiteness: Race and the Making of the American Working Class*, rev. ed. (London: Verso, 1999).

65.   John Finch, *Travel in the United States of America and Canada*. (London: Longman, Rees, Orme, Brown, Green, and Longman, 1833, 1844), quoted in Ignatiev, *How the Irish Became White*, p. 97.

66.   Seth Luther, *An Address delivered before the Mechanics and Working-men of the City of Brooklyn on the Celebration of the Sixtieth anniversary of American Independence* (Boston, 1836), pp. 18-20, quoted in Ignatiev, *How the Irish Became White*, p. 108.

67.   David Roediger, *The Wages of Whiteness: Race and the Making of the American Working Class*, rev. ed. (London: Verso, 1999); Noel Ignatiev, *How the Irish Became White*, p. 42; Theodore Allen, *The Invention of the White Race*. Vol. II.

68.   *Irish American* [New York City] January 6, 1850, quoted in Ignatiev, *How the Irish Became White*, p. 42.

69.   Ronald Takaki, *A Different Mirror*, p. 154.

70.   Joel Spring, *Deculturalization and the Struggle for Equality: Brief History of the Education of Dominated Cultures in the United States*. 3rd ed. (Boston: McGraw-Hill, 2001), p. 6; Ronald Takaki, *A Different Mirror*, pp. 28, 39.

71.   "Thomas Jefferson to Andrew Jackson, February 16, 1803," in Andrew A. Lipscomb and Albert E. Bergh, eds, *Writings of Thomas Jefferson*, 20 vols. (Washington D.C.: Carnegie Institution of Washington, 1904, 1926-1935), quoted in Takaki, p. 84, fn. 1, 443.

72.   "Jackson to Thomas Pinckney, February 16 and 17, 1814, and May 18, 1814," in John Spencer Basset, ed., *Correspondence of Andrew Jackson*, 6 vols. (Washington D. C). vol. 2, pp. 2-3, quoted in Ronald Takaki, *A Different Mirror*, p. 85

73.   Riordan, D. M. "What Shall We Do with the Indians?" in *Echoes of the Sunset Club, Comprising a Number of the Papers Read, and Addresses Delivered Before the Sunset Club of Chicago During the Past Two Years*. Compiled by W. W. Catlin. Chicago: Howard, Bartels & Co., 1891, 234-35 reprinted in Frederick W. Gleach, *Powhatan's World and Colonial Virginia: A Conflict of Cultures* (Lincoln: University of Nebraska, 2000), p. 201.

74.   Paul Johnson, *A History of the American People* (New York: Harper Collins, 1997), p. 252, ff 222; "Jefferson to Breckenridge, August 2, 1803," in P. L. Ford, ed., *Jefferson's Writings*, 10 Vol. (1892-1899), pp. 1136-1139.

75.   Quoted in Paul Johnson, *A History of the American People*, p. 371.

76.   Ronald Takaki, *A Different Mirror*, p. 168.

77.   Ibid., p. 169, ff9.

78.   Ibid., p. 169.

79.   Paul Johnson, *A History of the American People*, p. 379.

80.   Ibid., p. 380.

81.   Quotes in Takaki, *A Different Mirror*, p. 175, ff23.

82.   Ibid., p. 176. ff29.

83.   Ibid., p. 176, ff 27.

84.   Ibid., p. 177, ff 29.

85.   Ibid., pp 180-183.

86.   Johnson, *A History of the American People*, p. 385.

CHAPTER 5

THE GREAT DIVIDE
The Civil War to Modern
Racism

The key to the solution to the present difficulties is the abolition of slavery; not as an act of retaliation on the master, but as a measure of justice to the slave—the sure and permanent basis of a more perfect union.[1]

The Civil War was a contest between the agrarian/mercantile capitalists of the South and the entrepreneurial industrialists of the North both in terms of their economies and their ideologies. The South's weakness was the dependence of its ruling class on a plantation system that relied on slave labor as its source of power, income, and prestige. The intense cultivation of cotton wore out the land and necessitated expansion. Southern planters relied on New England and Britain to transport their goods and to produce textiles from the lucrative production of cotton. The South remained in a form of colonial dependency on industrialized capitalist economies. As long as production was high and profits soared there was little reason to change. The southern aristocracy championed its origins and ideology. In contrast, the North was establishing one of the fastest growing industrial

Race, Ethnicity, and Education: What is Taught in School, pages 119–147.
A Volume in: International Perspectives on Curriculum
Copyright © 2003 by Information Age Publishing, Inc.
All rights of reproduction in any form reserved.
ISBN: 1-59311-080-4 (paper), 1-59311-081-2 (cloth)

complexes in the world. The North attracted immigrants, expanded its labor supply, and increased its economic and political power as the nation expanded.[2]

THE POLITICS AND ECONOMICS OF LABOR

Two major regions, each divided into two variations, configured the United States politically and economically between the formation of the new republic and the Civil War. The differences between the North and South fractured along these lines in the antebellum period in ways that shaped the experiences of whites in all regions in relationship to non-whites.

New England

In New England the economy was dominated by small-scale, family owned and operated farms where self-sufficiency was prized. Closeknit, small communities practiced an exchange system that became more formalized in the 1820s as market activity increased and rural stores opened and began to hire wageworkers. The agricultural economy was not promising given that other regions had longer growing seasons and more fertile soil. At first families began to work in the home to produce goods to market. A non-agricultural base in lumber and fish contributed to the development of centers of maritime transportation to take advantage of marketing networks. In the first half of the nineteenth century large scale industry and commerce developed in these transportation centers and great family fortunes were accumulated using the shipping industry in the transatlantic slave trade. Even though there was very little slavery, indentured servitude took hold in the New England area.

The first textile mill was established in Rhode Island in 1793. Mills expanded with the industrial revolution in the early nineteenth century. Textile production grew as the steam engine fueled with coal made mechanized spinning operations possible. Other industries grew as well, such as the chemical industry to make bleaches and dyes for the cloth; the machine and die industry to make equipment; transportation expanded in order to deliver raw goods and take finished products to market. Coal and iron mines produced power and iron works produced building materials. Other variations on the mill idea produced saw mills for lumber and grain mills for grinding flour using water power. Paper mills were mechanized in the 1820s providing paper for books and pamphlets. Lowell, Massachusetts became the first industrial city with twenty-two mills by 1835. Over thirteen thousand workers, two-thirds women and one-third men, produced 2.2 million yards of cloth a week. The power weaving looms provided a model for industrial growth through corporate ownership of factories and the large scale, fully mechanized and integrated production of standardized goods.

Middle Atlantic States

The Middle Atlantic States were considerably more diverse than New England with Dutch, Huguenots, Swedes, Scotch-Irish, German, and English-Welsh Quakers. Large-scale commercial farms and tenant farms early provided a rich agricultural base but there was also iron manufacturing. An individualist-oriented entrepreneurial ideology encouraged mercantile development and the creation of trade zones as cities such as Philadelphia grew. Twelve percent was a common return for investments and nearly ten percent of the men identified themselves as merchants who traded and shipped goods. Successful merchants often cornered particular markets. Flour, for example, was exported to the South and indigo and rice were brought back to sell in the North.

Half of the white immigrant population in the Mid-Atlantic colonies and subsequent states, from the seventeenth to the nineteenth centuries, paid for their passage by serving four to seven years as indentured servants. Hundreds of thousands were apprenticed to pay for their passage and to learn trades. While young males were the majority of servant apprentices, one fourth were female. In the late seventeenth century the number of indentured and bonded immigrants dropped and, as in the South, slavery increased. At the time of the American Revolution both slavery and indentured servitude were common in the Middle Atlantic colonies. This pattern continued into the nineteenth century. Fifteen percent of the population was not free and thirty percent lived in poverty or close to poverty. The uneven class system is evident by the fact that the top ten percent of the taxpayers controlled ninety percent of the taxable property.

Class discrepancies and the creation of a white, skilled labor force contributed to racial, gender, and ethnic stereotyping. Internal class divisions allowed and encouraged the abuses of Jacksonian democracy. White society was also changing and a self-definition process was taking place in the workplace, home, and church. Young women and children were the first factory workers, but this changed. With Irish immigration the mills and factories became largely the workplace of immigrant male laborers. Competition and conflicts led to strikes and riots. Leaders such as Horace Mann argued that one solution was the Enlightenment idea of common public education. The Common School Movement started in Massachusetts in the antebellum period and took off after the Civil War. Conflict and competition in the workplace also encouraged a transient population with massive labor migrations that pushed families away from their place of birth in a westward movement and from rural areas to urban centers. Only two in five people stayed in any one community for an extended time.

By the mid-nineteenth century the stratification of society was noticeable. Concentric rings could be drawn around urban areas with the center occupied by the wealthy and each additional ring occupied by the less well to do. Cities became segmented. Communities could no longer operate through the traditional town meeting that promoted order and good government. Representative government took over in the cities with Tammany Hall style political machines and political parties with ward bosses and business alliances in a self-seeking competitive political order. The different social classes occupied different areas of the cities and subcultures developed with specific goals and identities. Trade unions grew among the skilled workers at first based on immigrants used to European craft shops and guilds. European immigrant skilled workers were often unsympathetic to rivals even as labor activism increased.

Religious revivalism grew in rural areas but also in urban areas along with crusades for temperance and abolitionism. In this period a distinct middle class was taking shape comprised of shop keepers, small manufacturers, bankers, and the like. This group specialized in "respectable" associations such as Protestant religious societies and clubs concerned with community affairs, politics, and the arts, as well as social reform issues. The middle classes specialized in creating the basis for a new competitive age through religious charitable activism that championed the establishment of an ideal middle class family life style that included the creation of public school systems that reinforced values in the young and taught them the skills necessary for survival in a changing social structure. This segment of society was concerned with social control and also with the rehabilitation of society and its motley inhabitants who would become "Americans." This group came to exert its influence over abolitionism and the ordering of the family with a woman's duty in the home, a man's responsibility in the workplace, and the child's proper place in school.

The Southern Contrast:
The Chesapeake Region and Lower South

In the Chesapeake region, the oldest colonial settlement, society was dominated by large plantations with elaborate mansions and a labor force of black slaves. Tenant farmers eked out a living in the tidewater area along the coast and subsistence farmers did the same in the backcountry. There were few cities and those that existed were not conducive to slave labor, which was almost entirely absent as inefficient in urban settings. The stratification of society continued from the codification of slavery in Virginia in the late seventeenth century to reproduce an unfree black substratum in the social structure that elevated the poor free population and diffused class conflict among whites. The reduced flow of white indentured servants in the eighteenth century increased the demand for slaves and the expanded slave trade. This produced a simple economy where slavery was a fixture typified by a small elite controlling a large population of blacks and a weak class of impoverished white free farmers.

Lower South Carolina and Georgia were more like the British settlements in the Caribbean with swampy land that supported perilous tropical diseases. Unlike the more typical monocultures of tobacco and cotton in the Chesapeake, the Deep South had other marketable crops including sugar, indigo, and rice. The largest plantations and largest numbers of slaves were in this area, which was linked to the Caribbean and Northern states with the exchange of slaves and good in ways that had similarities with the British imperial trade network.

The South was essentially outside the debate over the country's future direction due to its dependence on slavery as its means of production. Slavery was defended as necessary and as an ideal versus the North's increasing use of free labor. The South was a mercantilist offshoot of the national direction of development: it had advanced beyond a colonial status but it still produced staple crops for consumption outside its own center and educated southerners were consumers of manufactured goods as well as the financial and shipping services of those very metropolitan centers they refused to establish in their own territory. Licht cites the debate over whether the South was the consummate capitalist region, or the most aristocratic indicated by whether the dynamics were primarily on slavery as a labor system that was efficient, or if the dynamics were primarily on the slave-master relationship with the presence of large groups of poor white underclass. Were southern elites more lords than bosses?

In the pre-Civil War era the South was wealthier than the North in terms of the overall accumulation of wealth on the part of the elites but the North distributed the wealth to a greater extent. The South was a mercantilist outpost that did not develop an internally based economy with diversified producers and able consumers. As long as the exports that the South had to offer garnered such wealth and prosperity to the decision-making elite, there was little pressure for them to change. The North, on the other hand, garnered a vision of autonomous republican values composed of autonomous competing individuals. The South maintained an ostensibly Jeffersonian political vision of limited government. Southern leaders were wary of taxes, tariffs, and "Yankee" corporations. The modernizers of the North appeared to them to be staunch opponents of slavery and of all that maintained their very existence. While the southerners saw their conflict with the North as a defense of their institutions, the northerners saw the conflict in terms of keeping the Union together. They did not see the issues in terms of slavery and in point of fact did not defend the equality of humankind.

THE ELECTION OF 1860 AND THE DRED SCOTT DECISION

The campaign for the presidency in 1860 was not about the end of slavery. It was about restricting its extension, the power of the federal government over the states, and the legitimacy of the rule of white elites over working classes, slave and free. While Democrats charged Republicans with the desire to abolish slavery, the point was refuted by party spokesperson Horace Greeley in the *New York Tribune.* "Never on earth did the Republican party propose to abolish Slavery...Its objection with respect to Slavery is simply, nakedly, avowedly, its restriction to the existing states."[3] Initially, Abraham Lincoln only supported the restriction of slavery in the territories but he was drawn into the complex issues of the day.[4]

Slavery was prohibited by the Northwest Ordinance (1787) in all territories north and west of the Ohio River, present Ohio, Indiana, Illinois, Michigan, Wisconsin, and parts of Minnesota. The Louisiana Purchase of the vast territory from the Mississippi River to the Rocky Mountains from France in 1803 was mostly north and west of the southernmost point of the Ohio. The argument that the Northwest Ordinance did not apply to this territory resulted in the 1820 Missouri Compromise. Maine was then admitted as a free state, Missouri entered as a slave state, and slavery was prohibited in federal territories north and west of Missouri.

The Missouri Compromise promised that no laws could be passed that abridged the rights of states and allowed the extension of slavery within limits. The dynamics of slavery and the acquisition of territory became more vicious with the entrance of Texas into the Union in 1845 and as the United States declared war on Mexico in 1846 with the hopes of acquiring additional territory in California and New Mexico. The 1850 Missouri Compromise strengthened the contention that the Union was dependent on the absolute equality of the States. Southerners argued that the South was the savior of liberty in the name of slavery. Liberty in the South was not individual but embodied by the state, and the liberty of the elites in each state was to determine the destiny of the state as their natural right. The Compromise argued that refusing to:

> extend to the southern and western states any advantage which would tend to strengthen, or render these more secure, or increase their limits or population by annexation of new territory or States, on the assumption or under the pretext that the institution of slavery, as it exists among them, is immoral or sinful, or otherwise obnoxious, would be contrary to that equality of rights and advantages, which the Constitution was intended to secure alike to all

the members of the Union, and would in effect, disenfranchise the slave-holding States, withholding from them the advantages, while it subjected them to the burdens of government.[5]

The compromise also included a harsh new federal fugitive slave law that allowed slaves to be captured by federal commissioners, denied jury trial, or testimony in their own behalf before they were returned to their masters. Slave sales were banned in the District of Columbia, and California was admitted as a free state as a token to the North. In 1854 the Kansas-Nebraska Act repealed parts of the 1850 Compromise and opened up the territory held by the present day states of Kansas, Nebraska, the Dakotas, Montana, Colorado, and parts of Wyoming to slavery. A mini war called "Bleeding Kansas " broke out in 1856 between proponents of slavery and antislavery forces. It is likely that it had an impact on the Dred Scott case a year later and certainly showed the volatility of the issues.[6]

The Dred Scot Decision

The 1857 Dred Scott decision of the United States Supreme Court denied citizenship and humanity to blacks. It also nationalized slavery. The states' defense of slavery was, given the ruling, no longer relevant. Instead of using the power of the higher law of the federal government to eliminate slavery, it was used to extend it, make it inviolable, and to make it unconstitutional to curtail it or limit its extension. The case seemed an unlikely venue for such a drastic decision.

Dred Scott was born a slave in Virginia around 1800 but was brought to Alabama, and then St. Louis, Missouri by his owner. When his owner died, he was bought by an Army surgeon, Dr. John Emerson, and taken to Fort Armstrong in Illinois, a free state. Scott then moved with his master to Minnesota, a territory where the Missouri Compromise "forever prohibited" slavery. He was married in a civil ceremony in 1838, an unusual development. Scott and his wife were hired for profit when his master was transferred back to St. Louis. Eventually, Scott and his wife followed Emerson's family to St. Louis and were again hired out for profit to various people. They lived for a time in Texas before returning to Missouri. In 1846, Emerson died and his wife refused to sell Scott to himself. She apparently preferred the income Scott and his wife provided. Scott sued for his freedom on the basis of his residence in the free state of Illinois and free Wisconsin Territory. The case wound slowly through the state courts that consistently denied Scott his freedom. The case was finally appealed to the Supreme Court in December 1854.

Chief Justice Roger B. Taney's Court heard the case. While Taney was Attorney General under President Andrew Jackson, he had argued that blacks in the United States had no rights except those they "enjoy" at the "sufferance" and "mercy" of whites.[7] These attitudes foreshadowed the Dred Scott decision handed down in 1857. It declared that African Americans, slave or free, had no rights. Blacks had no right to citizenship; and no right that "a white person" was obliged to recognize. The decision further extended slavery throughout the territory of the United States by making slavery national rather than state-based, effectively abolishing the Missouri Compromise. It also ended a state's right to regulate slavery either inside or outside its own territory. The Lecompton Constitution of Kansas, framed that same year, followed the precedent that "the right of property is before and higher than any constitutional sanction, and the right of the owner of a slave to such slave and its increase is the same and as inviolable as the right of the owner of any property whatsoever." In 1864 a provision was added that the Kansas Constitution could be amended by two-thirds vote, but a clause affirmed, "no alteration shall be made to affect the right of property in the ownership of slaves."[8]

Democrats were not pleased with Taney's decision. Their argument for slavery was based on state's rights. Senator Stephen Douglas of Illinois in a speech on 22 March 1858 declared that "a fatal blow to States' Rights, subversive of the Democratic platform" had been struck. Douglas declared that: "I do not recognize the right of the President or his Cabinet, no matter what my respect may be for them, to tell me my duty in the Senate chamber." Douglas affirmed his belief in inequality in a speech on July 9, 1858:

> I am opposed to negro [sic] equality. I repeat that this nation is a white people—a people composed of European descendants—a people that have established this government for themselves, and their posterity, and I am in favor of preserving not only the purity of the blood, by the purity of the government from any mixture or amalgamation with inferior races.[9]

Black abolitionist Frederick Douglass actually welcomed the Dred Scott decision as the "beginning of a great cataclysm that would destroy slavery."[10] Douglass pointed out that the Supreme Court was not the highest authority over morality and that Taney's perverse views were subject to the power of "the Almighty." Taney "cannot pluck the silvery star of liberty from our Northern sky," he said. Fredrick Douglass pointed out that neither Taney nor the other forces that sought to perpetuate slavery could "change the essential nature of things—making evil good, and good evil."[11] The power of the southern elite was damaged by the Dred Scott decision. The position of African Americans sank to a new low. Lincoln commented that: "We shall lie down pleasantly dreaming that the people of Missouri are on the verge of making their state free; and we shall awake to the reality, instead, that the Supreme Court has made Illinois a slave state."[12]

PRO-SOUTH ARGUMENTS AND THE
COUNTER ARGUMENTS

Southern elites waged successful, if twisted, arguments, in defense of their life style as champions of states' rights and the legitimate rule of a privileged oligarchy. Southern arguments in support of slavery maintained that chattel slavery was in fact relative freedom and that wage labor was the true form of enslavement. John Calhoun argued that "slavery in its true light...[was] the most safe and stable basis for free institutions in the world." The South in this view restrained the excesses of the Northern and English conflicts between labor and capital.[13] By 1850 the arguments used to support the history of slavery in the United States seventy years later were directed to the public. In 1852, William Harper, a proslavery advocate published *Pro Slavery Argument*. Slavery "is as much in the order of nature that men should enslave each other as that animals should prey upon each other." Similarly, George Fitzhugh wrote in *Sociology for the South* (1854): "Slavery will everywhere be abolished, or everywhere be re-instituted." The *Richmond Inquirer* in 1856 proclaimed: "The great evil of Northern free society is that it is burdened with a servile class of mechanics and laborers unfit for self-government, and yet clothed with the attributes and powers of citizens . . . slavery is the natural and normal condition of laboring man, whether white or black."[14]

Jefferson Davis

The *New York Herald* called Jefferson Davis the "Mephistopheles of the South" in his attempt to transform magically slavery, a "moral and political evil," into a moral and political good by manipulating perspectives.[15] Davis was open to modern ideas and tended toward liberal views except on the subject of slavery. He was caught up in southern proslavery ideology even though he recognized that the South needed to advance economically in much the same way as the North in order to survive with its own lifestyle. Southerners needed to learn to become independent, to transport their own raw materials, and manufacture their own products. The South lacked a basic infrastructure. Its currency was not backed by a store of gold or silver. The means of transportation was geared toward moving raw products off the plantation to port cities such as Charleston and Savannah but it neglected to connect the states to each other either by rail or other means. To solve this problem meant centralization, urbanization, and industrialization as well as education. Gross contradictions were embedded in the choices. What needed to be done contradicted the very ideology Davis wanted to preserve. The modern world clashed with a world born of one satisfied with the old world.

Children needed to be taught the ways and values of the South. Davis lamented that educational materials and teachers often came from the North. The sons of planters who left the South for higher education as well as southern students learned viewpoints that contradicted traditional southern values. The planter class did not intend to work, and educating slaves and poor white workers required careful thought. It was not possible. Davis was caught in a contradiction, as was the South in general. To educate Southerners in order to modernize and industrialize jeopardized southern plantation culture and its traditional leadership. Poor southerners, slave and free, white and black, had no voice. Like the early Virginia elites, Davis opted for the consolidation of power. His alternatives at the time were limited. He chose stronger control over the dissemination of ideas rather than challenge southern elitism. Southern textbooks were to be rewritten in order to eliminate any opinions that conflicted with the plantation economy and slavery. Elitism was to be rewarded. He wanted to "indoctrinate their [the South's] mind with sound impressions and views." Davis wanted to eliminate "Yankee schoolteachers" and Yankee ideas.[16]

ATTEMPTS AT RECONCILIATION AND THE BIRTH OF THE CONFEDERACY

Even most Northerners opposed the militant abolitionist movements that dated from the 1830s after it became clear that sending African Americans back to West Africa was not going to solve the problem of free blacks since fewer than 1,500 were repatriated to Liberia by 1831. William Lloyd Garrison started publishing the *Liberator* on January 1 of that year. His motto was "I am in earnest—I will not equivocate—I will not excuse—I will not retreat an inch—and I will be heard."[17] The harsh rhetoric, nonetheless, attracted followers of moderate interest and sentiment changed.

Abraham Lincoln won the election in 1860. Only three days after his election, The South Carolina legislature authorized a convention on December 6 to decide the future of the state's relationship to the Union. On December 20, 1860, South Carolina seceded from the United States of America. The North at first reacted with a series of compromises. The most serious of which was the Crittenden Compromise that offered a constitutional amendment that would protect slavery and the slave trade in the southern states and in Washington D. C. A further stipulation disfranchised free "Negroes" in the North and South and provided that they be forced to leave the country. Even before the compromise was voted on Mississippi elected to leave the Union on January 7, 1861. On February 15, Georgia, Florida, Alabama, Louisiana, Texas, Arkansas, and Mississippi met to form a government. The Crittenden Compromise was rejected by both Houses of Congress, April 12, 1861.

Davis claimed that the Confederacy was born of "a peaceful appeal to the ballot box." That was a fiction. No referendum was held in any state. A total of 854 men, selected by legislatures, not the people, a select force of individuals representing the upper classes, made the decision. Representatives in various secession conventions decided the fate of nine million mostly poor southerners. While Davis did not want the impending conflict to be a rich man's war fought by the poor, that was exactly what it was. It was the wealthy and those with economic interests in the outcome not the rest of the whites who had nothing to gain who voted for secession. The African Americans, free and enslaved, had no choice, no voice, neither did poor whites. Alexander Stephans, the newly elected president of the Confederacy declared that the slave controversy was the immediate cause of the South's secession. His stand was made clear:

> Our Confederacy is founded upon the great truth that the Negro is not equal to the white man. That slavery—subordination to the superior race, is his natural and normal condition. This our new Government, is the first, in the history of the world based upon this great physical and moral truth.[18]

When South Carolina's forces trained its guns of Fort Sumter, Lincoln and his cabinet decided to send an expedition without arms or ammunition to negotiate in an effort to uphold the Union. When the fort was fired upon, the war began on April 12, 1861. The demise of slavery came more quickly than Frederick Douglass could imagine. President Lincoln signed legislation ending slavery in the territories on June 19, 1862. Taney's interpretation of constitutional powers was ignored, and within six months, January 1, 1863, the Emancipation Proclamation was issued. Slavery was no longer was protected under the Constitution and, in fact, had no protection at all. The Civil War took on a new dimension; slavery was now linked to the restoration of the Union. After 1863 the North was fighting to abolish slavery. This was consummated in 1865 with the adoption of the Thirteenth Amendment, which abolished slavery in all states of the Union.

Call to Arms and the End to Slavery

Frederick Douglass recruited African Americans through his newspaper with the call: "Men of Color, to Arms!" African Americans who optimistically joined the campaign did not find the same comradeship as in Bacon's Rebellion. They were segregated into "Negro" regiments with inferior equipment and support. They comprised approximately ten percent of the military; over a quarter of those enlisted lost their lives. African Americans were not allowed to serve as officers even though they received twenty Congressional Medals of Honor.[19] Black soldiers and veterans protested against this "insulting endorsement of the old dogma of Negro inferiority."[20] Before the war ended two hundred thousand black soldiers fought for the Union.

In early 1865 the United States Congress passed and sent on to the States the Thirteenth Amendment that constitutionally ended slavery. The next year the Fourteenth Amendment made all persons born in the United States citizens. The Dred Scott decision was nullified when the Fourteenth Amendment was ratified in 1868. Dred Scott did not live to see the outcome, but like Elizabeth Keys he was compensated. The sons of Dred Scott's first owner, Peter Blow, purchased Scott and his family and manumitted them into freedom. Scott remained a free man until his death in February 17, 1857, only nine months after having been freed. Chief Justice Taney died before his decision was overruled on October 12, 1864.

During the Civil War racist ideology defended class distinctions grounded in the belief that there was a hierarchy of races. Again, race took precedent over social class. The poor white wage laborer was subjected to continued exploitation. Hostility was directed away from the sources of their discontent and toward poor black laborers who were subjected to even lower wages. Poor white southerners, free and emancipated blacks, and northern rural and urban lower class whites suffered the highest mortality rates during the Civil War. Poor white southerners, free and emancipated blacks, and northern rural and urban lower classes were also casualties of the failure of Reconstruction after the war.

RECONSTRUCTION AND RETREAT

Radical Reconstruction and the backlash against legislated racism at the end of the nineteenth century have parallels in the Civil Rights movement one hundred years later and in the current politics of race. Legislation for equality laid the groundwork for political action in both cases, but implementing and reinforcing change were met with great resistance. The Thirteenth Amendment assured all African Americans freedom from involuntary servitude. The Fourteenth Amendment assured the right to citizenship. The Fifteenth Amendment provided self-determination with the right to vote. However, the dogma of race once unleashed was not to be reigned in easily. The purpose of Reconstruction between 1865 and 1877, in the eyes of radical Republicans, was to limit, if not strip, the planters' power. Slavery was abolished, schools were set up, former slaves acquired land, and the right to vote was briefly acquired along with the experience of holding an elected office. The aristocracy was temporarily displaced and the plantation economy destroyed.

The impact of the Civil War was felt to a much greater extent in the South than the North, not only because the South lost. The War was fought on southern soil, and there was considerable personal loss of property and capital. The end of slavery terminated a southern institution and it also constituted the loss of capital investment in labor. Freedom for slaves offered them the ability to choose their own hours for work, recreation, or personal time. They could also choose the pace of work ending the gang based slave labor, which as Walter Licht notes is, in economists' terms an inward shift in the labor supply curve.[21] Production needed to be completely reorganized. Even when production could be resumed, the main crop, cotton, had been devalued. Prior to the war the demand for cotton kept its value very high assuring enormous profits. With production curtailed during the war buyers of raw cotton turned elsewhere. India and Egypt proved to be new sources of cotton. When cotton production was resumed in the South, planters no longer controlled a flooded market and prices collapsed. Nonetheless, the social relations, the arrangement of power in the hand of planters, the value system, and economic activities in the South did not change. Licht points out that while the North witnessed a great boom in industrial growth after 1865, this growth did not occur in the South. The "New South" did not occur and industrialization had to wait.[22]

The agenda of radical Republicans was not shared by moderate Republicans and was opposed by conservative southern Democrat "Redeemers." A large portion of the southern white population sought to ignore, overturn, and destroy policies proposed by the radicals. The battles of the Civil War continued in a more covert fashion. African Americans and their supporters lost. Southern resistance, northern complacency, and the unwillingness of authorities to enforce legislation and punish civil rights violations left Reconstruction and the three Amendments meaningless.[23] The weak wording of the Amendments proved vulnerable to effective counter legislation with disastrous results for the rights of all Americans. The country entered the last decade of the century under the lengthening shadow of the color line.[24]

The planter class and its mythology were wounded by the Civil War but they were not left without the power to reorganize. Their prestige rose, if anything, in the eyes of poor southerners due to the effectiveness of racist propaganda. The conservative Democratic Party Redeemers recaptured state legislatures: North Carolina in 1870, Georgia in 1871, Texas is in 1873, Alabama and Arkansas in 1874, South Carolina in 1876, Louisiana and Florida in 1877, and Virginia in 1889.[25] Reconstruction was in a retreat by 1877. Left in its wake were permanent policies of repression based on racism. Power was manipulated through new forms of oppression at the ballot box, in the market place, and in housing.[26]

White Supremacists

Racist groups such as the Ku Klux Klan, founded immediately after Appomattox in 1867, terrorized both the black population and white sympathizers. The Union Leagues were a special target of violence for their promotion of suffrage among African Americans in the South. Black schools were burned and teachers assaulted.[27] The growth of white supremacy, racism, and a predilection for a violent disregard for both civil rights and the rule of law were not caused by Reconstruction policies alone. Radical Reconstruction provided a stimulus for the elaboration of antebellum racism. Racism came to serve as a badge of white respectability, as a defense of white culture. Violent acts and racial hatred toward African Americans and their white sympathizers were elevated to a duty that truly commanded race as the dominant identity over class. The glorification of the white race, white womanhood, protection of the white family, and white brotherhood created a sense of identity and sympathy with the "fallen" planter class. Those who disagreed faced violence. This included the right to segregate, exclude, terrorize, and kill African Americans and any Anglo-Europeans, northerners or southerners that associated with African Americans.. This was excused in terms of chivalry, humanity, and patriotism as well as states' rights.[28]

Racism replaced slavery as a tool for social control. African Americans were segregated and concentrated in enclaves at the bottom of society. Paternalistic race relations in a competitive agrarian feudal society, with its master-slave model, was eliminated and replaced by the superimposition of race over class in a free market competitive economy, where the possibility of escape from discrimination was denied African Americans. The social construction of the concept of race was complete. Legislation disenfranchised African Americans. Few of those affected noticed that it disenfranchised the poor and undereducated whites and that it served to reinstate the power of southern aristocrats over all laboring classes. The economic plight of the southern states, their devastation, lack of transportation, and lack of industry exacerbated social problems. Racism provided an outlet for frustration and violence and was used in both the North and South by those who benefited from low wages and a divided labor force.

Racism in the North

The North was not a haven for African Americans any more than the South was. Bombarded by racist literature and images, and faced with an influx of African Americans leaving the South as well as increases in European immigration, expanding industrialization, fluctuations in the economy, northerners and mid-westerners were also unsympathetic to the plight of freed African Americans. Politicians, who had sided with the abolitionists, announced the "political supremacy of the white race" along with southerners. Racist entertainment gained popularity with its message designed to mock and denigrate southern and black culture. African Americans were depicted as savages, criminals, and uncontrollable. The defenders of slavery depicted African Americans as "shiftless, child-like, dull-witted, and savage," as well as unassimilable and not equal. African Americans did not ascribe to their own inferiority. Figures like Frederick Douglass cited white prejudice not black faults: "Prejudice always blind to what it never wishes to see, and quick to perceive all it wishes, sees the whole race in the character of our worst representations, while it has no sight for our best." The savage attacks, however, took their toll.[29]

At the turn of the nineteenth to twentieth century overt racism in the United States reached a new high. Pseudoscientific ideas about the racial divisions of humanity came into full force and justified racist ideology. The revolution in production that had taken place in the nineteenth century expanded agricultural, industrial, and urban complexes with a scale of construction in transportation and communication previously unimaginable. A demographic revolution occurred during this period. The immigration of millions of Europeans to the United States and the internal migration of thousands of African Americans from the South to the North created urban centers and provided labor for their expansion and industry.

ECONOMIC DETERMINISM AND RACISM

Two comprehensive ideologies that grew out of the nineteenth century and became prominent in the twentieth century were economic determinism and racism.[30] Ideologies are belief systems that are comprehensively believed to be true based on faith more than factual evidence. Human beings assume ideological positions without realizing it, for many of our domain assumptions are taken for granted rather than consciously examined. Economic determinism is the belief that the social order is determined by the economic order, that social class determines one's place in society. Racism is based on the belief that biology determines a person's social status as inferior or superior. In the United States these ideologies became intertwined in ways that reproduced inequalities in society in spite of monumental transformations that included the Civil War, Reconstruction, mass migrations, industrialization and an unprecedented accumulation and concentration of wealth in an increasingly urbanized setting.

In the United States where social status, life style, and opportunities are dependent on income, the economy under capitalism is an important determinant of social life as well as the relatively open capacity for social mobility and individual advancement. Karl Marx, writing in the mid nineteenth century as industrial capitalism transformed English society and its social structure, argued that as capitalism advanced and established modern social classes the economy was the driving force behind society. During this same period, Americans were constructing biological determinism as debates over the practice of slavery in a free society escalated. Industrial capitalism in the North exploited a predominantly free labor market while agrarian capitalism in the South relied on not free labor. The origins and use of racial slavery in the South was a system of labor exploitation that created an elite whose status required the trappings of slavery as more than labor. The labor system also determined political power that was held by an aristocratic leisure class. Confronting slavery as purely an economic issue of exploitation was not expedient and, in fact, did not address the array of issues that remained unsolved after the North won the Civil War and allowed the southern planter elite to regain control in a transformed society, the New South.

Marx did not believe economic systems such as capitalism were permanent because he thought that the injustices of a class-based society would lead to revolution from below. Like the English Revolution in the seventeenth century, the Civil War was not a revolution from below. It was a revolution among elites fought, as most wars are, by non-elites. The South was not only a class-based society but also one characterized by a small number of ruling aristocrats who controlled a large number of not free workers. While the South lost the war, equality between former slaves and their masters did not take place. During Reconstruction, the politics of equality were slowly but effectively reversed with the help of northern capitalist and the ideological framework of biological determinism and racism.

Marx underestimated not only the success of capitalism but also the power of politics to mediate change in ways that reproduce social structure throughout the western capitalist world. As a representative democracy and a society based on law, the political structure of the United States was designed to balance the inequality of the economic order with equality before the law. There is constant adjustment and readjustment as social life adapts to political and economic change as well as new technologies. Economic determinism and the politics of caste are connected to racism and its persistence. Paradoxically, the ideology of economic determinism supports the idea that racial slavery was natural and that racism is natural and indestructible. In fact none of these ideas are natural. They are all products of the human imagination and made real as historical configurations built by human beings who create and reproduce culture in their own interests.

Racism is the false belief that different species of human beings exist, and that there are substantive innate differences between groups that comprise different races that are permanently unequal. In the United States this has been associated with extraneous physical characteristics such as skin color, hair color and texture, eye color, and facial features with light skin color associated with superiority, with thin features, light hair and eye coloring similarly privileged. The development of the ideology of racism is much more recent than the long trajectory of the history of the economic developments that established capitalism. However, capitalism as a way to organize labor in order to accumulate wealth and make money set up conditions that created the ideology of racism. The origin of capitalism as the world's most successful economic system was closely associated with European colonialism and the development of the slave trade. Capitalism and democracy are commonly taken as synonymous in general discourse. Developing countries, powerful western leaders insist, must take up capitalism if they want to be political democracies and part of the free world.

Political democracy preceded advanced capitalism in the United States, yet the correspondence between the rise of mercantile capitalism and the development of racial slavery was direct. Racism in the United States intersects with class and with capitalist interests. Racial slavery and the contradictions between the political philosophy of the United States and the practice of chattel bondage grew out of early agrarian and market capitalism in the western world. The perception of and maintenance of "racial" division has been useful to white elites in all regions of the country and has been played out in particularly vicious ways in areas where the population that has the economic and political power is predominantly classified as "white." The fiction of human races based on superficial observable characteristics, became a basis for class, gender, age, and ethnic discrimination. Skin color in the United States came to delineate and to mask economic status with its division of haves and have-nots. The affirmation of a color line visibly identified those groups deemed ineligible to achieve parity with the dominant group. This was justified by the extension of Enlightenment ideas about the scientific method misapplied to human differences, and emergent social sciences that accepted without question racial theories. Attempts to justify inequalities on the basis of natural social differences used Charles Darwin's notions of evolution, as adapted by Social Darwinists to create the ideology of biological determinism. Economic determinism adapted to biological determinism at the turn of the nineteenth to twentieth century supported an unthinking as well as conscious racism quite comfortably.

RACIAL DISCRIMINATION AND SEGREGATION
IN THE FAR WEST

The organization of Western hereditarian social thought and classification schema coincided with the end of Reconstruction and developed into the forms of racism and discrimination that prevailed in the first half of the twentieth century. In the late nineteenth century the after effects of the

Civil War and dislocations brought about by industrialization and urbanization, came up against fears about the efficacy of new populations. Labor
strikes in the 1870s and riots such as the Haymarket Affair in 1886 fed into
additional labor violence in the 1890s. This was met with a wave of nativism
that lashed out against new comers and elevated and solidified race theories of human difference. This period also witnessed the application of
these theories to enact anti-immigration legislation against ethnic white
populations. These laws first excluded individuals deemed "criminals,
lunatics, and idiots" in 1882. They were expanded to exclude "epileptics,
beggars, prostitutes and anarchists" in 1891. As compulsory school laws
were enacted and then enforced, similar exclusions on the basis of delinquency, poverty and disease were included in the texts of the laws. Intolerance was increasingly directed toward populations identified as somehow
"defective" based on the inflammatory rhetoric of proto-eugenicists such as
Richard Dugdale in his study of the Juke family as producing a defective
lineage in 1874. Compulsory school laws, mostly enacted after the Civil
War, had the effect of standardizing expectations if not practices. In 1909,
Leonard Ayres, an early proponent of applying scientific methods to public
education to increase its efficiency, drew to public attention the number of
children who did not advance with their classmates. His book, *Laggards in
the Schools,* implied that the "menace of the feebleminded" existed in open
public forums. Henry Goddard reinforced this issue in his works on the
feebleminded.[31]

The Chinese in California

At the turn of the nineteenth to twentieth century immigration was at its
height on both the East and West coast. The Asian experience on the West
Coast provides another window into racism in the United States over the
first half of the twentieth century. President Woodrow Wilson, as John
Blum in his book, *Woodrow Wilson and the Politics of Mortality* points out,
harbored a distaste "for those non-British newcomers to the United States,
whom he blamed in large degree for a degradation of American Democracy,"[32] Wilson acted on these beliefs, "with the support of the British,
[he] rejected a Japanese proposal at the Versailles Conference for the
inclusion of an amendment supporting racial equality in the Covenant of
the League of Nations."[33] That the Japanese wanted such an amendment is
understandable, for the Japanese, like the Chinese, who emigrated to the
United States, especially to California, in the nineteenth and early twentieth centuries faced severe discrimination and abuse.

By 1852 there were already 25,000 Chinese in California working as day
laborers, laundrymen, and domestics. When work on the transcontinental
railroad began, contractors found a ready supply of labor among the Chinese, and Chinese immigration increased, for the Burlingame Treaty

(1868) permitted Chinese immigration. However, the warm welcome the Chinese laborers experienced in the early 1860s turned to hostility. At about the time the work on the Union-Central Pacific Railroad was completed in 1869, it is estimated that the Chinese accounted for about ten per cent of California's total population and nearly a fourth of San Francisco's.[34] Competition for employment was keen, and the result was that the Chinese were viciously attacked in the "Sandlot Riots in San Francisco in July 1877. American workers saw them as a threat to their own well being because the Chinese were seen as willing to accept lower wages and a lower standard of living than what the American workers sought. As Oscar Handlin, the historian of immigration to the United States observed:

> There were occasional expressions of unfriendliness to the Chinese in the 1850s, but time intensified rather than relaxed the hostility. The Orientals, unlike European immigrants, rarely brought their families with them or intended to strike roots. Instead, they remained sojourners, striving to accumulate the savings that would take them back to their ancestral homes.[35]

The Chinese as a transient population did not become a part of the communities in which they lived not so much by choice but by the unfortunate facts of their lives. Unable to support themselves in China, they sought labor elsewhere and sent home a means for the survival of their kin. Often their only hope of returning to their family was in a casket on their death. The labor of the Chinese was welcome when there was work to be done since they could be hired for less than whites but they were not welcome when the task at hand was completed. Handlin tells us why: "Their strange appearance and their distinctive customs antagonized the whites..." He goes on to describe the conflict that was exploited by employers to keep wages down. Hostility, Handlin explains, came primarily from white laborers, "who feared their [Asian immigrants] competition." The result was "racist agitation, sparked by Denis Kearney and the Workingmen's Party of California, [which] ultimately led to a series of exclusion laws, beginning in 1882."[36]

Congress responded to the "Sandlot Riots" by enacting a bill that abrogated the 1868 treaty, but President Hayes, even though he "disapproved of the Chinese 'labor invasion' that had been stimulated by mining and railroad corporations," vetoed it.[37] He then appointed a commission that negotiated a new treaty that did not permit the United States to prohibit but did allow the regulation, limitation, and even the suspension of immigration of Chinese laborers. In 1879, the U. S. Congress enacted a law that prohibited Chinese immigrants from becoming naturalized citizens. In 1882, President Chester Alan Arthur signed the bill that Congress enacted to prohibit any further immigration of Chinese laborers. In his *History of the American People* published in 1901, Woodrow Wilson, then a professor of history at Princeton University, provided an assessment of what led to the 1882 exclusion act. It was a characterization of Chinese laborers that clearly reinforced stereotypes and hostility toward the Chinese as he expressed his own racist sentiments:

> The law that excluded Chinese immigrants had been passed at the urgent solicitation of the men of the Pacific coast. Chinese laborers had poured in there, first by hundreds, then by thousands, finally by hundreds of thousands, until the labor situation of the whole coast had become one almost of revolution. Caucasian laborers could not compete with the Chinese, could not live upon a handful of rice and work for a pittance, and found themselves being steadily crowded out from occupation after occupation by the thrifty, skillful Orientals, who, with their yellow skin and strange, debasing habits of life, seemed to them hardly fellow men at all, but evil spirits, rather.[38]

Wilson's claim that the Chinese "poured" in by "hundreds of thousands" was an exaggeration. Handlin reported that in 1880 there were approximately 105,000 Chinese in the United States, 95.5 per cent of whom were male and that in 1890 there were approximately 107,000, 96.4 per cent of whom were male.[39] There were not hundreds of thousands.

A treaty agreed upon in 1894 imposed a ten-year period during which no Chinese laborers would be permitted entry into the United States. When China terminated the agreement in 1904, a 1902 exclusion act was reenacted, and no terminal date was specified. There was not only an effort to restrict or eliminate Chinese laborers in California but also a determined effort to segregate their children and other "Oriental" children in the public schools. After the San Francisco schools opened after the 1906 earthquake, the San Francisco School Board ordered that Japanese, Chinese, and Korean children attend a separate "Oriental" school. In its resolution the San Francisco School Board expressed its conviction that "the co-mingling of such pupils with Caucasian children is baneful and demoralizing in the extreme, the ideas entertained and practiced by people of "Mongolian" or Japanese affiliations being widely divergent from those of Americans." Thus the Board resolved that it was

> determined in its efforts to effect the establishment of separate schools for Chinese and Japanese pupils, not only for the purpose of relieving the congestion at present prevailing in our schools, but also for the higher end that our children should not be placed in any position where their youthful impressions may be affected by association with pupils of the Mongolian race.[40]

The San Francisco School Board rescinded its order on 13 March 1907 after a conference with President Theodore Roosevelt.

The Japanese Experience in California

In 1890, when what may be termed "significant" Japanese immigration began, there were only 2,039 Japanese in the United States. During the decade of the 1890s it is estimated that between 25,000 and 160,000 Japanese immigrants came to the United States. During the following decade, immigration reached its peak at 130,000. The rate of immigration from Japan after that was about 10,000 a year until 1924 when further immigration of was prohibited. Notwithstanding the relatively small numbers of Japanese immigrants arriving in California, the San Francisco labor movement began the campaign against the Japanese. In 1892, Dennis Kearney who had earlier proclaimed "The Chinese Must Go," attempted to make a political comeback with the slogan, "The Japs Must Go." "In the same year," according to Roger Daniels, "a San Francisco newspaper launched a self-styled journalistic 'crusade' against the menace of Japanese immigration."[41] In 1894, a treaty between Japan and the United States provided that each nation would allow free entry of the other's citizens. It also allowed each nation to legislate against excessive immigration of laborers to protect its domestic interests. In 1900, Japan voluntarily restricted immigration to the United States. However, it did not restrict immigration to Hawaii, Canada, or Mexico, countries from which immigrants could easily enter the United States.[42] Japan's agreement to voluntarily restrict immigration did not quell anti-Japanese sentiment. In 1900, at a meeting sponsored by organized labor the mayor of San Francisco, James Duval Phelan, "effectively linked the anti-Chinese and the anti-Japanese movements" when he declared:

> The Japanese are starting the same tide of immigration which we thought we had checked twenty years ago...The Chinese and Japanese are not bona fide citizens. They are not the stuff of which American citizens are made.[43]

Anti-Japanese sentiment reached new and higher levels in 1905 when increased Japanese immigration (45,000 arrived between 1903 and 1905) seemed to give credence to earlier expressions of the threat the presence of Japanese presented. In February 1905, the *San Francisco Chronicle* with a streamer on its front page that read "THE JAPANESE INVASION, THE PROBLEM OF THE HOUR" began a concerted and deliberate anti-Japanese campaign." The *Chronicle* suggested that war with Japan was a real possibility (Japan had recently defeated Russia on land and at sea), that "every one of these immigrants...is a Japanese spy," and that Japanese men wanted American women. The California legislature responded to the *Chronicle's* campaign by passing a resolution that asked the U. S. Congress to limit Japanese immigration. According to the California legislators:

Japanese laborers, by reason of race habits, mode of living, disposition, and general characteristics, are undesirable . . . Japanese . . . do not buy land [or] build or buy houses...They contribute nothing to the growth of the state. They add nothing to its wealth, and they are a blight on the prosperity of it, and a great and impending danger to its welfare.[44]

When the San Francisco School Board announced its school segregation order on October 11, 1906, it received virtually no notice in the United States, "but nine days later the segregation order was front-page news in the Tokyo newspapers." Even though the order affected less than a hundred students, ninety-three to be exact, twenty-five of whom were United States citizens because they were born in the United States, the order transformed anti-Japanese sentiment in California into a national and international problem. The twenty-five Japanese-American students could expect no help from the federal government, for the Supreme Court's decision in *Plessy v. Ferguson* (1896) permitted the segregation of American citizens. However, the 1894 treaty with Japan that specified that the other would extend citizens of each nation rights protected the sixty-eight Japanese students who were not citizens.[45]

After President Roosevelt persuaded the San Francisco School Board to rescind its order, the United States and Japan entered into a "Gentlemen's Agreement" (1907-08) whereby Japan agreed not to allow Japanese laborers to immigrate to the United States. However, at the time, it was not widely noticed that the agreement allowed passports to be issued to "the parents, wives, and children of laborers already there." Subsequently, some Japanese laborers returned to Japan to marry and others engaged in proxy marriages arranged by friends or relatives in Japan. These brides known as "picture brides" by the nativists were seen as "just another aspect of a massive and diabolical plot to submerge California under a tide of yellow babies."[46]

The discrimination and prejudice toward the Japanese was intense and did not soon subside. The action of the San Francisco School Board and the sentiments expressed in the *San Francisco Chronicle* were understandably particularly offensive to the Japanese government. The author of an editorial in the *Chronicle* (November 6, 1906) uses language that is racist in tone and echoes the basic tenants of white supremacist doctrines:

There is, however, a deep and settled conviction among our people that the only hope of maintaining peace between Japan and the United States is to keep the two races apart. Whatever the status of the Japanese children while still young and uncontaminated, as they grow older they acquire the distinctive character, habits, and moral standards of their race, which are abhorrent to our people. We object to them in the familiar intercourse of common school life as we would object to any other moral poison.

The editorial explained: "We do not know that the Japanese children are personally objectionable in grades composed of pupils of their own age. We do not know whether they are or not." However, the editor continued to explain why the Japanese should not be educated in public schools with white children the argument that older Japanese boys are put in classes with younger children because of their lack of English:

> The most prominent objection to the presence of Japanese in our public schools is their habit of sending young men to the primary grades, where they sit side by side with very young children, because in those grades only are the beginnings of English taught. That creates situations, which often become painfully embarrassing. They are, in fact, intolerable . . .

The Chronicle's editors also took the English-only stance that teachers should not waste time teaching English to non-speakers. Excluding children on the basis of their English proficiency was declared to be a moral and legal right:

> We deny either the legal or moral obligation to teach any foreigner to read or speak the English language. And if we chose to do that for one nationality, as a matter of grace, and not to do the same for another nationality, that is our privilege.

Segregation in the West

The situation in California was directly likened to segregation in the South:

> While we deny any moral or legal obligation to give, at public expense, any education whatever to any alien, and consequently if we choose to give as a matter of grace to one and deny it to another, we have also as a matter of grace provided separate schools for the Japanese. In all the Southern states separate schools are provided for white and colored children. To say that we may exclude our own colored citizens from the schools attended by white children, but shall not exclude the children of aliens from such schools, is not only absurd but monstrous.[47]

The *Chronicle* was clearly telling its readers that if they wanted to teach English to some students who did know it and not teach it to others, it was their right to so discriminate. Discrimination or failure to serve effectively all students persisted in the San Francisco schools. As late as 1974, when the Supreme Court rendered the *Lau v. Nichols* decision, Justice William O. Douglas asserted that teaching students who did not understand English as though they did was not acceptable.

Even though President Roosevelt did persuade the School Board to rescind its order, the treatment of Japanese in California did not improve. Indeed, by 1911 prejudice against Chinese and Japanese immigrants was to be found beyond the West Coast of the United States. Jenks and Lauk who were associated with the United States Immigration Commission argued that:

> The Governments of China and Japan have really no reason to object to our wishing not to admit the working people of their races in large numbers. As a matter of fact, Americans are not admitted to China or to Japan on even terms with the natives there. They can go into the country as residents only in very limited communities; they are not permitted to buy land; and they are not admitted to citizenship in those countries. As a matter of fact, our country has treated the members, particularly, of the Japanese race, more liberally than the Japanese have treated the Americans. The Japanese have been allowed to buy land, in many instances in large tracts; and tho at the present time we are taking rather active measures to exclude them from coming in large numbers, up to date, at any rate, we have treated them more liberally than they have treated us.[48]

They also reported that in many instances the first jobs Japanese secured were jobs as strike breakers. That was "especially true of coal mining in southern Colorado and Utah in 1903 and 1904, and later in the case of the smelting industry in 1906.[49] They acknowledged that the Japanese, like the Chinese and the Hindus, "may not be considered in any way inferior to ourselves" but related "that they are not so easily assimilated as are the members of the European races," indicating "that they do not readily marry with our people nor our people with them."[50] Because they had become "almost a separate caste," it was "wise" to act "accordingly."[51]

In 1913 Progressive and Democratic politicians in California in order to win the farm and labor vote moved to enact legislation to prohibit Japanese from owning land. During a hearing on the bill, a former Congregational clergyman, ended his appeal for enactment of the bill with the following inflammatory statement:

> Near my home is an eighty-acre tract of as fine land as there is in California. On that tract lives a Japanese. With that Japanese lives a white women. In that woman's arm is a baby. What is that baby? It isn't a Japanese. It isn't white. It is a germ of the mightiest problem that ever faced this state; a problem that will make the black problem of the South look white.[52]

President Wilson did not object to the proposed legislation that was enacted but only expressed his hope "that the doing of the thing might be so modulated and managed as to offend the susceptibilities of a friendly nation *as little as possible.*[53] The California legislature was firm in its resolve not to allow those not eligible for citizenship, especially Japanese, to own land. However, the Alien Land Law of 1913 did not drive the Japanese from their land, for the law did not prohibit the Japanese from leasing land. Either through forming corporations that were owned by whites or by transferring the title of the land to their children who were born in the United States and thus were not aliens but citizens the Japanese were able to hold on to their farms. In 1920, after Californians realized that the 1913 Law did not have the effect for which they had wished, Californians voted three to one in favor of an initiative that denied Japanese the right to own or lease land or even to engage in sharecropping. Japanese immigrants were not considered eligible for citizenship according to the naturalization act, enacted after the Fourteenth Amendment was adopted, that specified that only "white persons" and aliens of African descent were eligible for citizenship.

RACE THEORY IN THE TWENTIETH CENTURY

Pseudo-scientists, popular publicists, politicians, respected scientists, and academics at the turn of the twentieth century used ideas of natural selection and survival of the fittest for their own political and economic advantage and to repress minority groups at home and to further rationalize imperialism abroad.[54] Social movements in public or state medicine, eugenics, mental hygiene, and social hygiene, at the turn of the century sought "scientific methods" to identify populations such as the "feebleminded" poor white, or immigrant. The place of incompetent, poor, and "ethnic" whites was in institutions.[55] The intelligence testing movement took off after World War I in efforts to identify normality and abnormality, and to legitimate the use of supposedly objective sorting mechanisms, such as standardized tests, in immigration policy, in the armed services, in hospitals, jails, and schools. In spite of the known bias against minorities, the use of standardized tests has escalated over the course of the century and still rides high on the escalating wave of accountability politics and anti-affirmative action.[56]

The view of divergent origins was not universally shared, European ethnologists and some Americans argued for the common origin of humankind. Variations of this hypothesis also had a political use. Divergences in looks and skills were accounted for by theories of degeneration (there was a single origin but some groups biologically were weakened and became inferior) and recapitulation (human development reflects evolutionary processes and some groups and individuals are not as advanced in this process hence the difference between savage and civil societies, stupid and smart people). Stereotypes of immigrant populations by nationality paralleled racist stereotypes during the Progressive Era, an era that witnessed the arrival of a significant number of immigrants from Eastern and Southern Europe. One's "ethnic" origin was viewed as a badge of savagery and shame, something to be shed, or educated out of if possible, as one "melted" into the "white population." This led to a series of policies concerning divisions among the white population, including movements such as the nativist movement, to protect society from impure foreigners; the testing movement, to uncover "defectives" in the general and school population; and the eugenics movement, to eliminate inferior types from the breeding population by sterilization and assignment to institutions. Children were singled out for special scrutiny as potentially defective and capable of degenerating the future of the human race. Child study advocates such as G. Stanley Hall and his students from Clark University employed his recapitulation theory to argue that children developed along the lines of evolution through stages. The hope for the future was in proper training and education. If not properly nurtured and educated, they could endanger humanity. The Mental Hygiene Movement and Child Guidance Movement sought to distinguish therapeutically deviant types and to promote proper parenting and schooling. These social efforts on the part of middle class, Protestant, Anglo-Saxon (white) society were *not* directed at the racially segregated non-white population of African heritage and others of mixed heritage deemed non-white or "Negro." Whites who threatened to degenerate the white race were subjects of interrogation and classification. They were at or near the bottom since they threatened to degenerate the hierarchy of races.

NOTES

1.   Editorial in the New York African American paper, *Anglo African*, April 20, 27, 1861. Reprinted in James M. McPherson, *The Negro's Civil War: How American Negroes Felt and Acted During the War for the Union.* (New York: Vintage 1967), p. 18, fn 2.

2.   Walter Licht, *Industrializing America: The Nineteenth Century.* (Baltimore: Johns Hopkins University, 1995), ch. pp. 78-101.

3.   New York, *Tribune*, September 7, 1860 quoted in James M. McPherson, *The Negro's Civil War: How American Negroes Felt and Acted During the War for the Union.* (New York: Vintage), 1965, p. 4.

4.   Ibid., p. 4.

5.   Quoted in Herbert Aptheker, *Abolitionism: A Revolutionary Movement.* (Boston: Twayne Publishers, 1989). p. 26.

6.   Paul Finkelman, *Dred Scott v. Sandford: A Brief History with Documents.* (Boston: Belford, 1997), p. 10.

7.   Ibid., p. 30.

8.   Harold M. Hyman and William M. Wiecek, *Equal Justice Under the Law, 1815-1875.* (New York: Harper & Row, 1982), pp. 203-231.

9. Paul Finkelman, *Dred Scott v. Sandford*, p. 49; Speech of Stephan A. Douglas at Chicago, July 9, 1858, in *Created Equal? The Complete Lincoln-Douglas Debates of 1858*, ed. Paul M. Angle. (Chicago: University of Chicago Press, 1958), pp. 20-21.

10. Paul Finkelman, *Dred Scott v. Sandford: A Brief History with Documents*. (Boston: Belford, 1997), p. 50.

11. Frederick Douglass, "The Dred Scott Decision: Speech at New York on the Occasion of the Anniversary of the Abolition Society," 11 May, 1857, reprinted in Paul Finkelman, *Dred Scott v. Sandford: A Brief History with Documents* (Boston: Belford, 1997), pp. 169-185.

12. Abraham Lincoln, "House Divided" speech, June 16, 1858, in *Collected Works of Lincoln*, 2: 467, 465; reprinted in Paul Finkelman, *Dred Scott v. Sandford: A Brief History with Documents* (Boston: Belford, 1997), pp. 185-195.

13. Herbert Aptheker, *Abolitionism: A Revolutionary Movement* (Boston: Twayne Publishers, 1989), p. 27.

14. Quoted in Aptheker, *Abolitionism*, p. 30.

15. Paul Johnson, *A History of the American People*. (New York: Harper Collins, 1997), p. 455-6.

16. Ibid.

17. Ibid., p. 449.

18. Quoted in James M. McPherson. *The Negro's Civil War: How American Negroes Felt and Acted During the War for the Union*. (New York: Vantage, 1967), pp. viii. The speech was reprinted in Edward McPherson, *The Political History of the United States During the Great Rebellion*, (Washington, n.p., 1865), pp. 103-4.

19. They fought in 39 major battles and 449 engagements. The record shows that four African American sailors and seventeen soldiers received the Congressional Metals of Honor even though they were denied officers' commissions. Herbert Aptheker, "Negro Casualties in the Civil War," *Journal of Negro History*, CCCII (January 1947): 12, 47-48; James McPherson, *The Negro's Civil War*, p. 237.

20. Meeting of Philadelphia African Americans on July 26, 1864, resolutions adopted, cited in McPherson, Ibid.

21. Walter Licht, *Industrializing America: The Nineteenth Century* (Baltimore: Johns Hopkins University Press, 1995), pp. 96-101.

22. Ibid.

23. Eric Foner, *Reconstruction: America's Unfinished Revolution, 1863-1877* (New York: Harper, 1988), p. 416; John Hope Franklin, *Reconstruction. After the Civil War*, 2nd ed., (Chicago: University of Chicago, 1961, 1994).

24. On a more recent view of this see, Lois B. Moreland, *White Racism and the Law* (Columbus, Ohio: Charles E. Merrill, 1970).

25. The bitterness was so great that southern states did not vote in Republican majorities in the House of Representatives or Senate, nor did they elect a Republican governor from Reconstruction until the 1999. In the case of Florida. Republican Governor Jeb Bush, elected in 1998, is the first Republican governor to serve with a majority Republican House and Senate since Reconstruction. There have only been four African American senators in our history. Two of these were in the Reconstruction period, Blanche K. Bruce (1875-1881) and Hiram Revels (870-1871) both of Mississippi. Edward Brooke (1966-1978) of Massachusetts and Carol Moseley-Braun (1992-1998) of Illinois are the two since. See Bernard A. Weisberger, "A Quartet to Remember: Since the Civil War the Nation has sent Just Four African American's to the Senate. Why?" *American Heritage* (April 1999): 16.

26.   Massey and Denton, *American Apartheid;* Handlin, *Race and Nationality;* Van den Berghe. *Race and Racism,* pp. 77-95; Thomas F. Gossett. *Race: The History of an Idea in America* (Dallas: So. Methodist Press, 1963).

27.   Foner, *Reconstruction;* John Hope Franklin, *Reconstruction After the Civil War* (Chicago: University of Chicago, 1961, 1994), p. 211.

28.   Franklin, *Reconstruction,* p. 211.

29.   Ottley and Weatherby, *The Negro in New York,* p. 130; James Weldon Johnson, *Black Manhattan* (New York: Atheneum, 1968, original 1930); James M. McPherson, *The Negro's Civil War: How American Negroes Felt and Acted During the War* (New York: Vintage, 1965), p. 100-110; John Hope Franklin, *Black Bourgeoisie* (New York: Collier, 1957).

30.   According to Hannah Arent in Ivan Hannaford, *Race: The History of an Idea in the West* (Baltimore, Johns Hopkins University Press, 1996).

31.   Leonard Ayres, *Laggards in Our Schools: A Study of Retardation and Elimination in City School Systems,* (New York: Charities Publication Committee, 1909); See Henry Goddard, *The Kallikak Family: A Study in the Heredity of Feeblemindedness* (New York: MacMillan, 1912); and *Feeblemindedness: Its Causes and Consequences* (New York: MacMillan, 1914).

32.   John Morton Blum, *Woodrow Wilson and the Politics of Morality* (Boston: Little, Brown and Company. 1956), p. 10.

33.   Michael Lind, *The Next American Nation: The New Nationalism & the Fourth American Revolution* (New York: Free Press, 1995) p. 104.

34.   Roger Daniels, *Concentration Camps U.S.A.: Japanese Americans and World War II* (New York: Holt, Rinehart, and Winston. 1972), pp. 3.

35.   Oscar Handlin, *The History of the United States,* Vol. Two (New York: Holt, Rinehart and Winston. 1968), p. 69.

36.   Ibid.

37.   Richard Hofstadter, William Miller and Daniel Aaron, *The United States: The History of a Republic* (Englewood Cliffs, New Jersey. 1957), p.485.

38.   Woodrow Wilson, *History of the American People,* Vol. V (New York: Harper and Brothers. 1901), p. 185.

39.   Handlin, *The History of the United States,* p. 69.

40.   Resolution of the San Francisco School Board (1905) as quoted in *Proceedings of the Asiatic Exclusion League* (San Francisco, 1908), pp. 8-9 reproduced in Sol Cohen. *Education in the United States: A Documentary History* Vol. V (New York: Random House. 1974), p. 2971. The School Board had announced in May 1905 that it planned in the near future to require all Japanese students, native and foreign born attend the separate schools that had already been established for Chinese students. The Board then explained that its reasoning was so that "our children should not be placed in any position where their youthful impressions may be affected by association with the Mongolian race." Daniels explained that: "The use of the term 'Mongolian' was dictated by an old California school law which permitted exclusion of children of 'filthy or vicious habits,' or 'suffering from contagious diseases,' and segregation in separate schools of American Indian children and those of 'Chinese or Mongolian descent." Daniels, *Concentration Camps U.S.A.,* p. 12.

41.   Roger Daniels, *Concentration Camps U.S.A.,* pp. 3,9.

42.   It is estimated that approximately 40,000 Japanese entered the United States by way of Hawaii (Hawaii was not then a state) between 1900 and 1908, "the period of heaviest immigration." Daniels, *Concentration Camps U.S.A.*, p. 6.

43.   ibid., p. 10.

44.   Quoted in Daniels. *Concentration Camps U.S.A.*, p. 11.

45.   Daniels. *Concentration Campus U.S.A.*, p. 14.

46.   ibid., p. 17.

47.   Quoted in Senate document no. 147, 59th Congress., 2[d] session (1906), p. 30 reproduced in Cohen. *Education in the United States*, p. 2972.

48.   Jeremiah W. Jenks and W. Jett Lauk. *The Immigration Problem* (New York: Funk and Wagnalls, 1911), pp. 201-202.

49.   ibid., p. 225.

50.   ibid., p. 200.

51.   ibid., p. 201.

52.   Quoted in Daniels. *Concentration Camps U.S.A.*, p. 15.

53.   Quoted in Arthur S. Link. *Woodrow Wilson and the Progressive Era, 1910-1917* (New Work: Harper and Row, 1954), p.85.

54.   Racist theories and propaganda gained legitimacy in the mid-nineteenth century. The social sciences as disciplines were influenced by Social Darwinism. Social Darwinism developed after the publication of Charles Darwin's, *The Origin of the Species*, in 1859, and its subsequent influence on the social theories of Herbert Spencer in his adaptation of natural selection to human populations. Francis Galton, Darwin's cousin, laid out the basis for the investigation of capability by class in his *Hereditary Genius*, 1869, which set others on the path to establish a science of human ability with a rank order system based on quantitative methods. Francis Galton, *Hereditary Genius* (London: MacMillan, 1869); Charles Darwin, *Origin of the Species* (London: J. Murray, 1859); Theresa Richardson and Erwin V. Johanningmeier, "Intelligence Testing: The Legitimation of A Meritocratic Educational Science," in Marc Depaepe, *The Development of Empirical Research in Education: Contributions from the History of Science* (Oxford: Elsevier Science, 1998): 699-714; Robert C. Bannister, *Social Darwinism: Science and Myth in Anglo-American Social Thought* (Philadelphia: Temple University Press, 1979); Richard Hofstadter, *Social Darwinism in American Thought* (New York: George Braziller, Inc., 1944, 1955); John Willinsky, *Learning to Divide the World: Education at Empires End* (Minneapolis: University of Minnesota, 1998), ch. 7, pp. 161-188.

55.   W. Lloyd Warner, "American Caste and Class," *American Journal of Sociology* XLII, No 2, (September 1936): 234-237; W. Lloyd Warner, Marchia Meeker, and Kenneth Eells, *Social Class in America: The Evaluation of Status* (New York: Harper, 1949/1960); Edward J. Larson, *Sex Race and Science: Eugenics in the Deep South* (Baltimore: Johns Hopkins University, 1995), argues that the sterilization programs largely targeted whites rather than blacks especially in the south as a outcome of the fear of the dilution of the superiority of the white race (p. 153).

56.   Richardson and Johanningmeier, "Intelligence Testing," pp. 699-714.

CHAPTER 6

EDUCATION AND THE MELTING POT
Ethnicity in the Era of Jim Crow

This is a happy story with a dole of sadness, like the surplus bread handed out to the poor. Like the rich man whose joy in richness is tainted with a worry that the poor might get too much . . .[1]

In *Racism: A Short History*[2] George Fredrickson identified "racism as the twin evil of ethnocentrism." Racism can be identified as hostility and discrimination against any group for any reason in a broad sense but overtly racist political regimes are cases where differences are elevated in a hierarchy that is invidious, unchangeable, and enforced by the power of the state in behalf of a dominant group. Overtly racist regimes are rare, but there is no shortage of discrimination and oppression in the world. Nowhere else were the political and legal potentialities of creating a racialized society, a society where the idea of race has been accepted as a domain assumption for the majority of the people, so realized as in the United States over such a long period of time. An "overtly racialized regime" requires characteris-

Race, Ethnicity, and Education: What is Taught in School, pages 149–179.
A Volume in: International Perspectives on Curriculum
Copyright © 2003 by Information Age Publishing, Inc.
All rights of reproduction in any form reserved.
ISBN: 1-59311-080-4 (paper), 1-59311-081-2 (cloth)

tics that Fredrickson found in the United States between 1895 and 1954 in "Jim Crow" laws that systematically discriminated against non-whites, most specifically against people of African descent in the Southern states. According to Fredrickson, these characteristics included:

1. The division between blacks and whites was an official ideology based on the idea that the differences between the dominant and subordinate group were permanent and unbridgeable.
2. The ideology was implemented through: a) laws against intermarriage, and b) enforced social segregation that barred integrated contact in public places. These laws went beyond custom or private acts of discrimination tolerated by the state.
3. The polity, once democratic, barred African Americans from public office and did not allow African Americans the voting rights accorded other citizens.
4. Access to resources, including economic opportunities, was limited; and most African Americans were kept in permanent poverty.[3]

The United States met the criteria of an overtly racist regime from the *Plessy v. Ferguson* Supreme Court decision in 1896 to the *Brown v. the Board of Education of Topeka* decision in 1954 when the Court ruled that "separate but equal" in public education was not equal and therefore unconstitutional. Subsequently, legally enforced segregation in the public arena began to crumble. The legally enforced division in society had a drastic effect on individuals and groups on each side of the color line. As pointed out in the case of antebellum racial slavery, the master-slave relationship based on white privilege and white supremacy was not simply dualistic white-black, but was complicated by the "plain folk," the often ill-treated white servant, the working classes whose only claim to privilege was that they could not be made hereditary slaves.[4] This triad of an elite dominant group over subordinate whites and a caste of black slaves at the bottom was reinforced by the reaffirmation of white supremacy in the transformation of racial slavery as an identifiable racial form of unpaid labor to overt racism that created a social caste below whites regardless of the free or not free status of African Americans at the turn of the century. Immigration reinforced this arrangement by supplying new people who were placed below the dominant group but above African Americans. They formed what Theodore Allen labeled a "buffer strata."[5]

Immigrants who were legally designated as "white" and therefore eligible for citizenship were privileged in comparison to Americans designated as not white. Even today when white people are confronted with the concept of white privilege, they often respond that they do not "feel privileged." In fact, neither whiteness nor any of its privileges were necessarily freely available to anyone outside the traditional dominant groups of native-born whites and the upper classes. Immigrants could not be made into a permanent caste below the native born but their status was uncertain. The melting pot was a bubbling cauldron of racialized and ethnocentric discrimination in the first half of the twentieth century.

THE WATERSHED

The legal end of the overtly racialized regime came with the elimination of the "white person" clause in the naturalization law in 1952. The end of legal segregation in public schools in 1954 did not immediately transform race-based practices in American society. R. A. Schermerhorn argued that new attitudes did not appear until the 1960s. In the first issue of *Ethnicity* (1974), he argued that to understand the effects of ethnicity it was necessary to undertake "an inquiry belonging to the sociology of knowledge." The "1960's, particularly the last part of that decade, constituted a watershed of the twentieth century, so that . . . the social facts before the late 1960's constitute one cluster that permits a special set of inferences [involving the color line], while the cluster of social facts *after* the late 1960s's requires a different set of inferences." The social facts or events of the late 1960s to which he referred were "sometimes called the Negro [sic] revolution, though [he] suggested that the terms 'revolt' or 'insurrection' would be closer to common usage."[6] This was the era when the African American community, for example the Black Power Movement, demanded the right for self-definition and rejected terms such as "Colored," or "Negro" that had been imposed by "whites." Almost coincident with that movement was the emergence of interest in ethnicity among other minorities as well as many Anglo-Europeans.

According to Schermerhorn, "a comparison of events and major social trends" before and after the "watershed" reveals why "ethnicity" was scarcely heard of before and why it gained currency after the "insurrection" with its sharply raised consciousness of discrimination, racism and its effects. Ethnic groups made their own comparisons with their experiences of discrimination and struggle to belong and achieve parity. Before the "watershed" there was "a pronounced rise of nationalism throughout Europe, partly abetted by American immigrants newly awakened to patriotism [not for America but] for their national homelands." It was not surprising then that "they became known as nationality groups in distinction from other minorities like the "Afro-Americans, Mexican Americans, [American] Indians" as well as religious groups such as "the Jews whose nationalistic identification with Israel," according to Schermerhorn, "was a delayed reaction."

During this era, the dominant ideology supported and promoted assimilation. "Popular opinion showed tolerance for European immigrants only when they were willing to give up their language and foreign customs:

self-effacement was the price of acceptance." The intellectuals saw "assimilation as inevitable in the long run and tacitly gave it approval." Even African American leaders "opted for integration as their long-term goal—this being just one variant of assimilation."[7] Assimilation or Americanization was viewed as "a simple, one-way movement toward a homogeneous set of beings called Americans." For Fredrickson, "African America identity is an example of a case in which ethnic identity is created by the racialization of people who would not otherwise have shared an identity." He observed "blacks did not think of themselves as blacks, Negroes, or even Africans when they lived in the various kingdoms and tribal communities of West Africa before the slave trade." American Indians have only taken on their collective identity because the dominant society is reluctant to recognize their own national tribal identities. There is also strength in unity. Individual tribes often regard themselves as superior and their enemies, including Europeans and sometimes each other, as unworthy of respect. However, they assimilated strangers and captives regardless of their culture.[8] Anglo-European practices of exclusion and enforced non-assimilation have not been universally shared.

AMERICAN DREAM, AMERICAN DILEMMA

Gunnar Myrdal's *American Dilemma* published in 1944 and testimony to the United States Congress at the end of Word War II show that on the other side of the color line, educational, economic, social, and political opportunities in the first half of the twentieth century were severely limited. The consequences of an overtly racialized regime placed intentionally powerful limits on the African American community. The limitations on educational opportunity were truly remarkable especially given that schooling is the primary vehicle for social mobility in the United States. When Myrdal investigated the support for education for whites and for blacks in the late 1930s, he reported "that Negro [sic] schools have lately been improving faster than white schools in the South—that is, in the sense that the *percentage* of increase in expenditures may have been greater for Negro [sic] than for white schools."[9] However, the improvements were not nearly great enough to overcome the already existing vast differences that had been established in the previous half century under segregation. The differences in funds provided for schools for whites and schools for African Americans were "as spectacular as it is well known." For the 1935-1936 school year, the average expenditure in ten southern states was $17.04 for black students and $49.30 for white students. Mississippi and Georgia spent about $9 for every black student and about five times as much for white students. The differences in expenditures affected all areas of public schooling for African Americans. African American teachers' salaries were lower than those of white teachers and their classes were larger. Less was spent on transportation of African American students than for whites. "Savings" were realized in African American schools in all areas by maintaining a school year that was "thirteen percent shorter than in white schools."[10]

Interestingly, it was not, according to Myrdal, unusual to meet "white persons even in the educated class who seriously believe that educational facilities for Negroes [sic] and whites are equal."[11] The existence of that belief is evidence of just how secure the demarcation of the boundary between whites and African Americans was in the first half of the twentieth century. While the boundary did not preclude interaction, its protocols did restrict what was said to whom, what was not said, and what was and was not seen. For those on the other side of the color line, opportunities to participate in American society at all levels in all areas were severely limited. That boundary and the difference were clearly there at the end of World War II. In early 1945 when the Senate Committee on Education and Labor held hearings on the proposal to provide federal funds for public education, the Senators heard of the vast differences in educational opportunity. As historian Diane Ravitch reported, the discrepancies were glaring:

> It was matter-of-factly noted in the record that in Copiah County [Mississippi] . . . the average salary for white teachers was $889.53, compared to an annual average for black teachers of $332.58; the length of the school term was eight months for whites and six months for blacks; of 91 white teachers in the county, 44 had no college degree, while of 126 black teachers, 122 had no college degree. The daily attendance rate for white children was forty-eight percent; for black children it was sixty percent at the Antioch School, the black parents dug down into their pockets to keep the school open for a seventh month.[12]

Deliberate segregation disallowed assimilation. As long as it was held that African Americans could not be assimilated into the body politic and that immigrants, unless Americanized, posed a threat to the American way of life, the "race relations" problem could not be solved. The United States would be a society that would continue to be divided by a color line—a society that assigned people on the basis of skin color to caste or caste-like status and assigned them to specific spaces and specific occupations. While blacks lived below the color line, many whites lived on the borderline. Not black but not fully privileged, they were only marginally allowed to join the white ethos. Their confusion reinforced the color line and their resentment fueled racism.

After the 1960s "watershed," according to Schermerhorn, "the current runs in the opposite direction." During this era, "cultural pluralism and separatism capture the imagination of countless persons to whom a merger with faceless masses looks increasingly unpromising." After the "watershed" those of European descent and those of African descent deny either that they are un-American or victims of a pathological culture.

White ethnics claimed the right to "cherish and revive the folk elements from their past or celebrate their culture heroes who distinguished themselves in the past; and black ethnics refuse to be intimidated by terms like 'exaggerated American' or 'distorted American,' as they are awakening to full awareness of their historic culture-building process and, in a delayed appreciation of Garvey's gross attempts at autonomy, are re-thinking their role as an ethnic group."[13] After the "watershed," the emphasis "on cultural pluralism and ethnicity implies a *renascence* of an older ethos for those of European descent" and a budding *nascence* of a newly formed ethos for the blacks." What was not earlier obvious but was clear by the 1970s was while "European immigrants were *losing* much of their culture," and "blacks [and others] were *gaining* much of theirs."

Upon their arrival in America, European immigrants, whatever their national origin, had "a distinctive ethos"—one they "gradually lost to the extent that assimilation took hold and a substitute culture tended to replace it." However, the process for African Americans was quite different as an involuntary immigrant population: ". . . forcibly separated from family and friends by their captors." In a sense, Europeans arrived with a culture they had to lose in order to become "white" and Africans "arrived as atomized individuals," forced from their culture. However, it is important not to underestimate the importance of mutual heritage and strength of culture that allows a people to survive and to maintain language and cultural patterns in perverse circumstances. The need for survival in the face of the rise of white supremacy and white privilege forged a black American culture. Unrelated individuals were turned from "a social category without group consciousness or social bonds" into a group with a culture and social bonds. As Schermerhorn noted: "subject to the same fate, as they were, they could not help but react in concert... they were gradually forming an ethos of their own."[14]

West African culture was inadvertently integrated into the lifeblood of the South and subsequently into the American psyche and is a strong aspect of the United States' cultural uniqueness. African immigrants had to adapt to their peculiar position as they became African Americans. African Americans, the reluctant immigrants, are, ironically, a quintessential ingredient in American life. As a writer in an antislavery newspaper observed in 1863, American history is juxtaposed with and in many ways is black history in that the "Negro" (sec) is "the observed of all observers; the talked of by all talkers; the thought of by all thinkers; and the questioned by all questioners."[15] White privilege was forged out of a contrast of status that could be identified visually. From Bacon's Rebellion to the American Revolution; from the Revolution to the Civil War; from the overtly racist regime of the American apartheid years to the Civil Rights Movement, the experiences of all Americans operated in relationship to black people in some way. White folks could not escape the presence of the not-white other, if not overtly then as the silent center.[16] The watershed occurs when the observations, talk, thought, and questions finally turn back on the underlying issue of the contradiction between the American dream, the myth, and the reality. Developing a society in which all were told by law that all had equal rights when in fact some did not can be said to be the essential tension in the making of modern societies, not just the United States.[17]

During the Civil Rights Era, the African American ethos emerged openly to resist the emphasis in American history and consciousness about their inferiority and the claims that their culture was pathological. Gunnar Myrdal's claim that "Negro [sic] culture in the 1940's [was] 'a distorted development, or a pathological condition of general American culture" indicates that assimilationism was still *the* dominant view.[18] Clearly, the dominant group concluded that the pathology needed to be "cured;" and, it was reasoned, it could be cured only if Americans would live up to their ideals and thereby reverse the vicious cycle of prejudice that so effectively created the life conditions that constituted the "pathological condition." If Americans would only abandon their prejudices and live up to their professed ideals, the "race relations" problem would be solved. In significant measure, that conclusion allowed the "problem" to be conceived of as a psychological not a social problem and thus the province of the psychologists not the public or public policy. Thus, the object of inquiry, attention, and treatment was the individual. The legal, political, social, and economic boundaries that confined the individual and prohibited him or her from participating in mainstream society could and would be ignored. The boundaries placed around African Americans gave rise to an ethnic consciousness. This same process—the process of maintaining boundaries to separate and distinguish people according to their real or imagined characteristics—can be viewed as ethnogenesis, the birth of ethnicity. Subordination creates ethnicity and the frames of the mind that accompany its formation.

SEGREGATION AND VIOLENCE IN AMERICA

The legal segregation of African Americans in the South was not unlike the discrimination aimed at other groups in other parts of the nation in the early twentieth century. Restrictive laws against Asians in California were reenacted against Hispanic groups and American Indians, sometimes with overt policies but just as often with covert social practices of segregation enforced by vigilante activities of whites supported by the sometimes perverse convictions of the popular culture. Places such as Indiana where blacks escaped on the Underground Rail Road to form black communities in the nineteenth century found their freedom increasingly restricted in the twentieth century.[19] The hostility was not limited to groups who would now come under the rubric of "people of color."

Political rivalries within the South in the late nineteenth and early twentieth century entailed great violence. W. E. B. DuBois' explanation in the 1930s was that "the propertied class sought to repossess the power of legal coercion essential to its exploitation of black labor." While this explanation is insightful, as Chester Flynn pointed out, it does not explain the incredibly broad support for vigilantism and the widespread patterns of brutality and violence among people who were otherwise "good and decent people." In some counties in the South and Midwest "every white male...reputedly joined" the Klu Klux Klan or White Caps, as these gangs of disguised men variously identified themselves.[20] Individuals who disagreed with vigilantism did not criticize the Klan for fear of attack or being labeled a "traitor to their race or section." Flynn explained the movement in terms of a "traditional folk movement aimed at upholding the white communities moral standards..." which were "literally" based on the "religious conviction with which whites subscribed to their racially defined caste system." There was near unanimity among whites in the efficacy of white dominance even though the violence ostensibly defending white racial unity betrayed the cavernous class divisions among whites. The former plantation elite in the South used white yeoman to perpetrate violence that supposedly maintained the "purity of the racial order." However, when violence threatened production and the economic interests of elites, their support waned. Planters were more interested in maintaining their dominance and did not want to sacrifice their political status as based on economic supremacy. Middle and working class whites were the soldiers who fought for both the class and racial supremacy of whites. Klan brutality was justified in moral terms that were not limited to violence against the black population. It was just as likely to turn against "immoral" whites. For example, in 1894 a white man named King, who was known for abusing his wife, was visited by the Klan, "inhumanely beaten," driven out of town and threatened with death if he returned. Another man was similarly treated when he married the town "scamp" several days after his wife died. Flynn noted that "attacks like these continued in Georgia off and on into the 1950s and were an especially common activity for the 'second' Klu Klux Klan, which grew powerful after World War I." Further, vigilante violence was not limited to the South, as so many of us are led to believe. "Long before the second Klan, this pattern of coercion was not peculiar to Georgia or even the South. It was common in the Midwest, chronic on the frontier, and appeared even in New England."[21]

This pattern of violence, rooted deep in American, English, and European history put immigrants at great risk in the early twentieth century. As "race" became a caste below "white," to be a "white person" was racialized in the sense of being exclusive and restricted to those with the moral credentials to qualify to "joint the club." Certain groups, now considered ethnic, even from Europe may or may not qualify as morally white. To be "ethnic" European was problematic in the first half of the twentieth century.

Immigration and Discrimination Against "Ethnic" Europeans and Asians

Fear of and discrimination toward immigrants, few of whom were accepted as "white persons," had been building since the 1890s. In the post-World-War-I era, the already existing racism was strengthened by the nation's adoption of nativism and isolationism—a fear of the non-native born and rejection of foreign involvement or entanglements. Americans' feared that even European immigrants would introduce un-American ideas such as unionism and socialism. Congress responded. In 1921 it acted to restrict immigration from the Far East, in compliance with anti-Chinese and Japanese propaganda on the Pacific Coast. Most significantly, Congress moved to limit immigration from Europe with Eastern and Southern Europe a particular target for exclusion. Specifying the number of "aliens," a term often used for unwelcome immigrants, who could be admitted to the U.S.A. from any one country allowed some groups more flexibility according to their current presence in the population. There could not be admitted more than three per cent of the current population of each group as indicated by the 1910 Census. In 1924, Congress moved to make immigration even more restrictive. Using a similar tactic Congress specified that the number of immigrants from a given country could not be more than two per cent of current citizens according to the 1890 Census. This law clearly restricted immigrants from Eastern and Southern Europe, for there were not many residing in the U.S.A. from those countries in 1890. The 1924 Immigration Act further specified that beginning in 1927 the total number of immigrants could not exceed 150,000. This law was also specifically written to completely exclude immigration from Japan and China.

The Immigration Acts of 1921 and 1924 were responses to pressure from American labor, which claimed that continued unrestricted immigration would drive the price of labor down and that immigrants would, as they often were, be used as strike breakers. At its national convention in 1901, the American Federation of Labor requested that the United States Congress "exclude not only Chinese but all Mongolians [sic]."[22] Pressure also came from American businessmen who feared radical socialist ideas that immigrants may bring. The relatively longstanding nativist movement and proponents of eugenics claimed that continued immigration would somehow dilute the American character and the American racial stock. In significant measure, the groundwork for the 1921 and 1924 Immigration

Acts was prepared by academicians from some of the nation's most prestigious universities: Henry P. Fairchild of Yale, Edward A. Ross of the University of Wisconsin, Jeremiah W. Jenks of New York University, Thomas N. Carver of Harvard, and Dean Leon C. Marshall of the University of Chicago, all of whom campaigned against immigration. After World War I, psychologists used their newly created tests of mental ability (intelligence tests) to support the eugenicists and to warn that continued immigration would weaken the nation.

The Immigration Commission Study of the "Problem"

On February 26, 1907 the United States Congress established the Immigration Commission to study what was then becoming known as "the immigration problem." In *The Immigration Problem*, Jeremiah W. Jenks and W. Jett Lauck who were associated with the Commission from its beginning undertook to present "the gist of the information collected in the forty-two volumes of the original material published by the Commission." They began by relating that the problem was "one of vital interest to the American people" and that President Roosevelt "considered it, with the possible exception of that of the conservation of the natural resources of the country, our most important problem."[23]

Jenks and Lauck specified 1883 as the year that divided the "old" immigrants from the "new" immigrants. Ninety-five per cent of the "old" immigrants came from Northern and Western Europe: England, Ireland, Scotland, Wales, Belgium, Denmark, France, Germany, the Netherlands, Norway, Sweden, and Switzerland. Between 1883 and 1907 the "character of immigration" changed markedly. Eighty-one percent of the "new" immigrants came from Austria-Hungary, Bulgaria, Greece, Italy, Montenegro, Poland, Portugal, Rumania, Russia, Servia, Syria, and Turkey. The problem was that the new immigrants differed "much more radically in type from the earlier American residents than did the old" immigrants. Consequently, that made the "problem of assimilation . . . much more difficult."[24]

Assimilation was rendered difficult because in many "industrial localities" the new immigrants were all but isolated from "native [born] Americans." "Immigrant workmen and their households not only live in sections or colonies according to race, but . . . attend and support their own churches, maintain their own business institutions and places of recreation, and have their own fraternal and beneficial organizations." Men experienced and suffered from "a sharp line of division in the occupations or the departments" in the mines and factories where they worked, "and in the case of unskilled labor the immigrant workmen are, as a rule, brought together in gangs composed of one race or closely related races." Women who worked in factories or as domestics had limited contact with native [born] Americans and "a considerable proportion of the children of foreign-born are also segregated in the parochial schools." Significantly, Jenks and Lauck noted that the tendency of the "old" immigrants to maintain "old customs and standards" that led "to congestion and unsanitary housing and living conditions" was not necessarily the fault of the "new" immigrants but was due to the native-born who were either "ignorant of conditions which prevail in immigrant sections" or "even when acquainted with them, . . . are usually indifferent so long as they do not become too pronounced a menace to the public health and welfare." The "native-born element" felt that there was "a certain stigma" attached "to working with recent arrivals or in the same occupations." They explained that the "aversion" native born Americans had to the immigrants was "psychological in its nature and arises from race prejudice or ignorance." Still, it was "one of the most effective forces in racial segregation and displacement." Jenks and Lauck effectively indicated that boundaries were being constructed that not only prohibited or retarded assimilation but also effectively created and maintained ethnicity. Neither the native born nor the immigrant was well served by the boundary between them. That boundary or the isolation made "the recent immigrant liable to serious physical and moral deterioration" The immigrants' "low standard of living," their ignorance "of proper measures for securing health and sanitation," and "the possible political and social manipulation of the recent immigrant population by unscrupulous leaders" constituted dangers to the native [born] Americans.[25] Economic exploitation of immigrants did not allow them to maintain a standard comparable to either native born residents or to old immigrants. Consequently, they had to live differently in different places— ghettos. Economic exploitation created not only physical but also social boundaries. It is within such boundaries that ethnogenesis occurred. Jenks and Lauck correctly predicted that the isolation of the "new" immigrants would "result in the establishment, perhaps in a modified form, of many Old World standards and institutions."[26]

While Jenks and Lauck urged "every effort should be made to promote assimilation of the immigrants and the distribution of immigrants from our overcrowded industrial centers to the rural districts,"[27] they advocated restriction of further immigration. Their reason was basically economic. They wanted to protect the American worker from competition, for it was easier to exploit new immigrants to the disadvantage of American workers. As Jenks and Lauck explained:

> The immigrants from South and East Europe have been mainly unskilled laborers, and, on the whole, have not shown the same readiness to join trade unions and to insist upon American working conditions as have those coming from the older immigrations from the north and west of Europe. Again, there is clearly a tendency on the part of some employers to segregate their

unskilled workmen into colonies under the leadership of a man of their own race. In this way, by keeping the gangs separated one from the other, they are able to avoid any display of race antipathy. They simplify supervision, and doubtless, in very many cases, they are able to prevent any organization into unions, so as to bring pressure for an increase of wages.[28]

They agreed with the Immigration Commission that "the measure of the wide development of a country is to a very great extent dependent upon the economic opportunity afforded to the wage-earning citizen for his material, mental and moral development, and this opportunity is dependent to a great extent upon a progressive improvement in his standard of living."[29] There was no question that the large number of immigrants was serving to depress wages and thus lower the American workers' standard of living. The use of immigrants to break strikes prevented American workers from bargaining for better wages. Jenks and Lauk reported that:

> On several occasions it is found that East European races have been introduced as strike-breakers; for example, in the coal mines of Colorado, New Mexico, and Washington, and in the metalliferous mines of Colorado. In these instances the keeping of the old scale of wages was only possible because of the failure of the strikes. In this way they, as in the coal regions of Pennsylvania, discouraged the efforts of the trade unions.[30]

While they began the above passage with "on several occasions," they concluded it with the claim that there had been "few such instances" of new immigrants suppressing the wages of American workers. Still, they concluded in favor of restricting immigration.

While Jenks and Lauck did favor the restriction of immigration, they acknowledged that the "educational, social, and political conditions" in the United States did serve to transform European immigrants' ways of living and thinking. They further indicated that "the investigations of the Immigration Commission...show that some changes in bodily form of the descendants of immigrants are very noteworthy." The Commission studied the "stature, weight, length of head, width of head, width of face, and color of hair of Bohemians, Slovaks, Poles, Hungarians, Russian Hebrews, Sicilians, Neapolitans, and Scotch."[31] The noted anthropologist of Columbia University, Franz Boas, who was in charge of the investigation for the Commission, summarized the changes in bodily form:

> The Bohemians, Slovaks, and Hungarians, and Poles, representing the type of Central Europe, exhibit uniform changes. Among the American-born descendants of these types the stature increases, and both the length and width of head decrease, the latter a little more markedly than the former, so that there is also a decrease of the cephalic index. The width of the face decreases very materially.[32]

Boas' fanciful descriptions of the ethnic stereotypes of Europeans extended to religion and specifically to Jews, revealing the potential in the

United States for anti-Semitism in that he identified Hebrews with a different biological type:

> The Hebrews show changes peculiar to themselves. Stature and weight increase; length of the head shows a marked increase, and the width of the head decreases, so that the cephalic index decreases materially; the width of the face also decreases.[33]

Italians, at the turn of the century, were in a similar place as were the Irish earlier in that their identity as "white" was not secure. Boas contributed to this mentality by elaborating a "Mediterranean type:"

> Sicilians and Neapolitans, representing the Mediterranean type of Europe, form another group, which shows distinctive changes. These are less pronounced among the Neapolitans than among the Sicilians, who are also purer representatives of the Mediterranean type, notwithstanding the many mixtures of races that have occurred in Sicily and the adjoining parts of Italy. The stature of the Sicilians born in American is less than that of the foreign-born. This loss is not so marked among the Neapolitans. In both groups the length of the head decreases, the width of the head increases, and the width of the face decreases.[34]

Boas went so far as to distinguish among regions within Italy. This type of biological determinism was highly popularized in public as well as professional arenas.

ELLWOOD PATERSON CUBBERLY: SCHOOLS AND IMMIGRANT CHILDREN

The fascination with body types and phenotypical characteristics identify a peculiarly American type of racialized division expounded by professional educators and others at the turn of the century. Ellwood Paterson Cubberley was a professor of education at Stanford University who helped to standardize school systems with his surveys and histories of education in the United States. Cubberley's views and ideology were first expressed in *Changing Conceptions of Education* (1909). This work reflected the general public perceptions but was specifically directed toward educators and educational reformers. It was written when many in the United States were well aware of the large number of immigrants coming to nation's shores. Many were then fearful of how this "great stream" of immigrants who were coming at an "alarming rate" would affect American life and institutions such as schools. They questioned whether the immigrants could be successfully assimilated into American life. The views Cubberley articulated in *Changing Conceptions* were views he, and subsequently other historians of education, continued to disseminate to prospective teachers and school administrators even after the end of World War II and even after the *Brown* decision in 1954. His characterizations of immigrants and other marginalized people were repeated in his subsequent works. *Public Education in the United States: A Study and Interpretation of American Educational History*, first published in 1919, revised in 1934, issued again in 1947 and still again in 1962 with renewed copyrights, was a standard text used in history of education courses throughout the United States for nearly half a century. Indeed, it was so dominant that when historians of education saw the need for a revised history of education, Cubberley, as indicated by Lawrence A. Cremin's *The Wonderful World of Ellwood Patterson Cubberley*, (1965) was the target. Cubberley was then criticized for not conceiving education in the broadest possible sense—as the transmission of culture— and for basically equating education with schooling. That Cubberley greatly contributed to the reinforcement, if not the creation, of cultural stereotypes that persisted was then overlooked, for historians of education were not then much interested in those who were not members of the dominant class.

Stigmatizing Immigrant Groups: Stereotypes and Propaganda

Through the first third, if not the first half, of the twentieth century it was common and even fashionable to catalogue with painstaking care the origins and characteristics of immigrants—those who were usually described by sociologists and historians as belonging to what many believed were members of various races[35]—and the degree to which they conformed to the ways of the dominant class—usually those who originally settled North America and subsequently created the United States and defined and dominated its culture (institutions and values). Those who readily conformed were accepted and easily assimilated into American life. Those who were not able or not allowed to conform basically because they lacked the requisite Anglo characteristics presented a problem. For example, Ellwood P. Cubberley observed in 1909 that:

> After 1880, southern Italians and Sicilians; people from all parts of that medley of races known as the Austro-Hungarian Empire—Czechs, Moravians, Slovaks, Poles, Jews, Ruthenians, Croatians, Serbians, Dalmatians, Slovenians, Magyars, Roumanians, Austrians, and Slavs, Poles, and Jews from Russia began to come [to the United States] in great numbers. After 1900, Finns from the north driven out by Russian persecution, and Greeks, Syrians, and Armenians from the south, have come in great numbers to our shores.

Cubberley exhibited in his views a distinctive characteristic of popular racism. He attributed the moral and behavioral traits of individuals to their "race" and extended that folly to the entire "ethnic group." Cubberley also implied that such characteristics not only were inborn but also were permanent traits that seriously limited the individual's ability to function either in schools as students or as citizens:

> These southern and eastern Europeans are of a very different type from the north Europeans who preceded them. Illiterate, docile, lacking in self-reliance and initiative, and not possessing the Anglo-Teutonic conceptions of law, order, and government, their coming has served to dilute tremendously our national stock, and to corrupt our civic life."[36]

Cubberley's characterization of German immigrants—"a picked and an educated class" with liberalism in politics and religion"—as different from and superior to Irish immigrants—"very poor and uneducated"—was essentially a restatement of what many Americans believed since the end of the eighteenth century. Indeed it is almost as though it came directly from Crevecoeur who in 1793 recorded the differences he observed among Germans, Scots, and Irish:

> From whence the difference arises, I know not; but out of twelve families of emigrants of each country generally seven Scotch will succeed, nine German, and four Irish. The Scotch are frugal and laborious; but their wives cannot work so hard as the German women, who on the contrary, view with their husbands, and often share with them the most severe toils of the field, which they understand better. They have therefore nothing to struggle against, but the common casualties of nature. The Irish do not prosper so well; they love to drink and to quarrel; they are litigious, and soon take to the gun, which is the ruin of everything; they seem beside to labor under a greater degree of ignorance in husbandry than the others; perhaps it is that their industry had less scope, and was less exercised at home.[37]

Cubberley was indeed continuing a tradition begun earlier. For example, in an 1851 article on immigration in the *Massachusetts Teacher,* teachers were instructed that the problems attendant to immigration required the attention of the nation's best and wisest minds. Immigration could either pollute the country with ignorance, vice, crime, and disease just as the Missouri River muddied the clear water of the Mississippi River, or the nation could act to protect itself from "the threatened demoralization" and take action to "improve and purify and make valuable this new element."[38] The *Massachusetts Teacher* instructed teachers that German immigrants "who are next in numbers [to the Irish], will give us no trouble." The "chief difficulty" was "with the Irish." The Germans were seen as "more abstinate, more strongly wedded to their own notions and customs than the Irish; but they have, inherently, the redeeming qualities of industry, frugality, and pride, which will save them from vice and pauperism, and they may be safely left to take care of themselves." The Irish, however, were different. The Irish simply did not know "the simple virtues of industry, temperance, and frugality."[39]

Cubberley related that the homeland of the Irish was primitive and that the Irish were lacking in modern methods known and practiced by the Germans, the English, and the Scandinavians. Despite their handicaps, the Irish were known for their "willingness, good-nature, and executive qualities." Scandinavians were "thrifty," and the English were credited with having "respect for law and order." The English, Irish, Germans, and Scandinavians were all recognized for the ease with which they assimilate."[40] Moreover, these immigrants were from "a race stock not very different from our own and all possessed courage, initiative, intelligence, adaptability, and self-reliance."[41]

Immigrants from Southern and from Eastern Europe were very different from those who hailed from Western or Northern Europe, according to Cubberly's view. Immigrants from Eastern and from Southern Europe—Southern Italians and Sicilians, Czechs, Moravians, Slovaks, Poles, Jews, Ruthenians, Croatians, Serbians, Dalmatians, Slovenians, Magyars, Roumanians, Austrians; and Slavs, Poles, and Jews from Russia—as well as Finns, Greeks, Syrians, and Armenians were seen as problematic. Their arrival in the United States "served to dilute tremendously our national stock, and to corrupt civic life." They were blamed for making the already complex American way of life even more difficult. To correct the threatening situation, Cubberley instructed prospective teachers and school administrators that: "Our task is to break up these groups or settlements, to assimilate and amalgamate these people as part of our American race, and to implant in their children, so far as can be done, the Anglo-Saxon conception of righteousness, law and order, and popular government, and to awaken in them a reverence for our democratic institutions and those things in our national life which we as the people hold to be of abiding worth."[42]

One can only wonder how many teachers would explain poor performance of their students with Cubberley's words: "so far as can be done," for Cubberley was clearly instructing them that there were significant and meaningful racial differences. On the other hand, there was little reason to expect that the assimilation would be successful, for most of the teachers in the lower grades were women, and female teachers, he explained, did not have "by nature the desire to learn about democracy's needs and problems."[43]

Cubberley's History of Education

In 1919 Cubberley published his successful history of education text, used in teacher training, in which he once again addressed how the character of the nation's immigrants had changed. There he expressed his belief that there were more immigrants available for the melting pot than could possibly fit. He was communicating a serious concern with the effects immigration was having on the nation. He basically claimed that the nation was in decline soon after immigration from southern and eastern Europe increased. It became, he wrote, "a great steam" and the stream, became a flood:

> Practically no Italians came to us before 1870, but by 1890 they were coming at the rate of twenty thousand a year, and during the five-year period 1906-10 as many as 1,186,100 arrived. After 1880, in addition people from all parts of that medley of races which formerly constituted the Austro-Hungarian Empire . . . and Japanese and Koreans from the Far East, began to come in numbers. . . .

Cubberley was obsessed with the pernicious character of different types of human beings and their character, which inevitably lacks "conceptions of righteousness, liberty, law, order, public decency, and government." According to Cubberley "these people" have come "to dilute tremendously our national stock and to weaken and corrupt our political life." The problems they are said to cause range greatly: "housing and living, moral and sanitary conditions, and honest and decent government, while popular education has everywhere been made more difficult." These newcomers presented problems everywhere from the "cities of the North, [to] the agricultural regions of the Middle and the Far West, and the mining districts of the mountain regions" Cubberley explained:

> The result has been that in many sections of our country foreign manners, customs, observances, and language have tended to supplant native ways and the English speech, while the so-called "melting-pot" has had more than it could handle. The new peoples, and especially those from the South and East of Europe, have come so fast that we have been unable to absorb and assimilate them, and our national life, for the past quarter century, has been afflicted with a serious case of racial indigestion.[44]

While some may have disagreed that the nation was suffering from "racial indigestion," there was widespread agreement that immigrants, newcomers, or aliens, as they were sometimes called, had to be digested. For example, in 1913 Joseph E. Park observed that "As a matter of fact, the ease and rapidity with which aliens, under existing conditions in the United States, have been able to assimilate themselves to the customs and manners of American life have enabled this country to swallow and digest every sort of normal human difference, except the purely external ones, like the color of the skin."[45]

Cubberley was again expressing a view that was very widely held: that there were races, that the races differed from one another, and that some were better or more desirable than others. In retrospect, it can be seen that there were two options: abandon the melting pot and the assimilationist theory that kept its fires burning or require it to do less melting. Americans were not yet ready to abandon the melting pot. The United States Congress enacted restrictive immigration laws in 1921 and 1924 so there would be fewer immigrants from racial stock different from the nation's racial stock to melt down.

Even after the enactment of the restrictive immigration laws of 1921 and 1924, the fascination with immigrants continued. In 1934 Cubberley instructed prospective public school teachers and administrators that the "American mixture" was very "great" and offered a catalogue that reflected and in all likelihood reinforced stereotypes and prejudices, for it assigned people, based on their country of origin, to specific occupations and, thus, to specific spaces, assignments that assured the subsequent development of ethnicity and the continuation of discrimination, prejudice and stereotyping. The fanciful detail of Cubberley's racial and ethnic profiling is shocking by today's standards. Everyone was classified. In some sense, even with the absurdity, Cubberley provides a window through which the diversity of the American polity can be seen:

> We buy our groceries of Knudsen and Larsen, our meats of Klieber and Engelmeier, our bread of Rudolf Krause, Petar Petarovich delivers our milk, Giuseppe Battali removes our garbage, Swen Swensen delivers our ice, Takahira Matsui is our cook, and Nicholas Androvsky has recently taken the place of Pancho Garcia as our gardener. We occasionally take dinner at a café managed by Schiavetti and Montagnini, we buy our haberdashery of Moses Ickelheimer, Isaac Rosenstein is our tailor, Azniv Arakelian sells us our cigars, and Thirmutis Poulis supplies our wants in ice cream and candies. Timothy Mehegan represents our ward in the city council, Patrick O'Grady is the policeman on our beat, Nellie O'Brien teaches our little girl at school, Nels Petersen is our postman, Vladimir Constantinovitch is our street-sweeper, Lazar Obichan reads our electric meter, Lorenzo Guercio sells potted plants and flowers on the corner, Mahoud Bey peddles second-grade fruit past our door, and Alexis Grablowsky mends and presses our suits and cleans our hats in a little shop two blocks down the street. The service garage, run by Pestarino and Pozzi, looks after our car. Emil Frankfurter is the cashier at our bank, Kleanthis Vassardakis shines shoes in our office building, and Wilhelmina Weinstein is our office stenographer.[46]

Then as now those not fully accepted by the dominant group were assigned to spaces and occupations designated by the dominant group, a practice that persists and a practice not peculiar to the United States. As Ramon Flechá has observed about attitudes and practices in Europe, where "ethnocentrism accepts the idea of people from different ethnicities living in the same territory while it rejects the idea of equal status." This more class-based approach justifies hierarchy as inevitable especially when addressing immigrant populations. "Immigrants are thus considered suited only for those positions that European people do not want." The concept of ethnocentrism in Europe also uses the idea of exchange theory where each ethnic group exchanges with the other what "each has to offer." For instance, European high technology can be exchanged for these nations' raw resources. This exchange also relates to human resources, as European executives and personnel can be exported to fill top managerial positions in non-Western countries.[47]

Once again Cubberley related that in many sections of the nation "foreign manners, customs, observances, and language have tended to supplant native ways and the English speech, while the so-called 'melting-pot' has had more than it could handle" and that the nation had been "afflicted with a serious case of racial indigestion."[48]

Teaching Teachers That American Civilization is Anglo-European

While Stuart G. Noble did not devote as much space to immigrants as did Cubberley, he did continue, as late as 1960, the tradition of teaching prospective teachers that American civilization was essentially an Anglo-Saxon civilization. He began the first chapter of his text with that clear message that the origin of the United States was predominantly English:

> The settlers of the thirteen original colonies were chiefly English-born and English-bred. There was a slight admixture of Swedes, Dutch, Germans, and French in the early population, but these elements, though significant locally, were not important in molding the life and character of the typical colonial community. The English outnumbered all other nationalities represented and in time placed an English stamp upon the culture of the period: The English language predominated, English customs and traditions came to prevail, and English ideas of religion, government, science, and education, when transplanted, took root and grew.

A vision of the Anglo-Saxon as a superior people was clear. The references to white supremacy go beyond privilege accorded superior institutions and cultural heritage. It is physical. To elevate white culture as the only moral, physical reality of the United States in tone eliminates others who do not partake of this heritage and "the other," becomes the "outsider," an "alien." What is transmitted is not only a myth but contains the essential message of white supremacy:

> Colonial American derived from England not merely its blood and sinews but also a cultural heritage of vast importance. From this source came the

experience of past ages in the form of beliefs, ideals, superstitions, and habits of living, all firmly fixed in the folkways of the English people. It is true that the early settlers came from all parts of England, rural and urban, that they represented different strata of society, that they held different religious beliefs, and that they belonged to both the ignorant and learned classes.

The mythical Anglo-Saxon stands above all others. While there were variations, Noble argued that "these significant differences are of minor importance when balanced against the fact that all, or nearly all, were children of a common tradition. The mother country, during the seventeenth century, planted on this side of the Atlantic the seeds of an Anglo-Saxon civilization." He was willing to acknowledge other Western Europeans. Out of an English base Noble added "to this, the French contributed important elements in the eighteenth century, and the Germans added much in later years." Noble found in the old ways, which are clearly historically inaccurate, that little change had occurred "until after the opening of the present century [twentieth]." Prior to that time, "America did little except appropriate, conserve, and improve upon the heritage which came, and has continued to come, from across the seas."[49]

According to Noble, the development of industry essentially created a situation that led to an "alarming rate" of immigration. He did not object if employers contracted with foreign labor and later deported them, but the absence of such practices he feared "opened the gates to the lower classes of immigrants and America became the land of liberty for the poor and oppressed of all nations." As the nineteenth century neared its end, "loose immigration laws admitted the horde [of immigrants] without discrimination," and "the problem of congestion of the foreign-born population in the slums of large cities was to become acute early in the new century."[50] In what seems a clear echo of Cubberley, Noble drew attention to the "hordes of immigrants" who overpopulated the cities. To make matters worse they "came largely from the backward European countries." They were "Italians, Greeks, Poles, Croats, Hungarians, and Russians." Noble explained that "the flood was threatening to inundate American institutions when the Quota Law of 1924 made a drastic restriction of immigration.[51]

While holding to the notion that "most of the immigrants who came in large numbers in the latter half of the nineteenth century were not familiar with the ways of the gentry," Noble did acknowledge that "when wealth and freedom from old-world restraints permitted them to rise to a higher social level, they began to take on the manners and behavior of the so-called better classes."[52] Like Cubberley, Noble questioned whether the melting pot could do its work. The earlier populations—the Irish and the Germans—were already absorbed into the general population, but the new groups consisted of "racial stock different from our own and so numerous." He feared they could not be assimilated. His evidence was that "they formed colonies in the larger cities, where they continued to speak their own languages and follow the customs of the lands from which they came." He admitted that their isolation was not entirely of their own doing but partly the work of "vicious leaders interested only in political exploitation." Noble was not optimistic, "even the schools were powerless to change them, for these institutions frequently served only the children of the foreign-born neighborhoods in which they were located." Somewhat ironically, "the familiar comparison of America to the melting pot of the nations was no longer an apt one."[53]

In Adolphe E. Meyer's *An Educational History of the American People* (1957), one finds considerably less discussion of immigrants. In his chapter on *The Cradle of the Common School*, he explained that immigration that once was a "trickle" became a "torrent" but did not describe the arrival in any manner that could be construed as prejudicial.[54] Indeed, in his explanation of the "national spirit" that developed in the middle of the nineteenth century, he appeared to criticize not the immigrants but the behavior and attitudes that accompanied the "national spirit" where pride in one's nation "enflamed aggressive and imperialistic phobias."

Meyer attributed the war with Mexico to this phobia. According to Meyer:

> . . . economically, the new [national] spirit revealed itself among merchants and industrialists in their cries for protection against alien competition, and among the laboring order in an accumulating resentment against the immigrant in their midst, and especially his lower level of living, his readiness to work for lesser wages, and what seemed to be a pigheaded resistance to Americanization. The national spirit flared up even in religion, particularly after his forties, as the number of Irish-Catholics mounted. Asserting that the glory of the Republic lay in its Protestant tradition, the spirit became polluted with intolerance—even, indeed, with anti-Catholic vendettas.[55]

IDENTIFYING THE AFRICAN AMERICAN "PROBLEM" FOR EDUCATORS

Those who read Cubberley's texts read that: "Only in the Southern States is there an absence of a large percentage of foreign-born, and there the problem of the Negro and his education takes the place of the foreign-born educational problem."[56] Cubberley's brief discussions of African Americans emphasized neither what African Americans contributed nor how they had been victimized but emphasized the problem they presented. They had value only before the Civil War. On the eve of the Civil War the four million African Americans were an asset to the south then valued at two billion dollars. After Appomattox "the four million blacks . . . .[had been] turned into a tremendous liability."[57] Before and after Appomattox, African Americans, in Cubberley's view, were a burden.

blacks, as they were freed and came under Union jurisdiction, were described as being "in a helpless, frightened, and destitute, condition.[58] Cubberley, clearly, did not empathize with the joy of being free.

After Appomattox and especially after President Rutherford B. Hayes ended Reconstruction in 1877 by removing federal troops from the South and ending military rule not much was done to address "the problem." Consequently, from the view of people such as Cubberley the problem grew worse. African Americans were systematically denied equality of educational opportunity as well as equality of economic, political, and social opportunity. For example, according to Cubberley, in 1886 in North Carolina, a state representative of the South, "considerably more than one fourth of the white population ten years of age and over, and about 70 per cent of the colored population, was illiterate." By 1900, conditions were not appreciably better. At best, Southern states were collecting taxes at a rate about sixty percent of what was collected in the North, and illiteracy in the South was three times greater than in the United States as a whole. Whatever was spent on schools for African Americans was less than the meager amount spent for whites. Private, or extra-governmental funds, such as those provided by the Slater Fund (established in 1882), the Anna T. Jeanes Fund (1908), the Phelps-Stokes Fund (1911), and the Julius Rosenwald Fund (1915), were used to provide separate or segregated educational arrangements and to keep African Americans on their side of the color line. Boundaries were clear, as were the penalties for crossing over them.

Cubberley instructed his readers that "the education of the Negro" was one of the "difficult problems [that] faces the South."[59] However, he argued, it was also a problem for the North due to migration out of caste-based segregation in the South. In the 1870s, eighty percent of the African American population lived in rural poverty in southern states; by the 1970s, eighty percent lived in urban poverty in northern states. This changed the character of the nation's cities and the workforce, and brought issues of race, ethnicity, and gender to the fore. The creation of inner city ghettos in the North took place between 1900 and 1940. Between 1900 and 1910, 197,000 African Americans migrated from the South to the North. Their migration increased during World War I when Northern factories recruited African Americans from the South as the demand for industrial production increased and European immigration decreased. Half a million African Americans left the rural South between 1910 and 1920 and came to cities such as Chicago, Detroit, Philadelphia, and New York.[60] They were met with poverty and racism from northern whites and immigrants who quickly learned the color status hierarchy.[61]

> With their large migration to the Northern cities at the time of and following the World War [I], the problem has now in part become one for the North as well. After nearly three-quarters of a century, the difficulties of the question

are still present and the complete answer has not been found, though the progress toward its solution has been remarkable.[62]

In the Defense of Segregation

Cubberley's reference to a solution was segregation. He saw the problem of African Americans as their problem of adjustment to freedom rather than the refusal of white society to accept blacks on equal terms.

No racial group in the United States offers so many problems of economic and social adjustment as does that of our ten million Negroes. In the South they constitute almost one third of the population; in Mississippi and South Carolina they number one half; and in the "black-belt counties" their proportion ranges from fifty to ninety per cent. In the seventy years since their emancipation took place, the illiteracy of the race has decreased from ninety-five to twenty per cent; approximately a million colored men, in 1930, were farmers of varying degrees of independence; and three quarters of a million own their own homes and one quarter million their farms. In the same period the death-rate among the Negroes has decreased one half, though it is still more than one and one half times that of the whites. Except in a few cities, the Negro teacher has completely supplanted the white as the teacher of the race[62] and as a people they are assuming an increasing responsibility for the education and progress of their members.[63]

In *An Introduction to the Study of Education,* Cubberley reported that illiteracy among African Americans—he variously labeled them as Negroes, colored children, or colored pupils—was over eighty percent in 1800 and down to sixteen percent by 1930. It was a significant increase, for, as he reported, "in 1865, the Negro race was practically an illiterate race" because legislative enactment in the south forbade the education of Negroes."[64]

In a paragraph introduced with the heading "The Negro Problem"—the subtext is that it is not a problem for all American but just for African Americans—he reported that the South generally forbade the education of both free and enslaved African Americans. South Carolina's attempt to integrate schools failed because of "political, social, biological and economic considerations."[65] Such reporting to prospective teachers indicated, though not very explicitly, that race was a real category and that there were meaningful biological differences between those assigned to one race or another.

The solution to the "Negro Problem,' not surprisingly, was education, and there was some reason to believe the problem could be solved. Progress had occurred: "When we look backward over the educational progress of the Negro we see that it has been noteworthy and highly satisfactory." There is no indication that he objected to a dual system of education, one for whites and one for African Americans. He did recognize that there were 48,000 African-American teachers and that over one thousand were teaching in colleges. Equally, important was his recognition that "the Negro had proved capacity for education." That "capacity for education" was the key to the solution of the "problem of the Negro." For Cubberley, "the ultimate solution to the problem of the Negro, of course, is very largely in terms of education." Still, it is clear that Cubberley, as the following statement indicates, had no difficulty with racially segregated education: "Colleges are training *their own race* for professional life as doctors, lawyers, ministers, bankers, and editors."[66]

Noble's estimation of what education could do for African Americans was not as optimistic as Cubberley's. For example, in his discussion of the efforts of the Freedman's Bureau and its attempt to provide education for African Americans he reported:

> It was inevitable that the movement should meet with disappointment. To begin with, the expectation that reform through literacy alone would immediately overcome the hereditary and environmental limitations of the Negro race was hardly to be justified.[67]

In that passage Noble was effectively endorsing racism—the belief that African Americans suffered from hereditary deficiencies that made them different from those who were white.

Meyer's discussion of African Americans focused not on the problems they presented to American society but on the problems they encountered. In his discussion of developments in the South "after Reconstruction," he related that "the newly found liberty of the Negro, moreover, was promptly curtailed, and though the Fourteenth and Fifteenth Amendments were there to assure him of his rights by various stratagems and deceits theses were made precariously small."[68] Meyer clearly explained that African Americans were denied equality of educational opportunity, especially in the South:

> The supreme and incontrovertible social fact in the situation was, of course, the presence of the Negro. Was he to be granted access to the public school on free and equal terms with the whites? Or was he to be set upon his bench in schools restricted to this race? Northerners in the main pressed for the former, but Southerners were pretty much opposed. Several Reconstruction governments, it is true, yielded on the matter and hazarded the establishment of a coracial public school. But the overwhelming bulk of whites would have no dealings with it and wherever it appeared, they went to great lengths to keep themselves and their children away. Such was the dominant sentiment, and so it smoldered long after Appomattox. In fact, by the end of the century every Southern state had declared itself, either in its constitution or in its statutes, for the maintenance of separate schools.

Significantly, while not explicitly stating that some adhered to the notion that there were races and that races differed from one another in significant ways, Meyer did address the issue of whether schooling African American children was a psychological question or a social question. It was one thing to debate the issue of schooling black children with white children but it was another to question whether black children could profit from education in the first place. Clearly, the next question was whether or not black children should be given the same subjects as white children. While "such questions no longer exercise us—science and democracy have seen to that. . . when they first were raised they resulted not only in strong feeling but in an array of answers which ranged from flat negatives to equally flat positives, with an aggregation of qualified negatives and positives in between."[69] Given the rise of special education and misclassification of children of African American, American Indian, and Latino descent in these classes it seems that the issues were not quickly dismissed. Meyer must have been somewhat optimistic in his claim that "such questions no longer exercise us" but his views and assessment were indeed very different from his predecessors, Cubberley and Noble.

Defining the American People and Their Place in School for Teachers

Both Cubberley's book and Noble's book were available after the *Brown* decision. Neither contained any reference to that decision. Even more interesting is the omission of any reference to *Plessy v. Ferguson* in either of their texts. Meyer, however, not only discussed those decisions but also pointed out that the first recorded legal action that sanctioned separating African American students from white students "occurred not in Dixie, but in Boston, when in 1849, a Negro, Benjamin Roberts, took his case to the state's highest bench in an attempt to obtain damages from the city for its refusal to admit his five-year-old Sara to the white primary school of the district where he chanced to be a resident." However, the court ruled against him and upheld racial segregation in Boston's public schools. That was an important decision, for, as Meyer explained: "The Roberts decision had developed into a powerful precedent."

In his discussion of "Some Current Cultural Difficulties" Meyer was very clear about the problems African Americans confronted in terms of "intercultural" frictions with white culture. Meyer thought that this was primarily a southern problem, as is typical of people from other parts of the country. Meyer recognized that these issues "to some extent [occur] in other parts of the land as well." He reported:

There, too, Negroes are not always welcome in hotels and restaurants and other public places; not every employer will hire them; and certain hospitals have refused them assistance of any kind. In great towns like New York, the pressure from the whites has crowded the Negroes into segregated habitation which—in the past at any rate—has given rise to segregated Negro schools. Religious organizations have also practiced segregation.[70]

For Cubberley, Native-Americans were the only "true" Americans but he effectively contradicted himself and revealed his values by stating that the Native-Americans needed to be "merged into the general population and become citizens, not tribesmen." He acknowledged that the Native-Americans were forced to live on reservations and that some children received elementary education administered by either Protestant or Catholic mission schools. Native-Americans were "true" Americans but the were also "wards" of the federal government. The education he recommended for Native-Americans was to be according to one's gender. He emphasized the importance of vocational instruction in "agriculture, carpentry, black-smithing, engineering, masonry, automobile mechanics, printing, painting, and shoe repair for boys; and home training, cooking, nursing, sewing, laundering, and poultry raising for the girls."[71]

Cubberley reported that "scattered along an arctic coastline of almost four thousand miles live several thousand primitive people of another race, the Eskimo." He instructed future teachers "there is no doubt that the natives of Alaska are being developed in education and industry so as to become an important factor in the economic life of the territory." In fact, "some of them are comparatively wealthy from hunting, sealing, and fishing and own modern homes and gasoline propelled fishing vessels." The sub-text of his discussion was that the relative prosperity of the Eskimos [sic] was due to education. He praised the Alaskan school service by pointing out that it "demands teachers with much more than professional qualifications alone, a teacher, community leader, an arbitrator of disputes, supervisor of reindeer industry, censor of morals, preserver of peace, public health nurse and a chief medical advisor all in one." He reported: "from the time Alaska was purchased from Russia, in 1867, until 1884 the U.S. government ignored the educational needs of the territory, leaving the Natives entirely to missionary enterprise." Cubberley only endorsed public education, education sponsored by and provided by the government.[72]

In the *Founding of the American Public School System*, first published in 1940, Paul Monroe reported how "the German migration of the late forties added a progressive influence to education." He further reported that "the immigrant elements as a whole made the educational problem more distinct, and by accentuating the tests to which our political and social structure must be subjected directed the attention to the native population of the significance of education." Immigrants did contribute to the building and development of the relatively new nation: "many of the immigrants were employed on the great public works of the times, the building of rail-roads and canals." As to the public unrest that frequently characterized the period of massive immigration, Monore reported that "much of the responsibility for this condition approaching anarchy was popularly attrib-uted to the untrained and unbridled foreign element, unfamiliar with American conditions and amenable only to force, much as illiteracy, igno-rance, and civic instability are attributed to it today." Educated immigrants, he indicated, became "citizenized," literate, accustomed to American ways and subservient to their employers.[73]

In *The Development of Education in the Twentieth Century* (1949), Adolphe E. Meyer devoted less attention to immigrants and more attention to Afri-can Americans than did his predecessors. Meyer was aware of discrimina-tion and certainly did not endorse it. In his discussion of minority group discrimination, he reported that "minority groups of Irish, Poles, and Ital-ians, most of whom were unskilled and poorly educated, had to live in seg-regated quarters. They toiled as day laborers, eking out their paltry pay, and finding it almost impossible to belong to our society."[74] In his discus-sion of intercultural education, Meyer reported how the early settler viewed the indigenous peoples: "In the eyes of the white-skinned immi-grant, the Indian appeared of low and inferior stock, and it wasn't long before he had to suffer for the color of his reddish skin."[75] Meyer pro-jected the color consciousness of his own era backward in time.

In his account of educational psychology and its findings concerning racial differences, Meyer reported that the first "first comprehensive data regarding differences between whites, Negroes [sic], and native [born] Americans" were compiled during World War I. He was referring to the world's first comprehensive group intelligence testing program conducted by the U.S. Army called the Army Alpha and Beta tests for their two ver-sions. The first intelligence tests were developed in France originally by Alfred Binet to find out why some children lagged behind others in school. Henry Goddard, a eugenicist who was director of Vineland Training School for the Feebleminded, brought the scale of developmental tasks to the United States. It was adapted as a group test during the war to test the ability of future soldiers. In the tests, to the dismay of the authors, poor whites did not fare much better than non-whites. Meyer conceded that the Army Alpha and Beta group intelligence tests concluded that whites "were superior in their ability to do abstract thinking." However, he correctly qualified these conclusions: "that in no case do the differences appear to be large enough to warrant any general claim for racial superiority." Meyer reported that it was "demonstrated that, despite lower averages, there are relatively few whites with intelligence superior to that of the highest of the Negroes [sic]; and again, there are correspondingly few Negroes [sic] with a lesser intelligence than that of the dullest the whites."[76]

NOTES

1.   Opal Moore, "A Happy Story," in Charles H. Rowell, ed., *Ancestral House: The Black Short Story in the Americas and Europe* (Boulder: Westview, 1995), p. 419.

2.   George M. Fredrickson, *Racism: A Short History* (Princeton: Princeton University, 2002).

3.   Ibid.

4.   Philip Morgan, *Slave Counterpoint: Black Culture in the Eighteenth Century Chesapeake and Lowcountry* (Chapel Hill: North Carolina Press, 1998).

5.   Theodore Allen, *The Invention of the White Race*, Vol II. (New York: Verso, 1997).

6.   R. A. Schermerhorn, "Ethnicity in the Perspective of the Sociology of Knowledge," *Ethnicity*, Vol 1 (1974), p. 3.

7.   It may be that the extent to which assimilation as a goal or ideal was not as widely accepted as some have believed. Diane Ravitch has observed that "Soon after the passage of the [Civil Rights Act of 1964], changes began to occur that altered racial relations and affected subsequent public policy. Though it was not immediately apparent, the nature of the civil rights movements changed. As an interracial movement led by blacks, its goal had been a public policy in which the state treated persons as individuals, without regard to race, color, creed, or national origin. After this goal was written into law, the movement itself was transformed by the political climate into a black movement, dedicated to advancing the interests of blacks as a minority group. The nationalist strain that had always existed among blacks and within black organizations came to the fore, calling attention to the need of blacks for group recognition, for assertion of their own history and culture, for a legitimate and respected place among American ethnic groups." See: *The Troubled Crusade: American Education 1945-1980* (New York: Basic Books, 1983), pp. 145-6.

8.   Fredrickson, *Racism*.

9.   Gunnar Myrdal. *An American Dilemma: The Negro Problem and American Democracy*. Twentieth Anniversary Ed. (New York: Harper & Row, 1962), p. 342.

10.   Ibid., pp. 339-340.

11.   Ibid., p. 339.

12.   Ravitch, *Troubled Crusade*, p. 4.

13.   Schermerhorn, "Ethnicity in the Perspective of the Sociology of Knowledge," pp. 4-5.

14.   Ibid., p. 5.

15.   *Principa*, June 11, 1863, an antislavery paper quoted in James M. McPherson, *The Negro's Civil War: How American Negro's Felt and Acted During the War for Union* (New York: Vintage, 1967), p. ix.

16.   Ibid.

17.   George Lefebvre, *The Coming of the French Revolution*, R. R. Palmer, Trans. (Princeton: Princeton University Press, 1947, 1975) argues that this contradiction of the English, American, and French Revolutions are the causes of the tensions of modernity, pp. 214-5.

18.   Schermerhorn, "Ethnicity in the Perspective of the Sociology of Knowledge," pp. 4-5.

19.   Stanley Warren, "The Evolution of Secondary Schooling for Blacks in Indianapolis, 1869-1930," pp. 29-50; Emma Lou Thornbrough, "The History of Black

Women in Indiana," pp. 67-85; both in Wilma Gibbs, ed., *Indiana's African American Heritage: Essays From Black History News and Notes* (Indianapolis: Indiana Historical Society, 1993).

    20.   Chester L. Flynn Jr., *White Land, Black Labor: Caste and Class in Late Nineteenth Century Georgia* (Baton Rouge and London: Louisiana State University Press, 1983), pp. 30-31.

    21.   Flynn, *White Land, Black Labor,* pp. 44-46; See fn 30 on "White Capping" in Ohio and Indiana. Robert Maxwell Brown, "Historical Patterns of Violence in America," in Hugh D. Graham and Ted R. Gurr, eds., *Violence in America: Historical and Comparative Perspectives: A Report to the National Commission on the Causes of Violence and Its Prevention* (Washington,D.C: U.S. Government Printing Office, 1969); Edward P. Thompson, "Rough Music:Le Charivari Anglais," *Annales : Economic; Sociétés; Civilization* XXVII (March-April, 1972): 286-87.

    22.   Roger Daniels, *Concentration Camps U.S.A.: Japanese Americans and World War II* (New York: Holt Rinehart, and Winston, 1972) p. 10.

    23.   Jeremiah Whipple Jenks and W. Jett Lauck. *The Immigration Problem: A study of American Conditions and Needs (New York, London: Funk & Wagnalls Co. original 1912 [1911], 6ᵗʰ printing 1926),* pp. 24-25. Studies that decried the large numbers of immigrants began as early as 1892 with Z. Sidney Sampson's *The Immigration Problem* (New York: D. Appleton & Co., 1892); Robert De Courcey Ward, an early social scientists with the settlement movement funded by the Charity Organization Society conducted a study in 1904, *The Immigration problem, its present status and its relation to the American race of the future* (New York: The Charity Organization Society, 1904). Studies were so numerous and public attention heightened enough that Mary Katherine Kay wrote: *The Immigration Problem: A Bibliography* (Madison, WI: n.p., 1909). Jenks and Lauck's book went through six printings between 1911 and 1926. Before the first World War ended James Murphy Ward published his version of *The Immigration Problem* (Popular Bluff, MO.: Republican Printing, 1917). The National Industrial Conference Board published its study, *The Immigration Problem in the United States,* in 1923. The issue also heightened Canada's interest in immigration witnessed by Charlotte Whitton's 1924 work: *The Immigration Problem for Canada* (Kinston: The Jackson Press). In 1928 Edward Rieman Lewis questioned the very integrity of the country in his *America, Nation or Confusion: A Study of Our Immigration Problems* (New York and London: Harper and Brothers, 1928). The recent demographic shifts in the United States have provoked similar responses one hundred years later.

    24.   Jenks and Lauck, *The Immigration Problem,* pp. 24-25.

    25.   Ibid., p. 76.

    26.   Ibid., pp. 73-75.

    27.   Ibid., p. 340.

    28.   Ibid., p. 207-208.

    29.   Ibid., p. 339.

    30.   Ibid., p. 206.

    31.   Ibid., pp. 266-267.

    32.   "Reports of the Immigration Commission,: Vol. 38 quoted in Jenks and Lauck. *The Immigration Problem,* p. 268.

    33.   Ibid.

    34.   Ibid.

    35.   What are now correctly seen as nationalities were often called races.

36.   Ellwood P. Cubberley. *Changing Conceptions of Education* (Boston, MA: Houghton Mifflin, Co., 1909), pp. 14-15. Cubberley repeated and expanded on these characterizations in *Public Education in the United States: A Study and Interpretation of American Educational History* (Boston, MA: The Riverside Press, 1919), p. 337-338. They were repeated in the revised edition in 1934. (pp. 485-486).

37.   Michel-Guillaume Jean de Crevecoeur, *Letters from an American Farmer,* 1793, Letter III, in *Willard Thorp, Merle Curti, and Carolos Baker, American Issues Volume I: The Social Record,* rev. ed. (New York: J. B. Lippincott, 1955), p. 169.

38.   Immigation *The Massachusetts Teacher* Vol. 4 (October 1851) in Michael B. Katz ed., *School Reform: Past and Present* (Boston: Little Brown and Co., 1971), p. 169.

39.   Ibid., pp. 169-170.

40.   Cubberley, *Changing Conceptions*, p. 13.

41.   Ibid., pp. 13-14.

42.   Ibid., pp. 15-16.

43.   Ibid., p. 67.

44.   Ellwood P. Cubberley, *Public Education in the United States: A Study and Interpretation of American Educational History* (Boston, Massachusetts: Houghton Mifflin Co., 1919), pp. 337-338.

45.   Robert E. Park, *Racial Assimilation in Secondary Groups with Particular Reference to the Negro, Publications of the American Sociological Society,* Vol. VIII (1913) reproduced in Everett Cherrington Hughes, *et. al.* eds., *Race and Culture: The Collected Papers of Robert Ezra Park,* Vol. I (Glencoe, IL: The Free Press, 1950), p. 208.

46.   Ellwood P.Cubberley, *Public Education in the United States: A Study and Interpretation of American Educational History.* Rev. ed. (Boston, MA: Houghton Mifflin Co., 1934), pp. 486-487.

47.   Ramón Flecha, Modern and Postmodern Racism in Europe: Dialogic Approach and Anti-Racist Pedagogies, *Harvard Educational Review,* Vol. 69, No. 2 (Summer 1999), p. 157.

48.   Cubberley. *Public Education in the United States.* rev. ed., p. 486.

49.   Stuart G. Noble, *A History of American Education.* rev. ed. (New York: Rinehart and Company, Inc., 1954), pp. 3-4. The first edition was published in 1938. A fifth printing appeared in April 1960. In developing and reporting the notion that the United States was essentially an Anglo-Saxon civilization, Noble relied on John R. Commons, *Race and Immigrants in America* (New York: The Macmillan Co., 1907); Charles A. and Mary R. Beard, *The Rise of American Civilization* (New York: The Macmillan Co., 1927); and Allan Nevins, *American Social History as Recorded by British Travelers* (New York: Henry Holt and Co., 1929).

50.   Noble, *A History of American Education,* p. 295.

51.   Ibid., p. 371.

52.   Ibid., p. 303.

53.   Ibid., pp. 372-373.

54.   Adolphe E. Meyer, *An Educational History of the American People* (New York: McGraw-Hill, 1957). pp. 139-140.

55.   Ibid, p. 147.

56.   Cubberley, *Public Education,* p. 340 and Public Education, rev. ed., p. 486.

57.   Cubberley, *Public Education,* rev. ed., p. 431.

58.   Ibid., p. 437.

59.   Ibid., p. 431.

60.   Ronald Takaki, *A Different Mirror: A History of Multicultural America* (Boston: Little Brown and Co., 1993), ch. 6 especially on the Irish.

61.   Douglass S. Massey and Nancy A. Denton, *American Apartheid: Segregation and the Making of the Underclass* (Cambridge: Harvard University Press, 1993), pp. 27-29.

62.   At his point, Cubberley quoted the following from G. S. Dickerman in *History of Negro Education,* Bulletin 38, 1916, United States Bureau of Education, p. 262: This change has not been an unmixed blessing, and the schools have not always prospered as a result. While white teachers were in their management they themselves often became deeply interested in the children and ambitious for the prosperity of the school. Having considerable influence in the community, they were able to secure more favorable attention than would be given to the Negro teachers. With the change, the schools under Negro teachers had no effective advocates, and so were constant losers. The amazing contrast between the public schools for white children and those for Negroes in nearly all parts of the South tells the story of this misfortune."

63.   Cubberley. *Public Education* rev. ed., p. 684.

64.   Ellwood P. Cubberley. *An Introduction to the Study of Education* Revised by Walter Crosby Eells (Boston: Houghton Mifflin Co., 1933), p. 450.

65.   Ibid.

66.   Ibid., pp. 451-452.

67.   Noble, *A History of American Education*, p. 324.

68.   Meyer, *An Educational History of the American People*, p. 217.

69.   Ibid., p. 219.

70.   Ibid., p. 370.

71.   Ellwood P. Cubberly, *An Introduction to the Study of Education*, revised by Walter Crosby Eells (Boston: Houghton Mifflin Co., 1933), p. 453.

72.   Ibid., p. 456.

73.   Paul Monroe, *Founding of the American Public School System: A History of Education in the United States From Early Settlement to the Close of the Civil War* (New York: Hafner, 1971, 1940), p. 224.

74.   Adolphe Meyer, *Development of Education in the Twentieth Century*, 1949, pp. 556.

75.   Ibid., p. 555.

76.   Ibid., p. 477.

CHAPTER 7

CIVIL RIGHTS MOVEMENT
The Long Road to Freedom

. . . the Reconstruction generation had passed from the scene and even within the black community, memories of the period had all but disappeared. Yet the institutions created or consolidated after the Civil War—the black family, school, and church—provided the base from which the modern civil rights movement sprang. And for its legal strategy, the movement turned to the laws and amendments of Reconstruction. 'The River must bend, and the longest road must terminate.' Rev. Peter Randolf, a former slave, wrote these words as the dark night of injustice settled over the South"[1]

Some may believe, understandably, that the modern Civil Rights Movement began with the *Brown* decision in May 1954 or in December 1955 when Rosa Parks, secretary of the Montgomery, Alabama branch of the National Association for the Advancement of Colored People (NAACP), refused to surrender her seat on a bus to a white man. The Revered Martin Luther King, Jr. led the subsequent bus boycott until a year later when the U. S. Supreme Court ruled that racial segregation on public busses was unconstitutional. There is no question that those developments were significant, but the history of the modern Civil Rights movement dates back to the early years of the twentieth century when the short-lived Niagara Movement and then the National Association for the Advancement of Col-

Race, Ethnicity, and Education: What is Taught in School, pages 181–217.
A Volume in: International Perspectives on Curriculum
Copyright © 2003 by Information Age Publishing, Inc.
All rights of reproduction in any form reserved.
ISBN: 1-59311-080-4 (paper), 1-59311-081-2 (cloth)

ored People were founded. Both the Niagara Movement and the NAACP were founded during the Progressive Era (an era that is usually considered to have begun in the late 1880s or early 1890s and to have ended in 1914 with the beginning of World War I), and can rightfully be considered to be progressive. Ironically, the Progressive Era is also the era during which Jim Crow laws were enacted and the era during which labor's attempts to organize were actively and sometimes brutally suppressed. As August Meier and John H. Bracey, Jr. have observed, the NAACP did embrace the progressive agenda, but most accounts of progressivism tend to give little or no attention to either race or the NAACP.[2] Somehow, the coincidence of those two eras is often overlooked. Progressives were reformers but many leading progressives believed people of color, especially African Americans, Asians, Native Americans, and Mexicans to be inferior and therefore not eligible for legal rights and protections enjoyed by others. For example, in 1901 the Supreme Court had to decide whether people in the territories the nation acquired as a result of the Spanish-American War were entitled to rights and protections guaranteed by the Bill of Rights. The Court ruled that they did not.

The Progressive Era coincides with the "dark night of injustice that settled over the South" and the nation after the failure of Reconstruction. The United States enacted laws that made the South into the world's first "overtly racist regime" with an official ideology that sanctioned legal, political, and economic discrimination against African Americans.[3] The South began to enact Jim Crow laws—laws that required racial segregation—in the 1880s. They were typically versions of laws that had been enacted in the North before the Civil War. They were given legal sanction at the national level in 1896 when the United States Supreme Court ruled in *Plessy v. Ferguson* that Homer Plessy, who was considered to be an African American,[4] could be required to sit in a railroad coach reserved for African Americans. The decision was consistent with the social and political climate of the era and was handed down at a time when, as Jennings Wagoner, Jr., observed "most Northerners, including many who in earlier decades had been zealously involved in Southern affairs, had turned their attention away from the plight of the southern black."[5] Booker T. Washington had delivered his famous "Atlanta Compromise" speech, a year earlier, in which he argued that it would be "the extremist folly" for African Americans to press for "social equality" and promised whites that: "In all things that are purely social we can be as separate as the fingers, yet one as the hand in all things essential to mutual progress."[6] Washington was offering or hoping that in exchange for not pressing for social and political equality African Americans would receive economic opportunity and access to the jobs that were being given to recently arrived immigrants. His hope was not realized.

Plessy v. Ferguson gave the states "the power to *require* segregation"[7] and the right to establish standards to determine who was and who was not white. States did exercise these rights. Mississippi had ruled that people of Chinese ancestry were not white (though the Supreme Court ruled in 1898 that children born in the United States of Chinese parents were citizens) and could not attend white schools. In 1927 in *Gong Lum v. Rice* the Court sided with the state of Mississippi and ruled that Chinese Americans were "members of the 'colored races'."[8] The Supreme Court effectively held that there were two classes of citizenship: white and not white. States controlled by whites had the authority to segregate those they classified as not-white. Jim Crow laws required separate railroad cars, schools, hospitals, restrooms, drinking fountains, and even separate cemeteries. Throughout the Progressive Era and even after World War I and World War II, minorities who were considered to be not white, especially African Americans but also Asians, the American Indian nations, and Latino/a peoples were systematically denied the right to vote, suffered discrimination in employment and housing, and were subjected to mob violence. *Plessy v. Ferguson* was a decision that governed the lives of many minorities for nearly sixty years. The failure of Reconstruction (1863-1877) and the success of *Plessy v. Ferguson* made the Niagara Movement, the National Association for the Advancement of Colored People and the Legal and Education Defense Fund (LDF) that grew out of the NAACP necessary.

THE NIAGARA MOVEMENT

An early attempt to organize a movement to counter the setbacks in civil and political rights suffered by African Americans in the Post-Reconstruction era occurred in July 1905 when "twenty-nine Negro intellectuals met at Niagara Falls (on Canadian soil, since they were discriminated against in the Buffalo hotel were reservations had been made for the conference)."[9] Led by W. E. B. DuBois, their plan was to build a national organization with offices throughout the United States that would combat Booker T. Washington's policies that they considered to be too gradualist and too conciliatory. They felt the need for an organization that would combat the various forms of segregation and discrimination African Americans were increasingly facing on a day-to-day basis. At the end of the three-day conference, the group issued its "Declaration of Principles of the Niagara Movement." Under its nineteen headings, the "Declaration" provided not only what the members' complaints were but also what their commitments and duties were.[10]

The members of the conference opened with the theme of progress and the accomplishments of African Americans during Reconstruction. The main three themes coincide with Eric Foner's observation that family, church, and education comprised the fundamental framework developed in the Reconstruction period that formed the basis for the Black Power and Civil Rights Movements in the 1960s.[11] The end of slavery allowed African Americans to control family relations, to strengthen their home life as well as individual and collective ties to each other. Strengthening the family included the ability to buy property as well as the ability to protect it. Family life was closely related to the church. Religion was an important aspect of African American communal life during slavery. The church was a forum for discourse and the center of intellectual and spiritual life. Reconstruction advanced the ability of the church to serve both as a community resource and as the venue where political concerns were considered and plans of action agreed upon. African American churches produced eloquent spokesmen for the rights of African Americans. For example, it has been observed that it was not all unusual that the meetings held during the Montgomery bus boycott "were held in church buildings, and were presided over by ministers."[12]

The Declaration of the Principles of the Niagara Movement

Religion was closely tied to education. Denied a formal or informal education blacks long sought avenues to secure literacy and advancement. In the late eighteenth century free blacks in the North created mutual benefit associations to provide schooling for their children. Reconstruction reinforced the effort to support learning in the arts and literature. The conference attendees maintained that these signs of progress were a refutation of the assaults on black intelligence and capacity advanced by those who had dismantled Reconstruction. It was a "demonstration of constructive and executive ability in the conduct of great religious, economic and educational institutions," in the words of the Declaration.[13] The nineteen principles in the Declaration were arranged around three themes:

1. social issues and objectives;
2. economic conditions and their remedy; and
3. political concerns and strategies to resolve problems.

Social Issues and Objectives

Education was a central pillar of hope in terms of accomplishing the social objective of equality in society. The Niagara Movement stood solidly behind the expansion of free, public, compulsory education. Participants in the Niagara Movement were concerned with the lack of high school and college opportunities for African American children, especially in the South. "High school training should be adequately provided for all, and college training should not be the monopoly of class or race in any section of our common country," they asserted. They urged the black community to demand advanced education including "well-equipped trade and technical schools for the training of artisans, and the need of adequate and liberal endowment for a few institutions of higher education." Education, they maintained should be extended to the public so that informed opinions could be formed on the subject of civil "rights, republican government, and human brotherhood." They noted with alarm that knowledge of the principles of the country seemed to be in a state of "regression," and "we pray God that this nation will not degenerate into a mob of boasters and oppressors, but rather will return to the faith of the fathers, that all men were created free and equal, with certain unalienable rights."

The movement was also concerned with child welfare issues popularized by the Juvenile Court movement of the Progressive era. They favored "orphanages and farm schools for dependent children, juvenile reformatories for delinquents, and the abolition of the dehumanizing convict-lease system." They clearly sided with educational and rehabilitative solutions to dependency and delinquency over punitive incarceration. In terms of health and welfare, it was stressed that all children should be raised in decent housing and in safe locations where they could grow up healthy "in physical and moral cleanliness."

Economic Conditions and Their Remedy

Clearly, economic discrimination prohibited African Americas from achieving their social goals. Freed from slavery many blacks in the South were reduced to tenant farmers, which "amounts to peonage and virtual slavery." Black labors as well as efforts toward establishing black small business were crushed. "Everywhere," they noted, "American prejudice, helped often by iniquitous laws, is making it more difficult for Negro-Americans to earn a decent living." Their analysis of labor issues was very sophisticated, identifying the "development of two opposite classes of men," managers and owners and exploited laborers. The problem was that the laboring classes were also divided with white unionized workers in opposition to a surplus labor force of strikebreakers those hired only under emergency circumstances. This practice, they correctly identified, afforded black workers with "neither protection nor permanent employment," The practice, in fact, served to rouse the ire of labor unions who proceeded to "boycott and oppressing thousands of their fellow-toilers, simply because they are black." They concluded that "these methods have accentuated and will accentuate the war of labor capital, and they are disgraceful to both sides." African Americans, they noted, were doomed to poverty by these configurations. This combination of ideology and overtly discriminatory policies constitute an important aspect of George M. Fredrickson's identification of this era as overtly racist.

Political Concerns and Strategies to Resolve Problems

The difficult racialized politics of the day held center stage for protest and complaint as well as a target for activism and change. The collapse of the Thirteenth, Fourteenth, and Fifteenth Amendments due to a lack of enforcement resulted in the loss of suffrage for African Americans. The Niagara Movement rejected the overt violence of segregation and rejected paternalism as an aspect of this same violence. "We believe that no man is so good, intelligent, or wealthy as to be entrusted wholly with the welfare of his neighbor." They demanded just rewards for accomplishments. Courts, including the activities and decision of judges and juries, were admonished for their partial and self-serving verdicts. Segregation in the "church of Christ" was singled out as "wrong, unchristian, and disgraceful to the twentieth century civilization."

The people were called on to protest and agitate against these circumstances, not just for African Americans but for all citizens: "We demand upright judges in courts, juries selected without discrimination on account of color and the same measure of punishment and the same efforts at reformation for blacks as well as white offenders." Uneven power was the issue. "We repudiate the monstrous doctrine that the oppressor should be the sole authority as to the rights of the oppressed."

The strategies to change these circumstances were through complaints, agitation, protest, and demands. "We refuse to allow the impression to remain that the Negro-American assents to inferiority, is submissive under oppression and apologetic before insults. Through helplessness we may submit, but the voice of protest of ten million Americans must never cease to assail the ears of their fellows, so long as America is unjust." Injustice included the creation of the color line which was discrimination simply "based on race or color...which is barbarous, we care not how hallowed it be by custom, expediency, or prejudice." They acknowledged that "differences made on account of ignorance, immorality, or disease are legitimate methods of fighting evil" while they argued that "discriminations based simply and solely on physical peculiarities, place of birth, color of skin, are relics of that unreasoning savagery of which the world is and ought to be thoroughly ashamed."

The Declaration defined oppression in uncompromising terms, noting the tendency of whites to ignore the issues and to contribute to them through ignorance, inattention, and perverseness. Blacks faced legitimate problems through no fault of their own. They were "stolen, ravished and degraded, struggling up through difficulties and oppression." These circumstances are rejected by whites who respond in a manner that is so inappropriate that it is outrageous. When African Americans need sympathy, they receive criticism. If they need help, find hindrance. When they need protection, they are faced with mob-violence. When a person needs justice, they are given charity. The need for justice is met with "cowardice and apology." Those who "need bread and are given stones." "The nation," they observe, "will never stand justified before God until these things are changed."

The answer had to be in social activism, "for to ignore, overlook, or apologize for these wrongs is to prove ourselves unworthy of freedom." The movement then was not just about black people but all people. "Persistent manly agitation is the way to liberty, and toward this goal the Niagara Movement has started and asks the co-operation of men of all races." This recognizes that the road to redemption is not just a path for African Americans but is one shared by all people. The accomplishments of Reconstruction were not won alone: "with deep thankfulness the help of our fellowmen from the abolitionist down to those who to-day still stand for equal opportunity," is recognized. Certain duties were pledged that are also universal: the duty to vote; to respect the rights of others; to work; to obey the laws; to be clean and orderly; to send our children to school; [and] to respect ourselves, even as we respect others." The Declaration ends with the solemn transmission: "this statement, compliant and prayer we do submit to the American people and Almighty God—1905."[14]

Spread of the Movement

By September 1905, DuBois, was able to report in J. Max Barber's *Voice of the Negro* that the Niagara Movement consisted of "54 men resident in 18 states of the United States." The membership included "ministers, lawyers, editors, business men and teachers." He reported that "the honor of founding the organization" belonged to F. L. McGhee, that C. C. Bentley "planned the method of organization," and that W. M. Trotter "put the backbone into the platform." DuBois then communicated the principles of the constitution of the Niagara Movement. The principles were not only for African Americans but for all Americans. The principles effectively constituted what later was seen to be the American the creed. The principles included:

a. freedom of speech and criticism,
b. an unfettered and unsubsidized press,
c. manhood suffrage,
d. the abolition of all caste distinctions based simply on race and color,
e. the recognition of the principle of human brotherhood as a practical present creed,
f. The recognition of the highest and best training as the monopoly of no class or race,
g. belief in the dignity of labor, and
h. a united effort to these ideals under wise and courageous leadership.[15]

The Niagara Movement's second meeting was held in August (16th to 19th) 1906 in Harper's Ferry, West Virginia, the site of John Brown's raid. At that meeting, DuBois once again enumerated the movement's demands for true equality and for civil rights. While violence was rejected, homage to John Brown was paid: "We do not believe in violence, neither in the despised violence of the raid nor the lauded violence of the soldier, nor barbarous violence of the mob, but we do believe in John Brown, in that incarnate spirit of justice, that hatred of a lie, that willingness to sacrifice money, reputation, and life itself on the alter of right. And here on the scene of John Brown's martyrdom we consecrate ourselves, our honor, our property to the final emancipation of the race which John Brown died to make free."[16]

The third meeting of the Niagara Movement was held in August (26th to 29th) in Boston where once again the demands for civil rights were articulated as well as a commitment to democratic processes. Then, a call was made to "the 500,000 free black voters of the North" to "vote with the white laboring classes, remembering that the cause of labor is the cause of black men, and the black man's cause is labor's own."[17] In the following months, meetings were held in Washington, D. C., Baltimore, Maryland, New York City, Minneapolis, Minnesota, and Cleveland, Ohio. In the following year the members of the Niagara Movement met in Oberlin, Ohio. That was its last meeting. According to Gunnar Myrdal, the Niagara Movement "never grew to be anything more than a feeble junto." It seems that "it was not discreet for ambitious young Negroes to belong to this movement, for "it had against it Booker T. Washington and all his Negro and white friends."[18] It did, however, lay the "groundwork" for the founding of the National Association for the Advancement of Colored People (NAACP).[19] The Niagara Movement's agenda and many of its members became part of the NAACP.

THE NATIONAL ASSOCIATION FOR THE
ADVANCEMENT OF COLORED PEOPLE

The founding of the National Association for the Advancement of Colored People was occasioned by the attention given by the press to the race riot that occurred in the summer of 1908 in Springfield, Illinois. Scores of African Americans were killed or wounded, and others were chased out of the city. The writer William English Walling issued "a challenge to the nation." Walling maintained "there was a need for a revival of the spirit of the Abolitionists to win liberty and justice for the Negro in America." Mary White Ovington answered the challenge. In January 1909, she met with Walling and Dr. Henry Moskowitz in New York City where the plans were made that soon led to the formation of the NAACP. Oswald Garrison Villard, president of the *New York Evening Post* drafted the call for a conference to be held on the one hundredth anniversary of Abraham Lincoln's birth, February 12, 1909. Fifty-three people signed the call that asked "all believers in democracy to join in a national conference for the discussion of present evils, the voicing of protests, and the renewal of the struggle for civil and political liberty." Six were African Americans: "William L. Bulkley, a school principal of New York, Mrs. Ida B. Wells-Barnett of Chicago, Dr. Dubois of Atlanta, Rev. Francis J. Grimké of Washington, Bishop Alexander Walters and Dr. J. Milton Waldron of Washington." Jane Addams of Hull House in Chicago, the philosopher John Dewey, William Dean Howells, Lincoln Steffens, Florence Kelley, and Charles Edward Russell were among the forty-seven white signers of the call.

Founding the NAACP

The call was answered, and on May 31 and June 1, 1909 a meeting was held in New York. Less than two weeks after the 1909 conference, DuBois reported that observers of the meeting must have "looked into each other's faces with apprehension" when they witnessed "some two or three hundred persons of all shades assembled in the United Charities building." Dubois noted: "the conference did not look dangerous." Well known white participants included: Florence Kelley, Anne Garlin Spencer, Oswald Garrison Villard, William Hayes Ward, Charles Edward Russell, Lillian D. Wald, John E. Miholland, and Rabbi Stephen S. Wise. The question was less about the presence of whites than the presence of blacks and whether they were capable of acting in their own self-interest. DuBois noted the necessary qualities as being "earnest and unselfish" and capable of "the poise and balance necessary for a great forward movement of practical and efficient betterment?" Perhaps not surprisingly, Booker T. Washington, was absent, while among those present were J. M. Waldron, Bishop Alexander Walters, Monroe Trotter, J.M. Barbaer, W. L.Bulkeley, Ida Wells-Barnett, W. A. Emilau, R. R. Right, Jr., and L. M. Hershaw—all persons who mean much within the veil, but are less known without."[20]

DuBois reported that before turning to a discussion of the importance of the right to vote and Ida Wells-Barnett's discussion of the thousands of people (3,284 to be exact) who had been "murdered by mobs in this country in twenty-five years," the conference began with emphasizing the very points around which the real race argument centers today, *viz.*, from the standpoint of modern science, are Negroes men?" He reported that Professor B. G. Wilder of Cornell University and Professor Livingston Farrand of Columbia University clearly indicated, "that the whole argument by which Negroes have been pronounced absolutely and inevitably inferior to whites is utterly without scientific basis."[21]

At the 1909 conference DuBois made the case for voting rights and equality of economic opportunity for African Americans—concerns that continue to the present day. He argued that the practice of training two sets of workers and extending the franchise to one (white) and not the other (African American) was a form of "madness" that would result in "conflict and oppression." It would lead to a nation "half slave and half free," and then, he suggested, "either the slave will rise through blood or the freeman will sink."[22] At the same meeting, J. Max Barber argued that politics was more important than economics, that the solution of the race problem was the franchise:

> If you will give a man the right to vote, if you will put the ballot in his hands, if you will give him the right to protect himself, and if he will see that the proper man goes to Congress, a man who will see that American citizens are protected in their rights, then you will get these other things. If you want to solve the race problem, you have to get men who have the right to vote, to say who shall be the governor or the judge, with the right to sit on juries to protect themselves, the right to punish sheriffs for doing what they have done in office.[23]

George Frazier Miller argued that the solution was for African Americans to abandon their loyalty to the Republican Party and turn to Socialism, a system in which "everyone has the right to work and every man the full reward of his labors."[24] Miller's argument was not persuasive. It was not until the era of Franklin D. Roosevelt that African Americans began to turn to the Democratic Party in significant numbers. In the early 1940s when the Communist Party was active in the United States and actively recruited African Americans, it "continually criticized the NAACP for its lack of radicalism."[25]

J. Milton Waldron urged that the position of President Taft who urged the African American to make himself "useful to the business interests of the community and keep out of sight and out of public office where he is by reason of his numbers or prominence offensive to white people" be rejected. To follow the advice of President Taft, according to Waldron, "may make slipshod servants of Negroes but it will not train them into good citizens or noble men." Like Miller, he did not want African Americans who had the franchise to vote automatically for the Republican Party. He wanted the African American who had the franchise to exercise his (women did not yet have the franchise) right to vote "not as a partisan, for his political salvation in the future depends upon his voting for men and measures, rather than with any particular party."[26]

Waldron agreed that chattel slavery was no longer legal but insisted "the practice in thought and speech of looking at Negroes from the chattel plane still persists." For Waldron there was no question about what was needed to solve the race problem. Nothing less than true equality was required. According to Waldron:

In the first place we claim that the early friends of the Negro grasped the true solution, which is that his needs and possibilities are the same as those of the other members of the human family; that he must be educated not only for industrial efficiency and for private gain, but to share in the duties and responsibilities of a free democracy; that he must have equality of rights, for is own sake, for the sake of the human race and for the perpetuity of free institutions. America will not have learned the full lesson of her system of human slavery until she realizes that a rigid caste system is inimical to the progress of the human race and to the perpetuity of democratic government.

Waldron explained that the "gulf" the "old slave oligarchy" between African Americans and "free white labor" had persisted and that it could only be eliminated when it was realized that the interests of laborers and of African Americans who were also laborers were one and the same. He rejected the claim that the African American had to "look to the business men of the South alone for protection and recognition of his rights."[27]

At the 1909 meeting in New York a committee was formed. That committee then went on to hold several "mass meetings" that led to another conference in May 1910 in New York. At the second New York meeting the NAACP was formed with Moorfield Storey as its chair. W. E. B. DuBois was named Director of Publicity and Research and editor of the organization's journal, *The Crisis*. Its leadership, African American and white, included the entire political spectrum, "from socialist intellectuals like W. E. B. Dubois to politically conservative Republicans like Moorefield Storey of Boston (a past president of the American Bar Association)."[28]

The editorial board[29] promised that the editorial page of the *Crisis* "will stand for the rights of men, irrespective of color or race, for the highest ideals of American democracy, and for reasonable but earnest and persistent attempts to gain these rights and realize these ideals."[30] Its first editorial announced that its purpose was "to set forth those facts and arguments which show the danger of race prejudice, particularly as manifested today toward colored people."[31] By 1918, the circulation of the *Crisis* was 100,000, considerably more than the 1,000 copies that were sold after its first issue.[32]

THE LEGAL REDRESS COMMITTEE AND THE LEGAL DEFENSE AND EDUCATION FUND

From its very beginning the NAACP focused on "securing the basic citizenship rights guaranteed by the Fourteenth and Fifteenth Amendments of the Constitution."[33] In practical terms, its goal was to end all legally required and enforced segregation. That meant reversing all that *Plessy* allowed. During its first year, the NAACP sought to secure better economic opportunities for African Americans, better police protection in the South, and carried on, through the *Crisis*, its campaign against lynching, a campaign that would last for at least half a century. The NAACP continually lobbied for executive, judicial, and legislative actions and decisions that would end the discrimination African Americans experienced throughout the nation. Its strategy was to use investigation and exposure through *The Crisis* to keep issues before the public. Its Legal Redress Committee did enjoy some success with the courts. By 1923, the Legal Redress Committee's attorneys, white and black, achieved three important successes before the United States Supreme Court. In 1915, in *Guinn v. United States* the Court ruled that the grandfather clauses in the Maryland and Oklahoma constitutions to be in violation of the Fifteenth Amendment and therefore void. The grandfather clauses, aimed at African Americans, specified that those whose grandfathers had not voted in an election were not eligible to vote. In 1917, in *Buchanan v. Warley* the Court overturned a Louisville, Kentucky ordinance that specified that African Americans could only reside in designated sections of the city. In 1923, in *Moore v. Dempsey* the NAACP successfully argued that an African American who had been convicted of murder in an Arkansas court was entitled to a new trial because African Americans were not allowed to serve on the jury.

While the successes of the Legal Redress Committee were significant, they should not be construed to mean that the life conditions of African Americans were significantly improving. 1915 was the year that the Legal Redress Committee prevailed in *Guinn* but it was also the year that the movie *Birth of a Nation* appeared. Based on Thomas Dixon's writings, "it told a most sordid and obviously distorted story of black emancipation, enfranchisement, and debaucher of white womanhood. And it did more than any other single thing to nurture and promote the myth of black domination and debauchery during Reconstruction."[34] Just a few years earlier, President Wilson, who during his campaign for the presidency claimed that he wanted "justice done to the colored people in every matter," issued an executive order that established segregated lunchrooms and rest rooms for federal employees in the nation's capital.[35]

The Post-World-War-II Climate

In 1940 the Legal Redress Committee gave way to the Legal Defense and Educational Fund, Inc. (LDF), with Thurgood Marshall as its chief counsel. Unlike the Legal Redress Committee it qualified for tax-exempt status, making contributions to it were tax deductible. While it had close ties to the NAACP, it was functionally and legally an independent entity. Clearly, LDF's most notable success was the 1954 *Brown* decision that declared racially segregated schools to be unequal and therefore unconstitutional. The *Brown* case was built on a series of cases that NAACP and LDF attorneys successfully argued during the previous decades, at a favorable time. In the post-World-War-II era the persistent efforts of LDF's attorney's was significantly aided by a changed political climate. As Jack Greenberg observed, "international and political developments inspired hope."[36] Given that 900,000 African Americans served in the armed forces in World II, it became increasingly difficult to justify denying them the rights and freedom for which they had fought, often with distinction. It became increasingly difficult and embarrassing for the United States to object to European colonialism while the United States itself treated people of color in ways not significantly different from how colonial powers treated the non-white people they colonized. The nation's adversary in the Cold War, the Soviet Union, took every opportunity to point out to the rest of the world how the United States treated people of color. Whatever credibility scientific racism had was all but completely undermined as the nation learned what Hitler's Nazi Germany had done in its name. When the cases that constituted *Brown* were argued, President Truman's solicitor general filed a friend of the court brief that reminded the Court of the nation's differences with the Soviet Union and suggested that "It is in the context of the present world struggle between freedom and tyranny that the problem of racial discrimination must be viewed."[37]

Government Action: The President's Committee on Civil Rights

Even before the end of World War II, there were significant signs that governmental action against specific racial groups was beginning to be questioned at the highest levels. In 1943, the Supreme Court did uphold a case that placed curfews on Japanese-Americans but also expressed the view that "distinctions between citizens solely because of their ancestry are by their very nature odious to a free people whose institutions are founded upon the doctrine of equality."[38] In 1944, the Court allowed the removal of Japanese-Americans from the West Coast but did indicate "all legal restrictions which curtail the civil rights of a single racial group are immediately suspect." Such restrictions, it indicated, were not necessarily unconstitutional but had to be subjected "to the most rigid scrutiny."[39]

After the War (December 1946), President Truman appointed the President's Committee on Civil Rights. Its charge was: "To inquire into and to determine whether and in what respect current law-enforcement measures and the authority and means possessed by Federal, State, and local governments may be strengthened and improved to safeguard the civil rights of the people."[40] Even before this Committee issued its report, Truman used his office to campaign for the end of Jim Crow. He became the first president to accept an invitation to address the NAACP. On June 29, 1947, on the steps of the Lincoln Memorial he effectively told the 10,000 people in his audience that it was time to end all that Jim Crow allowed. As David McCullough observed, he wanted an end to "the whole caste system based on race or color."[41]

The Committee's report, "To Secure These Rights," issued in 1947 clearly stated how extensive and brutal discrimination was. In 1946 six blacks were lynched by mobs. Twenty-two others were rescued from such mobs and all but one of the would-be victims were black. In spite of this lawlessness, members of lynch mobs were rarely arrested or prosecuted. If prosecuted they were rarely convicted. Police brutality in the South was legendary. Prisoners were subjected to illegal searches, beatings, pistol whippings, and other third-degree interrogation tactics. There was no guarantee of a fair trial in some communities due to the fact that minorities were excluded from legal counsel and could not serve on juries. Voting rights were unconstitutionally restricted in many states in ways that prevented or minimized black participation. Inventions such as poll taxes or requirements that prospective voters interpret the state constitution to the satisfaction of local officials were used to disfranchise blacks. The voting electorate was kept small and unrepresentative. In the 1944 election only 18.3 percent of potential voters in the eight poll-tax states had voted, compared to 68.7 percent in the other forty states.

In spite of legal proclamations, discrimination in the armed forces persisted. Blacks were barred from enlistment in any branch of the Marine Corps except as stewards. Fully eighty percent of black sailors were cooks or stewards. In the United States Army, African Americans were limited to ten percent of the population in all of its sectors. Only a tiny proportion of officers in any of the services were black.

Unfair trade practices limited employment. When hired, often wage discrimination occurred. Whites and blacks with the same education were paid differently for the same work, just as men and women were similarly unfairly paid. Blacks were routinely excluded from hotels, restaurants, and other places of public accommodation making it difficult to travel. Health care facilities discriminated against African Americans. Many hospitals did not admit black patients or permit black doctors on their staff. Most medical schools barred African Americans from applying. "Medical schools graduate approximately 5,000 students a year, but only about 145 of these are Negro. And of these 145, 130 are from two Negro schools."

School segregation, was enforced by law in seventeen states and the District of Columbia, "Whatever test is used—expenditure per pupil, teachers' salaries, the number of pupils per teacher, transportation of students, adequacy of school buildings and educational equipment, length of school term, extent of curriculum—Negro [sic] students are invariably at a disadvantage.[42]

Civil Rights as an Issue for All Americans

The President's Committee concluded that civil rights was an issue not just for African Americans and Jews but for all Americans. Among its recommendations was the elimination of segregation, based on race, color, creed, or national origin. Congress was to enact a law stating that discrimination and segregation, based on race, color, creed, or national origin, in the rendering of all public services by the national government is contrary to public policy. Congress was to further enact a law prohibiting discrimination or segregation in interstate transportation. Similarly discrimination and segregation were to be outlawed "in all public or publicly supported hospitals, parks, recreational facilities, housing projects, welfare agencies, penal institutions, and concessions of public property." Restrictive covenants in housing were to be outlawed. Finally, it was recommended that "equal access to places of public accommodation" be granted.[43]

Truman did not hesitate to act on his Committee's recommendations. The day after *To Secure These Rights* was issued, October 30, 1947, the United States Solicitor General supported the LDF's claim that "court enforcement of restrictive covenants was unconstitutional" by filing a friend-of-the court brief.[44] The executive branch of the nation's government was now clearly on the side of those who sought an end to racial segregation. On February 1, 1948, President Truman sent a message to Congress, requesting "comprehensive civil rights laws, adequate to the needs of the day, and demonstrating our continuing faith in the free way of life." Specifically, he wanted an end to the poll tax that effectively prohibited African Americans from voting in the seven states of the Old South, legislation that would make lynching a federal crime, an end to discrimination in all forms of interstate travel, and a Fair Employment Practices Commission that would have the power to end discrimination not only by employers but also by labor unions. He also wanted Congress to consider the claims of Japanese Americans who had been confined to camps during World War II "solely because of their racial origin." He also indicated that he had ordered the Secretary of Defense to end discrimination in the armed forces.[45]

On July 28, 1948, Truman acted to end racial discrimination in the armed forces when he issued Executive Order 9981. In that order he stated:

> It is hereby declared to be the policy of the President that there shall be equality of treatment and opportunity for all persons in the armed services without regard to race, color, religion, or national origin. This policy shall be put into effect as rapidly as possible, having due regard to the time required to effectuate any necessary changes without impairing efficiency or morale.[46]

Executive Order 9981 also banned racial discrimination in federal employment. Truman also ordered the Federal Housing Administration to end its practice of not insuring homes in areas that were racially mixed.[47] Congress did not act on Truman's Committee's recommendations. However, those recommendations were implemented in 1964 and 1965 when Congress passed the Civil Rights Act and the Voting Rights Act.

Court Rulings: Mendez v. Westminister

The rulings of a United States District Court and the United States Circuit Court of Appeals (Ninth Circuit) in the *Mendez v. Westminister*[48] cases (1946 and 1947, respectively) are significant not only because they show that the segregation of those considered not to be white was indeed a national problem but also because the judicial decisions show that the climate that permitted discrimination was changing. Gonzalo Mendez, William Guzman, Frank Palomino, Thomas Estrada, and Lorenzo Ramirez, all citizens of the United States claimed on behalf of their children and "some 5,000 persons similarly affected, all of Mexican or Latin descent" that the school authorities' practice of requiring such children to attend segregated schools denied them rights guaranteed by the Fourteenth Amendment. In its decision the Circuit Court acknowledged that there were "other discriminatory customs, shown by the evidence, existing in the defendant school districts as to pupils of Mexican descent and extraction" but declined to discuss them. However, it did rule, "the allegations of the complaint (petition) have been established sufficiently to justify injunctive relief against all defendants, restraining further discriminatory practices against the pupils of Mexican descent in the public schools of defendant school districts." The school districts appealed the decision, and on April 14, 1947 the United States Circuit Court of Appeals upheld the District Court's decision. The rulings in the *Mendez v. Westminister* case(s) are interesting because the courts did not rule explicitly against racial segregation. The California Constitution of 1879 as amended in 1943 explicitly allowed segregation of American Indian, Chinese, Japanese and "Mongolian" children in its public schools according to section 8003:

> The governing board of any school district may establish separate schools for Indian children, excepting children of Indians who are wards of the United States Government and children of all other Indians who are descendants of the original American Indians of the United States, and for children of Chinese, Japanese, or Mongolian parentage.

This stipulation was made more onerous in that the next section, 8004, further stipulated that other schools could not make up for the exclusion by admitting the children. Law required segregation:

When separate schools are established for Indian children or children of Chinese, Japanese, or Mongolian parentage, the Indian children or children of Chinese, Japanese, or Mongolian parentage shall not be admitted into any other school.[49]

California law allowed the state to require segregation, and the Courts did not question or challenge that. However, California law did not explicitly allow segregation to occur through administrative action, as was the case in the *Mendez* case. Moreover, California law did not specify that school districts had the power to establish separate schools for children of Mexican or Latin parentage.

The Appeals Court in the *Mendez* case(s) avoided ruling on segregation and declined to consider the friend of the court brief filed by Thurgood Marshall, Robert L. Carter, and Loren Miller that argued that the court "should strike out independently on the whole question of segregation, on the ground that recent world stirring events have set men to the reexamination of concepts considered fixed." However, in a footnote (note no. 7) the Appeals Court observed:

it used to be taught that mankind was made up of white, brown, yellow, black and red men. Such divisional designation has little or no adherents among anthropologists or ethnic scientists. A more scholarly nomenclature is Caucasoid, Mongoloid and Negroid, yet this is unsatisfactory as an attempt to collectively sort all mankind into distinct groups.

The Appeals Court did not rule on segregation but the California legislature did. On June 14, 1947, just two months after the Appeals Courts decision, the Governor of California approved the legislatures' act that repealed Sections 8003 and 8004 of the California Education Act. It became law on September 19, 1947.

THE LEGAL DEFENSE FUND AND THE ROAD TO BROWN

Clearly, the Legal Defense Fund's most notable success was the 1954 *Brown* decision. *Brown* was important for what it did and for what it symbolized. It only ruled that racially segregated schools were unequal and therefore unconstitutional but symbolically it signaled an end to Jim Crow and promised the elimination of the color line in all aspects of American life. *Plessy* effectively endorsed white supremacy and the subordination of people of color. *Brown*, at the time, gave hope to those that believed that the subordination of people of color was wrong and should be ended. However, it took years for the National Association for the Advancement of Colored People and the Legal Defense Fund to reach the point where the attorneys had some confidence that they could successfully present arguments that would end racial segregation in American public education. While working to end racial segregation in education, the LDF attorney's were working in other areas and meeting with some success. Their victory in *Smith v. All-wright* (1944) known as the "White Primary Case" gave African-Americans the right to vote in primary elections. In that case Thurgood Marshall and W. J. Durham presented evidence to show that since 1859 only two Republicans had been elected in Texas general elections. Thus, to win a primary election was tantamount to win the general election, and to disallow African-Americans from voting was effectively to allow them to participate in a contest that was already decided. *Smith v. Allwright* that overturned *United States v. Classic* (1935) was important because it established that the right to vote in primary elections was a constitutional right. Political parties could no longer claim that they were private parties and thus not subject to either the Fourteenth or Fifteenth Amendments. Another victory was won on May 3, 1948 when the Supreme Court overturned a 1926 ruling and ruled that courts did not have the authority to enforce covenants that specified to whom property owners could and could not sell their property. Restrictive covenants usually required buyers of property to agree not to ever sell to African Americans or Jews. However, at times such covenants included Asians, Mongolians, Turks, and Indians.

The Margold Report

The road to *Brown* can easily be traced back to 1930 and the Margold Report. The Margold Report was the result of a small committee headed by Nathan Margold. It set the course the LDF attorneys were to follow. However, it was, as Greenberg related, followed with "frequent deviation." When the report was written, there was no question that educational facilities and opportunities provided for African Americans were far from being equal, but Margold argued that the action against segregation must be bold:

> . . . it would be a great mistake to fritter away our limited resources on sporadic attempts to force making of equal divisions of school funds in the few instances where such attempts might be expected to succeed. Such an effort would eliminate only a minor part of discrimination and only temporarily. It would not establish new principles or have any general effect. . . . *We should be leaving wholly untouched the very essence of the existing evils.* If we boldly challenge the constitutional validity of segregation if and when accompanied irremediably by discrimination, we can strike directly at the most prolific sources of discrimination.[50]

Margold's argument was that segregation was unconstitutional because when segregation existed, inequality existed. He believed that an effective argument against segregation could be based on Supreme Court's earlier decision in *Yick Wo v. Hopkins* (1886) when the Court held that a San Francisco ordinance was unconstitutional because it was clearly aimed at Chinese and deprived them of their constitutional rights.

LDF attorneys could argue that the educational facilities and programs provided for people of color, mostly African Americans, were in fact not equal. Demonstrating inequality in educational facilities was not a formidable task. In some places there were schools for whites but none for African Americans. In other places there were separate schools but by every measure they were clearly not equal. In 1940 in the South the annual expenditure for white students was more than twice as much as for African American students. Expenditures for African American students increased during the 1940s, but as late as 1952 the expenditure for white students was almost fifty percent more than it was for African Americans.[51] It could also attack *Plessy* directly, that *Plessy* was wrong, and that separate was unequal and therefore unconstitutional. Attacking *Plessy* directly was more problematic than arguing that the separate facilities were in fact not equal. Moreover, a ruling by the Supreme Court that *Plessy* was wrong would have meant that the government had no right to consider race and no right to decide to which race a person belonged. That was explicitly stated in the *Plessy* decision: "The power to assign to a particular coach obviously implies the power to determine to which race the passenger belongs, as well as the power to determine who, under the laws of the particular State, is to be deemed a white and who a colored person . . ."[52] Moreover, it was believed that the cost of providing truly equal education would be so great that it would bring an end to segregation.

LDF attorney's also had to decide whether to begin at the bottom or the top of the educational ladder. Margold's focus was on elementary schools and high schools, but LDF's campaign began at the top of the educational ladder, with graduate and professional schools. As Greenberg reported, "higher education remained the model case of inequality: Whites had graduate and professional schools and blacks had virtually nothing."[53] In 1947 when LDF was focusing its attention on the lack of equal educational opportunity in higher education, African Americans comprised ten percent of the population but received only one percent of advanced degrees. Of the 3,375 doctoral degrees awarded, only eight were awarded to African Americans and integrated universities awarded these.[54]

By the time *Brown* was initially argued in 1952 LDF had won a number of cases in the 1930s and 1940s that they believed established important precedents, although they had failed to secure a direct ruling on *Plessy*. In these cases the NAACP and LDF attorneys were arguing that African-Americans were being denied equal educational facilities and opportunities to which they were legally entitled.

More Court Action

Pearson v. Murray (1936)

In 1936, Donald Murray wanted to study law at the state's law school that was reserved for whites; there was no law school for African Americans. Maryland wanted to award him a scholarship to enable him to attend an out-of-state law school, but he wanted to study in state. NAACP/LDF attorneys, Thurgood Marshall and Charles Houston won the case in the Maryland State court. Because the injury to Murray was "present and personal," he was entitled to immediate relief. Maryland had two choices: either admit him or immediately establish a law school for African Americans. Clearly, Maryland could not immediately establish a new law school. It could either admit Murray or appeal the case. However, Maryland did not appeal the case and admitted Murray to the University of Maryland Law School. It was a victory but it did not establish a national precedent.

Missouri ex rel. Gaines v. Canada (1938)

Lloyd Gaines applied to Missouri's all-white law school and was denied admission; there was no law school for African Americans. The NAACP attorneys won the case in the United States Supreme Court. However, Lloyd Gaines disappeared, and thus Missouri did not have to admit him. Subsequently, Missouri established a law school for African Americans.

Sipuel v. Oklahoma State Regents (1948)

Ada Lois Sipuel sought admission to Oklahoma's all-white law school, and she was denied. In 1946 the LDF's attorneys failed to secure a court order that would require her admission. The Oklahoma State Supreme Court denied her admission and ruled that she should have asked for a separate law school for African Americans. The court also indicated that she could have a scholarship to attend an out-of-state laws school. LDF appeared to have won in the United States Supreme Court. It ruled "the State [Oklahoma] must provide [legal] education to her in conformity with the equal protection clause of the Fourteenth Amendment and provide it *as soon as* it does for applicants of any other group." However, the Oklahoma court ordered that "'unless and until the separate school of law for Negroes . . . is established and ready to function' authorities were required to enroll her in the University of Oklahoma *or* 'not enroll any applicant of any group in said class until said separate school is established and ready to function.'" The Oklahoma authorities then roped off a section of the state capitol and declared it to be a separate law school for Ms. Sipuel. LDF went back to the Supreme Court with the hope that the Court would order an end to segregation. However, the Supreme Court indicated that it only ordered Oklahoma to treat Ms. Sipuel equally, that it did not order Oklahoma to admit her to the all-white law school.[55] The Supreme Court effectively refused to rule on *Plessy*.

Sipuel was instructive for LDF. It taught LDF that any attempt to win by arguing that racial segregation was unconstitutional "presented a big risk." Subsequently, LDF argued not only that segregation was unconstitutional but also that the education provided for African Americans was not equal to that provided for whites and that the segregation had damaging psychological and educational effects.[56] In 1949 the Oklahoma legislature acted to allow African Americans to enroll in white professional and graduate schools if no such programs were offered in African American schools. Although the legislature specified that such students were to be segregated, Ms. Sipuel was admitted to the law school and was not segregated from the other students.[57]

Sweatt v. Painter (1950) and McLaurin v. Oklahoma State Regents (1950).

These were argued together before the Supreme Court. *Sweatt* was occasioned when the University of Texas Law School refused to admit Herbert Marion Sweatt. In *Sweatt* LDF presented evidence to demonstrate that higher education facilities and opportunities provided for African Americans were not nearly equal to those provided for whites:

> White plant was valued at more than $72,000,000, black at $4,000,000; per capita black investment was one-quarter of that for whites. Whites had 106 fields of specialization, blacks only 49, including mattress making, auto mechanics, carpeting, laundering, and dry cleaning. Whites could get graduate degrees in 40 fields, blacks in 13. Texas gave whites 212 doctorates between 1940 and 1945; no black institution qualified to grant a doctorate. The University of Texas library had more than 750,00 volumes, and the African-American school had about 82,000.[58]

Rather than admit Sweatt to the all-white law school, Texas established a separate school for Sweatt in a basement of a building. LDF presented evidence to demonstrate that the hastily created school was not equal to the school to which Sweatt sought admission:

> The University of Texas [law school] had 65,000 volumes, the black school none of its own. The university had sixteen full-time faculty, the black school none, other than three of the white school's faculty who were supposed to teach at the black school. The university had 850 students; if Sweatt had gone to the black school he would have been alone. The university had a moot court, legal aid clinic, law review, honor society, and scholarship fund. The black school had none of these.[59]

Besides arguing that the two schools were clearly not equal, LDF argued that placing African Americans in separate schools that were never equal was unconstitutional because it clearly discriminated against African Americans. That argument was based on *Yick Wo v. Hopkins*, an argument proposed by Margold in 1930. As it did in *Sweatt* and in *Sipuel*, LDF used materials from anthropologists, psychologists, and sociologists to argue that segregation damaged those who were segregated and that segregation was therefore unconstitutional. Thurgood Marshall was directly attacking the separate but equal doctrine established in *Plessy*. He declared: "They can build an exact duplicate but if it is segregated, it is unequal."[60]

LDF explicitly asked the Court to overrule *Plessy*. The Supreme Court ruled for Sweatt but it did not overturn *Plessy*. It acknowledged that the tangible as well as the "qualities that are incapable of objective measurement"—"reputation of faculty, experience of the administration, position and influence of the alumni, standing in the community, traditions and prestige" of the separate school for Sweatt were not equal to the University of Texas Law school.[61]

The Case of George McLaurin

George McLaurin was an African American schoolteacher who applied to the University of Oklahoma's School of Education graduate program. In 1948 a three-judge federal court ruled that Oklahoma was in violation of the U. S. Constitution because Oklahoma had no opportunities for African Americans to earn graduate degrees. However, The University of Oklahoma was not ordered to admit McLaurin because the governor sent a letter to the court indicating that he would propose legislation to allow African Americans to attend white universities. The governor may have been responding to political pressure, for earlier in the year approximately a thousand of the twelve-thousand student body at the University of Oklahoma protested segregation by burning a copy of the Fourteenth Amendment and sending the ashes to President Truman.[62] Even before the law was enacted McLaurin was admitted, but restrictions were placed upon him. He was not permitted to sit in the classroom with other students but had to look into the classroom from a small room next to the classroom where the other students sat. In June 1949 Oklahoma legislated that African Americans were to be admitted to professional programs in white schools if no such program existed for African Americans but they were to be segregated from the other students. By the time *McLaurin* reached the Supreme Court, McLaurin had a seat in the classroom, but every attempt was made to segregate him within the institution. In the classroom, the library, and the cafeteria he was required to sit in a designated seat.

The Legal Defence Fund believed that *McLaurin* was indeed a segregation case. The LDF won, but the Court did not rule on the constitutionality of *Plessy*. The Court's conclusion was that:

. . . the conditions under which this appellant [McLaurin] is required to receive his education deprive him of his personal and present right to the equal protection of the laws. . . . We hold that under these circumstances the Fourteenth Amendment precludes difference in treatment by the state based upon ace. Appellant, having been admitted to a state supported graduate school, must receive the same treatment at the hands of he states as students of other races.[63]

The Court ruled that the restrictions placed on McLaurin constituted a handicap that not only affected his education but also would affect the education of his students. The argument asserts that as society becomes more complex the need for trained leadership increases and that the appellant's case was the "epitome of that need, for he is attempting to obtain an advanced degree in education, to become, by definition, a leader and trainer of others." The students who would come under his influence were directly affected by the education of their teacher. "Their own education and development will necessarily suffer to the extent that his training is unequal to that of his classmates." Therefore, "state-imposed restrictions which produce such inequalities cannot be sustained.[64]

The Court made a statement about the importance of education in an increasingly complex society. It was a view that was to be found in the *Brown* decision. However, these decisions did not immediately give African Americans access to colleges and universities. In the 1970s LDF was still going to court in its attempts to get the Department of Health Education and Welfare to use the authority Title VI of the Civil Rights Act of 1964 gave it.

After *Sweatt* and *McLaurin* LDF moved from its attack on segregated professional and graduate education to attack segregation at the undergraduate level and in elementary schools and in high schools. While they failed to convince the Court to overturn *Plessy*, they believed they learned from how the Court had been reasoning how to win at the lower levels. They would "go after the intangibles."[65] That meant attacking segregation. By June 1950 LDF had decided "to make desegregation, not equalization, the focus of all future cases."[66]

FROM BROWN TO THE CIVIL RIGHTS ACT

What has come to be known as the *Brown* decision is, in fact, the name that has been given to five school segregation cases that were first argued before the Supreme Court in 1952. Four of the five cases were filed and argued by LDF: *Oliver Brown, et al. v. Board of Education of Topeka, Shawnee County, Kansas, et al.*; *Harry Briggs, Jr. et al. v. R. W. Elliott, et al.* (South Carolina case); *Dorothy E. Davis, et. al. v. County School Board of Prince Edward County, Virginia, et al.*; and *Francis B. Gebhart, et al. v. Ethel Louise Belton, et al.*

(a Delaware case). The fifth case, *Spotswood Thomas Bolling, et al. v. C. Melvin Sharpe, et al.* (a District of Columbia case) was argued by James M. Nabrit, Jr.

On May 17, 1954, Chief Justice Earl Warren read the Court's decision. The most significant part of that decision came very near the end of the decision when Chief Justice Warren announced that "We conclude that in the field of public education the doctrine of 'separate but equal' has no place. Separate educational facilities are inherently unequal." To the surprise of many there was no dissenting opinion; it was a unanimous decision. Almost immediately, the Voice of America broadcast the decision throughout the world in thirty-four different languages.[67] The Court had ruled that even if all "tangible" factors in separate facilities were truly equal, the segregation of "children of the minority group" deprived them of equal educational opportunity. According to Warren, education had become essential for the maintenance of a democratic society and for individuals so they could succeed and contribute to society:

> Today, education is perhaps the most important function of state and local governments. Compulsory school attendance laws and the great expenditures for education both demonstrate our recognition of the importance of education to our democratic society. It is required in the performance of our most basic public responsibilities, even service in the armed forces. It is the very foundation of good citizenship. Today it is a principal instrument in awakening the child to cultural values, in preparing him for later professional training, and in helping him to adjust normally to his environment. In these days, it is doubtful that any child may reasonably be expected to succeed in life if he is denied the opportunity of an education. Such an opportunity, where the state has undertaken to provide it, is a right, which must be made available to all on equal terms.

The *Brown* decision, or what is now referred to as *Brown I*, neither overruled *Plessy* nor granted immediate relief to the plaintiffs or to any of the other children attending unequal segregated schools in the seventeen states that required segregation and the four states that permitted it.[68] In *Brown I* the Court only ruled on the "constitutionality of segregation in public education." The Court, recognizing that "because these are class actions, because of the wide applicability of this decision, and because of the great variety of local conditions," and because "the formulation of decrees in these cases presents problems of considerable complexity" postponed ruling on how and when the decision—how to desegregate or how to integrate public schools would be implemented. So that decisions could be made on implementation the case was restored to the docket. The Attorney General of the United States was "again invited to participate" and "the attorneys General of the states requiring or permitting segregation in public education" were allowed to participate as friends of the court. That led to what is now known as *Brown II,* which was decided on May 31, 1955.

The *Brown II* Decision

Some believed that *Brown I* ended the career of Jim Crow, but *Brown II* showed Jim Crow's career would not soon end. As Jack Greenberg wrote, in *Brown II,* "the Court spoke with forked tongue."[69] While the Court indicated that "constitutional principles" could not be set aside simply because some disagreed with the decision and directed that school authorities were to "make a prompt and reasonable start toward full compliance" and do so "at the earliest practicable date," it also agreed that districts may need time to deal with a variety of problems related to "administration, arising from physical condition of the school plant, the school transportation system, personnel, revision of school districts and attendance areas into compact units to achieve a system of determining admission to the public schools on a nonracial basis, and revision of local laws and regulations which may be necessary in solving the foregoing problems." The Court further ordered that the federal district courts were to "enter such orders and decrees consistent with this opinion as are necessary and proper to admit to public schools on a racially nondiscriminatory basis *with all deliberate speed* the parities to these cases." "With all deliberate speed" proved not to mean either immediately or even soon. The district courts were in charge but were given no clear guidelines and no deadlines. As the 1950s came to an end, LDF had already filed more that sixty cases in order to end racial segregation in elementary and in high schools and most were still pending. As of June 1960, five southern states—Alabama, Georgia, Louisiana, Mississippi, and South Carolina—had managed not to admit any African American student to a school with white students.[70] Enforcement was to be gradual. As Hugh Davis Graham noted, "'with all deliberate speed' had led to a decade of southern intransigence marked by the barest tokenism."[71] Linda Brown's father won in the Supreme Court but she was graduated from racially segregated schools in Topeka. A decade after *Brown,* the vast majority of African Americans who attended school in the South were still attending segregated schools; only 2.3 percent of southern African American school children were enrolled in desegregated schools.[72] Districts only began to desegregate after they had no choice but to respond to court rulings. Consequently, LDF had to file case after case, and there were many. For example, at the end of 1965, LDF had 185 school cases, four times as many as it had in 1961. Those who disagreed with *Brown I* and who wanted to resist found some hope in *Brown II* and often found support from important political leaders.

A notable indication of resistance, if not defiance, appeared on March 12, 1956 when nineteen U. S. Senators and seventy-seven members of the U. S. House of Representatives signed the "Southern Manifesto" and had it entered into the Congressional Record. Only three Senators from the South declined signing it: Lyndon B. Johnson from Texas and the two Senators from Tennessee, Albert Gore, Sr. and Estes Kefauver. Signers of the "Manifesto" claimed that *Brown* was "a clear abuse of judicial power," that the Court had infringed upon the rights of the Congress and the several states. They further observed that Connecticut, Illinois, Indiana, Massachusetts, Michigan, Minnesota, New Jersey, New York, Ohio, Pennsylvania, and other states in the north had held to the doctrine of separate but equal in education until, "exercising their rights as Sates through the constitutional processes of local self government, changed their school systems." The signers supported those who were lawfully resisting and commended their motives.[73]

The Segregation and Desegregation Mandates: *Plessy versus Ferguson* and *Brown v the Board of Education*

When the decision in *Brown I* was rendered, it was widely reported in the media that *Plessy* had finally been overturned and that the dissent of Justice John Marshall Harlan who argued that the Constitution was "color-blind" and neither knew or tolerated "classes among its citizens" had finally been heard. However, as Jack Greenberg explained, "Nominally, the Court's only legal directive in *Brown* was that states might no longer segregate the races in schools."[74] Chief Justice Warren was indeed aware of *Plessy* and even discussed it. However, *Brown* did not directly and explicitly overturn *Plessy*. In *Plessy* the Court denied that assigning African Americans to separate facilities would produce a stigma of inferiority on those so segregated. It argued that that was so only if those who were segregated chose "to put that construction on it." Warren argued that the racial segregation of children "generates a feeling of inferiority as to their status in the community that may affect their hearts and minds in a way unlikely to be undone." He maintained his position was "supported by modern authority" and rejected the contrary finding in *Plessy*. Warren's argument was based on what social scientists knew about the consequences of segregation, knowledge that was not available at the end of the nineteenth century. Thus, the reasoning in *Brown* turned out to be essentially the same reasoning that was applied in *Plessy*. Warren had relied "on the same constitutional logic and transient social science that had underpinned *Plessy*, in effect substituting the egalitarian psychology of the 1950s for the racist sociology of the 1890s."[75] Had Warren sided with Harlan's dissent in *Plessy* and maintained that the Constitution was color-blind, he would have taken away governments' ability to make and acknowledge racial distinctions and to make color conscious rulings. Siding with Harlan would also have limited the Court's power. As Graham observed, "Because *Brown* had stopped short of holding unconstitutional all racial classifications by government as impermissibly color-conscious per se, then, the Court was able to maximize its newly claimed authority and jurisdiction while minimizing limitations on its discretion in enforcing its decree and affording remedies.[76]

While Warren argued in *Bolling* that racial classifications "must be scrutinized with particular care, since they are contrary to our traditions and hence constitutionally suspect," his position in *Brown I* essentially held that racial classifications were not unconstitutional. Warren's argument and decision not only maintained governments' right and power to make and uphold "color-conscious" actions and policies but also gave the courts the power to determine "what state behavior was acceptable and when it became unacceptable." In his arguments before the Supreme Court in 1955, Marshall claimed that the issue before the court was "whether or not race can be used" and indicated that all his side wanted was "the striking down of race."[77] Marshall did not get what he wanted. After *Brown I* and *Brown II*, and especially after enactment of the 1964 Civil Rights Act, not only the federal courts but also American society would become increasingly explicitly color conscious. The courts would attend not only to how an individual might be denied her or his rights but also how classes of people—usually people of color—were denied their rights or were somehow mistreated by state action or placed at a disadvantage as a consequence of earlier state action. As Graham observed, "by imbedding in its implementation decree in *Brown II* a presumption against Harlan's color-blind Constitution, however, the Court ironically linked enforcement to class actions that would ultimately require *more* not less, government classification by race."[78]

Brown and the 1964 Civil Rights Act

While the "only legal directive in *Brown* was that states might no longer segregate the races in schools," the consequences of the decision reached far beyond segregation in public schools. Many believed that it did indeed overturn *Plessy* and embrace Justice Harlan's claim that the Constitution was colorblind. Consequently, those who wanted to end Jim Crow and extend civil rights to all Americans had reason to believe that turning to the judicial system was an effective way to secure social justice. In addition, however, *Brown* set loose a movement for social justice that was no longer argued by attorneys in the courts. The movement that led to the Montgomery bus boycott, to sit-ins at lunch counters and to other disruptive but nonviolent forms of resistance to Jim Crow was fueled by discontent with the lack of basic social justice. New organizations came to the fore, and they were organizations that challenged the *status quo* not in the controlled atmosphere of the courtroom but in ordinary public venues such as lunch counters in drug stores, five and dimes, department stores, and bus terminals. *Brown* served as the foundation for that phase of the civil rights movement that achieved enactment of the 1964 Civil Rights Act.

By the time the 1964 Civil Rights Act was enacted, it was clear to the federal courts that the executive and legislative branches of the federal government were on the side of chasing Jim Crow out of all aspects of American Society. However, that was not the case ten years earlier. When *Brown* was decided, Dwight D. Eisenhower was president and a significant number of in the U. S. Congress, as indicated by the "Southern Manifesto" were opposed to the decision. It was widely believed that Eisenhower was less than enthusiastic about the *Brown* decision. When the case was before the Court but not yet argued, he invited Chief Justice Warren to a dinner party and sat him next to John W. Davis, the lead counsel for the defense team. Besides telling the guests what a great American Davis was, Eisenhower, in a private moment, tried to get Warren to understand the southern view. He told Warren that the southerners were "not bad people" and related, "all they are concerned about is to see that their sweet little girls are not required to sit in school alongside some big overgrown Negro."[79] Though he did not openly reject it, he did not endorse it. He related, "I think it makes no difference whether or not I endorse it. The Constitution is as the Supreme Court interprets it; and I must conform to that and do my very best to see that it is carried out in this country." His observation that "it is difficult through law and through force to change a man's heart," was certainly not a statement that encouraged people to accept and to comply with the Court's ruling.[80] In fact, it has been reported that he may have suggested that he had hoped the Court would rule not to end racial segregation in the public schools. Through the 1950s, states and communities with support from significant parts of the political and legal establishment did all they could to delay complying with the Court's decision if not actually defying it. If the Supreme Court had insisted upon immediate compliance, upon immediate desegregation of schools, there may have been massive defiance, defiance that the Court may not have been able to overcome.

THE CIVIL RIGHTS ACT OF 1964

The *Brown* decision did set in motion a movement that, while often viciously resisted in some parts of the nation, did nevertheless culminate in the Civil Rights Act of 1964. As its eighteen thousand words suggest, it was the most comprehensive and complex civil rights act ever enacted by the

Congress. The Civil Rights Act of 1883 specifically disallowed Congress from using the Fourteenth Amendment to enact legislation that would prohibit private discrimination. However, with the 1964 Act, Congress got around that provision by making illegal "discrimination or segregation carried on under cover of any custom or usage required or enforced by officials of the State."[81] Its provisions reflected those issues and concerns that advocates of civil rights had sought to have addressed since the beginning of the Niagara Movement and the founding of the NAACP. Title I of the act strengthened federal safeguards designed to guarantee all Americans the right to vote. This title was further strengthened when Congress enacted the Voting Rights Act of 1965. Title II banned discrimination in hotels, restaurants, theatres and other such places. This title soon gave access to virtually all establishments that served the public. For example, in 1968 there was a ruling that the Civil Rights Act of 1964 did cover drive-in restaurants.[82] Title III gave the United States Attorney General the power to sue in order to end segregation in public facilities. Title IV directed the United States Commissioner of Education to conduct a survey to determine whether equality of educational opportunity obtained in the nation. Title V continued the Civil Rights Commission that was created in 1957 as a fact-finding agency. Title VI specified that "No . . . person shall, on the grounds of race, color, or national origin be excluded from participation in, be denied the benefits of, or be subjected to discrimination under any program or activity receiving Federal financial assistance." Title VII banned discrimination in employment on the basis of race, color, national origin, religion, or sex. It was the only title that mentioned sex.

Title IV and Title VI Proved to be Almost Immediately Significant

The report of the survey ordered by Title IV, *Equality of Educational Opportunity Report* (now commonly known as the Coleman Report), and the subsequent discussions of it changed how equality of educational opportunity was defined and determined. Title VI may not have seemed important then. However, in 1965 Congress passed the Elementary and Secondary Education Act (ESEA) Title VI of The Civil Rights Act and Title I of ESEA served as a powerful carrot and stick for those school districts that were resisting desegregation. Title I of ESEA provided funds for school districts with educationally disadvantaged students. It was the most important title, for most of the nation's school districts were eligible to receive funds and approximately three-fourths of the appropriated funds were in Title I. When Congress reauthorized ESEA in 1966 it authorized an expenditure of twelve billion dollars. That meant that the nation's public schools were eligible for a portion of the nine billion dollars to improve the education for poor children. However, to qualify for ESEA funds school districts not only had to demonstrate they that served poor children—a task that was relatively easy, especially for major urban school districts—but also to demonstrate that they were not in violation of Title VI.

The U. S. Office of Education in HEW was responsible not only for the disbursement of Title I funds but also for developing guidelines to determine whether districts qualified under the provision of Title VI of the Civil Rights Act. As early as April 1965, the first guidelines were developed. School districts in which there was no segregation of either students or faculty were permitted to file an "assurance of compliance." Districts that were in the process of desegregating under court order were to file a copy of the order and a report on how much segregation of students and faculty existed and a report on the progress being made toward desegregation. Still other districts were allowed to submit a plan indicating how they would voluntarily desegregate by the fall of 1967. These districts were allowed to develop new compact attendance districts or to implement free-choice plans, whereby students were allowed to choose the school they wanted to attend.[83]

Title I as a carrot and Title VI as a stick did have some modest effect. During the first year Title I was in effect, "the proportion of black children attending school with whites rose from 2 percent to 6 percent, and 1,563 districts started to desegregate, more in a single year than in the preceding decade."[84] Many districts, especially in the Deep South, filed free-choice plans. Those plans proved either to effect token integration or to maintain segregation. A study by the U. S. Civil Rights Commission reported that there were 102 free-choice districts in which no African American students were attending school with whites.[85] In significant measure free-choice plans did not work because African-Americans were hesitant to face angry mobs protesting their attendance and they often had good reason to believe that local law officials would not protect them from the mobs. Boycotts, bomb threats, bombings riots, near riots, or the presence of angry mobs when African Americans registered or attempted to register or enrolled occurred in Alabama, Georgia, North Carolina Kentucky, Tennessee, South Carolina, Maryland, and, of course, Little Rock which became a national crisis.[86]

To increase the rate of desegregation the Office of Education revised its guidelines in March 1966. Besides all but prohibiting free-choice plans, the new guidelines established "performance criteria"—some saw them as quotas—for each school district for the 1966-67 school year. School districts that had integrated 8 to 9 percent of its African American students into white schools were required to double that number. Districts that had 4 to 5 percent of its African American students were required to triple that number. Districts that had adopted free-choice plans and failed to integrate any of its students were required to make a "very substantial start." According to the Office of Education, it was not sufficient for school districts to demonstrate that they were not discriminating; they were now required to implement plans that would desegregate schools. The Office of Education was challenging what came to be known as the "Briggs dictum," a 1955 ruling of a federal district court in South Carolina that held that schools were not constitutionally required to integrate students, that school districts were only required not to discriminate. By maintaining that only governmentally required and enforced segregation was unlawful and maintaining that all students had the right to choose the school they wanted to attend the court was providing a legal foundation for free-choice plans. It admitted that governmentally enforced segregation was illegal but giving sanction to voluntary segregation.[87] For the Office of Education the Civil Rights Act was color conscious, not colorblind.

A Marker of Change in American Society

The Civil Rights Act turned out to be an Act that now serves as a marker of a change in American society. For example, Diane Ravitch observed that "soon the passage of the [Civil Rights Act of 1964], changes began to occur that altered racial relations and affected subsequent public policy. Though it was not immediately apparent, the nature of the civil rights movement changed." According to Ravitch, "as an interracial movement led by blacks, its goal had been a public policy in which the state treated persons as individuals, without regard to race, color, creed, or national origin." However, after legal changes "the movement itself was transformed by the political climate into a black movement, dedicated to advancing the interests of blacks as a minority group." Ravitch argued that there had always been a "nationalist strain" in the black community that called for "attention to the need of blacks for group recognition, for assertion of their own history and culture, for a legitimate and respected place among American ethnic groups."[88]

What had been seen as a movement that sought to create a color blind society became a movement that increasingly became and encouraged color consciousness. Those who had long campaigned for its enactment believed that their goal of making the nation a color-blind society was achieved when on July 2, 1964 President Johnson signed it into law. He then related that the Act did "not restrict the freedom of any American so long as he respects the rights of others" and that it did "not give special treatment to any citizen."[89] Then, some believed that the government no longer had the power to classify people by race or color and, at the same time, gave the federal government the power to protect all citizens against discrimination as they sought to exercise their rights. However, the act "marked a turning point in the evolution of the civil rights movement as well as in the large issue of he role of race and group consciousness in American life."[90] Indeed, the irony was and is that if the position taken by Justice Harlan that the Constitution and therefore society is or should be color blind, then it becomes very difficult, if not impossible, to know whether those who have been deprived of rights and opportunities because of their color are still be deprived. Discrimination occurred and continues to occur on the basis of color. There is no way to know whether people of color are being denied their civil and political rights unless one looks to see if they are. Color consciousness cannot be avoided; it may be necessary. Not long after passage of the 1964 Civil Rights Act the Courts on their long road toward the full implementation of *Brown* handed down decisions that clearly recognized and ruled for group rights and relief.

By 1964 there was no doubt about the position of President Johnson's administration, and the federal courts were beginning to require school districts to end the dual systems of schooling. The "Briggs dictum," judge John Parker's claim that Constitution did not require integration but only forbade segregation was set aside by the courts, and the position of HEW was upheld. Significantly, school districts were ordered, as was the case in *United States and Stout v. Jefferson County Board of Education* (1966), not simply to desegregate the schools but to integrate them. In *Jefferson* Judge Wisdom indicated his dissatisfaction with the pupil-placement plans and free-choice plans that resulted in minimal desegregation and required that the schools in Jefferson County be racially balanced, according to the recently established HEW guidelines. Judge Wisdom indicated that the "patience of the Court" was being taxed and that "the time has come for foot-dragging public school boards to move with celerity toward desegregation."[91] Now it was not enough to demonstrate that school officials were not discriminating against students because of their race. Remedies were now not focused on the individual but on the class. Now, in order to integrate the schools, to create a racially balanced system, school officials had to be color conscious, not color blind.

Green v. New Kent County Board of Education (1968)

In *Green v. New Kent County Board of Education* the LDF won "a smashing victory," for the Supreme Court not only ruled that the freedom of choice plans did not work but instructed school districts that they had an "affirmative duty" to "convert to a unitary system in which racial discrimination would be eliminated root and branch." To establish and to maintain a unitary system school officials have to be aware of race, of color, in order to be certain that students are not racially segregated.

Swann v. Charlotte-Mecklenburg Board of Education (1971)

Swann v. Charlotte-Mecklenburg Board of Education is the case in which the Court in a unanimous decision effectively ruled that if busing was required to integrate a school system, then busing was required. In Charlotte, African Americans were so concentrated close to the town's center that there was no way to draw school attendance zones that would be contiguous and racially balanced. John Finger, an expert witness in the case, proposed non-contiguous zones by paring schools near the center of the city with schools in outlying areas. The proposed zones were designed to have approximately the same racial composition as the community at large, twenty-nine percent African American and seventy-one percent white. It was a plan that was conscious of color in the community and proposed integration on the basis of being quite conscious of color. After the *Swann* decision, LDF was able to achieve widespread desegregation. The federal court decisions after 1964 did make a significant difference. In 1964 about 2 percent of African American children in the South attended schools with white children. By 1972 about 60 percent of African American children in the South were attending school with white children.

In the *Swann* decision, Chief Justice Warren Burger wrote: "Neither school authorities nor district courts are constitutionally required to make year-by-year adjustments of the racial composition of student bodies once the affirmative duty to desegregate has been accomplished and racial discrimination through official action is eliminated from the system."[92] School districts that were once thoroughly integrated or desegregated because of demographic changes—either the movement into an area or the movement out of area by a group either white or non-white—have become resegregated. Now, Burger's dictum stands in the way of those who are committed to racially integrated school systems and those who would want to undo the resegregation.

Implications of the *Jefferson, Green,* and *Swann* Decisions

The *Jefferson, Green,* and *Swann* decisions were crafted not only to end discrimination or assure equality of treatment but also somehow to compensate for damages brought about by past discrimination and thereby shape the future. Moreover, those decisions mark a turning point in the civil rights movement and in popular opinion. In the early 1940s a mere 2 percent of whites in the South and only 42 percent of whites in the North believed that the African American children and white children should attend the same schools. A generation later, by 1972, 70 percent of whites in the South and 90 percent of whites in the North believed that African American and white children should attend the same schools. However, at almost the same time, 1966-68, the federal government's program of action aimed at school integration was beginning to lose support from African Americans as well as whites.[93]

Graham has argued that there are two phases of the civil rights era. During Phase I, up to 1965, the goal was to end discrimination. Then, equal treatment was the goal. However, after 1965 there was "a shift of administrative and judicial enforcement from a goal of equal treatment to one of equal results." President Johnson was among those who endorsed the emphasis on "results." He expressed this view in a speech delivered to the graduates at Howard University, June 4, 1965:

> It is not enough just to open the gates of opportunity. All our citizens must have the ability to walk through those gates . . . This is the next and the more profound stage of the battle for civil rights. We seek not just freedom but opportunity. We seek not just legal equity but human ability, not just equality as a right and a theory but equality as a fact and equality as a result . . . to this end equal opportunity is essential, but not enough, not enough.[94]

The shift was from a goal of equal treatment with positive assistance, such as special recruitment and training efforts, to a goal of equal results or a proportional distribution of benefits among groups. For some, who did not understand the intent of the legislation, that shift meant a reverse form of prejudice. In this view, "affirmative action" reduced the rightful position of privilege reserved for whites in that it constituted a commitment to "preferential treatment" and a commitment to "racial quotas" that acted against white self-interest.[95]

NOTES

1.   Eric Foner, *Reconstruction: America's Unfinished Revolution, 1863-1877*, (New York: Harper & Row, 1988), p. 612. Quotation from former slave, Peter Randolf, in *From Slave Cabin to the Pulpit, Boston, 1893*, quoted in Foner, p. 131.

2.   August Meyer and John H. Bracey, Jr. "The NAACP as a Reform Movement, 1909-1965: To reach the Conscience of America, " *The Journal of Southern History*. Vol. 59, No. 1 (February 1993), p. 4.

3.   Ibid.; George M. Fredrickson, *Racism: A Short History* (Princeton: Princeton University Press, 2002), pp. 99-101.

4.   Homer Plessy was born free into a French-speaking family in 1862. He was one-eighth African American and appeared to be European-American.

5.   Jennings L. Wagoner, Jr., "The American Compromise: Charles W. Eliot, Black Education and the New South," in Ronald K. Goodenow and Arthur O. White, eds., *Education and the Rise of the New South* (Boston: G. K. Hall, 1981), p. 26.

6.   Booker T. Washington, *Up From Slavery* in Louis Harlan ed., *The Booker T. Washington Papers* (Urbana: University of Illinois Press, 1972), pp. 322-323.

7.   Jack Greenberg, *Crusaders in the Courts: How a Dedicated Band of Lawyers Fought for the Civil Rights Revolution* (New York: Basic Books, 1994), p. 57. Emphasis in the original.

8.   Brook Thomas, ed., *Plessy v. Ferguson: A Brief History with Documents* (Boston: Bedford Books, 1997), p. 37.

9.   Gunnar Myrdal. *An American Dilemma: The Negro Problem and Modern Democracy* (New York: Harper and Row. 1962), p. 742.

10.   "Declaration of Principles of the Niagara Movement," July 13, 1905, Buffalo, New York. Reproduced in Howard Brotz, ed., *Negro Social and Political Thought, 1850-1920* (New York: Basic Books, 1966), pp. 533-537. Original brochures in the Schromberg Collection, New York Public Library.

11.   Eric Foner, *Reconstruction*, p. 612.

12.   Joseph R. Washington, Jr. *Black Religion: The Negro and Christianity in the United States* (Boston: Beacon Press, 1964), p. 2.

13.   "Declaration of Principles of the Niagara Movement," July 13, 1905.

14.   Ibid.

15.   Reproduced in Herbert Aptheker ed., *A Documentary History of the Negro People in the United States, Vol. II: From the Reconstruction Era to 1910* (New York: The Citadel Press, 1951), pp. 904-906.

16.   W.E.B. DuBois, "Resolutions of the Niagara Movement," August 15, 1906. DuBois' 1906 Niagara Address is reproduced in Aptheker, *A Documentary History of the Negro People*, p. 909; and Brotz, ed., *Negro Social and Political Thought*, pp. 538-539. Original brochures in the Schromberg Collection, New York Public Library.

17.   Address of Third Annual Meeting of Niagara Movement, 1907 in Aptheker, *A Documentary History of the Negro People*, p. 914.

18.   Myrdal, *An American Dilemma*, p. 742.

19.   Aptheker, *A Documentary History of the Negro People*, p. 897.

20.   *The Survey* (June 12, 1909) reprinted in Aptheker. *A Documentary History of the Negro People*, p. 917.

21.   Ibid.

22.   W. E. B. Dubois, "Politics and Industry," in Aptheker. *A Documentary History of the Negro People*, p. 917.

23.   In Aptheker, *A Documentary History of the Negro People*, p. 921.

24.   Ibid., p. 922.

25.   Meier and Bracey, "The NAACP as a Reform Movement," p. 16.

26.   "Proceedings of the National Conference, 1909," New York (n. d., n. p.) in Aptheker, *A Documentary History of the American People*, p. 924.

27.   Ibid., p. 923.

28.   Meier and Bracey, "The NAACP as a Reform Movement," p. 7.

29.   The other members of the editorial board were: O. G. Villard, J.M. Barber, Charles E. Russell, Kelly Miller, William S. Braithwaite and Mary D.MacLean.

30.   *The Crisis* (November 1910) in Aptheker. *A Documentary History of the Negro People*, p. 925.

31.   Reproduced in Aptheker, *A Documentary History of the Negro People*, p. 927.

32.   John Hope Franklin and Alfred A. Moss, Jr., *From Slavery to Freedom* (New York: Alfred A. Knopf, 1994), p. 317.

33.   Meier and Bracey, "The NAACP as a Reform Movement," p. 4.

34.   Franklin and Moss, *From Slavery to Freedom*, p. 325.

35.   Ibid., p. 324.

36.   Jack Greenberg, *Crusaders in the Courts*, p. 68.

37.   Ibid., pp. 164-165.

38.   Quoted in Jack Greenberg, *Crusaders in the Courts*, p. 60.

39.   Ibid., p. 61.

40.   Ibid., p. 61.

41.   David McCullough, *Truman* (New York: Simon & Schuster, 1992), p. 570.

42. Diane Ravitch, *The Troubled Crusade: American Education 1945-1980* (New York: Basic Books, 1983), pp. 231-32.

43. Quoted in Jack Greenberg, *Crusaders in the Courts*, pp. 61-62.

44. Ibid., p. 62.

45. McCullough. *Truman* , pp. 586-587.

46. Quoted in Gail Buckely, *American Patriots: The Story of Blacks in the Military from the Revolution to Desert Storm* (New York: Random House, 2001), p. 339.

47. Ravitch. *The Troubled Crusade*, p. 25.

48. *Mendez et. al. V. Westminister School District of Orange County et. al.* argued in the Unites States District Court of the Southern District of California, Central Division, ruled on February 19, 1946 and *Westminister School District of Orange County et. al. v. Mendez et. al.* Argued in the United States Circuit Court of Appeals, Ninth Circuit, ruled on April 14, 1947.

49. Reprinted in Sol Cohen, ed., *Education in the United States: A Documentary History, Vol. V* (New York: Random House, 1974), pp. 2978-2979.

50. Quoted in Greenberg, *Crusaders in the Courts*, p. 59.

51. Greenberg, *Crusaders in the Courts*, p. 116.

52. Reprinted in Waldo E. Martin, Jr., *Brown v. Board of Education: A Brief History with Documents* (Boston: Beford/St.Martins, 1998), p. 79.

53. Greenberg, *Crusaders in the Courts.*, p. 63.

54. Ibid., p. 79.

55. Ibid., pp. 64-65.

56. Ibid., p. 66.

57. Ibid., p. 67.

58. Ibid., p. 71

59. Ibid.

60. Quoted in Greenberg, *Crusaders in the Courts*, p. 76.

61. Ibid., p. 77.

62. Ibid., p. 66.

63. Reproduced in Martin, *Brown v. Board of Education*, p. 120.

64. Ibid., p. 119.

65. Greenberg. *Crusaders in the Courts,* p. 78.

66. Ibid., p. 118,

67. Richard Kluger, *Simple Justice: The History of Brown v. Board of Education and Black America's Struggle for Equality* (New York: Vintage Books, 1977), p. 708.

68. The seventeen states that required segregation were: Alabama, Arkansas, Delaware, Florida, Georgia, Kentucky, Louisiana, Maryland, Mississippi, Missouri, North Carolina, Oklahoma, South Carolina, Tennessee, Texas, Virginia, and West Virginia. The four states that permitted segregation were: Arizona, Kansas, New Mexico, and Wyoming.

69. Greenberg, *Crusaders in the Courts*, p. 206.

70. Ibid., p. 255.

71. Hugh Davis Graham. *The Civil Rights Era: Origins and Development of National Policy, 1960-1972* (New York: Oxford University Press, 1990), p. 366.

72. Ibid., p. 372.

73. Reproduced in Martin, Jr. *Brown v. Board of Education.* "The Southern Manifesto," appeared in *The Congressional Record*, 84th Congress, 2[d] session, March 12, 1956, pp. 459-64, pp. 220-221.

74. Jack Greenberg, *Crusaders in the Courts*, p. 116. Soon afterwards the Supreme Court struck down state laws that required racial segregation on beaches, busses, parks, and golf courses citing Brown by *per curiam* decisions that cited *Brown*.

75. Graham, *The Civil Rights Era*, p. 367.

76. Ibid., p. 368.

77. Ibid., p. 370.

78. Ibid., p. 371.

79. Quoted in James T. Patterson, *Grand Expectations: The United States, 1945-1974* (New York: Oxford University Press, 1996), p. 393.

80. Eisenhower's statements are quoted in Greenberg, *Crusaders in the Courts*, p. 213.

81. Quoted in Greenberg, *Crusaders in the Courts*, p. 315.

82. Greenberg, *Crusaders in the Courts*, p. 374.

83. Ravitch. *The Troubled Crusade*, p. 163.

84. Ibid., p. 164.

85. Ibid.

86. Greenberg, *Crusaders in the Courts*, p. 217.

87. Ravitch, *The Troubled Crusade*, p. 165.

88. Ibid., pp. 145-146.

89. Quoted in Ravitch, *The Troubled Crusade*, p. 142.

90. Ravitch, *The Troubled Crusade*, p. 142.

91. Quoted in Jack Greenberg, *Crusaders in the Courts*, p. 382.

92. Ibid., p. 389.

93. Graham, *The Civil Rights Era*, p. 455.

94. Quoted in Ravitch, *Troubled Crusade*. See Lee Rainwater and William L. Yancey, *The Moynihan Report and the Politics of Controversy* for the full text of the president's speech and Daniel Patrick Moynihan's "The Negro Family: The Case for National Action," which influenced the text. p. 161.

95. Graham, *The Civil Rights Era*, pp. 456-457.

CHAPTER 8

THE POLITICS OF EDUCATIONAL OPPORTUNITY AND IDENTITY

I saw the best minds of my generation destroyed by/madness, starving hysterical naked,/dragging themselves through the negro streets at dawn/looking for an angry fix,/angelheaded hipsters burning for the ancient heavenly/ connection to the starry dynamo in the machin/ery of night,/who poverty and tatters and hollow-eyed and high sat/up smoking in the supernatural darkness of/cold-water flats floating across the tops of cities/contemplating jazz,[1]

The post-World-War-II era can be said to have had two sides: one apparent and one hidden. The apparent side was the side of affluence. Many Americans enjoyed unprecedented opportunities. Real income reached new highs and home ownership increased significantly. Americans created a consumer culture and a new landscape—suburbia. However, African Americans were excluded from that culture and were systematically and deliberately kept off the suburban landscape. While enjoying their unprecedented affluence, Americans were also living under the threats the Cold

Race, Ethnicity, and Education: What is Taught in School, pages 219–252.
A Volume in: International Perspectives on Curriculum
Copyright © 2003 by Information Age Publishing, Inc.
All rights of reproduction in any form reserved.
ISBN: 1-59311-080-4 (paper), 1-59311-081-2 (cloth)

War presented: the specter of the atomic bomb and the political repression of the McCarthy hearings. The *Brown* decision in 1954 was a sign that America's institutions were about to be transformed, especially its schools. However, the federal government did virtually nothing to enforce the *Brown* decision. Americans did soon attend to their public schools. On October 5, 1957 Americans learned about *Sputnik*. The Soviet Union had successfully launched the first man-made Earth satellite. The space race was on. Americans were told that their schools had to be reformed. Those who had spent nearly a decade criticizing the quality of the nation's schools secured instantaneous credibility. Americans turned to promoting excellence in their schools and preparing students to join a new technical elite. Soon, however, it became clear that a population that had long been ignored had to be recognized. The priorities and politics of American society were being rearranged. By the early 1960s it was clear that the new priority was equality of educational opportunity.

EQUALITY OF EDUCATIONAL OPPORTUNITY

While the notion that true equality of educational opportunity necessarily meant that equality was not obtained unless results were indeed equal, was not universally accepted, it has had consequences for public education policy. A good example is the report that United States Commissioner of Education was directed to produce when Congress passed the Civil Rights Act of 1964. Title IV, Section 402 of the Civil Rights Act directed the Commissioner to "conduct a survey and make a report to the President and the Congress, within two years . . . concerning the lack of availability of equal education opportunities for individuals by reason of race, color, religion, or national origin in public educational institutions at all levels in the United States, its territories and possessions, and the District of Columbia."[2] In July 1966, Harold Howe II, the United States Commissioner of Education presented the report *Equality of Educational Opportunity Report (EEOR)*, (now known as the *Coleman Report*, for the chief investigator was James Coleman). Significantly, when Coleman completed the survey and reviewed the data, the criteria he used to determine whether equality of educational opportunity was obtained were different from those to which he adhered when he began the survey.

Coleman and his associates examined the educational opportunities available to what were identified as six racial and ethnic groups: "Negroes, American Indians, Oriental Americans, Puerto Ricans living in the continental United States, Mexican Americans, and Whites other than Mexican Americans and Puerto Ricans often called 'majority' or simply 'white'."[3] They collected data to answer questions in four major areas concerning segregation, public school efficacy, student achievement, and the characteristics of schools associated with achievement. Coleman tried to ascertain how much segregation existed among the various racial and ethnic groups in the nation's public schools. Secondly, he tried to determine whether all public schools offered equal educational opportunities by collecting information on laboratory facilities; textbooks; libraries, curricula; teacher characteristics, such as training and education, experience, salaries, attitudes, and verbal ability; and several student characteristics, such as socioeconomic status, parents' education, academic goals, and other attitudinal measures. Third, Coleman measured student achievement or learning by examining students' performances on standardized tests. Fourth, he tried to determine whether academic achievement was related to the characteristics of the schools students attended.

The Coleman Report

The *Coleman Report* established that ten years after the Brown decision significant segregation persisted. If the measure of equality was integration, then inequality persisted. Most of the nation's children continued to attend racially segregated schools. Of all the minority groups studied, African American children were the most segregated. Nearly two-thirds of African American first graders attended schools that were between ninety and one hundred percent African American. Nearly half of African American twelfth graders attended schools in which half or more of the students were African American. Of all groups, white children were the most segregated—eighty percent of white students in both the first and the twelfth grades attended schools that were between ninety and one hundred percent white.

That Coleman and his associates documented the extent to which white students had successfully avoided desegregated schools is not surprising. Resistance to integration was very strong in many communities, and *Brown II* did appear to many to sanction delay. What was surprising was the failure of the investigators to find significant differences between African American and white schools. That the survey was ordered indicates that there was the belief that the quality of African American schools differed significantly from that of white schools. Even Coleman had believed the study would show "striking" differences. Before the *Coleman Report* was completed he predicted that:

> . . . the study will show the difference in the quality of schools that the average Negro child and the average white child are exposed to. You know yourself that the difference is going to be striking. And even though everybody knows there is a lot of difference between suburban and inner city schools, once the statistics are there in black and white, they will have a lot more impact.[4]

There was also an expectation, especially in the North, that the *Report* would "establish that southern states systematically discriminated against the Negroes in the provision of school facilities," but "the tabulated data do not support the presumption of gross discrimination in the provision of school facilities in the South"[5] The pattern of gross discrimination that was so evident in the South before and even after World War II had been remedied. In some measure, this was due to the belief that if the schools to which African Americans were assigned were equal to those attended by white students, it would be possible to avoid integration.

However, there were documented differences in minority schools: "There are fewer physics laboratories, there are fewer books per student in libraries, texts are less often in sufficient supply. Schools are less often accredited, students who fail a subject are less likely to repeat a grade, they are less often schools with intensive testing, academically related extracurricular activities are less, the curriculum less often is built around an academic program."[6] Such differences, however, were not as "striking" or as "significant" as had been expected. The conclusion was that "these differences in facilities and programs must not be overemphasized," for in many instances they were "not large." Moreover, it was determined that "regional differences between schools are usually considerably greater than minority-majority differences."[7]

The difference in achievement between minority and majority groups was significant. The difference between African Americans and whites was found to be "progressively greater for the minority pupils at progressively higher grade levels."[8] At the sixth grade, the "grade level gap" in achievement was 1.6 years. By the time students entered high school. It was 2.4 years. At the end of high school, it was up to 3.3 years. Minorities were at a disadvantage when they entered school and when they left school.

The achievement differences could not be explained by the inequalities between the schools the students attended. As Coleman noted, "it appears that variations in the facilities and curriculum of the schools account for relatively little variation in pupil achievement insofar as this is measured by standardized tests."[9] It seemed clear that "whatever may be the combination of nonschool factors—poverty, community attitudes, low educational level of parents—that placed minority students at a disadvantage in verbal and nonverbal skills when they enter the first grade, the fact is that the schools have not overcome it."[10] One implication was that the schools were not totally responsible for differences in achievement of the groups studied, but Coleman was not willing to relieve schools of the responsibility. Since then, public schools have been charged with the responsibility for teaching all students in a way that will not show differences between identifiable groups of students. That is one of the reasons why there is now so much emphasis on testing as well as concern about whether the tests used are culturally fair.

Outcome of the Coleman Report

After publication of the *Equality of Educational Opportunity Report*, Coleman wrote that while it may have seemed "flat," it was "not as uncontroversial as it appears" and suggested, "Some of its findings, though cautiously presented, have sharp implications."[11] His discussion of the implications show that he was proposing a revolutionary change in the definition of equality of educational opportunity. Its "principal focus of attention was not on what resources go into education, but on what product comes out." To have equality of educational opportunity meant not just that schools were equal "in some formal sense" but that all children would leave school with the skills they needed to compete successfully either in the job market or in college, "that is, verbal and reading skills, and analytical and mathematical skills." To achieve equality of opportunity, the consistent and predictable relationship between social class or membership in a minority group and educational achievement had to be overcome. As Coleman explained, "Equality of educational opportunity implies, not merely 'equal' schools, but equally effective schools, whose influences will overcome the differences in starting point of children from different social groups."[12]

In a subsequent discussion of the *Report*, Coleman acknowledged that "not just to offer, in a passive way, equal access to educational resources, but to provide an educational environment that will free a child's potentialities for learning from the inequalities imposed upon him by the accident of birth into one or another home and social environment" was "a task far more ambitious than has ever been attempted by any society."[13] Coleman emphasized that to undertake such an ambitious task required a new approach to educational policy. To allocate additional resources to schools to maintain the status quo in organization and operation would not improve matters, for "*per pupil expenditures, books in the library, and a host of other facilities and curricular measures show virtually no relation to achievement if the 'social' environment of the school—the educational backgrounds of other students and teachers—is held constant.*"[14]

The Coleman Report's Challenge to Educational Policy and Practice

Three points that Coleman raised challenged the conventional thinking about educational policy and practice. The first was essentially a restatement of a claim that educators and social theorists had been making since the beginning of the twentieth century: The family did not have access to the resources necessary for preparing their children for the requirements of a complex technological society, and the school was the institution prepared to teach children the values, knowledge, and skills necessary for competing successfully in a complex and impersonal social order. He pointed out that traditionally the school was "a supplement to the family in bringing a child into his place in adult society" and argued "the conditions imposed by technological change and by our post-industrial society, require a far more primary role for the school, if society's children are to be equipped for adulthood."[15] If children were to be properly equipped for adulthood in school, it was necessary to lessen the influence of the family and increase the influence of the school "by starting school at an earlier age, and by having a school which begins very early in the day and ends very late."[16] That recommendation was endorsement of Title I of the Elementary and Secondary Act that Congress (1965) had recently enacted. Over three-fourths of the funds in ESEA were devoted to Title I that was to provide funds for programs for disadvantaged students.

Coleman's second point effectively raised questions about the widespread attachment to the "neighborhood school." Adherence to it ensured that "the social and racial homogeneity of the school environment," that was strongly related to the differential achievement that he wanted to eliminate, would persist. For some, the way to overcome that "homogeneity" was through busing. However, Coleman did not endorse busing, for he believed that an "incidental effect" of busing "would be to increase the segregation within schools, through an increase in tracking."[17]

Coleman's third point was a call for "new kinds of educational institutions, with a vast increase in expenditures for education—not merely for the disadvantaged, but for all children." While he did not then offer any specific suggestions for new kinds of education, he did suggest that new forms of schooling worthy of consideration "might be in the form of educational parks, or in the form of private schools paid by tuition grants (with Federal regulations to insure racial heterogeneity), public (or publicly subsidized boarding schools (like the North Carolina Advancement School), or still other innovations."[18] Improved teaching methods had to be developed so tracking could be avoided. Tracking was only necessary because current methods were suited only to a narrow range of students. Better methods would allow teachers to teach a greater range of students effectively and thereby "make possible the informal learning that other students of higher educational levels can provide."[19]

Recommendations

Coleman's recommendations were based on what was found in the *Equality of Educational Opportunity Report*—that students had an effect on each other in school. There it was reported that student achievement was related to the educational attainment and aspirations of other students in the school. They found that:

> . . . children from a given family background, when put in schools of different social composition, will achieve at quite different levels. This effect is again less for white pupils than for any minority group other than Orientals. Thus, if a white pupil from a home that is strongly and effectively supportive

of education is put in a school where most pupils do not come from such homes, his achievement will be little different than if he were in a school composed of others like himself. But if a minority pupil from a home without much educational strength is put with schoolmates with strong educational backgrounds, his achievement is likely to increase.[20]

SOCIAL SCIENTISTS RESPOND TO
THE COLEMAN REPORT

Ironically, the *Equality of Educational Opportunity Report*, which was the largest social science research project ever devoted to the issue of race in the United States, allowed some social scientists to argue that the power of public education to reduce inequality had been greatly overestimated. Inequality was due to the social conditions in which children were reared, and the school, it was concluded, had very limited power to redress the inequalities children in such conditions experienced. However, educators and policy makers did not immediately recognize the full impact of Coleman's findings.

Patrick Moynihan and Thomas F. Pettigrew, with support from the Carnegie Corporation, offered a seminar on equality of opportunity at Harvard. Their seminar "became the focus of an extraordinary welling up of intellectual excitement,"[21] drawing "fifty to sixty faculty members, and other interested groups."[22] "Harvard," according to Hodgson, "had seen nothing like it since the arms-control seminars of the late 1950s, at which the future strategic policies of the Kennedy administration were forged and the nucleus of the elite that was to operate them in government was brought together."[23] Christopher Jencks, who had recently begun work on a study of "The Limits of Schooling," supported by the Carnegie Corporation, joined the seminar. With the help of Theodore Sizer, dean of Harvard's Graduate School of Education, Jencks organized the Center for Educational Policy Research. The Carnegie Corporation and the federal government funded the center, and it became the site for several years of intensive study of the data Coleman had collected. In the spring of 1972, Moynihan and Frederick Mosteller published a set of papers—*On Equality of Educational Opportunity*—that had originated in the 1966 seminar. Later in the year, Jencks and his associates published a second volume of papers devoted to Coleman's data and issues—*Inequality: A Reassessment of the Effect of Family and Schooling in America*. Mosteller and Moynihan focused on inequality among individuals. The different foci of the two books led to different outlooks and recommendations, but each work was a forceful challenge to the traditional notion that society could rely solely on its public schools to reduce inequality in American society.

The Frederick Mosteller's and
Patrick Moynihan's Response: Progress

Mosteller and Moynihan neither contradicted nor challenged Coleman's findings. They acknowledged that his data might contain some biases and minor inaccuracies, but they discounted the possibility that refined data would alter any conclusions by pointing out that "it is the experience of statisticians that when fairly 'crude' measures are refined, the change more often than not turns out to be small."[24] They also noted that the Coleman Report had effectively changed how "equality of opportunity" was defined:

> Stated briefly, before EEOR 'equality of opportunity' was measured in terms of school inputs, including racial mixture. By inputs, we mean physical facilities of schools and training of teachers; by racial mixture, the Supreme Court's emphasis on integration. With the publication of EEOR it became increasingly the practice, even the demand, that equality be measured by school outputs; that is to say, by the results of academic achievement.[25]

While Mosteller and Moynihan did not deny the new definition of equality of educational opportunity and while they maintained that the dissatisfaction, disappointment, and even the "cultural despair" of some groups were understandable, they chose to emphasize how much progress had been made in satisfying the requirements of the classical notion of equality of educational opportunity. They acknowledged that at the end of the 1960s racial tensions were "higher than at any time in our history" and that the dissatisfaction with public education had reached the "point of crisis,"[26] but they nonetheless emphasized how much had been accomplished. In the middle third of the twentieth century, the nation had made "extraordinary progress:"

> There were no two areas of social policy in which progress toward a social ideal largely conceived and widely propounded was more conspicuous than those of equality of educational opportunity and equality of the races. The nation entered this period bound to the mores of case and class. The white race was dominant. Negro Americans, Mexican Americans, Indian Americans, Indian Americans, Oriental Americans, were all somehow subordinate, somehow something less than fully American. (Puerto Ricans had barely touched the national consciousness.) Education beyond a fairly rudimentary point was largely determined by social status. In a bare third of a century these circumstances have been extensively changed.[27]

Significantly, the changes were the results of deliberate actions. The nation had decided to eliminate inequality in two areas of society and had made progress toward doing so. While African Americans once claimed that desegregation was not proceeding quickly enough, by the end of the

1960s some charged, "the new unitary school systems continued to discriminate against blacks in various ways, that blacks still did not receive 'quality' education, and that special federal funds were not being used for educational purposes."[28] The nature of the charges—the differences between the two kinds of charges—was, according to Mosteller and Moynihan, a significant social change. That some problems had not been solved and that there were new ones were simply signs that the situation was "normal enough." There was "a long way to go," but advances had been made. They acknowledged "the difference between the kind of equality we have and the kind we want" but they also wanted "to take stock of advances when they have occurred."[29]

The Christopher Jencks Report: Inequality

While Mosteller and Moynihan admitted that inequalities still persisted but chose to emphasize how much progress had been made toward achieving equality, Jencks emphasized how impossible it seemed to be. He questioned whether the nation wanted to eliminate inequalities, especially economic inequalities. Americans, he charged, had "no commitment to ensuring that everyone's job is equally desirable, that everyone exercises the same amount of political power, or that everyone receives the same income."[30] Jencks did not focus on the inequality among racial and ethnic groups, for that inequality was not nearly as great as that which existed among individuals with any of the groups. It was "quite shocking" to learn that white workers earned fifty percent more than African American workers, but Jencks was "even more disturbed by the fact that the best-paid fifth of all white workers earns 600 percent more than the worst-paid fifth." Such differences made the differences between groups seem "almost insignificant."

Jencks was very clear about what he was advocating. He explicitly indicated "the decision to emphasize individual rather than group differences was made on political grounds." He was interested in achieving equality of opportunity, but he was "far more interested in a society where the extremes of wealth and poverty are entirely eliminated than in a society where they are merely correlated with skin color, economic origins, sex, and other such traits."[31]

Jencks challenged the widely held notion that educational reforms and extension of educational opportunities would eliminate poverty. The belief that middle class children rarely wound up poor and that poor children could be made into middle class children in the public schools was, according to Jencks, a belief without foundation. Jencks and his associates found no evidence to support the belief that more or improved education would have a positive effect on the other elements that comprised a child's life conditions. Economic and social inequalities could not be reduced through educational reforms. Jencks reported his conclusion:

> We have seen that educational opportunities, cognitive skills, educational credentials, occupational status, income and job satisfaction are all unequally distributed. The association between one variable of inequality and another is usually quite weak, which means that equalizing one thing is unlikely to have much effect on the degree of inequality in other areas.[32]

Jencks' Challenge to School Reform

Conventional school reforms simply were not powerful enough to "make adults more equal." Schools appeared not to have as much influence on children as their homes, the street, and television. Typical reforms focused on how resources were allocated, new curricula, and pupil assignment while what made a difference—"the way teachers and students actually treat each other minute by minute"—was beyond the control of the reformers. Moreover, whatever influence a school did have on a child, it was, Jencks claimed, unlikely "to persist into adulthood."[33]

Jencks did not see much promise in conventional school reforms but he was not opposed to educational reform. However, his was not a plan to do better what was already being done, but a call to adopt a new conception of schooling and to assign a new purpose to schooling. The conventional conception of the school as a factory that took in children as raw material and processed them into "employable adults" had to be abandoned. Rather than focusing upon schools as instrumental or preparatory institutions and evaluating them in terms of their "long-term effects" on students, he urged that the school be conceived not as means to ends but as ends in themselves and that they be evaluated in terms of their "immediate effects on teachers and students." To describe such schools, it was appropriate and useful to adopt "a language appropriate to a family rather than a factory."[34] Because it was generally accepted that families could be judged in a number of ways, it seemed appropriate to have a variety of ways to judge schools. That meant that schools should be characterized by diversity of purpose and procedure. The principle of uniformity disallowed the possibility of satisfying all portions of the public, but the principle of diversity would allow the public to be satisfied. There were no good reasons, Jencks believed, not to allow people to choose what kind of schooling they wanted for their children. For him, "the ideal system is one that provides as many varieties of schooling as its children and parents want and finds ways of matching children to schools that suit them." Whatever parents and children wanted seemed appropriate, for not even professional educators, according to Jencks, had a better understanding of the long-term effects of school than did parents. Moreover, "since the character of an individual's schooling appears to have relatively little long-term effect on his development, society as a whole rarely has a compelling interest in limiting the range of educational choices open to parents and students."[35]

Jencks clearly preferred one kind of schooling to others but he was not willing to argue that his preference should be *the* preference for all. He did not "believe that schools should be run like mediocre summer camps" and valued "ideas and the life of the mind."[36] Others, however, preferred "discipline and competitive excellence," high reading and math scores," teaching children to behave properly," or something else from a "nearly endless" list of possibilities. What was important, he maintained, was that children be allowed to feel that they were "doing something purposeful." One way to do that was to engage then in "activities that contributed to their becoming more like grownups."[37]

FALTERING COMMITMENT TO EQUAL OPPORTUNITY IN EDUCATION

In the years following the publication of the *Equality of Educational Opportunity Report* and the various analyses of it, the commitment to providing increased resources to achieve true equality of educational opportunity all but disappeared. The recommendations Mosteller and Moynihan offered did call for more research *"for the purposes of improving national, state, and local educational policy,*[38] They did recommend *"increased family-income and employment-training programs, together with plans for the evaluation of their long-run effects on education."*[39] They were effectively recommending that attempts be made not to overcome the effects of the social environment but to change the conditions in which children are reared. That recommendation was also a tacit admission that public schools, as presently and traditionally organized, had limitations. While not rejecting the importance of schooling, they were certainly looking to alternatives to solve the problems of inequality. Thus, they recommended *"that new kinds of schools be developed and evaluated, and that in existing schools new sorts of educational policies substantially different from those of the past be tried in a research and development manner."*[40] They urged *"that the electorate maintain persistent pressure on its government agencies, school boards, legislatures, and executives to set specific targets, develop and revise programs, and report on progress toward local, state, and national goals in education with an attitude that optimistically expects gains, but, knowing their rarity, appreciates them when they occur."*[41]

Funding Issues in the Provision of Equality of Opportunity

Shortly after the publication of *Equality of Educational Opportunity Report*, Moynihan argued that increases in funding for education had been sufficient and that little was to be gained by increasing what was already enough. During the decade that had just ended, the nation had increased its expenditures for education "at a rate almost half again that of the Gross National Product, GNP, itself."[42] While the GNP was increasing at the rate of 6.8 percent, education expenditures were increasing at an annual rate of 9.7 percent. The conclusions of a study conducted by the Rand Corporation for the President's Commission on School Finance was "devastating to whatever is left of conventional wisdom." There was a point after which additional expenditures on schools made little or no difference on achievement. The policy implications were that:

> . . . increasing expenditures on traditional educational practices is not likely to improve outcomes substantially. There seem to be opportunities for significant redirections and in some case reductions in educational expenditures without deterioration in educational outcomes.[43]

The Rand researchers reported, "*research has found nothing that consistently and unambiguously makes a difference in student outcomes.*"[44] Their review of "variants" of existing systems of public education also failed to find anything that was consistently related to how well students achieved. Their review of compensatory educational programs was, Moynihan claimed, "wrenching." Such studies would not allow educators to argue that increased funding would enable them to make significant gains. "Production functions," or the law of diminishing returns, worked in education just as it worked in other sectors of the society. As Moynihan explained:

> Typically, in an early state increments of input have a high marginal utility which gradually diminishes until the exchange of input for output is no longer equal, and finally to the point where no additional output results. It seems to be the case that, over a considerable range of public services, we are traversing a segment of a production function which is virtually asymptotic. (The Rand report puts it with respect to education, that we are in a 'flat area.')[45]

Educators had to face the prospect of no longer receiving increased funds to solve their problems. They also had to recognize the possibility that the problems they were trying to solve were not educational problems, for the Rand report concluded, "There is good reason to ask whether our educational problems are, in fact, school problems."[46]

Any attempt to equalize expenditures for education would only raise the total cost for public education because the political system functioned in a way that insured that those with less would receive more and worked against any attempt to appropriate less for those with more. The cost of equalization would be staggering. A study conducted in Pennsylvania indicated that a thirty-five percent increase–$1,052,263,235—would be required to insure that all districts had funds equal to eighty percent of those expended by the districts with the highest rates of expenditures. According to Moynihan, government, whether federal, state or local, had to stop the fiscal hemorrhage.

Moynihan was not the only one to suggest that it would be difficult to defend increases for education. With Mosteller, he was able to point out that a study published by the First National City Bank, *Public Education in New York*, showed that there was no positive relationship between school expenditures and student achievement. The "preliminary evidence" gathered from 150 schools showed that "there is no statistical correlation between the aggregate amounts of money spent per pupil and the improvement in reading scores from one year to the next." The finding that "the race/poverty nexus appears to correlate highest with low reading levels"[47] confirmed the findings of the Coleman Report.

Inequality Outside of School: The Workplace

In 1972, the economist Lester C. Thurow argued, "our reliance on education as the ultimate public policy for curing all problems, economic and social, is unwarranted at best and in all probability ineffective."[48] He reported that since World War II there had been a greater distribution of education in society but that the distribution of income did not change in any corresponding way. While the bottom fifth of the white male population had increased its share of education from 8.6 percent to 10.7 percent between 1950 and 1970, its share of the income dropped from 3.2 to 2.6 percent. The highest fifth of the same population experienced a decrease in its share of education for the same period from 31.1 percent to 29.3 percent but its share of income for the same period increased from 44.8 percent to 46.3 percent. The conventional wisdom, or what Thurow described as "wage competition theory," held that such a redistribution of education would lead to a redistribution of income, but that clearly did not occur.

Examination of the experience of African Americans revealed a similar pattern. Thurow reported, "from 1952 to 1968, the mean education of black male workers rose from 67 percent to 87 percent of that of white male workers—yet median wage and salary incomes rose only from 58 percent to 66 percent."[49] However, that increase could be "traced to black emigration from the South, where incomes for blacks were lower than they were elsewhere. Commonly held assumptions about inequality, equality, and their causes seemed to be crumbling in the early 1970s, or as Jencks observed, "many popular explanations of economic inequality are largely wrong."[50]

Disassembling National Policy on Educational Opportunity

By the mid 1970s, the national policy on equality of educational opportunity that had been assembled in the late 1950s and early 1960s was clearly being disassembled. As David Cohen and Michael Garret described it, this policy

> . . . rested on the idea that poverty, unemployment and delinquency resulted from the absence of particular skills and attitudes—reading ability, motivation to achieve in school and the like. There was also an assumption that schools inculcated these skills and attitudes and that acquiring them would lead to economic and occupational success. In other words, this policy assumed that doing well in schools led to doing well in life. Finally, the emerging policy, which came to be called compensatory education, assumed that providing schools with more resources would enable and induce them to remedy students' deficiencies.[51]

By the mid 1970s, the studies, discussions, and controversies inspired by the Coleman Report itself and what Cohen and Garret described as "the stream of negative Title I evaluations," all gradually eroded the assumptions underlying compensatory policy."[52] As the climate of opinion about the effectiveness of the specific compensatory strategies changed, the support for "categorical" programs was weakened and the support for "general aid"—aid that may or not be devoted to disadvantaged pupils—was somewhat improved. In the political arena, however, the erosion of those assumptions made a difference when resources were allocated. As Hodgson reported:

> "The Jencks report" was freely cited by the Nixon administration's Office of Management and Budget on Capitol Hill in justification of cutting the budget for fiscal 1974. There was a widespread feeling that "Coleman and Jencks" provided a respectable rationale for giving a low priority to spending on education.[53]

The ideas of reformers and educators who were committed to providing equality of educational opportunity for all children may have been challenged and perhaps even seriously discredited in some sectors, but the problems they were trying to address certainly have not disappeared. Equality, inequality, achievement, integration, desegregation strategies, family-social background, the special problems of handicapped children, and the needs and rights of non-English speaking students have continued to command the attention of educators and lawmakers.

Charges that the compensatory educational programs failed were answered by arguments that they were frequently based on incorrect and unjust assumptions. During the 1960s, it was, As Ricardo L. Garcia, observed, "popular to label students from ethnic minority or low socioeconomic backgrounds 'culturally deprived'."[54] Theories of cultural deprivation frequently maintained that the culture and language of students from outside mainstream American society were inferior or invalid because they differed from that of the dominant middle-class white students. Some compensatory programs were accordingly designed not to build on what students knew but to replace one culture and linguistic background with those of the dominant middle class. That approach either denied or simply ignored all that educators claimed about the relevance of the structure of knowledge just a few years earlier. According to Garcia, it also "ignored the fact that ethnic minority and poor students have cultures, languages, and ethnic group heritages that cannot easily be replaced by those of another culture.[55] Such criticisms of compensatory programs are not claims that schools are necessarily ineffective. Rather, they are charges that schools have frequently violated the time-honored principle that dictates that teachers teach children in terms of what they know. If it is assumed that children know little or nothing or that what they know is not worthwhile, often because the teachers do not know what they know, effective teaching is extraordinarily difficult, if not impossible.

THE STRUGGLE TO REBUILD CONTINUES: BILINGUAL EDUCATION, SPECIAL EDUCATION, AND HELP FOR LOW-INCOME FAMILIES

Even while the effectiveness of compensatory programs was being challenged, action was being taken to insure that true equality of opportunity would be extended to all children regardless of their handicap or their ethnic and linguistic backgrounds. In the late 1960s and early 1970s, the special problems of children from non-English speaking families began to receive the attention they needed from educators and legislators. In 1967, Senator Ralph Yarborough of Texas introduced bilingual educational legislation to Congress. In January 1968, Congress enacted the Bilingual Education Act (Title VII of the Elementary and Secondary Education Act). It did not require all school districts to introduce bilingual education programs, but it did recognize that many children needed instruction in their native language as well as English if they were to progress satisfactorily in school. The act provided funds for school districts that wanted to implement programs. However, in 1970, the Department of Health, Education and Welfare (DHEW), using the 1964 Civil Rights Act as a basis, directed all school districts with enrollments of more than 5 percent non-English speaking children to provide language programs that would insure that all children would have the opportunity to achieve in school.

Bilingual Education

Advocates of bilingual education programs who maintained that special programs were necessary to insure that all children would have equal opportunity at academic achievement received affirmation of their position when the Supreme Court rendered its decision in *Lau v. Nichols* (1974). The Court then unanimously agreed that the schools of San Francisco were not offering equal educational opportunity to Chinese-speaking students. To claim that non-English speaking students could benefit from instructional and curricular strategies designed for English-peaking students was, the Court declared, "a mockery of public education" and a violation of the 1964 Civil Rights Act. In 1975, the Office of Civil Rights of DHEW issued a set of guidelines, generally known as the "Lau Remedies" for implementing the Lau decision. The guidelines specified that school districts had an obligation: to identify the student's primary and home language; to diagnose the student's educational needs and prescribe and implement appropriate programs to satisfy those needs; to insure that programs do not track students on the basis of English language proficiency; to insure that teachers are culturally sensitive and linguistically proficient; to prohibit ethnically identifiable schools and classes; and to notify parents of school programs in the appropriate language. Curiously, the task force that wrote the "Lau Remedies" argued against English as a Second Language (ESL) programs as an effective remedy. Yet, the basis of the Court's decision in *Lau* was, as Diane Ravitch has observed, "the failure of the San Francisco schools to provide ESL to all Chinese children in the system."[56] In this case, the Court did not order a remedy. The Department of Health Education and Welfare designed the remedy.

While the Supreme Court declared bilingual programs be implemented and basically accepted a Coleman-like definition of equality of opportunity that focused on the opportunity to achieve academically, bilingual education has been a confusing and controversial issue for many. Even in the 1980s, Ravitch was able to ask: "Was the purpose of bilingual education to provide a *transition* to the regular English-language school program or was its purpose to *maintain* the language and culture of non-English speaking children?"[57] Some of the controversy is about the best way to teach English to non-English-speaking students—whether they should be taught to read and then to speak English or vise versa. In some measure, such controversies reflect the differences among psychologists and students of linguistics about language acquisition. However, some of the controversies have cultural and political aspects. Some argue that "maintenance models," that allow children to maintain proficiency in their native language while becoming proficient in English, are appropriate. Others argue that the emphasis should be on "transitional models," that phase out use of the native language in school as proficiency in English is acquired. However, the issues attendant to bilingual education are not simply questions about the best way to teach students English. The assumption that culturally different, or non-English-speaking students, needed language remediation has not helped their educational progress but has, according to Garcia, resulted in "innumerable cognitive and emotional problems."[58]

Education for All Handicapped Legislation:
Special Education Takes Off

The efforts to extend equality of educational opportunity to children from racial and ethnic groups and to children from low-income families did lead to efforts to assist other children, especially handicapped children. As Erwin L. Levine and Elizabeth M. Wexler observed:

> The problems of handicapped children, particularly related to securing an adequate education, represent a phenomenon which had its roots in the civil rights movements of the 1960s. In that decade many blacks believed they were getting less than they were entitled to in education, employment, housing and accommodations and came together to obtain their rights. They confronted the system on executive, legislative and judicial fronts. Many of those who advocated more government for educating handicapped children saw themselves as part of the mainstream of politics, in the same manner as did the major civil rights groups, and set about to organize themselves in advancing the cause of the handicapped.[59]

The cause of handicapped children, that began to receive national attention in the 1960s after President Kennedy appointed the President's Panel on Mental Retardation, and secured help from Congress in 1966 when it authorized the Office of Education to establish a Bureau of Education for the Handicapped (BEH) and created the National Advisory Committee on Education and Training of the Handicapped. Each of these organizations was expected to serve as an advocacy agency and to work for increased funding and legislation to benefit the handicapped.[60] The handicapped won further benefits and rights in 1973 when Congress passed the Rehabilitation Act. Section 504 of that Act guaranteed the handicapped access to all programs in all institutions that received federal funds. Perhaps the greatest victory for the advocates of the handicapped occurred in 1975 when President Gerald Ford signed the Education for All Handicapped Children Act into law, popularly known as Public Law 94-142. Its enactment was a clear sign that the nation had realized that more than half of the nation's eight million handicapped children were not receiving "appropriate educational services which would enable them to have full equality of opportunity" and that one million handicapped children were "excluded entirely from the public school system."[61]

Since its enactment, most discussions of Public Law 94-142 focused on the "mainstreaming" requirement—the belief that the law specified that all children, no matter what their disability, had to be placed in regular classrooms with non-handicapped children. It should, however, be noted that the law does not specifically require that all handicapped children be "mainstreamed." In fact, the law did not necessarily require the states to implement any new programs, practices, or procedures unless those states accepted federal funds to finance the cost of providing special services for handicapped children. However, once a state accepted federal funds, it was obligated to provide all handicapped children with "a free appropriate public education which emphasizes special education and related services designed to meet their unique needs." Acceptance of federal funds required states to identify handicapped children, prepare written individualized education plans (IEP's) for each handicapped child, and to provide the "least restrictive environment" for the handicapped child. For many, "least restrictive" meant the traditional classroom.

In testimony to a House Subcommittee on Select Education Hearings, on House of Representatives Bill (H. R.) 6692, 1977, the Council for Exceptional Children maintained that the cost of overcoming the logistical and physical problems of effecting mainstreaming should be paid just as the cost of ending racial desegregation in the schools had been and was being paid. It was beneficial for all children to learn about people who are different and to learn to live and to work with them. Mainstreaming was, the Council maintained, beneficial for non-handicapped children as well as for handicapped children. The Council had to so argue because by 1977, mainstreaming had become "a red flag for many who feared that having handicapped children mixed with 'normal' children would have an ill effect on the latter."[62] Harold Perry, president of the Council, even emphasized to the subcommittee that the Council did not advocate the mainstreaming of all handicapped children: "To say that we are going to put every retarded child, every learning disability child, every emotionally disturbed child, into a regular classroom full time is foolish, first of all; it is incorrect, most of all."[63]

If there were agreement about the definition of "appropriate education," there would be little difficulty in interpreting and implementing the provisions of Public Law 94-142, just as there would be few, if any, controversies about public education. The lack of agreement among educators, the public, and legislators about the meaning of "appropriate education" resulted in a number of appeals to the judiciary. In some instances, the courts ruled that Public Law 94-142 required school districts to provide services for the handicapped even though those services are not specifically stated in the law. As Martha McCarthy reported:

> For example, school districts have been judicially required to provide extended-year programs for severely handicapped children who would suffer

substantial regression from an interruption in their educational programs (*Armstrong v. Kline*, 1980). Also, school districts have been required to support residential placements for disabled students even though the placements have been made in part for non-educational reasons (*North v. District of Columbia Board of Education*, 1979) and catheterization (*Tatro v. State of Texas*, 1980) for handicapped children who need such services in order to participate in the educational program.[64]

In 1982, the Supreme Court handed down its first ruling interpreting Public Law 94-142. In the *Rowley* case, the Court declined to specify which services a school district must provide for handicapped students and overturned the rulings of lower courts that a school district was obligated to provide a sign language interpreter for a student who, without such assistance, was doing above average work in school. Rather, the Court indicated that its role was not to specify what appropriate education was but only to insure that the school district did develop an IEP according to the procedures specified in the law. The Court further decreed that "the intent of the Act was more to open the door of public education to handicapped children on appropriate terms than to guarantee any particular level of education once inside."[65]

AFFIRMATIVE ACTION

After the *Brown* decision, and especially during the late 1960s and early 1970s, many attempts were made to open the door to equality of educational opportunity and economic opportunity to those who previously faced a closed door. There remains disagreement as to whether that door has been truly opened for all. The attempts to open the door to all have presented many new responsibilities and challenges to schools and their teachers. Those attempts raised questions about educational policy from a local level to a state and national level. It is, however, clear, as expressed in *Brown*, that public education is important to the nation and is no longer solely a responsibility of local and state governments.

Striving For Equal Outcomes Rather than Opportunity

When President Johnson told the graduating class at Howard University that "equality as a right and a theory" was not enough and that "equality as a fact and equality as a result" was what was sought, it is doubtful that he was in favor of establishing quotas or racial preferences. During the early 1960s civil rights leaders, Bayard Rustin and Martin Luther King, Jr., for example, spoke out against racial preferences. President Kennedy thought it would be "a mistake to begin to assign quotas on the basis of religion, or race, or color, or nationality" As Vice-President, Johnson agreed with his president, telling Mexican-Americans in Los Angeles: "We are not going to solve this problem by promoting minorities. That philosophy is merely another way of freezing the minority group status system in perpetuity." Yet, after the Civil Rights Act of 1964 and the Voting Rights Act of 1965 were enacted, there was the question as to how "equality as a fact and equality as a result" was to be achieved.[66] One answer was Johnson's War on Poverty or his vision of the Great Society. That meant a program of social reform that would in all likelihood benefit African Americans disproportionately but would benefit all poor Americans—a program that was mostly, if not completely, colorblind. Such a program would in time disperse all people of color into all the socio-economic classes and professions.[67] However, as earlier noted, the civil rights movement was transformed from a movement that sought a colorblind society to one that became increasingly color conscious—from a movement dedicated to ending discrimination and protecting individual rights to one that "evoked new theories of compensatory justice and group rights."[68] One explanation is that it may have been an all but impossible vision to achieve. Ever since the Naturalization Act of 1790, the first Census in 1790 and every Census since then, residents of the United States have been classified and have classified themselves as either white or as a person of color—nonwhite. Another is that once the decision is made that citizens will not be discriminated on the basis of race or ethnicity, it becomes necessary to maintain records of who is enrolled in a school, who applies for a job, and who is hired. To prove that discrimination has not or is not occurring it becomes necessary to have proof, to keep records and counts. Still another, is the recognition that to overcome institutional racism—practices that may not be deliberately designed to discriminate but in fact do discriminate—it becomes necessary to establish procedures that will ensure that opportunity is extended to all regardless of race or ethnicity. Finally, there is the claim that preference must be given to certain groups to compensate for earlier practices that have the effect of excluding or disqualifying them for equal participation. Consequently, in what may be seen as phase two of the civil rights movement, Americans were introduced to "affirmative action," which Lind has defined as "a vague term, which could be (and eventually was) taken to mean hiring by the numbers to prove compliance."[69]

From The Wagner Act of 1935 to Affirmative Action

The term "affirmative action" appears to have had its origin in the Wagner Act of 1935, where "it was used to define the obligation and authority of the National Labor Relations Board to redress an unfair labor practice by ordering the offending party 'to cease and desist from such unfair labor practice, and to take such *affirmative action*, including reinstatement of employees with or without back pay, as will effectuate the policies of this Act'."[70] Affirmative action," as a term appeared again on March 7, 1961 when President Kennedy issued Executive Order 10295, an order that created the President's Committee on Equal Employment Opportunity (PCEEO). At the time, it was all Kennedy could do to fulfill his campaign promise to be aggressive on civil rights, for his victory was very narrow and he clearly had no support for civil rights legislation in the Congress. Vice President Johnson was assigned the responsibility for drafting the order and was designated as chair of the committee. It was not an assignment that he wanted but he had no choice for vice-president Nixon had held such a post during the Eisenhower administration.

In many respects, there was not much new in Kennedy's order. Like previous presidential orders issued by Truman and like the Eisenhower President's Committee on Equal Employment Opportunity, Kennedy's order was "to establish rules of procedure, receive complaints, hold hearings, receive and review reports, and sponsor conferences" and was "to survey the federal agencies to identify employment patterns and trends."[71] At the time, "affirmative action" was commonly understood to mean nothing more that the implementation of programs to recruit minorities for positions and to develop various training programs for minorities so they could advance to better positions. Kennedy's order was rooted in the traditional liberal position that held that applicants should be hired without regard to race or ethnicity and while employed they should be treated just as all others were. The liberal establishment wanted nothing more than an end to discrimination. According to Graham:

> The most strident public demands of the Americans for Democratic Action, the NAACP, the National Urban League, the Congress of Racial Equality, the Southern Christian Leadership Conference, the Political Action Committee of the AFL-CIO—indeed of the entire spectrum captured under the umbrella of the Leadership Conference for Civil Rights—called consistently for racially neutral anti-discrimination. The civil rights lobby with its roots deep in Jewish philanthropy and social protest as well as black resistance, remained extremely wary of such historically unpleasant notions as racial or ethnic quotas, and job and admissions applications that required minority group identification.[72]

The liberal establishment was not in favor of any preferences or privileges that would not be available to all Americans. As late as 1963, when Kennedy delivered his civil rights message to Congress he invoked Justice Harlan's claim in *Plessy* that the Constitution was "colorblind."

Like previous such presidential orders, Kennedy's was rooted in the tradition that assumed that those who were charged with discrimination were innocent until proven otherwise and required that plaintiffs and prosecution to produce the proof of their complaint when the needed proof or evidence was "possessed by the powerful organizations whose motives and behavior were the subject of the complaint."[73] The order's use of "affirmative action" has been described as "vague" and "casual" but it turned out to be "laced with the irony of unintended consequences."[74] The order did specify that prospective bidders, contractors, and subcontractors provide a Compliance Report. Those who desired to benefit from government contracts had to show that they were in compliance, "to ensure that applicants are employed, and that employees are treated during employment without regard to their race, creed, color, or national origin."[75] Thus, to demonstrate compliance data had to be collected, records had to be assembled and maintained.

The Kennedy-Johnson order directed that a census of minority employment in all federal agencies be undertaken, and Johnson required that the census be submitted within sixty days. However, it was an order with which agencies could not easily comply. For example, the report from the Department of Health, Education and Welfare (HEW) indicated that it could only "count Negro heads visually," for the department's policy did not permit "recording of employees' race, creed, color, or national origin."[76] Still agencies managed to make reports that indicated that African Americans were "slightly *over*represented in federal employment" but that they were "crowded into the lower grades."[77]

THE CLASSIFICATION AND IDENTIFICATION OF MINORITIES IN FEDERAL POLICY

Heads of federal agencies soon realized that they had to develop systematic ways to identify their applicants and employees by race. The President's Committee on Equal Employment Opportunity's first compliance form for government contractors had two columns, one for "Negroes" and one for "Other." The second column was included "in the event that such groups (Oriental, Spanish-American, Puerto Rican, American Indian) constitute an identifiable factor in the local labor market."[78] Contractors were to calculate and record the percentage of African Americans. However, by June 1962 the forms the President's Committee for Equal Employment Opportunity developed for "government employees added optional regional categories for Spanish speaking, Mexican and Puerto Rican origin, Oriental origin, and American Indian."[79] The supposed practice of not recording applicants' race was being abandoned by 1963. Eventually, the federal government would construct racial and ethnic categories into which all Americans would be placed.

Mandates for Race and Ethnicity in The Construction of Federal Standards: Statistical Directive 15

Beginning with first census in 1790 and in every census after the first, the race of every American has been recorded. Typically, from 1790 to 1960, the census enumerator assigned a race to them. That occurred once every ten years. In 1960, the Bureau of the Census turned to self-identification. However, now it is likely that Americans are asked to indicate their race and/or ethnicity several times a year. When making an application for employment, admission to an educational institution, enrolling in school, applying for a loan or scholarship, or applying for a mortgage, they are asked, not required, to indicate their "race/ethnicity" and gender. Currently, the form is likely to ask the applicant about ethnicity and race. Under ethnicity, the applicant is asked to indicate whether he/she is or is not Hispanic or Latino. Under race, the applicant is asked to indicate whether he/she is American Indian or Alaskan Native; Asian; Black or African American; Native Hawaiian or Other Pacific Islander; or White.[80]

The construction of the five "races" used to classify Americans can be traced back to 1973 when then Secretary of Health, Education, and Welfare (HEW) Caspar Weinberger "asked the Federal Interagency on Education (FICE) to develop consistent rules for classifying Americans by ethnicity and race."[81] The FICE recommended that people be assigned to one of five races: American Indian or Alaskan Native, Asian or Pacific Islander, Back, White, and Hispanic. The FICE's recommendations were forwarded to the Office of Management and Budget (OMB); and on May 12, 1977 the Office of Management and Budget issued "Directive No. 15: Race and Ethnic Standards for Federal Statistics and Administrative Reporting." The "Directive" provided definitions of the racial and ethnic categories and indicated that "standard classifications for record keeping, collection, and presentation of data on race and ethnicity in Federal program administrative reporting and statistical activities" were being provided.

The racial and ethnic categories were developed to satisfy the "needs expressed by both the executive branch and the Congress to provide for the collection and use of compatible, non-duplicated, exchangeable racial and ethnic data by Federal agencies." In a report in 1977 the Office of Management and Budget tried to explain why categories were created and how they were used. Data on race and ethnicity had been used extensively since the 1960s to monitor and enforce laws in "education, employment, housing and mortgage lending, health care, voting rights, and the administration of justice." Further, "these legislatively based priorities created the need among Federal agencies for compatible, non-duplicative data for population groups that historically had suffered discrimination on the basis of their race or ethnicity." The Office of Management and Budget explained that it had issued its "current set of categories for use in the collection and presentation of data on race and ethnicity in order to establish compatible, non-duplicative data. They further noted that the new set of categories also "implemented the requirements of Public Law 94-311 of June 16, 1976, which called for the collection, analysis, and publication of economic and social statistics on persons of Spanish origin or descent.[82] The reason for the determination of the categories was for the convenience of data collection. It also to contribute to the enforcement of equal opportunity.

Formalizing Five Racial Classifications

The now familiar set of five ethnic and racial categories was formalized by the Office of Management and Budget in 1977. The five categories included:

1. American Indian or Alaskan Native
2. Asian or Pacific Islander
3. Hispanic
4. White
5. Black

The category of "American Indian or Alaskan Native" is described as "a person having origins in any of the original peoples of North America, and who maintains cultural identification through tribal affiliation or community recognition." This is a geographic designation of origin and self-identified cultural definition. Could an American Indian or Alaskan Native also be "Asian or Pacific Islander?" The description for Asian or Pacific Islander is geographic but includes many unrelated cultures, languages and heritages. The descriptor states that an "Asian or Pacific Islander" is "a person having origins in any of the original peoples of the Far East, Southeast Asia, the Indian subcontinent, or the Pacific Islands. This area includes for example, China, India, Japan, Korea, the Philippine Islands, and Samoa." The term "original peoples," is confusing because a person could trace his/her origin from "Asia" and also from North America. The third classification, "Hispanic," is also unclear. A "Hispanic" person is defined in terms of origin but also in terms of an assumed culture "a person of Mexican, Puerto Rican, Cuban, Central or South American or other Spanish culture or origin, regardless of race." What about Brazilians who are Portuguese, African, and Indigenous? The specific reference to race places origin and culture over the perception of the fourth and fifth categories, which are identified by dissimilar criteria.

The fourth and fifth categories refer to "White," and "Black." To be "White" is a designation of origin that harbors domain assumptions and evades the obvious and problematic character of the historical use of "white person" in the United States. It is not a cultural designation, nor is it racial. To be "White" is to be "a person having origins in any of the original peoples of Europe, North Africa, or the Middle East." This includes people who may or may not consider themselves "white" as well as people who would not necessarily be "treated" as a "white person" given the changing social and political construction of race in the United States. The definition of "Black" is one of the two categories where race is a mentioned and it is the only category where race is a defining characteristic. It is the only category where the designation of the descriptor is repeated: to be black is to be black. To be black is to be "a person having origins in any of the black *racial* [author's emphasis] groups of Africa."

Continuing Contradictions in Classification: One Step Up or Two Steps Back?

The problems with the classification of human beings for purposes of management multiply in the current age just as they have in the past. The use of statistics in the elimination of discrimination becomes entangled in the politics of classification. The Office of Management and Budget's categories are likely a very good indicator of how Americans view race. As Melissa Nobles reported, those who developed the categories "relied on their own personal understanding of race, not on expert testimony or opinion."[83]

Before the issuance of "Directive 15" people from the Indian subcontinent, according to the FICE, were considered white. However, the Office of Management and Budget decided that people from the Indian subcontinent were not white but were Asian or Pacific Islander.[84] The Office of Management and Budget's categories, as Michael Lind has observed, "reflect political and bureaucratic imperatives, not cultural realities." Thus, he has suggested "there might just as well be three official races in the America—Eurasian-American, African-American, American Indian/Mestizo—or eight: American Indian, Mestizo, Black, Indo-European, Turko-Arabic, Malay, Mongoloid, Mulatto."[85] Lind's observation that "race is an arbitrary category that is bound to grow more arbitrary as intermarriage produces growing numbers of Americans with ancestors in several of today's officially defined racial groups"[86] was confirmed during and after the taking of the 1990 Census. The Office of Management and Budget's categories, described by David Hollinger as the "ethno-racial pentagon,"[87] did not allow either individuals to indicate their ethnic or racial heritages as they wished or the government to ascertain how the composition of the nation had changed. Consequently, in 1993 the Office of Management and Budget began a review of the then current standards for collecting, analyzing, and reporting all government data related to race and ethnicity. In 1994 the Office of Management and Budget established the Interagency Committee for the Review of Racial and Ethnic Standards, a committee with representatives from more than thirty federal agencies to recommend how better data on the nation's racial and ethnic composition could be secured.

Revising Statistical Directive 15: Change and No Change

On October 30, 1997, the Office of Management and Budget published in the *Federal Register* revisions to "Directive 15." The OMB split the "Asian or Pacific Islander" category into two categories: "Asian" and "Native Hawaiian or Other Pacific Islander," and expanded the "Native American or Alaskan Native" category to included the original peoples of South America and Central America. They also modified the text of the other categories. During and after the 1990 Census there were complaints by people who objected to being asked to indicate one "race." "Directive 15" issued in 1977 indicated that people were to make one selection. The 1997 revision allowed people who saw themselves as multiracial to select more than one race. The revised categories, to be used by all federal agencies no later than January 1, 2003 are as confusing and problematic as in the past. Few of the fundamental problems are addressed while other problems are added. Often the reason for the change is unclear or self-serving.

The designation of "American Indian or Alaska Native" remains essentially the same with the addition of Central America: "a person having origins in any of the original peoples of North and South America (including Central America), and who maintains tribal affiliation or community attachment." Immigration has increased from Mexico, Latin and Central America, as well as South America, due to poverty, civil wars, and United States' involvement in wars on drug trafficking. Many of the immigrants are not Hispanic in that they do not trace their heritage, language, culture, or identity to Spain or Portugal. The new category adds a token recognition to an eclectic population that often would not identify with each other necessarily or American Indians either. The former category of "Asian" was reduced by creating a new category of "Native Hawaiian, or Other Pacific Islander." Asians are "a person having origins in any of the original peoples of the Far East, Southeast Asia, or the Indian subcontinent." This includes "Cambodia, China, India, Japan, Korea, Malaysia, Pakistan, the Philippine Islands, Thailand, and Vietnam."

"Native Hawaiian or Other Pacific Islander" is reserved for "a person having origins in any of the original peoples of Hawaii, Guam, Samoa, or other Pacific Islands." The use of "original peoples" remains in the definition. It remains problematic because of the intermingling among people from varoius places making a person's origin indeterminate or difficult to prove. This is especially the case when tribal origins, as in Hawaii, entitle a person to certain privileges. It is to the advantage of dominant groups to make it difficult to claim indigenous identity if it means recognizing treaty rights to land, property, and political power for a minority.

The category of "Hispanic" has added "or Latino/a." Hispanic is a designation created by Spain that refers to people influenced by Spain or Portugal. Latino/a is a term favored by France to refer to people who speak a Romance or Latin based language. The OMB designation further specifies "a person of Cuban, Mexican, Puerto Rican, South or Central American, or other Spanish culture or origin, regardless of race." This would exclude people from other Latin language groups such as the Italian and French. The category is further qualified in that "the term, 'Spanish origin,' can be used in addition to 'Hispanic or Latino/a.'" Clearly, this is an effort to pacify the political implications of placing an exclusive boundary around a group that is in reality a collection of groups that differ from one another. Government agencies, such as the Bureau of the Census, have long attempted to create a nomenclature that is adequate and have not thus succeeded in part because this is a heterogeneous group.

Perhaps not surprisingly, the category "white" has not changed: "a person having origins in any of the original peoples of Europe, the Middle East, or North Africa," remains. In contrast the category "black" has added "or African American" but the definition of "a person having origins in any of the black racial groups of Africa," remains the same with the same problems. However there is another addition where "terms such as 'Haitian or Negro' can be used in addition to 'black or African American.' In this case the effort to expand the terminology in order to capture the diverse nature of any population that might come under such a category actually reverts to archaic terms used prior to the Civil Rights Movement.

Law Enforcement and Classification by Race

In a 1997 report the Office of Management and Budget indicated that the standards were developed so that civil rights laws could be enforced. The federal government needed data "to monitor equal access to housing, education, employment opportunities, etc., for population groups that historically had experienced discrimination and differential treatment because of their race or ethnicity." The categories, according to the OMB, "represent a political-social construct" and "are not anthropologically or scientifically based." The categories were not designed to "designate certain population groups as 'minority groups.'"[88]

While such data on race and ethnicity are collected, the placement of an individual into one or more of the categories is not done by the government but by the individual, for "self-identification is the preferred means of obtaining information about an individual's race and ethnicity, except in instances where observer identification is more practical (e. g., completing a death certificate). "Directive 15" did not establish criteria or qualifications (such as blood quantum levels) . . . to be used in determining a particular individual's racial or ethnic classification.[89]

While "Directive 15" and its revision have a "white" category, the other categories were not designed to indicate "nonwhite." "Directive 15" specified that "the designation 'nonwhite' is not acceptable for use in the presentation of Federal Government data" and "is not to be used in any publication of compliance or statistical data or in the text of any compliance or statistical report." The Directive did not prohibit any agency from collecting data with additional categories other than those set forth by the Office of Management and Budget. However, if data were collected with the use of additional categories, it had to be collected in a way that allowed the date to "be aggregated into these [Directive 15's] basic racial/ethnic categories." Thus, according to the Federal Government, all human beings have a place in one or more of OMB's categories.

THE CENSUS AND RACIAL CLASSIFICATION: TWO HUNDRED YEARS

As noted, every census since 1790 has not only attempted to determine how many people resided in the United States but also attempted to determine the racial composition of the nation. A review of the racial categories used in the census and the directions given to census enumerators (census takers) reveals not only "that race is not an objective category, which the censuses simply count" but also that race is "a fluid and internally contradictory discourse, partly created by and embedded in institutional processes, including those of the census itself."[90] The terminology used in the following discussion reflects the conflicting, confusing, and sometimes offensive nature of the categories used by the census. The 2000 Census clearly employed the categories established by Office of Management and Budget's 1997 revision of "Directive 15." After asking the person's name, telephone number, sex, age, and date of birth the person was asked to indicate whether he/she was "Spanish/Hispanic/Latino/a." If the person marked yes, he/she was asked to mark one of the additional boxes: "Mexican, Mexican American, Chicano;" "Puerto Rican;" "Cuban;" or "Other Spanish/Hispanic/Latino/a." If the person marked "other," he/she was asked to print the name of the group with which he/she identified. The next question asked about the person's race, and the directions indicated that one or more of the fifteen categories were to be marked. The fifteen categories were: "White, Black, African American, Negro, American Indian or Alaska Native, Asian Indian, Chinese, Filipino, Japanese, Korean, Vietnamese, Native Hawaiian, Guamanian or Chamorro, Samoan, Other Pacific Islander, Other Asian, or Some Other Race." Those who marked American Indian or Alaska Native were asked to indicate the "name of enrolled or principal tribe. "Those who marked Asian, Other Pacific Islander, or Some other Race" were asked to indicate their race.

The first six censuses did not include nearly as many racial categories as the 2000 Census. The 1790 Census counted free white males, free white females, all other free persons, and slaves. The second and third Censuses (1800 and 1810) specified that all other free persons did not include "Indians not taxed." The fourth Census (1820) added a category for "free colored persons." The fifth and sixth Censuses (1830 and 1840) contained only three categories: free white persons, free colored persons, and slaves.

Melissa Nobles pointed out that "the 1850 census marked a watershed in census-taking," for it reveals "the influence of race science in the development and justification of race inquiries." Of significance was the addition of the "mulatto" category under color.[91] It was added due to the influence of Josiah Nott who argued for multiple races and believed in polygenesis. He argued for collecting vital statistics—fertility rates and mortality data—because he believed such data would demonstrate that racial mixture would weaken a race. He believed that he could prove the inferiority of African Americans. The enumerators of the 1850 Census were given very specific instructions. For the slave-population schedule the enumerators were instructed: "Under heading 5 '*Color*,' insert in all cases, when the slave is black, the letter B; when he or she is a mulatto, insert M. The color of all slaves should be noted." For the free-population schedule the enumerators were instructed: "Under heading 6, entitled "*Color*," in all cases where the person is white, leave the space blank; in all cases where the person is black insert the letter B; if mulatto, insert M. It is very desirable that these particulars be carefully regarded."[92]

The 1860 Census added a category for Native Americans. The 1870 Census and the 1880 Census added a category for Chinese. The 1870 and the 1880 enumerators were told that "Mulatto" was generic and included "quadroons, octoroons, and all persons having any perceptible trace of African blood." When counting mulattos, they were to be "particularly careful," for "important scientific results" depended on their making correct determinations.[93]

The 1890 Census included eight categories: White, Black, Mulatto, Quadroon, Octoroon, Chinese, Japanese, and Indian. The enumerators were instructed to "Write *white, black, mulatto, quadroon, octoroon, Chinese, Japanese, or Indian*, according to the color or race of the person enumerated." The enumerators were instructed to be "particularly careful" when distinguishing among blacks, mulattoes, quadroons, and octoroons and were give definitions for each. A person with "three-fourths or more black blood" was black. A person with "three-eighths to five-eights black blood" was a mulatto. A person with "one-fourth black blood" was a quadroon. A person with "one-eighth or any trace of black blood" was an octoroon.[94] The year 1920 was the last in which the census attempted to count mulattoes, a person with "some proportion or perceptible trace of Negro blood." Enumerators were then to distinguish between "full-blooded Negroes" and mulattos.

The 1920 and the 1930 Censuses added four additional categories: Filipino, Hindu, Korean, and Other. The only census to include a category for Mexicans was in 1930. Thus, before and after, Mexicans were white, but in 1930 they were not. In 1930, mulattos and any person with any amount of "Negro blood" were to be counted as a "Negro." People with "mixed Indian and Negro blood" were to be counted as "Negroes" unless "the Indian blood predominates and the status of an Indian is generally accepted in the community." Those with "mixed white and Indian blood" were to be counted as Indians, "except where the percentage of Indian blood is very small, or where he is regarded as a white person by those in the community where he lives." Enumerators were informed: "Practically all Mexican laborers are of a racial mixture difficult to classify." The rule for classifying a person as a Mexican was that individuals who were born in Mexico or whose parents were born in Mexico were Mexican. It appears that if it was clear to the enumerator that the person was "definitely not white, Negro, Indian, Chinese, or Japanese," then that person was Mexican. The nonwhite parent was to be used to determine the race of those were a "mixture of white and nonwhite." "Mixtures of colored races" were to be classified "according to the race of the father." However, individuals who were a mixture of Indian and Negro were to be classified as "Negro."[95]

The instructions given to 1930 Census enumerators clearly reflected "the racial status quo in American law, society, and science."[96] In the 1920s and 1930s several southern states adopted what came to be known as the "one-drop rule." They enacted legislation or modified existing laws that essentially ruled that any person with an African-American heritage or any other mixed heritage not considered to be white was deemed not white. For example, the 1935 Georgia State Code defined white persons as those who had "no ascertainable trace of either Negro, African, West Indian, Asiatic Indian, Mongolian, Japanese, or Chinese blood in their veins."[97] How one could conclusively prove that he/she had no such ancestors seems to be a question that was not addressed.

The 1940 and the 1950 Censuses counted as "Negroes" all persons of "mixed white and Negro blood." A percentage was not then specified but it did not matter how "small the percentage." The percentage was not specified. No distinction between "Negroes" and mulattoes was made. Mulattoes were "Negroes." Those with a mixture of "Indian and Negro blood" were counted as "Negroes" unless "the Indian blood predominates and the status of an Indian is generally accepted in the community."[98] No percentage was specified. Those with a mixture of "white and Indian blood" were counted as Indians" unless the unspecified percentage was very small or unless the person was "regarded as a white person by those in the community where he lives." Mixed races persons were classified "according to the race of the father, except Negro-Indian.

The year 1960 marked a turning point in the census, for then "self-identification replaced enumerator identification."[99] The categories provided for those being counted included: White, Negro or Black, American Indian, Japanese, Chinese, Filipino, Hawaiian, Korean, and Other. Definitions for color and race were provided for those completing the 1960 Census forms. Those definitions indicated that Puerto Ricans, Mexicans, and all others of Latin-American descent were white "unless they are definitely of Negro, Indian, or other nonwhite race." "Negro" was to be marked for Negroes and "for persons of mixed white and Negro parentage." Those with "mixed Indian and Negro blood" were to be marked as Negro unless the person completing the form knew "that the Indian blood very definitely predominate[d] and that he is regarded in the community as an Indian." "American Indian" was to be marked for "fullblooded" Indians and for those who had one-fourth or more Indian blood. Those "regarded as Indian in the community where they live[d]" were to be marked as Indian. People from India, unless they were of "European stock" were to be marked as "Hindu." There were instructions to make certain that people distinguished between Asian Indians and American Indians. In general, the race of the father was to be used to determine the race of "persons of mixed white and nonwhite races."[100]

In 1980, the Census Bureau provided even more categories than in 1970: White, Negro or Black, Japanese, Chinese, Filipino, Korean., Vietnamese, American Indian, Asian, Indian, Hawaiian, Guamanian, Samoan, Eskimo, Aleut, and Other. In 1990, there were still more categories: White, Black or Negro, American Indian, Eskimo, Aleut, Chinese, Filipino, Hawaiian, Korean, Vietnamese, Japanese, Asian, Indian, Samoan, Guamanian, Other Pacific Islander, and Other.

The Formal Designation of Race and Ethnicity Have Never Been and Are Not Fixed

The review of the categories used in the censuses shows that race is certainly not a fixed concept. It is indeed fluid. What is considered to be a race and how one's race has been determined have varied. It is also highly questionable whether the counts of the various groups tell very much. There is no way to tell how reliable the enumerators were or what their prejudices or inclinations were. Self-identification may be more reliable, but it is necessary to recognize that how people view themselves often changes over time.

The varied nomenclature, the progression and regression in terminology, surrounding race and ethnicity tell more about the perceptions of dominant groups than about the subordinate groups whom others define. If the varied terminology is an impediment to the development of social policies that eliminate discrimination, the connections between individual biography and collective cultural identities as they coincide with systems of privilege and subordination need to be identified. The category of race is pernicious since its historical implications and use have been harmful and have had disastrous implications for all inhabitants of the United States. Race, with its implications of biological permanence, is harmful. Ethnicity is more useful as a cultural designation but it also has tendencies that could make it a replacement for the more negative aspects of race in the sorting of individuals and groups according to immutable characteristics that are no longer considered biological but of social origin.

NOTES

1.   Allen Ginsberg, Howl in Allen Ginsberg, *Howl and Other Poems*, William Carlos Williams Intro. (San Francisco: City Lights Books, 1956, 1959, Feb. 2001), p. 7.

2.   James S. Coleman, *et. al. Equality of Educational Opportunity* (Washington, DC: U. S. Government Printing Office, 1966), p. iii.

3.   Ibid.

4.   Quoted in Frederick Mosteller and Daniel P. Moynihan eds., *On Equality of Educational Opportunity* (New York: Vintage Books, 1972), p. 8.

5.   Ibid., p. 10.

6.   Coleman. *Equality of Educational Opportunity*, pp. 121-122.

7.   Ibid., p. 122.

8.   Ibid., p. 21.

9.   Ibid., p. 22.

10.   Ibid., p. 21

11.   James Coleman, "Toward Equal Schools or Equal Students?" *The Public Interest*, No. 4 (Summer, 1966): 71.

12.   Ibid., p. 72.

13.   James Coleman, "Toward Open Schools," *The Public Interest*, No. 9 (Fall, 1967): 21.

14.   Coleman, "Equal Schools," p. 73.

15.   Ibid., p. 75.

16.   Ibid., p. 74.

17.   Ibid.

18.   Ibid.

19.   Ibid., p. 75.

20.   Coleman, *Equality of Educational Opportunity*, p. 22.

21.   Godfrey Hodgson, *America in Our Time: From World War II to Nixon* (New York: Vintage Books, 1978), p. 449.

22.   Mosteller and Moynihan, *On Equality of Educational Opportunity*, p. 13.

23. Hodgson, *America in Our Time*, p. 449.

24. Mosteller and Moynihan, *On Equality of Educational Opportunity*, p. 13.

25. Ibid., p. 6.

26. Ibid., p. 59.

27. Ibid., pp. 58-59. Emphasis in original.

28. Ibid., p. 63.

29. Ibid., p. 13.

30. Christopher Jencks, et. al., *Inequality: A Reassessment of Family and Schooling in America* (New York: Harper Colophon, 1973), p. 3.

31. Ibid., p. 14.

32. Ibid., p. 253.

33. Ibid., pp. 255-256.

34. Ibid., p. 256.

35. Ibid.

36. Ibid., p. 257.

37. Ibid.

38. Mosteller and Moynihan, *On Equality of Educational Opportunity*, p. 53. Emphasis in original.

39. Ibid., p. 56. Emphasis in original.

40. Ibid., Emphasis in original.

41. Ibid., p. 57. Emphasis in original.

42. Daniel P. Moynihan. "Equalizing Education: In Whose Benefit?" *The Public Interest*, no. 29 (Fall 1972): 70.

43. Ibid., p. 73. Emphasis in original.

44. Ibid., Moynihan's emphasis.

45. Ibid., pp. 79-80.

46. Ibid., p. 73.

47. Mosteller and Moynihan, *On Equality of Educational Opportunity*, p. 32.

48. Lester C. Thurow, "Education and Economic Equality," *The Public Interest*, No. 289 (Summer 1972): 81.

49. Ibid., pp. 69-70.

50. Jencks, *Inequality*, p. 8.

51. David K. Cohen and Michael S. Garet, "Reforming Educational Policy with Applied Social Research," *Harvard Educational Review*, Vol. 45 (February 1975): p. 21.

52. Ibid., p. 23.

53. Hodgson, *America in Our Time*, p. 461.

54. Ricardo L. Garicia, *Teaching in a Pluralistic Society: Concepts, Models, Strategies*, (New York: Harper & Row, 1982), p. 20.

55. Ibid., p. 21.

56. Ravitch *The Troubled Crusade*, p. 275.

57. Ibid., p. 273.

58. Garcia, *Teaching in a Pluralistic Society*, p. 29.

59. Erwin I. Levine and Elizabeth M. Wexler, *PL 94-142: An Act of Congress* (New York: Macmillan, 1981), pp. 11-12.

60. Ravitch, *Troubled Crusade*, p. 307.

61. P. L. 94-142 reprinted in Levine and Wexler. *PL 94-142*, p. 192.

62. Levine and Wexler, *PL 94-142*, p. 139.

63. Ibid., p. 140.

64.   Martha M. McCarthy, "The Pennhurst and Rowley Decisions: Issues and Implications," *Exceptional Children*, Vol. 49 (April 1983): 520-521.

65.   Quoted in McCarthy, "The Pennhurst and Rowley Decisions," p. 520.

66.   Michael Lind, *The Next American Nation: The New Nationalism & the Fourth American Revolution* (New York: Free Press, 1996), pp. 109-110.

67.   Ibid., p. 108.

68.   Graham, *The Civil Rights Era*, p. 4.

69.   Lind, *The Next American Nation.*, p. 110.

70.   Quoted in Graham, *The Civil Rights Era*, p. 33. Graham's emphasis.

71.   Ibid., p. 41.

72.   Ibid., p. 34-35.

73.   Ibid., pp. 41-42.

74.   Graham, *The Civil Rights Era*, p. 41.

75.   Quoted in Graham, *The Civil Rights Era*, p. 42.

76.   Graham, *The Civil Rights Era*, p. 61.

77.   Ibid., p. 61. Graham's emphasis.

78.   Quoted in Graham, *The Civil Rights Era*, p. 62.

79.   Graham, *The Civil Rights Era*, p. 62.

80.   Applicants for positions with the federal government may also be asked to indicate whether they have a "targeted disability." For example, applicants for positions with the National Archives and Records Administration are asked to do so and are informed that "The Equal Employment Opportunity Commission [EEOC] targets the following disabilities for extra recruitment efforts: Deaf, Blind, Missing Extremities, Partial/Complete Paralysis, Convulsive Disorders, Mentally Retarded, Mental Illness or Distortion Limb/Spine."

81.   Lind, *The Next American Nation*, p. 119.

82.   *Federal Register* (July 9, 1997), Part II, pp. 36873-36946. Available at <http://www.whitehouse.gov/omb/fedreg/directive15.html.>

83.   Melissa Nobles, *Shades of Citizenship: Race and the Census in Modern Politics* (Stanford. California: Stanford University Press, 2000), p. 80.

84.   Lind, *The Next American Nation*, p. 119.

85.   Ibid.

86.   Ibid., p. 10.

87.   David A. Hollinger, *Postethnic America: Beyond Multiculturalism* (New York: Basic Books, 1995), pp. 32-33.

88.   *Federal Register* (July 9, 1997).

89.   Ibid.

90.   Melissa Nobles. *Shades of Citizenship*, p. 1.

91.   Ibid., pp. 35-36.

92.   U. S. Census Bureau. Reproduced in Nobles. *Shades of Citizenship*, p. 187. Italics in the original.

93.   Ibid., pp. 187-188.

94.   Ibid., p. 188. Italics in the original.

95.   Ibid., pp. 188-189.

96.   Ibid., p. 69.

97.   Quoted in Nobles, *Shades of Citizenship*, p. 70.

98.   U. S. Census Bureau, Reproduced in Nobles. *Shades of Citizenship*, p. 189.

99.   Nobles, *Shades of Citizenship*, p. 78.

100.   U. S. Census Bureau, Reproduced in Nobles. *Shades of Citizenship*, p. 190.

CHAPTER 9

CONCLUSION
Understanding the Past for Today and All Tomorrows

> But I got news for them. They us. I never tell them that but inside I know it. They us, just like we is ourselves. Cut any of them open and you see if you don't find Munford Bazille or Hatti Brown there. You know what I mean?"[1]

The Challenge of the future is to avoid the pitfalls of the past. Citizens of the United States of America are situated on the brink of many conflicting choices in an unsettled world. Issues of political and economic dominance, the use of violence and war to achieve national and ideological goals and competition over rightful leadership are as critical today, if not more so, as in any time in history. Are the racial categories of the past being transformed into new immutable ethnic disparities based on class, cultural and national differences? In the confusion of the moment can we learn from each other how to see through the myths of our past living in our present? Can American exceptionalism be transformed into a collective identity as world citizens on the planet Earth? Can manifest destiny be regrouped into a global political and economic consciousness? What form would such a consciousness take? What is the role of the United States and what is the

Race, Ethnicity, and Education: What is Taught in School, pages 253–279.
A Volume in: International Perspectives on Curriculum
Copyright © 2003 by Information Age Publishing, Inc.
All rights of reproduction in any form reserved.
ISBN: 1-59311-080-4 (paper), 1-59311-081-2 (cloth)

responsibility of American (U.S.) citizens in this endeavor? There are no singular answers to these questions. Many of the answers projected today sound disarmingly close to the rhetoric of the past. They were not solutions but the door to divisions.

MYTHS OF DESTINY AND EXCEPTIONALITY: THE PAST IS NOT OVER

Citizens of the United States envisioned themselves as products of the Anglo-Saxon tradition and as their natural heirs. The New World was supposed to champion and improve upon the Old World's political potential and move it toward national freedom and republican government. This reflected a faith in individualistic democracy as not only good for the United States but also a universal goal for all humanity. These beliefs were closely related to the concept of manifest destiny—the belief that the United States would rise not only politically but also economically to promote democracy throughout the world through commerce, agriculture, and industry. Today it is through global markets, high technology, and military power. The ideological dual political and economic missions of the past required a strong foreign policy but did not necessarily encourage the use of force and conquest in their original forms. The founders of the Republic at the end of the eighteenth century turned to revolution and armed conflict as a necessary evil.[2] This attitude changed at the end of the nineteenth century. After the collapse of the Soviet Union much of the dream of world leadership was realized.

The Role of Government

By the beginning of the twentieth century policymakers' social attitudes were easily compatible with a new "modern" role for government. "Drawing support from Social Darwinism and "scientific" racism, America's dominant groups felt confident of their own superiority. Moreover, they had grown accustomed in domestic affairs to calling upon government to enforce and maintain their prerogatives."[3] In the Progressive era governmental power crushed those ethnic groups that were perceived as threats to social stability, just as on the frontier, federal troops squashed the last great Indian resistance at Wounded Knee in 1890. In the South, state governments enforced Jim Crow laws against African Americans. That created apartheid, and the Supreme Court sanctioned the system with its separate-but-equal doctrine in *Plessy v. Ferguson.* In northern cities, governmental power clashed with strikers who were branded as radical "new immigrants." In the Far West, laws to restrict the immigration of the Chinese were enforced. Thus far in the contemporary period we have not enacted draconian laws.

As Emily S. Rosenberg has pointed out, "concepts of racial mission, so well rehearsed at home were easily transferred overseas."[4] While the arguments of the past are outdated, the underlying assumptions of rightness and destiny are contemporary. A century ago editor Theodore Margurg argued:

> We have brushed aside 275,000 Indians, and in place of them have this population of 70,000,000 of what we regard as the highest type of modern man...
> [W]e hold to the opinion that we have done more than any other race to conquer the world for civilization in the past few centuries, and we will probably go on holding to this opinion and go on with our conquests.[5]

Because governmental power had consistently supported Anglo-Saxon dominance at home in the name of advancing republicanism and progress, so it seemed natural for policymakers to adopt a similar activist role and rationale abroad. Senator Albert Beveridge urged President William McKinley not to shirk the "white man's" burden of history. God, he argued:

> . . . has not been preparing English speaking and Teutonic peoples for a thousand years for nothing but vain and idle self contemplation and self admiration. No! He has made us master organizers of the world to establish system where chaos reigns. He has given us the spirit of progress to overwhelm the forces of reaction throughout the earth. He has made us adept in government that we may administer government among savage and senile people. Were it not for such a force as this the world would relapse into barbarism and night. And all our race He has marked American people as His chosen nation to finally lead in the regeneration of the world."[6]

Theodore Roosevelt, who became President a little over one hundred years ago, agreed. Drawing on America's own history, he argued that when the United States government fought "wars with barbarous or semi-barbarous peoples," it was not violating the peace but merely exercising a "most regrettable but necessary police duty which must be performed for the sake of the welfare of mankind."[7]

Progressivism and Progress As Regressive

Crusades to dominate those who were not Anglo-Saxon also found support from the burgeoning Progressive movement, of which President Theodore Roosevelt, Indiana's Senator Beveridge and other turn-of-the-century imperialists considered themselves a part. Progressivism, a reform impulse that profoundly reshaped American domestic life and foreign relations from the 1890s through World War I, comprised a loose and often contradictory coalition of crusaders against corruption in government, conservationists, Anglo-Saxon supremacists, muckraking journalists, social welfare workers, efficiency experts, middle-class professionals, and advocates of business regulation.[8] These themes are not foreign to contemporary politics.

The seeds of American exceptionalism and manifest destiny can be found as early as 1782 in J. Hector St. John de Crèvecoeur's *Letters from an American Farmer.* In those letters Crèvecoeur, who can be credited with first introducing the notion that America was a melting pot myth, wrote:

> Here [America] individuals of all [European] nations are melted into a new race of men, whose labours and posterity will one day cause great changes in the world. Americans are the western pilgrims who are carrying along with them the great mass of arts, sciences, vigour, and industry which began long since in the East; they will finish the great circle. The Americas were once scattered all over Europe; here they are incorporated into one of the finest systems of population which has ever appeared, and which will hereafter become distinct by the power of the different climates they inhabit. The American ought therefore to love this country much better than that wherein he or his forefathers were born.[9]

It is not surprising that Crèvecoeur's work is still readily available in bookstores. He was one of the sources of myths and an inspiration for those who wanted to perpetuate the idea of a melting pot but who also did not really want it to melt, if it meant accepting immigrants.

The belief in American superiority reached a high point as the nineteenth century ended and the twentieth began. We see a new cycle of this belief in progress today. Then, American leaders were quite willing to use government to support what they believed was their obligation, or right, to impose upon others the American way. Rosenberg reported that:

> . . . the overproductive thesis (which mistakenly presumed a fairly inelastic domestic demand) did provoke a reassessment of government's role. Accepting the proposition that government had new responsibilities to enlarge foreign markets a State Department memo of 1898 stated that the "enlargement of a foreign consumption of the products of our mills and workshops has, therefore, become a serious problem of statesmanship as well as of commerce . . . and we can no longer afford to disregard international rivalries now that we ourselves have become a competitor in the world-wide struggle for trade." If only they could take charge and attack social problems in a scientific way, the new professionals believed, they would bring order and progress at home and abroad.[10]

At this time the United States saw the Philippines (we did take them) as a "gateway to the Orient."[11] Possession of the Philippines would also advance American Protestant missionary efforts in those Catholic islands and on the Asian mainland. "The Christian view of politics," explained one missionary in 1901, "emphasizes the burden of Government and the responsibility of domination, and thereby transforms empire from an ambition to an opportunity. Blindly and unworthily, yet, under God, surely and steadily, the Christian nations are subduing the world, in order to make mankind free."[12]

Instruments of Righteousness

The doctrine of America's inevitable destiny incorporated the idea that the United States was God's instrument for righteousness of good over evil. Unlike the founders of the Republic, Roosevelt's and Beveridge's America needed force. President Roosevelt, the Rough Rider, loathed those who would be "flapdoodle pacifists and molly coddle outfit," who might lack Beveridge's "manly athleticism." (Americans, they maintained, should not be afraid to die for their cause and should fear dishonor or the perishing of the nation more than death itself.) "Every nation, even the evil nation, must follow conscience and use force to defend its judgment" was a view espoused by Captain Alfred Mahan whose colonial and expansionist theories rooted in the American experience and British naval colonial policy were popularized by Roosevelt as a friend and admirer. Mahan's optimism held that since "God would never permit a just cause to go down in defeat" the nation was assured of success.[13] Americans never lose wars in the permanent victory myth. By the beginning of the twentieth century, the United States' aggressive expansionist policies resulted in the acquisition of Florida from Spain; Louisiana from the French; the Pacific Northwest from England; Northern Mexico including what is now Texas, California, Arizona, New Mexico and parts of Colorado from Mexico, as well as Hawaii, parts of the Caribbean, Puerto Rico, Panama and the Philippines.[14]

Imperialism appeals to those who believe in America's inevitable progress. American exceptionalism was justified as a God given mission and was consistent with nineteenth conceptions of biological growth. America, conceived of as Anglo, then European, fed into white supremacy at home and abroad. As Charles Darwin's theory of natural selection was adapted to social life by Herbert Spencer, it found its way into economic, political, sociological, and educational thought. William Graham Sumner led the field in adapting natural evolution to social evolution. Sumner, an economist and sociologist at Yale University, is interesting because he used Spencerian evolution for the core of his theories to argue for a strict laissez-faire approach to social governance. He was also an anti-imperialist as were many major leaders in social reform, humanitarian causes. This included literary figures such as Mark Twain; and educators such as David Starr Jordan, President of Stanford University; and Jane Addams, the founder of Hull House in Chicago. Sumner argued:

> Expansionism and imperialism are at war with the best traditions and principles and interests of the American people, and . . . they will plunge us into a network of difficult problems and political perils, which we might have avoided, while they offer us no corresponding advantage in return.[15]

Sumner's anti-imperialism, however, was not derived from a position that favored pluralism. His view of history, even though he was opposed to war, reinforced Anglo-European privilege and superiority. The dominance hierarchy was conceptually static, and these views were consistent with Eurocentric American public policy and fostered the Anglo-European consensus about what it means to be an American that Lind identified.

Sumner argued that social evolution was more or less automatic and natural like biological evolution. Humans acquire folkways and collective habits that favor survival on an instinctual level. In civil society these habits become conscious and can be contemplated but should not be interfered with. "The social order is fixed by the laws of nature precisely analogous to those of the physical order," Sumner declared. "The most that man can do is by his ignorance and conceit to mar the operation of social laws."[16] Inequality between human beings was inevitable, according to Sumner. Inequality resulted from competition, which in turn developed individual talents. Interference by government, according to Sumner, penalized the hardworking and rewarded the incompetent. Franklin Giddens of Columbia University succeeded Sumner in promoting ideas of evolutionary progess in social life.

Education and Heredity

Two psychologists introduced the social theories that attributed individual and group success to heredity into education, G. Stanley Hall at Clark University and Edward Thorndike at Columbia University. While no scientific techniques existed to measure the relative influence of heredity and environment in determining human character and behavior, sweeping generalizations were accepted as factual and scientific. Hall and Thorndike individualized the theory of natural inequality, inevitable progress, and manifest destiny in individuals where heredity became the major factor in success and failure in school and in life. Anglo-European dominance made it seem natural that the ruling groups and individuals in society were "naturally" white. Interference with this "natural" order seemed, as it was to Sumner, futile. To interfere with a selected group of the American people as the "real" Americans who carried the destiny of the nation on their shoulders was believed to be a costly mistake.

PUBLIC EDUCATION AS A GATEKEEPER

Public education has been distorted by the politics of institutional racism and ethnocentrism. Institutional racism in the twentieth century still has the potential to revert to open racism. "New hereditarian" pseudo-science returned with a vengeance to counter the effects of the *Brown* decision and the Civil Rights Movement that culminated in the 1964 Civil Rights Act. William Shockley's and Arthur Jensen's theories justifying race and racism in the 1960s followed in the racist tradition of the Progressive era. They were recited some thirty years later by Richard J. Herrnstein and Charles Murray in *The Bell Curve* (1994) who used similar themes of impending cultural destruction that were popular in the anti-abolition debates and anti-Reconstruction campaigns.[17] The continuation of this thread of racism follows directly, often with little variation or even new data, from the flawed racial thinking of the last century.[18] The media in the late 1990s still projected negative images of nonwhites and celebrated the genealogy of whiteness.[19] The doctrine of white supremacy continues to inhibit the ability of all Americans to perceive their own needs and to act on them. In this way the civil rights of all Americans and all the children in the future are diminished.

Reifying Hierarchies of Classification

Americans are socialized in and out of school to believe that the borders and classifications associated with the conceptualization of race, ethnicity, and exceptionality in the United States are primordial, natural, universal, and inevitable. Modern disciplines, science, technology, and the power of the nation-state affirm an objective reality that all are led to believe is beyond our intervention.[20] The examination of the bargaining processes and the trajectory of forms of knowledge as well as concepts of social privilege, access, and opportunity involve what can be termed boundary work.[21] In boundary work attention is drawn to the origin, establishment, and legitimation of ideas in relationship to power structures. The social and historical mechanisms that construct the social identities of race and ethnicity shape experienced reality and opportunities for advancement in the United States. Who benefits or is harmed by the invention of stratified classification systems is directly related to the class and status associated with the power of the group constructing the typology as well as the power of groups so identified to react.[22]

Attempts to classify formally all that lives are very recent and coincide with the rise of the modern disciplines of biology, and the behavioral and social sciences. Prior to the Enlightenment religious belief systems precluded the idea of classifying life forms. The order of nature and social order were part of theological doctrines and were believed to be beyond human intervention. The Enlightenment offered a new found freedom to pursue science, to understand the Creator's universe and even to intervene in its workings. Understanding, it was believed, would allow control. However, it was not until after the 1850s that the secular aspect of the pursuit of science superceded the sacred.[23] Humans became subjects of study and worthy of classification.[24] In the nineteenth century, humans were no longer apart from the natural world but were part of it. As part of it, they were, it was claimed, subject to the laws of nature. They were to be studied just as all other natural phenomena were studied. The social science disciplines were created and legitimated categories of sameness and difference between social groups. Given the establishment of racial oppression and slavery in the colonial period, this endeavor took on special consequences and dynamics in the United States. The application of the theory of evolution to society was used in the social construction of concepts of race as well as for the validation for a particularly virulent form of pro-white and anti-black racism that took hold of the country in the twentieth century.[25] The distribution and redistribution of power along the borders of class, race, and ethnicity are central processes in the racialized politics of the United States. The historical projection of white as exceptional in the eighteenth century was a major factor in the construction of race in the nineteenth century and more recently as fuel for the politics of ethnicity in the twenty-first century.[26]

WHITENESS AND HIERARCHY

"What is whiteness?" "Who is a white person?" and, "What is white privilege?" are questions that underlie the history of the concepts of race and ethnicity in the United States based on an Anglo-Saxon ideal type. Deviations from the ideal of whiteness form the shifting boundary of a color line based on white privilege in the United States.[27] As history tells us, chattel bonded servitude predated the arrival of Africans in the southern colonies of British North America in the early seventeenth century. Servitude took many forms in the various colonies of British North America in the 1600s but only assumed a peculiar socio-political status as grounded in caste distinctions based on white skin privilege in the southern states. A white skin "color line" formed as slavery became identified with a dark complexion, and racial slavery emerged as distinct from white servitude in the eighteenth century.[28] This was well before the "scientific" association of phenotype with the conception of race or races one hundred years later.

Biology and Racism

The idea of biological race in a modern sense did not exist prior to the nineteenth century. Historian Theodore Allen argued that oppression and slavery in Ireland and American colonies in the eighteenth century was racial.[29] However, he used a pre-nineteenth century non-biological definition of "race" as a socially differentiated subordinated group, not a physically defined genetic group. The borderline of racial oppression in Allen's sense is determined by the relative position of the highest member of the subordinated group as beneath the lowest member of the emergent dominant group. This occurred in Ireland in the sixteenth century with the English suppression of the Celtic tribes of Ireland and Scotland. Clearly, phenotype is not a factor in this example of "racial" oppression.[30] In post-colonial studies the term "ethnicity" or ethnic oppression is used "to account for human variation . . . rather than the discredited generalizations of race."[31] The persistence of racism in its modern sense, in spite of being discredited, is a case in point. It does make sense to use "racial oppression" and "racial slavery" because of the extreme bias that racism imposed on the historical fact of the enslavement of Africans in the United States with its parallel in the suppression and enslavement of the Irish by the English in Ireland. The Irish, in a sense became "white" in the nineteenth century along with other groups differentiated by the rise of racism and the increasing significance of the color line in the United States.[32] Contrary to many historical misconceptions as we have seen, *slavery was not caused by racism*. The belief in race and institutional racism persists because of the political and economic usefulness of class differentiation masked by the shifting borders of racial types of oppression. That extreme forms of caste-like suppression of groups can occur with or without phenotypic differences is witnessed in the treatment of American Indians and Mexican Americans.

Modern racism, prejudice, and discrimination were not factors in the invention of extreme forms of labor, class and gender oppression that characterized the plantation economy.[33] Skin color became a signifier, a sign of inferior status due to divisions in the labor force in the southern economy. The not free dark skinned slave, of African or Anglo-African heritage, was juxtaposed with the free landowner, wage laborer, or partly free light skinned servant of Anglo-European heritage.[34] This distinction was reshaped into the idea of a human race and multiple human hierarchical subspecies in the mid nineteenth century. Proto-psychocultural as well as sociobiological explanations for slavery came to public attention in the 1830s during the Abolition Movement. Imagined racial differences were used as a way to defend slavery. In spite of emancipation and enactment of the Thirteenth, Fourteenth, and Fifteenth Amendments guaranteeing freedom, citizenship, and civil rights to African Americans, the racial differentiation increased after the Civil War. This differentiation and suppression were further developed during Reconstruction and the Progressive era reconstitution of the New South. Racism, individual and institutional, justified segregation in the twentieth century.[35]

Historical Writing On Slavery

Historical writing on slavery and racism as well as the studies of the relative place of white versus black people are controversial and often politicized. Early southern historians were often elites who sought to explain their society in a favorable light. However, the arguments that absolve white society of responsibility by suggesting that slavery occurred "unaware" hardly work. Social policies cannot be driven by social forces outside of human agency.[36] Early justifications for modern as opposed to classical slavery borrowed from the idea that captives in war forfeited their lives and in lieu of being killed could be enslaved by the victor. This justification was used by John Locke in the seventeenth century and was popular in both the northern colonies as well as the southern colonies.[37] Phenotype or skin color was not a factor. Most servant/slaves were Irish or Scottish Celts and a few captured Indians or Africans from the Caribbean colonies in the southern and northern colonies. Almost every person in New England had at one time been in a position of servitude in some form.[38] The justification of slavery after the introduction of pseudo-scientific ideas of race is significantly different. Similarly, claims of the biological inferiority of Africans and African Americans, their natural affiliation with positions of servitude, and the conviction that it is instinctive to reject dark skin as obviously unattractive or repulsive are modern concepts not ancient ones as some argue.[39] Apologist historians also argue that the emergence of white supremacy, lifetime hereditary bonded servitude, and hereditary slavery made Virginians especially appreciative of freedom and thus rose to power and influence in behalf of freedom and democracy in the America Republic. That argument assumes that there was a mass of free white propertied landowners or middle classes and that there was a community of interest among those designated as whites. That was not the case. The majority of whites were not landowners.[40] Recent publications and popular media continue the myth that slavery increased "our moral worth, our ability to claim ourselves a democracy and as an inclusive society...It [slavery] made this country more humane."[41]

Legal racial rhetoric in the nineteenth century also supported slavery and limited the ability to enforce civil rights. Thomas Ross observed that the rhetoric of "white innocence," and the abstraction of the black experience by taking slavery, discrimination and oppression out of context so it is unrecognizable, "did not create the conditions of subjugation" but it did condition choices that avoided any ability to "mitigate . . . subjugation."[42] The rhetoric of race built into the *Dred Scott* (1856) case that dehumanized slaves and extended slave territory, *Civil Rights* cases (1883) that rendered all but meaningless the Thirteenth and Fourteenth Amendments that allowed Reconstruction to fail and *Plessy v. Ferguson* (1896) that legalized segregation constituted a "symptom of the disease of racism that gripped legal culture, and the larger culture of nineteenth century America."[43]

Ethnicity and Civil Rights: Following the Dream

The claim that there were multiple subspecies of human beings was widely accepted in the United States by men of science as well as in popular thought by the early twentieth century, and the impact has lingered for one hundred years. Racism flourished along the borderline of *de jure* (legal) Jim Crow segregation in the South and *de facto* (in fact) segregation in the rest of the country in the first half of the twentieth century. Immigration at the turn of the century also greatly contributed to the formation of categories of exceptionality of mostly white non Anglo-Saxon "ethnics" who did not appear to conform to America's dominant cultural ideals. After World War II, the concept of ethnicity emerged with the Civil Rights movement and the attempts to dismantle overt and covert racial discrimination.[44]

The concept of multiple human species was first applied to minorities, or not white "people of color." It was broadly associated with the biological implications of race as well as cultural components of social identity. As biological science has definitively disproved the genetic reality of races, race remains a social construction reflecting the long-term effects of racism. Ethnicity as a cultural designation has been used to explore the unique characteristics of various subcultures in American society as well as those of the dominant culture including exceptional white subcultures and those based on class and gender as well as regional exceptionalism.

Whiteness and non-whiteness are not absolutes but constitute a contested terrain and a social construction based on relations of power. The color line drawn in the colonial South has nonetheless remained as part of the fabric of society in the United States. The language of social categories based on concepts of exceptionality and differentiation are fluid. Even the privilege accorded whiteness is in practice often elusive and limited to elites due to their social class and gender. Yet, the practices of discrimination along the boundaries of race, ethnicity, and exceptionality remain strong components of social life and are embedded in institutional practices.

The study of ethnicity and culture in the first years of the twenty-first century are no longer strictly identified with subcultures and the non-white population but have turned to the examination of the dominant culture and what it means in a society undergoing rapid demographic change and increased diversity. Neither the "white" nor the "not-white" populations now studied are homogeneous. It is not clear what the outcome will be. It is clear that the concepts of race, ethnicity, and exceptionality are not benign. It is also clear that the implementation of beliefs about race, ethnicity, and exceptionality as introduced into social policies are mediated by complex relations of power among, between, and within groups. The trajectory of constructed beliefs and practices that continue to maintain race, ethnicity and exceptionality as aspects of human identity and social structure in the United States has had a profound impact on public schooling.

ETHNICITY: INDETERMINATE STRUCTURES AND POWER SYMBOLS

Ethnicity emerged in the post-World-War-II era. The Civil Rights Movement's challenge to racism brought other forms of discrimination by class, race, gender, ability, and disability to the nation's attention. Ethnicity was used as a mediator. African Americans tested the grounds of what it meant to be an ethnic group rather than a racial group. Demographic change and awareness of other minorities heightened: Chicano, Mexican, Chinese, Japanese, Korean, Vietnamese, Filipino, Puerto Rican cultures seemed to fit better with ethnicity than race. Current immigration from Latin America, Africa, the Middle East, and Far East heighten this perception as new languages, cultures, and religions visibly change the daily context of the market place and school, as well as discourse over the politics of difference. Ethnic classifications potentially mask continued inequality based on profiling that is based on a group's perceived ability to conform to the standards of whiteness, white privilege, and white values.[45]

U.S. Exceptionalism

In the United States social, political, and economic historical divisions took a peculiar form. The struggle for the survival of identity and access to freedom was symbolically subsumed under the umbrella of "white person." In the United States throughout the twentieth century the existence of racial divisions of humanity was often taken for granted. This was not nec-

essarily the case in England or Europe. The issues have been greatly exacerbated by demographic changes where Hispanic, Asian, American Indian,
Middle Eastern, and other peoples have dispersed the visibility of African
Americans and the race problem as a black/white binary issue. This has
not necessarily benefited the majority of African Americans, or Latinos
(especially Mexican Americans), the largest traditionally oppressed groups
in the United States, just as it has not necessarily rectified the horrendous
treatment of the aboriginal first nations, American Indians.

Sociological and historical research on race relations originated in the
Chicago School of Sociology in the 1920s, expanded after World War II
and blossomed during the Civil Rights Movement. "Ethnic studies" and
multicultural education grew in the 1970s. Over the past five to ten years
the focus has changed among some researchers who now study a new field,
which consists of critical race theory, legal studies, history, and social science and education.[46] Researchers in this new field examine the problems
of members of out groups and their patterns of exceptionality and explore
the dynamic of "whiteness" as the underlying counterpoint in the dialectic
relationship between dominant and subordinate cultural relations in the
United States. The study of "minorities" has usually taken place within the
framework conceived by the dominant group who often are Anglo-European, middle to upper class, Protestant, and patriarchal, who traditionally
conceptualized, both formally in academic circles and informally in social
policy, members of subcultures as deviant given their own standards and
values.

The end of the "Second Reconstruction" of the Civil Rights movement
opened the door for a new crisis and a new terminology. The attention
given to ethnicity and culture effectively masked racial oppression in the
face of deindustrialization, the reversal of the opportunity structures that
had sustained "white" middle and working class relations, as new waves of
immigrants challenge the status quo in a global world market that has displaced many people from the Middle East, Latin America, Asia, and Africa
as well as Eastern Europe. Violent confrontations and the potential for violence both small and large scale are a fact of post-modern life.

Schools Caught in the Middle

Schooling was early imbued with the cultural politics of the day. Special
education expanded rapidly as more children with handicapping conditions were allowed to enter school. As desegregation was mandated and
eventually implemented, the overrepresentation of minorities in classes for
the mentally retarded and later the over representation of middle and
upper class white children in classes for the gifted became apparent and
remain a problem embedded in a variety of institutional practices: for

example, tracking and the pervasive use of standardized tests and biases built into public education. These problems remain widespread especially with non-English speaking groups relegated to an inferior education.[47]

Popular sentiment and public awareness of diversity shifted as emergent fields of scholarship in the last thirty years sought to address social problems and to reform school policy. Policy makers, educators, and parents became embattled over efforts to mediate racial and ethnic inequality. Educational reform faltered and opinions splintered with negative publicity, critical reports, and confused priorities as massive demographic changes swept the country accompanied by a worldwide economic transformation from an industrial to a high technological post-industrial economy in the 1970s and 1980s.

The Black Power Movement of the Civil Rights Era in the 1960s spawned other movements identified by their cultural, linguistic, and "ethnic" heritages such as the American Indian Movement, the Chicano Movement, and the Women's Movement that had an impact on schools. In universities, the field of Ethnic Studies emerged. Departments that studied the history and perspective of particular groups in Black Studies, American Studies, Women's Studies were created. Human relations approaches evident from the inter-cultural education movement in the 1930s grew even more popular. Advocates for multicultural education in the 1970s first sought to identify and increase understanding between groups. Multicultural education also sought changes in pedagogical practices used to teach minorities and the culturally different as well as children with mental and physical exceptionalities. New or add-on curriculum and policies contributed to minor alterations in school practices and often led to controversies over mainstreaming, bilingual education, and multicultural education itself. More recently and parallel to this approach a movement emerged for the significant restructuring of schooling in a pluralistic society concerned with equity, justice, and equality of educational opportunity.

WHITE TEACHERS IN PLURALISTIC SCHOOLS

Malcolm X observed: "we can't teach what we don't know, and we can't lead where we won't go." Gary Howard acknowledged this point in his book with a similar title. He addressed the issue of white identity among teachers in multiracial schools in a climate of demographic change that has transformed the school population in the United States over the past ten years. That transformation will continue to reshape dramatically the nation's population in the next decade and into the foreseeable future.[48] Students of color will constitute forty percent or more of the school population by the year 2010. The largest urban districts already have predominantly multicultural student populations. The trend for teachers is in the opposite direction. The vast majority of teachers are not only white but also products of relatively isolated white neighborhoods and white institutions of higher education.[49] Increasing diversity in populous states that are traditionally multicultural such as New York, California, Texas, and Florida is not surprising, but as globalization, trade agreements, civil unrest and wars undermine traditional economies, and migration escalates and does not necessarily follow the traditional patterns. Mexican workers once migrant are seeking new venues for opportunity in the South and Midwest as permanent residents. This has led to the opening of a Mexican Consulate in Indianapolis as well as studies by the governor to determine the impact of this population that has grown by seven hundred percent in some counties. West Africans, Southeast Asians, and Arabs from the Middle East are part of the changing cultural climate teachers must address. As Howard and others pointed out and the 2000 Census confirmed, "diversity is not a choice, but our responses to it certainly are."[50]

Addressing White Dominance in Teaching

The movement to address the importance of white dominance in teaching has grown. The problem with taking on an issue such as this is that white people often do not see themselves as having a culture much less one that is dominant. Howard used the analogy of not really noticing the air that we breathe or a fish taking water for granted within a fishbowl. Concepts of white identity are immersed in the historical assumption of the natural authority and rights of "white persons" as true Americans. The unquestioned belief in white supremacy is embedded in one's consciousness and reinforced in institutions in harmful ways that are not noticed and seen as natural. This operates in three ways.

Projecting a Monocultural World View
First, an Anglo-European worldview is projected as the only correct and accurate perception of reality. Howard called this the "assumption of rightness." The assumption of rightness as reinforced in school and everyday practices makes it difficult for most people who pass as white to comprehend the experiences of those who do not experience what they do. This projection onto others of one's own perspective fundamentally hampers the teacher-student exchange with any child. It is part of the mechanism that reinforces the superiority and success of children from families that match the dominant ideal and relentlessly devalues the culture, perspectives and experiences of children who do not match the ideal. It is one way that schools reproduce social class inequality and limit the potential of children from minority backgrounds on the basis of race or ethnicity as

well as on the basic of gender and ability. There have been many names for this process. Lisa Delpit called it part of a "silenced dialogue" in which the dominant discourse silences people of color and assures their failure by neglecting to tell everyone the rules of the game. Joel Spring called it deculturalization—school practices that serve to replace a child's home culture with one favored by the dominant culture. That some groups cannot become "white" is somehow used to justify their failure to perform and be successful. The persistence of the idea of race and the superiority of whites is troubling. From its origin arguments for white supremacy have persisted. Howard likened this phenomenon to a "crazy uncle" who is locked away in our collective social reality:

> This old relative has been part of the family for a long time. Everyone knows he has been living with us, because we bring him food and water occasionally, but nobody wants to take him out in public. He is an embarrassment and a pain to deal with, yet our little family secret is that he is rich and the rest of us are living, either consciously or unconsciously, off the wealth and power he accumulated in his heyday. Even though many of us may disapprove of the tactics he used to gain his fortune, few of us want to be written out of the will. The legacy of racism, which has been fueled and legitimated by our assumption of rightness, has haunted the house of collective White Identity for centuries. How we deal with this specter [is the question at hand].[51]

The Legitimation of the Consequences of Universalizing Whiteness

Second, white people do not necessarily intentionally perpetuate racism and racist practices that discriminate. In the California Newsreel production, *Color of Fear*, Victor, one of the participants in a weekend seminar on racism comments that it is not the members of openly racist organizations that he fears as a black man. It is rather the well meaning, generous, often "open minded" middle class white person who does not understand what is going on and in his or her ignorance continues the processes that keeps the crazy uncle alive, well, and tolerated in public policy and in school classrooms. What Howard described as a "luxury of ignorance" again on the part of whites is a luxury because people who are victims of discrimination cannot chose to ignore the effects of racism. Whites, however, have the choice to come forward or not come forward. It is always possible to disappear back into the safety of white identity. It is possible to ignore what is going on without any obvious immediate harmful consequences. Privileged groups who consider their opinions validations of natural universal truths, even if they sincerely desire to do what is right in the terms that they are capable of understanding, still do not have any necessary motivation to become aware of their own misperceptions. Similarly, "the luxury of ignorance" serves to maintain whites' belief in the melting pot and colorblind perspectives. The melting pot ideal that was popularized early in the twentieth century was coincident in time with the enforcement of Jim Crow legislation. The melting pot metaphor represented the belief that the masses of immigrants from southern and eastern Europe who flooded into Ellis Island and other ports of entry should lose their culture, language, and Catholic religion and adopt the proper ways of western Europeans in the Anglo-Saxon tradition. Not everyone was willing or able to subscribe to this ideal and, as pointed out earlier, a paradigm shift occurred in the Second Republic when Anglocentrism gave way to Eurocentrism. Yet, it is clear that the African American population who could trace their heritage in North America back to the seventeenth century were not intended as candidates for assimilation. The formation of a legally enforced rigid caste system based on the false claims of racial inferiority was created, and African Americans were assigned to it.

The solution to the color line in the post segregation era was to be "color blind" to race as configured in the United States. Colorblindness is also a luxury of whites. It is a promise to not notice that discrimination occurs in a regular pattern and reproduces the inequalities embedded in the unfair practices of the past. The luxury of ignorance allows white people to pretend that people of color experience the same world they do and that whites have been right as assumed all along. In the *Color of Fear*, David, the representative white, middle class male, locked in the shadow of his own worldview at first denies the experiences and feelings of his non-white peers as wrong headed. He stands firmly and resolutely behind a melting pot and colorblind ideology. Only gradually when he raises the issue of this daughter's struggle to compete successfully for admission to college under the current high stakes admission policies and he is treated with sympathy, does he begin to see how he might have reacted if they had brushed off his concerns with the comment that she should try harder and become more competitive.

The Persistence of Psycho-Biological Over Social Explanations

Third, white people do not display arrogance and ignorance because of some flawed gene. White dominance has to be taught carefully, directly, and indirectly. It has to become intergenerational and embedded in concepts of reality through systems of socialization that reinforce it and through formal education based on the assumption that the dominant white view is the right view. The belief that the white view is the right view, the belief in assimilation as represented by the melting pot metaphor and the colorblind orientation constitute the mechanics of continued white domination. This is a trajectory that Howard called the "legacy of white privilege."[52] Teachers continue these practices in part because the texts they are given to use often fail to distinguish between myths and reputable histories. Additionally, teachers are often not given the opportunity to study history and literature to enable them to make critical judgments. Teachers fear reprisals from cautious administrators and supervisors whose knowledge is no greater than that of the teachers. Parents, who have also been taught myths, fear the consequences of critical histories or even accurate versions of their own often recent or distant immigrant backgrounds, which they have romanticized, have learned to forget, or are embarrassed about. In spite of admonitions to encourage critical thinking, textbooks contribute to distortions through nationalistic legends that teach that there is only one true path, the "American way." America's example is allowed to represent the greater good for humanity.

The Misuse of Religious Values

Howard wrote about the ways in which the assumption of rightness in the United States is often justified through the use of and misuse of religion. Images from a Judeo-Christian heritage are used to reinforce American exceptionalism and white supremacy. Howard amusingly described a school board meeting in Seattle at which the board's policy on the teaching of foreign languages was discussed. At the meeting a frustrated father opposed to foreign language instruction argued, "If English was good enough for Jesus Christ, it's good enough for my kids!" Christianity is not the only religion to be used to the advantage of various factions in society where the interests of one group are portrayed as not only right but as blessed by the one and only true God. "If Jesus is one of us, he must have spoken English." The resentment of town's people or teachers to newcomers in "our" town or school, is a case in point. "They" don't belong "here."[53]

Anglo-Saxon America is historically portrayed in Biblical terms with romantic or wild landscapes. Early American artist, George Caleb Bingham, depicted "Daniel Boone Coming through the Cumberland Gap" in the image of Joseph and Mary. Boone in his buckskin suit and rifle leads a white horse with a woman cloaked in a shawl. The forward group forms a trinity. Their white faces shine before the "wild" background, and emergent figures follow out of the gloomy terrain of mountains and stark branches. They come toward a new beginning.[54] American Indians were depicted as kin to the landscape as either "children of nature" or "ruthless savages."[55] Explorers of the Oregon Trail, Meriwether Lewis and William Clark, were depicted in oil on canvas by Charles Marion Russell (1912) as they meet the Flathead Tribe in 1805.[56] Fierce wolves and the mounted warriors brandish spears skyward as their spotted Appaloosa horses charge, stop, and whirl are contrasted with the stationary figures of the white men bringing "civilization" and order to the wilderness. A vast empty Montana valley, waiting to be taken, stretches toward snowcapped mountains. Clouds shape the horizon flecked with the golden glow of a sun setting to the West, toward destiny.

The wilderness theme of empty land given by God to a chosen people is as pervasive as it is misleading.[57] The indigenous peoples of the Americas, the first nations, civilizations, territories, and villages that first aided the newcomers are given little attention and even less credit. In children's texts we read token words of thanks about Squanto, giver of corn, at the first Thanksgiving in New England. The cartoon of the "beautiful" Princess Pocahontas represents a "noble savage" who helped Captain John Smith and married John Rolfe in Virginia. The image of the "faithful" Sacajawea, the guide who led Lewis and Clark to Oregon through the Louisiana Purchase to that Montana valley described above, is acknowledged on a coin that is not often used. Little is taught about United States' policy in the Jacksonian Age of Democracy that included genocide against the Native American people. Silence replaces the horrors of the Cherokee Trail of Tears or what in Indiana is described as the Trail of Death. "America" the vision goes, beckoned new immigrants from far off lands to offer opportunities as a "free people" dedicated to "life, liberty, and the pursuit of happiness." Yet, Americans are not depicted as diverse in the heroic images of our past. America's mythic heroes encounter only romantic or savage "others" in passing who somehow appear to not count. The Spaniards, who founded the first fort and community with a school in Saint Augustine in what is now Florida; Mexicans who settled Texas, California, and a significant portion of the South, Southwest, and Far West; the French who controlled the central portion of the nation from New Orleans to the St. Lawrence River and Ohio Valley; and Dutch pioneers in the Hudson Valley and New York, whose settlements preceded them are silenced in the origin myths.

Cultural Fictions and their Uses

Stephen J. Hartnett in his study of the rhetoric of "cultural fictions" in the antebellum period debates over slavery and emancipation reported that slavery, modernism, capitalism, and continental expansion intersect. As stories in the making, "much like fiction," rhetoric defines versions of reality and serves to give experience meaning. The stories express and form habits of thought and behavior that reflect the way people rationalize their experiences and project their own interests.[58] Historic arguments over slavery and racial privilege and discrimination also illustrate the contentious nature of democratic processes as the dialogue oscillates between dissent and assent. Contradictions reveal multiple perspectives and competing principles that waver between democracy and what Americans, we are told, left behind in England, despotism.

The democracy-despotism duality remains prominent in spite of the myth of historic closure. The promise of freedom for all is countered by the history of slavery and the practice of segregation that still limits and regulates access to participation in American life. The rhetorical claims of equal participation by "the people," democracy, are contradicted by the reality of voting patterns and participation in governance by a few, oligarchy. The notion of manifest destiny as a calling and right is contradicted by the facts of imperialism and genocide as a legacy of settlement and continental expansion. The potential problem continues today with economic globalization. The right to democratic dissent in a free society is suppressed by limited access to usable information for most people, in spite of expanded media. Sound bites and the cultural noise of a consumer society overshadow debates over issues. When issues are debated, the presence of contradictory "cultural fictions" makes it difficult to judge truth or just claims to reality.[59]

AMERICA AS "EUROPE'S DREAM" REVISITED

The historic idea of American exceptionalism is part truth and part fiction but it serves real purposes. American history and identity, as noted, contain stories that serve as umbrella myths that are points of pride that serve to unify as well as divide. An early and persistent claim of citizens of the United States is that their country is a very special place with singularly special people. American exceptionalism maintains that the United States of America not only is different from all other countries or nations but also has superior institutions, a better way of life, and holds the moral high ground, which gives it the right in various ways to make all other nations conform to its views and principles. Those who subscribe uncritically to American exceptionalism usually, not always, tend to view various forms of diversity, culture, and experience as a threat to what they believe the United States has been and should be in the future. There is a great deal of resistance to changing the rules of American identity by those who feel they have a stake in traditional versions of American history. This tends toward a static perception of an immutable identity and past, a safety net and rallying point for those who feel in control and are content with the status quo.

The contradictions in American history and life are played out in the idea of exceptionalism. The origins of the concept reveal the template that formed the divisions in American society as they took root and as they remain embedded in conflicting versions of American identity and American history. Examining the formation of exceptionalism also has implications for interpretations of what the future should entail, whether it should be static or regressive, exhibit gradual and progressive change, or demand significant transformation.

The United States of America in a certain sense was "an extension of the European imagination—the dream of Europe."[60] It emerged as a nation professing the belief that all human beings have inherent rights. In 1776, the Declaration of Independence asserted the right of the people to throw off tyrants in that "all men are created equal, that they are endowed by their Creator with certain unalienable rights…" The Constitution of the United States and its Bill of Rights also affirm that governments derive their power from the consent of the governed rather than by divine or other authority. Turgot, a contemporary of the American Revolution, spoke in 1778 of the awesome potential of the United States. This potential remains:

> This people [U.S.A.] is the hope of the human race. It may become the model. It ought to show the world, by facts, that men can be free and yet peaceful, and may dispense with the chains in which tyrants and knaves of every colour [sic] have presumed to bind them, under the pretext of the public good. The Americans should be an example of political, religious, commercial, and industrial liberty. The asylum they offer to the oppressed of every nation, the avenue of escape they open, will compel governments to be just and enlightened…*But to obtain these ends for us, America must secure them to herself* and must not become, as so many… have predicted, a mass of divided powers, contending for territory and trade, cementing the slavery of people by their own blood.[61]

The dangers that were predicted two years after the Declaration of Independence did not materialize. The United States has struggled with avoiding becoming "a mass of divided powers contending for territory and trade." The United States has grown into a great power but its greatness is limited and divided, structurally flawed in spite of Reconstruction, the long road to Brown through the dark night of racial segregation and by an attitude of righteousness and exceptionality. The Civil Rights movement is not over; the danger is not past. The goal of providing universal political, religious, commercial, and industrial liberty for all has not yet been achieved.[62]

"The Dark Beast Struggles Toward Bethlehem to Be Born"

America is not finished. Humanity struggles to become truly civilized. The human struggle against barbarism is not a struggle against someone else it is a struggle with ourselves.[63] To achieve and secure justice and enlightenment, to be free and peaceful, to end oppression and tyranny as a model for other nations, America must seek to secure these goals for all citizens as well as justice for all nations. White dominance nationally, as seen in western colonialism and imperialism, was based on the belief of the physical superiority of white people and the structural superiority of Western culture. This is not only questionable; it has been demonstrated to be patently false. The United States is the dominant world power but non-western nations have also developed sophisticated modern economic and technical capacities. We are slowly learning to recognize the contributions of civilizations and cultures that prize harmony with nature and elevate spiritual and social values over economic and technical dominance. The era of the belief in innate structural white supremacy cannot be sustained. Yet, the entrepreneurial capacity and cultural power of the dominant group in the United States are not likely to diminish. In whose interests dominant groups wield the instruments of power is questioned. If it is in ways that are only to the advantage for those in power and detrimental for those who are powerless, the direction will be in Turgot's words like "cementing the slavery of people by their own blood." Whether the current international power configuration is just a "transitory phase," also remains to be seen. Citizens of the United States need to see the perspective of other people as important for its own welfare in the human global community. It is up to the citizens of the United States to chart its future. The United States and Anglo-European perspective may well continue to dominate education, science, technology, and enterprise, but whether this is done in fairness and justice or through tyranny will soon be up to the citizens of the future, who are now in school.

What we teach school children about themselves and their past can affect their future. The past can present new possibilities as in Charles Rowell's *Ancestral House*, in which it is shown that the idea of sharing a legacy is not about a single race or ethnicity, or single racial or ethnic construct.[64] The ancestral house is where "warring people ancient and modern become the one person who represents new possibilities in the Americas as multiracial, multicultural and with a new world of infinite possibilities."[65] "The past in time present and future" is passing through the "maelstrom of history."[66] Wilson Harris drew on the wounds of slavery and the African Diaspora to find emancipation. He urged us to escape from the "victim and captive," to reach out, "to pioneer" and ultimately to become the person in control at the helm of the ship.[67] To know our part in history, our own and collective ancestral house, is to reorient the slave ship of our past to all of our benefit, for regardless of our role as perpetrator, observer, or victim, we are all held as captives if we remain ignorant and act in ignorance. Omissions and misunderstanding are the mechanisms of the projected and self-inflicted cruelty of racism and ethnocentrism as it survives and shapes our lives. Through knowledge we can "begin to cool the water of the maelstrom," to become masters of our own destiny and to allow others to do the same in peace. What we teach in school is a gatekeeper for the future of humanity.

NOTES

1.   Charles H. Rowell, ed., Introduction, *Ancestral House: The Black Short Story in the America's and Europe.* (Boulder: Westview, 1995), pp. xxiii-xxiv, quoted from Ernest J. Gaine's "Three Men."

2.   While the ruling planter class in the Old South glorified war, it was not generally glorified. Merle Curti, *The Growth of American Thought* (New York: Harper & Row, 1964), p 654.

3.   Emily S. Rosenberg, *Spreading the American Dream: American Economic and Cultural Expansion, 1890-1945* (New York: Hill and Wang, 1982), p. 40.

4.   Ibid., p. 41.

5.   Quoted in Rosenberg, *Spreading the American Dream,* p. 41.

6.   Senator Albert Beveridge of Indiana, Congressional Record 56, Cong I session January 9, 1900 ,711.

7.   Rosenberg, *Spreading the American Dream,* p. 41

8.   Ibid., pp. 41 and 42.

9.   J. Hector St. John Crèvecoeur, *Letters from an American Farmer and Sketches of Eighteenth–Century America* (New York: Penguin Classics, 1986), p. 70.

10.   Rosenberg, *Spreading the American Dream,* p. 43.

11.   Ibid.

12.   Ibid., pp. 43, 44.

13.   Merle Curti, *The Growth of American Thought,* pp. 653, 654.

14.   Ibid., p. 655.

15.   Dated 1899, quoted in Curti, *Growth of American Thought,* p. 641.

16.   William Graham Sumner, Reply to a Socialist in *The Challenge of Facts and Other Essays* (New Haven. CT: Yale University Press, 1914), pp. 55-62.

17.   William Shockley, "Proposed Research to Reduce Racial Aspects of the Environment-Heredity Uncertainty," *Science,* 160 (April 26, 1968): 443; Arthur Jensen, "Social Class, Race and Genetics: Implications for Education," *American Educational Research Journal,* 5 (1968): 1-42; Richard C. Herrnstein and Charles Murray, *The Bell Curve: Intelligence and Class Structure in the United States* (New York: Free Press, 1996).

18.   Stephen Jay Gould, *The Mismeasure of Man* (New York: W. W. Norton, 1981).

19.   John Gabriel, *Whitewash: Racialized Politics and the Media* (New York: Routledge, 1998); Everette E. Dennis, Edward C. Pease, *The Media in Black and White* (New York: Transaction, 1997); Toni Morrison, *Playing in the Dark: Whiteness and the Literary Imagination* (New York: Random House, 1992).

20.   James Baldwin, "A Talk to Teachers," from an article, "The Negro Child— His Self Image," in the *Saturday Evening Post,* December 21, 1963. The original was delivered as a lecture on October 16, 1963.

21.   Theresa Richardson and Donald Fisher, eds., *The Development of the Social Sciences: The Role of Philanthropy* (Stamford, CT: Ablex, 2000), p. 15; Donald Fisher, "Boundary Work: Toward A Model of the Relation between Knowledge/Power," *Knowledge in Society,* 10, 2 (1988): 156-176.

22.   Alan Weider, "South Carolina School History Textbooks' Portrayal of Race: An Historical Analysis," in *Race and Education: Narrative essays, Oral Histories and Documentary Photography* (New York: Peter Lang, 1997), Ch. 10, pp. 126-127; Francis

Fitzgerald, *America Revisited: History School Books in the Twentieth Century* (Boston: little Brown, 1979).

23.   The opening to study nature was still based in theology until the mid to late nineteenth century. For example, William Paley, *Principles of Mental and Moral Philosophy* (Bridgeport, CN: M. Sherman, 1827, original 1785), espoused a common sense moralism based on a combination of Christian theology, scientific observation, and ethics identified with the moderate utilitarian philosophy espoused by Jeremy Bentham, *The Utilitarians* (Garden City, N.Y: Anchor Books, 1973) and Scottish Realism. Paley's influence was furthered by his pocket watch analogy in the introduction to *Natural Theology* (Trenton, N.J.: D. Fenton, 1824, first published in 1802). In the analogy, "man" encounters a watch and observes its workings and in doing so inevitably must conclude that it is the work of a "skilled artificer." The perfect operation of the watch in accordance with the laws of nature offered proof, according to Paley, of Gods existence. Jeremy Bentham's utilitarian philosophy and William Paley's moral theology prevailed in proto-scientific academic and popular thought until the "revolution" of the 1850s when the study of life and the universe moved away from its base in theology and turned to a naturalistic grounding. This occurred with the publication of Charles Darwin's *Origin of the Species* in 1859; Rudolf Virchow's, *Die Cellularpathologie* in 1858, (which established that all cells are derived from other cells); and Louis Pasteur's disproof of the spontaneous generation of organisms (all organisms come from other organisms), completing the establishment of the idea of genetic continuity over creationism. Robert Bannister, *Social Darwinism: Science and Myth in Anglo-American Thought* (Philadelphia: Temple University, 1979), pp. xiii-xiv, 13, 14, 19, 26, 36, 62. Herbert Spencer's adaptation of Darwin's natural selection to social theory in *Social Statics* (New York: D. Appleton, 1865) created a comprehensive cosmology that restated a moral sense doctrine against Paley and Bentham. See a review of *Social Statics* in the *Atlantic Monthly* 16 (1865), p. 383.

24.   Theresa Richardson, *The Century of the Child: The Mental Hygiene Movement in the United States and Canada* (Albany: State University of New York Press, 1989).

25.   Ibid.; Bannister, *Social Darwinism*; William Graham Sumner, with Albert Galloway Keller ed. *Science of Society* (New Haven: Yale University Press, 1927, original 1874).

26.   George Fredrickson, *The Arrogance of Race: Historical Perspectives on Slavery, Racism, and Social Inequality* (Middletown: Wesleyan, 1988); also Fredrickson, *The Black Image in the White Mind* ((New York: Harper and Row, 1971); A. Leon Higginbotham, *In the Matter of Color: Race and American Legal Process* (New York: Oxford, 1978), p. 375; David Roediger, *Toward the Abolition of Whiteness, Essays on Race, Politics, and Working Class History* (New York: Verso, 1994), and "White Looks: Hairy Apes, True Stories, and Limbaugh's Laughs," in Mike Hill, ed., *Whiteness: A Critical Reader* (New York: New York University, 1997), pp. 35-46; Alexander Saxton, *The Rise and Fall of the White Republic* (New York; Verso, 1990); Matt Wray and Annalee Newitz, "Introduction" in Matt Wray and Annalee Newitz, eds., *White Trash: Race and Class in America* (New York: Routledge, 1997), p. 4; Barbara Fields, "Slavery, Race, and Ideology in the United States of America," *New Left Review*, 95 (1990): 181; Thomas Gossett, *Race: The History of an idea in North America* (Dallas, TX: Southern Methodist University Press, 1963).

27.   Martha R Mahoney, "The Social Construction of Whiteness," pp. 330-333; Luther Wright, Jr. "Race and Racial Classifications," pp. 321-322, both in Richard Delgado and Jean Stefancic, eds., *Critical White Studies: Looking Behind the Mirror*

(Philadelphia: Temple University Press, 1977). Ian F. Haney López, *White by Law: The Legal Construction of Race* (New York: New York University, 1996).

28. Higginbotham Jr., *In the Matter of Color*, p. 375. Theodore Allen, *The Invention of the White Race: The Origin of Racial Oppression in Anglo-America*, Vol. II (New York: Verso, 1997), pp. 177-99; Theodore Allen, *The Invention of the White Race:* Vol. 1 *Racial Oppression and Social Control* (New York: Verso, 1994, 2000); Eric Williams, *Capitalism and Slavery* (Chapel Hill: University of North Carolina, 1944).

29. Allen, *The Invention of the White Race*, Vol. I. and Vol. II.

30. Allen, *The Invention of the White Race*, Vol. II.

31. Bill Ashcroft, Gareth Griffiths, and Helen Tiffin, eds., *Key Concepts in Post Colonial Studies* (London: Routledge, 1998), p.80.

32. Noel Ignatiev, *How the Irish Became White* (New York: Routledge, 1995); also see Karen Brodkin, *How Jews Became White Folks & What that Says About Race in America* (New Jersey: Rutgers, 1994).

33. This view coincides with Allen's argument as well as Williams' whose 1944 publication set off a controversy among historians. See Barbara Lewis Solow and Stanley L. Engerman eds. *British Capitalism and Caribbean Slavery: the Legacy of Eric Williams* (New York, 1987); Joseph Boskin, *Into slavery Racial Discrimination in Virginia Colony* (Philadelphia: Temple, 1976), pp. 101-112; James M. McPherson, Laurence b. Holland, James M. Banner, Nancy Weiss, and Michael D. Bell, eds., *Blacks in America: Bibliographic Essays* (Garden City, NY: Prentice Hall, 1971). More contemporary proponents of psycho-cultural historical arguments that racism caused slavery and that there are physical explanations for slavery and racism include: Winthrop Jordan, *White Over Black: American Attitudes Toward the Negro, 1550-1812* (Chapel Hill: North Carolina University Press, 1968); see the critique in Allen, Vol. I, 1994, p. 75; Carl N. Degler, *Out of Our Past: The Forces that Shaped Modern America* (New York: Harper & Row, 1959); "Slavery and the Genesis of American Race Prejudice," *Comparative Studies in Society and History*, Vol II, No. 1 (October 1959); *Neither Black nor White: Slavery and Race Relations in Brazil and the United States* (New York: MacMillan, 1971), also *In Search of Human Nature: the Decline and Revival of Darwinism in American Social Thought* (New York: Oxford, 1991) defends biological explanations for human behavior including slavery. This perspective is refuted by Dorothy Ross in her review in *American Historical Review* (April 1992): 608-9. The socio-biological views of geneticists Stanley Garn, *Human Races* Rev. 2nd Printing (Springfield Ill: University of Illinois, 1962); and Theodosius Dobzhansky, *Mankind Evolving: The Evolution of the Human Species* (New York: Yale, 1962) are used by Jordan and Degler. Both geneticists stress that genetics cannot offer any explanation or insight into the history of racism and prejudice. See Allen, *The Invention of the White Race*, Vol. I, p. 237, fn. 51. Most recently genetic research on DNA has proven that there is one human race with a gene pool that is nearly identical. Phenotypic differences in skin color are meaningless. There are more genetic differences between tall and short people than between people of European heritage and African heritage.

34. Theodore W. Allen, *The Invention of the White Race*, Vol. II and Vol. 1 *Racial Oppression and Social Control.*

35. Allen, *The Invention of the White Race*, Vol. I and Vol II; John Hope Franklin, *From Slavery to Freedom: A History of Negro America* (New York: Knopf, 1967); Edmund Morgan, *American Slavery-American Freedom: the Ordeal of Colonial Virginia* (New York: Norton, 1975), Reginald Horsman, *Race and Manifest Destiny* (Cambridge, MA: Harvard, 1981).

36.   Ulrich B. Phillips, *Life and Labor in the Old South* (Boston: Little and Brown Co., 1929) argues that slavery originated "unaware."

37.   Edmund S. Morgan, *Religion and Domestic Relations in 17th Century New England* (New York: Harper, 1944), pp. 110-1, 117-8, 128-9.

38.   Ibid.

39.   There is no "ancient pedigree of white racial prejudice" as argued by Ward M. McAfee, *Religion, Race, and Reconstruction: the Public School in the Politics of the 1870s* (Albany: SUNY, 1998), p. 78, citing Carl Degler, *Neither Black Nor White*.

40.   Edmund Morgan, *American Slavery-American Freedom: The Ordeal of Colonial Virginia* (New York, 1971); Morgan, "Slavery and Freedom: The American Paradox," *Journal of America History* (June 1972), pp. 5-6; Ira Berlin, "Time and Space and the Evolution of Afro-American Society on Mainland North America," *American Historical Review* 85 (1980): 44-78; Thomas R. Dew, *The Proslavery Argument* (Charleston: SC: 1852, reprint Negro Universities 1968); Edmund Burke, *An Account of European Settlements in America*, 2 Vols. (New York: Arno, 1972, original 1758). This is refuted by Jackson Turner Main, *The Social Structure of Revolutionary America* (Princeton: Princeton University Press, 1965); also "The Distribution of Property in Post-Revolutionary Virginia," *Mississippi Valley Historical Review* 41 (1954-5): 241-58; Gloria Main, "Inequality and Early America: The Evidence from Probate Records of Massachusetts and Maryland," *Journal of Interdisciplinary History* 7 (1976): 559-81; T. J. Wertenbaker *Patrician and Plebeian in Virginia, or the Origin and Development of Social Classes of the Old Dominion* (New York, 1910, 1958); Russell R Menard, *Economy and Society in Early Colonial Maryland* (New York: Garland, 1985); Allan Kulikoff, *Tobacco and Slaves: The Development of Southern Cultures in the Chesapeake, 1680-1800* (Chapel Hill: University of North Carolina, 1986).

41.   Eric Adler, Knight Ridder Newspapers, "Scholars: Slavery Shaped America, and History Without Slavery: U.S. May Never Have Been," *Tampa Tribune*, March 2, 1999, p. 1A, 17A cites Ira Berlin, *Many Thousands Gave: The First Two Centuries of Slavery in America* (Cambridge, MA.: Belknap Press of Harvard, 1998); and Orlando Patterson, *Rituals of Blood: Consequences of Slavery in Two American Centuries* (Washington: De Civitas/Counterpoint, 1998). Patterson is quoted.

42.   Thomas Ross, "The Rhetorical Tapestry of Race," in Delgado and Stefancic, eds., *Critical White Studies*, pp. 89-97.

43.   *Ibid.*, p. 89; *Dred Scott v. Sandford*, 60 U.S. 393 (1856); *The Civil Rights Cases*, 109 U.S. 3 (1883); *Plessy v. Ferguson*, 163 U.S. 537 (1896); U.S. Const. Amends, CIII & XIV.

44.   Bill Ashcroft, Gareth Griffins and Helen Tiffin, *Race and Colonialism: Key concepts in Post-Colonial Studies* (London: Routledge 1998), pp. 80-90.

45.   Cornel West, *Race Matter*, Gary Orfield and Carole Ashkinaze, *The Closing Door: Conservative Policy and Black Opportunity* (Chicago: University of Chicago, 1991); Doug Massey and Nancy Denton, *American Apartheid: Segregation and the Making of the Underclass* (Cambridge, MA.: Harvard University Press, 1993). DNA evidence shows that race is not a biological concept but remains a social construction of great importance in U.S. life and social relations.

46.   Allen, *Invention of the White Race*, Vol. II; Lopez, *White by Law*, Delgado and Stefancic, eds., *Critical White Studies*; Joe L. Kincheloe, et. al. eds., *White Reign: Deploying Whiteness in America* (New York: St. Martins, 1991); Matt Wray and Annalee Newitz, eds., *White Trash: Race and Class in America* (New York: Routledge, 1997); Mike Hill, ed., *Whiteness: A Critical Reader* (New York: New York University, 1997);

Matthew Frye Jacobson, *Whiteness of a Different Color: European Immigrants and the Alchemy of Race* (Cambridge, MA.: Harvard University Press, 1998); Richard Dryer, *White* (London and New York: Routledge, 1997).

47. Lauri Olsen, *Made in America: Immigrant Students in Our Public Schools* (New York: New Press, 1997).

48. Gary Howard, *We Can't Teach What We Don't Know: White Teachers, Multiracial Schools* (New York: Teachers College, Columbia University, 1999), p. 4.

49. *Ibid.*, p. 2; William H. Watkins, *The White Architects of Black Education: Ideology and Power, 1865-1954* (New York: Teachers College, Columbia University, 2001); Laurie Olsen, *Made in America*: Lisa Delpit, *Other People's Children: Cultural Conflict in the Classroom* (New York: New Press, 1995); Sonia Nieto, *Affirming Diversity: The Sociopolitical context of Multicultural Education* (New York: Longman Publishing U.S.A., 1996); National Center for Education Statistics, 1993.

50. Howard, *We Can't Teach*, p. 2.

51. Ibid., p. 52.

52. Ibid., pp. 59-62.

53. Ibid., pp. 58-59.

54. George Caleb Bingham, "Daniel Boone Coming through the Cumberland Gap," Oil Painting, Washington University St. Louis.

55. Oliver LaFarge, "Myths that Hide the American Indian," *American Heritage* (October 1956).

56. Charles Marion Russell, "Detail of an Oil Painting, original Montana Historical Society, Helena, Montana," reprinted in the *Worldbook Encyclopedia* (Chicago: Worldbook Inc., 1988), Vol. 20, p. 150.

57. Henry Nash Smith, *Virgin Land: The American West as Symbol and Myth* (New York: Vantage, 1950).

58. Hartnett, *Democratic Dissent*, p. 4.

59. Ibid., p. 2.

60. Patrick Gerster and Nicolas Cords, "Introduction to Lewis B. Wright, The Colonial Search for a Southern Eden," in Gerster and Cords, eds., *Myth and Southern History*, Vol. 1, *The Old South* (Urbana: University of Illinois, 1989), p. 17.

61. Cited in Patrick Cords and Nicolas Gerster, eds., *Myth and the American Experience* (New York: Glencoe Press, 1973), p. 92.

62. Norman F. Cantor, *The American Century: Varieties of Culture in Modern Times* (New York: Harper Collins, 1997), p. 508.

63. The quote is cited in Ignatiev and Garvey, *Race Traitor.* Walter Benjamin in *Illuminations* Trans. Harry Zohn, Intro. Hannah Arendt (New York: Harcourt, Brace & World, 1969), pp. 298-299, noted in response to the Holocaust: "there is no document of civilization which is not at the same time an act of barbarism." See Robert A. Williams, "Documents of Barbarism: The Contemporary Legacy of European Racism and Colonialism in the Narrative Traditions of Federal Indian Law." in Richard Delgado, *Critical Race Theory: The Cutting Edge.* (Philadelphia: Temple University Press, 1995), pp. 98-109.

64. Rowell, Introduction, *Ancestral House*, pp. xv-xxxviii.

65. Ibid.

66. Ibid.

67. Wilson Harris, "Appendix A," in Rowell, "Introduction," *Ancestral House*, pp. xxvi-xxvii.

BIBLIOGRAPHY

Adair, Douglass, "Jefferson Scandals," in Douglas Adair, ed., *Fame and the Founding Fathers: Essays by Douglass Adair.* New York: Trevor Colbourn, 1974, pp. 160-191.

Adair, Douglass, ed. *Fame and the Founding Fathers: Essays by Douglass Adair.* New York: Trevor Colbourn. 1974.

Adler, Eric. Knight Ridder Newspapers. "Scholars: Slavery Shaped America, and History Without Slavery: U.S. May Never Have Been." *Tampa Tribune,* March 2, 1999, pp. 1A, 17A.

Allen, Theodore W. *The Invention of the White Race: Racial Oppression and Social Control.* Vol. I 1994. London, New York: Verso, 2000.

Allen, Theodore W. *The Invention of the White Race: The Origin of Racial Oppression in Anglo-America.* Vol. II London, New York: Verso, 1997.

Angle, Paul M. ed. *The Complete Lincoln-Douglas Debates of 1858.* Chicago: University of Chicago, 1958.

Anyon, Jean. *Ghetto Schooling.* New York: Teachers College Columbia University, 1997.

Aptheker, Herbert. *Abolitionism: A Revolutionary Movement.* Boston: Twayne Publishers, 1989.

Aptheker, Herbert. "Negro Casualties in the Civil War." *Journal of Negro History,* CCCII (January 1947): 12, 4-48.

Aptheker, Herbert. ed. *A Documentary History of the Negro People in the United States, II: From the Reconstruction Era to 1910.* New York: The Citadel Press, 1951.

Argall, Governor Samuel. "Proclamation." 10 May 1618, 18 May 1618. Ref. No XXIII, List No. 7. Library of Congress in Susan Myra Kingsbury, *The Records of*

Race, Ethnicity, and Education: What is Taught in School, pages 281–299.
A Volume in: International Perspectives on Curriculum
Copyright © 2003 by Information Age Publishing, Inc.
All rights of reproduction in any form reserved.
ISBN: 1-59311-080-4 (paper), 1-59311-081-2 (cloth)

the Virginia Company of London. Vol. II. Washington DC: U.S. Government Printing office, 1933, p. 33.

Ashcroft, Bill, Gareth Griffiths, and Helen Tiffin, eds., *Key Concepts in Post Colonial Studies.* London: Routledge, 1998.

Ayers, Edward L. *The Promise of the New South: Life After Reconstruction.* New York: Oxford, 1992.

Ayres, Leonard. *Laggards in Our Schools: A Study of Retardation and Elimination in City School Systems,* New York: Charities Publication Committee, 1909.

Bailey, Thomas A. "The Mythmakers of American History." *Journal of American History,* Vol LV (June 1968): 5-21.

Baldwin, James. "Talk to Teachers" from The Negro Child—His Self Image. *Saturday Evening Post,* December 21, 1963.

Ball, Charles. *Slavery in the United States: A Narrative of the Life and Adventures of Charles Ball, A Black Man.* Lewistown: John W. Shugert, 1836 in Yuval Taylor ed. *I was Born a Slave: An Anthology of Classic Slave Narratives, 1770-1849.* Vol I. Chicago: Lawrence Hill Books, 1999, pp. 260-486.

Ball, Edward. *Slaves in the Family* New York: Ballantine Books, 1999.

Bannister, Robert C. *Social Darwinism: Science and Myth in Anglo-American Social Thought.* Philadelphia: Temple University Press, 1979.

Barot, R., H. Bradley, and S. Fenton, "Rethinking Ethnicity and Gender," in R. Barot, H. Bradley, and S. Fenton, eds. *Ethnicity, Gender and Social Change.* London: Macmillan Press Ltd. 1969, pp. 3-4.

Barot, R., H. Bradley, and S. Fenton, eds., *Ethnicity, Gender and Social Change.* London: Macmillan, 1969.

Beard, Charles A. and Mary R. Beard, *The Rise of American Civilization.* New York: The Macmillan Co., 1927.

Beard, Charles A. and Mary R. Beard, *A Basic History of the United States.* New York: Doubleday, Doran & Co., 1944.

Bell, Derrick. *Faces at the Bottom of the Well: The Permanence of Racism.* New York: Basic, 1992.

Bentham, Jeremy. *The Utilitarians.* Garden City, NY: Anchor Books, 1973.

Berlin, Ira. *Many Thousands Gave: The First Two Centuries of Slavery in North America.* Cambridge, MA: Belknap of Harvard, 1998.

Berlin, Ira. "Time and Space and the Evolution of Afro-American Society on Mainland North America." *American Historical Review.* 85 (1980): 44-78.

Berube, Maurice R. "The School Culture Wars in American School Reform: Progressive, Equity, and Excellence Movements." Westport, CN: Praeger, 1994.

Beveridge, Senator Albert. *Congressional Record.* 56 Cong. I Sess. January 9, 1900, p. 711.

Bingham, George Caleb. "Daniel Boone Coming through the Cumberland Gap." Oil Painting, Washington University, St. Louis.

Blassingame, John W. *The Slave Community: Plantation Life in the Antebellum South,* Revised and Enlarged. New York: Oxford, 1979.

Blum, John Morton. *Woodrow Wilson and the Politics of Morality.* Boston: Little Brown & Co., 1956.

Boskin, Joseph. *Into Slavery: Racial Discrimination in the Virginia Colony.* Philadelphia: Temple, 1976.

Broadus, Mitchell. *The Rise of the Cotton Mills in the South.* Baltimore: Johns Hopkins Press, 1921.

Brodkin, Karen. *How the Jews Became White folks and What that Says about Race in America.* Piscataway, NJ: Rutgers University Press, 1994.

Brook, Thomas, ed., *Plessy v. Ferguson: A Brief History with Documents.* Boston: Bedford Books, 1997.

Brown, Robert Maxwell. "Historical Patterns of Violence in America." in Hugh D. Graham and Ted R. Gurr, eds., *Violence in America: Historical and Comparative Perspectives: A Report to the National Commission on the Causes of Violence and Its Prevention.* Washington, D. C.: U.S. Government Printing Office, 1969.

Buckley, Gail. *American Patriots: The Story of Blacks in the Military from the Revolution to Desert Storm.* New York: Random House, 2001.

Buckley, Thomas E. "Unfixing Race: Class, Power and Identity in an Interracial Family." *Virginia Magazine of History and Biography.* CII (1994): 340-380.

Burke, Edmund. *An Account of European Settlements in America.* 1758 New York: Arno, 1972.

Burke, Edmund. "Letter to Hercules Langrishe, 3 January 1792." in *The Works of the Right Honorable Edmund Burke,* 6th ed. Boston, 1880, 4: 241-306, 4: 249-52, 4:305.

Burkholder, Mark A. and Lyman L. Johnson, *Colonial Latin America,* 4th ed. New York: Oxford, 2001.

Byerly, Victoria. *Hard Times Cotton Mill Girls: Personal Histories of Womanhood and Poverty in the South.* Ithaca, NY: ILR Press, 1986.

Caldwell, Charles. *Thoughts on the Original Unity of the Human Race. 1830.* 2nd ed. Cincinnati: J.A. & U.P. James, 1852.

Caldwell, Dan. "The Negroization of the Chinese Stereotype in California." *Southern California Quarterly,* 53 (June 1971): 128.

Canny, Nicolas P. "The Ideology of English Colonization: From Ireland to America," *William and Mary Quarterly,* 3rd series, Vol. 30, No. 4 (October 1973): 598.

Cantor, Norman F. *The American Century: Varieties of Culture in Modern Times.* New York: Harper Collins, 1997.

Cohen, David K. and Michael S. Garet. "Reforming Educational Policy with Applied Social Research." *Harvard Educational Review,* Vol. 45 (February 1975): 21.

Cohen, Louis, John Thomas, and Lawrence Manion, eds. *Educational Research and Development in Britain 1970-1980.* NFER: Nelson Publishing Co. Ltd., 1982.

Cohen, Sol. ed., *Education in the United States: A Documentary History.* Vol. V. New York: Random House, 1974.

Colburn, David R. and Jane L. Landers. eds. *The African American Heritage of Florida.* Gainsville: University of Florida Press, 1995.

Colfax, Richard H. *Evidence Against the Views of the Abolitionists Consisting of Physical and Moral Proofs of the Inferiority of the Negroes.* New York: J. T. M. Bleakley, 1833.

Coleman, James S. et. al. *Equality of Educational Opportunity.* Washington, D. C.: U. S. Government Printing Office, 1966.

Coleman, James. "Toward Equal Schools or Equal Students?" *The Public Interest,* No. 4 (Summer, 1966): 7.

Coleman, James. "Toward Open Schools." *The Public Interest,* No. 9 (Fall, 1967): 21-75.

Commanger, Henry Steele. ed. *Noah Webster's American Spelling Book.* New York: Teacher's College Press, 1962.

Commons, John R. *Race and Immigrants in America.* New York: The Macmillan Co., 1907.

Cords, Nicolas and Patrick Gerster, eds. *Myth and the American Experience.* New York: Glencoe, 1973.

Craft, Maurice and Alma Craft. "Multicultural Education" in Louis Cohen, John Thomas, and Lawrence Manion. eds. *Educational Research and Development in Britain 1970-1980.* NFER: Nelson Publishing Company Ltd., 1982, pp. 445-446.

Crèvecoeur, J. Hector St. John. *Letters from an American Farmer and Sketches of Eighteenth-Century America.* New York: Penguin Classics, 1986.

Crèvecoeur, Michel-Guillaume Jean de. "Letters from an American Farmer, 1793, Letter III." in Willard Thorp, Merle Curti, and Carolos Baker, eds., *American Issues Volume I: The Social Record,* rev. ed. New York: J. B. Lippincott, 1955.

Cubberley, Ellwood P. *An Introduction to the Study of Education* Revised by Walter Crosby Eells. Boston: Houghton Mifflin Co., 1933.

Cubberley. Ellwood P. *Changing Conceptions of Education.* Boston, Massachusetts: Houghton Mifflin, Co., 1909.

Cubberley, Ellwood P. 1919. *Public Education in the United States: A Study and Interpretation of American Educational History.* 1919, Boston, MA: The Riverside Press, 1934.

Curti, Merle. *The Growth of American Thought.* 1943. 3rd ed. New York: Harper and Row, 1964.

Curtis, Edmund and R. B. McDowell, eds. "Remonstrance of the Irish Princes to Pope John XXII, 1317." in *Irish Historical Documents.* London, Methuen, 1943, p. 41.

Cuvier, George. *Recherches sur les ossemens fossiles,* Vol. 1. Paris: Deterville, 1812.

Dahlie, Jorgen and Tissa Fernadno. eds. *Ethnicity, Power and Politics in Canada.* Toronto: Methuen Publications, 1981.

Daniels. Roger. *Concentration Camps U.S.A.: Japanese Americans and World War II.* New York: Holt, Rinehart, and Winston, 1972.

Daniels, Roger and Harry H. Kitano. *American Racism: Exploration of the Nature of Prejudice.* Englewood Hills NJ: Prentice-Hall, 1970.

Darwin, Charles. *Origin of the Species: By Means of Natural Selection or the Preservation of Favoured Races in the Struggle for Life.* 1859. Introduction by Julian Huxley New York: Mentor Book, New American Library, 1958.

Davis, David Brion. *The Problem of Slavery in Western Culture.* Ithaca, NY: Cornell University, 1966.

Davis, David Brion. *Slavery and Human Progress.* New York: Oxford, 1984.

Declaration of Independence, United States of America, Ratified July 4, 1776.

"Declaration of Principles of the Niagara Movement, July 13, 1905, Buffalo, New York." in Howard Brotz, ed. *Negro Social and Political Thought, 1850-1920.* New York: Basic Books, 1966.

Degler, Carl N. "Slavery and the Genesis of American Race Prejudice," *Comparative Studies in Society and History,* Vol II, No. 1 (October 1959).

Degler, Carl N. *In Search of Human Nature: The Decline and Fall of Darwinism in American Social Thought.* New York: Oxford, 1991.

Degler, Carl N. *Neither Black nor White: Slavery and Race Relations in Brazil and the United States.* New York: Macmillan, 1971.

Delger, Carl N. *Out of Our Past: The Forces that Shaped Modern America.* 1970 3rd ed. New York: Harper & Row, 1984.

Delgado, Richard. *When Equality Ends: Stories About Race and Resistance.* Boulder, CO: Westview Press, 1999.

Delgado, Richard, ed., *Critical Race Theory: The Cutting Edge.* 1995. Philadelphia: Temple University Press, 1999.

Delgado, Richard and Jean Stefancic. eds. *Critical White Studies: Looking Behind the Mirror.* Philadelphia: Temple University Press, 1997.

Delgado, Richard and Vicky Palacious, "Mexican Americans as a Legally Cognizable Class Under Rule 23 and the Equal Protection Clause." *Notre Dame Law Review* 20 (1975): 393.

Delpit, Lisa. "The Silenced Dialogue: Power and Pedagogy in Educating Other People's Children." in Lois Weiss and Michelle Fine, eds., *Beyond Silenced Voices: Class, Race and Gender in United States Schools.* Albany, NY: State University of New York Press, 1993.

Dennis, Everette and Edward C. Pease. *The Media in Black and White.* New York: Transaction, 1997.

Dew, Thomas R. *The Proslavery Argument.* 1852. Charleston: SC: Negro Universities 1968.

Dewey, John. "The Influence of Darwinism on Philosophy" in John Dewey, *The Influence of Darwinism on Philosophy And Other Essays in Contemporary Thought.* New York: Peter Smith, 1910.

Dickerman, G. S. *History of Negro Education,* Bulletin 38, United States Bureau of Education, Washington D. C. : U.S Government Printing, 1916.

Dobzhansky, Theodosius. *Mankind Evolving: The Evolution of the Human Species* New York: Yale, 1962.

Douglas, Davidson M. *Reading, Writing & Race: The Desegregation of the Charlotte Schools.* Chapel Hill, NC: University of North Carolina, 1995.

Douglas, Stephan A. "Speech at Chicago, July 9, 1858," in *Created Equal? The Complete Lincoln-Douglas Debates of 1858,* Paul M. Angle, ed., Chicago: University of Chicago Press, 1958, pp. 20-21.

Douglass, Frederick. "The Dred Scott Decision: Speech at New York on the Occasion of the Anniversary of the Abolition Society, 11 May 1857." in Paul Finkelman, *Dred Scott v. Sandford: A Brief History with Documents.* Boston: Belford, 1997, pp. 169-185.

Douglass, Frederick, *Autobiographies.* New York: Library of America, Penguin, 1994.

Durant Jr., Thomas J. and David Knottnerus. eds. *Plantation Society and Race Relations: The Origins of Inequality.* New York: Praeger, 1999.

Dryer, Richard. *White.* London: Routledge, 1997.

'Editorial,' *Anglo African,* April 20, 27, 1861, in James M. McPherson, *The Negro's Civil War: How American Negroes Felt and Acted During the War for the Union.* New York: Vintage , 1967, p. 18,

Ericksen, Thomas Hylland. *Ethnicity and Nationalism: Anthropological Perspectives.* London: Pluto Press, 1993.

Essex Historical Collections. Vol. III. October 1975.

"Ethnography and Ethnology," *Encyclopedia Britannica,* 9th ed. Chicago: R. S. Peale,1891, pp. 613-626.

Equiano, Olaudah. *The African: The Interesting Narrative of the Life of Olaudah Equiano.* 1789. London: The X Press, 1998.

"Ethnography and Ethnology." *Encyclopedia Britannica.* 9th ed. Chicago: R. S. Peale, 1891.

Fausz, John Frederick. "The Powhatan Uprising of 1622: A Historical Study of Ethnocentrism and Cultural Conflict." Diss. College of William and Mary, 1977.

Federal Register (July 9, 1997), Part II, pp. 36873-36946. Office of Management and Budget, Executive Office of the President . Washington D. C.: U. S. Gov., 1997.<http://www.whitehouse.gov/omb/fedreg/directive_15.html>.

Feagin, Joe R. and Hernán. *White Racism: The Basics.* New York: Routledge, 1995.

Fields, Barbara. "Slavery, Race, and Ideology in the United States of America." *New Left Review,* 95 (1990): 181.

Finch, John. *Travels in the United States and Canada.* 1833 London: Longman, Rees, Orme, Brown, Grun and Longman, 1844.

Finkelman, Paul. *Dred Scott v. Sandford: A Brief History with Documents.* Boston: Belford, 1997.

Finley, Moses I. *Ancient Slavery and Modern Ideology.* 1983. Harmondsworth, England. expanded ed. Princeton, NJ: Markus Wiener, 1998.

Fisher, Donald. "Boundary Work: Toward A Model of the Relation between Knowledge/Power." *Knowledge in Society,* 10, 2 (1988): 156-176.

Fitzgerald, Francis. *America Revisited: History School Books in the Twentieth Century.* Boston: little Brown, 1979.

Flecha, Ramón. "Modern and Postmodern Racism in Europe: Dialogic Approach and Anti-Racist Pedagogies." *Harvard Educational Review,* 69, 2 (Summer 1999):157.

Flynn Jr. Chester L. *White Land, Black Labor: Caste and Class in Late Nineteenth Century Georgia.* Baton Rouge and London: Louisiana State University Press, 1983.

Foner, Eric. *Reconstruction, America's Unfinished Revolution, 1863-1877.* New York: Harper & Row, 1988.

Franklin, Benjamin. "Proposals Relating to the Education of Youth in Pennsylvania," in Ed. Thomas Woody. *Educational Views of Benjamin Franklin.* New York: McGraw-Hill, 1931.

Franklin, Benjamin. "Idea of the English School," in Thomas Woody, ed., *Educational Views of Benjamin Franklin.* New York: McGraw-Hill, 1931.

Franklin, John Hope. *From Slavery to Freedom: A History of Negro Americans,* 3rd ed. New York: Alfred A. Knopf, 1967.

Franklin, John Hope and Alfred A. Moss, Jr., *From Slavery to Freedom.* New York: Alfred A. Knopf, 1994.

Franklin, John Hope. *Reconstruction. After the Civil War,* 1961. 2nd ed. Chicago: University of Chicago, 1994.

Franklin, John Hope. *Black Bourgeoisie.* New York: Collier, 1957.

Fredrickson, George M. *Racism: A Short History.* Princeton: Princeton University, 2002.

Fredrickson, George M. *White Supremacy: A Comprehensive Study in American & South African History.* New York: Oxford University Press, 1971.

Fredrickson, George M. *The Arrogance of Race: Historical Perspectives on Slavery, Racism, and Social Inequality.* Middletown: Wesleyan, 1988.

Fredrickson, George M. *The Black Image in the White Mind.* New York: Harper and Row, 1971.

Gabriel, John. *Whitewash: Racialized Politics and the Media.* New York: Routledge, 1998.

Galton, Francis. *Hereditary Genius.* London: MacMillan, 1869.

Garcia, Eugene E. *Hispanic Education in the United States. Raíces y Alas.* Boulder, CO: Rowman & Littlefield, 2001.

Garicia, Ricardo L. *Teaching in a Pluralistic Society: Concepts, Models, Strategies.* New York: Harper & Row, 1982.

Garn, Stanley. *Human Races* Rev. 2nd ed. Springfield Ill: University of Illinois, 1962.

Garvey, John and Noel Ignatiev, "The Editors Reply," *Race Traitor,* No 6 (Summer 1996): 37.

Garvey, John and Noel Ignatiev, Race *Traitor.* London: Routledge, 1996.

Gay, Peter. *The Enlightenment: The Rise of Modern Paganism.* New York: Alfred A. Knopf, 1966.

Genovese, Eugene. *Roll Jordan Roll: The World the Slaves Made.* New York: Vintage, 1974.

Gibbs, R. W. "Obituary for Morton," *Charleston Medical Journal* 1851, cited in Stephen Jay Gould, *Mismeasure of Man.* 1981. New York: Norton, 1996.

Gibbs, Wilma. ed. *Indiana's African American Heritage: Essays from Black History. News and Notes.* Indianapolis: Indiana Historical Society, 1993.

Ginsberg, Allen. "Howl" in Allen Ginsberg, *Howl and Other Poems,* 1956. Intro. William Carlos Williams. San Francisco: City Lights Books, Feb. 2001, p. 7.

Giroux, Henry and Peter McLaren. *Between Borders: The Politics of Cultural Studies.* New York: Routledge, 1994.

Glazer, Nathan and Daniel P. Moynihan. "Introduction." in Nathan Glazer and Daniel P. Moynihan, eds., *Ethnicity: Theory and Experience.* Cambridge, MA: Harvard University Press, 1975.

Glazer, Nathan and Daniel P. Moynihan. *Beyond the Melting Pot: The Negroes, Puerto Ricans, Jews, Italians, and Irish of New York City.* 1963 2ed. Cambridge, MA: The M.I.T. Press and Harvard University Press, 1970.

Gleach, Frederic W. *Powhatan's World and Colonial Virginia: A Conflict of Cultures.* Lincoln, NE: University of Nebraska, 1997.

Gobineau, Count Joseph Arthur de *The Moral and Intellectual Diversity of Races, with Particular Reference to Their Respective Influence in the Civil and Political History of Mankind.* Philadelphia: J. B. Lippincott, 1856.

Goddard, Henry. *The Kallikak Family: A Study in the Heredity of Feeblemindedness.* New York: MacMillan, 1912.

Goddard, Henry. *Feeblemindedness: Its Causes and Consequences.* New York: MacMillan, 1914.

Goodenow, Ronald K. and Arthur O. White. eds. *Education and the Rise of the South.* Boston: G. K. Hall, 1981.

Gossett, Thomas. *Race: The History of an idea in North America.* Dallas: Southern Methodist University Press, 1963.

Gould, Stephan Jay. *The Mismeasure of Man.* New York: W. W. Norton, 1981.

Graham, Hugh Davis. *The Civil Rights Era: Origins and Development of National Policy, 1960-1972.* New York: Oxford University Press, 1990.

Grantham, Dewey W. *The South in Modern America: A Region at Odds.* New York: Harper Perennial, 1994.

Greenberg, Jack. *Crusaders in the Courts: How a Dedicated Band of Lawyers Fought for the Civil Rights Revolution.* New York: Basic Books, 1994.

Greenfield, Gary A. and Don B. Kates, Jr., "Mexican Americans, Racial discrimination, and the Civil Rights Act of 1866," *California Law Review* 63 (1975): 662.

Guenbault, J. H. *Natural History of the Negro Race.* 1833. Charleston, SC: D. J. Dowling, 1837.

Hale, Grace Elizabeth. *Making Whiteness: The Culture of Segregation in the South, 1890-1940.* New York: Pantheon, 1998.

Hall, Perry A. *In the Vineyard: Working in African American Studies.* Knoxville, Tennessee: University of Tennessee Press, 1999.

Handlin, Oscar. *Race and Nationality in American Life.* Boston: Little and Brown, 1957.

Handlin, Oscar. *The History of the United States,* Vol. 2. New York: Holt, Rinehart and Winston. 1968.

Handlin, Oscar, Arthur Meier Schlesinger, Jr., Samuel Eliot Morison, Frederick Merk, and Paul Herman Buck. *Harvard Guide to American History.* Cambridge, MA: Harvard University Press, 1954.

Hannaford, Ivan. *Race: The History of an Idea in the West.* Baltimore: Johns Hopkins University Press, 1996.

Hartnett, Stephen John. *Democratic Dissent and The Cultural Fictions of Antebellum America.* Urbana-Champaign, IL: University of Illinois, 2002.

Hening, William Waller. *The Statutes at Large: Being a Collection of All the Laws of Virginia..."* 13 vols. Richmond: State of Virginia, 1809-1823.

Hitt, Jack. "Goodbye Columbus! Gavin Menzies is an Amateur Historian with a Bold New Book Declaring that the Chinese Discovered the New World in 1421.Was There Really a Chinese Junk Near Sacramento?" *The New York Times Magazine.* sect. 6 (January 5, 2003): 18-21.

Hero, Rodney E. *Latinos and the U.S. Political System: Two-Tiered Pluralism.* Philadelphia: Temple University, 1992.

Herrnstein, Richard C. and Charles Murray, *The Bell Curve: Intelligence and Class Structure in the United States.*New York: Free Press, 1996.

Higginbotham, A. Leon. *In the Matter of Color: Race and American Legal Process.* New York: Oxford, 1978.

Hill, Mike. ed. *Whiteness: A Critical Reader.* New York: New York University Press, 1997.

Hodgson, Godfrey. *America in Our Time: From World War II to Nixon.* New York: Vintage Books, 1978.

Hofstadter, Richard. *The American Political Tradition and the Men Who Made It.* New York: Vintage Books, 1976.

Hofstadter, Richard. *Social Darwinism in American Thought.* 1944. New York: George Braziller, Inc., 1955.

Hofstadter, Richard, William Miller, and Daniel Aaron. *The United States: The History of a Republic.* Englewood Cliffs, New Jersey. 1957.

Hollinger, David A. *Postethnic America: Beyond Multiculturalism.* New York: Basic Books, 1995.

Horsman, Reginald. *Race and Manifest Destiny.* Cambridge, MA: Harvard University Press, 1981.

Howard, Gary. *We Can't Teach What We Don't Know: White Teachers, Multiracial Schools.* New York: Teachers College, Columbia University, 1999.

Hughes, Everett Cherrington, et. al. eds. *Race and Culture: The Collected Papers of Robert Ezra Park.* Vol. I Glencoe, IL: The Free Press, 1950.

Hughes, Robert. *American Visions: The Epic History of Art in America.* New York: Alfred A. Knopf, 1997.

Hyman, Harold M. and William M. Wiecek, *Equal Justice Under the Law, 1815-1875.* New York: Harper & Row, 1982.

Ignatieff, Michael. "The burden: With a military of unrivaled might, the United States rules a new kind of empire. Will this cost America its soul—or save it?" *The New York Times Magazine.* sect. 6 (January 5, 2003): 22-27, 50, 53-54.

Ignatiev, Noel and John Garvey, eds. *Race Traitor.* New York: Routledge, 1996.

Ignatiev, Noel. *How the Irish Became White.* New York: Routledge, 1995.

Immigration and Naturalization Act of 1952, 8, 101 (a) (23), 66 Stat. 169 (codified as amended at 8 U.S.C. § 1101[a][23][1988]).

Immigration and Nationality Act § 1101 (a) (23) (1952).

"Jackson, Andrew to Thomas Pinckney, February 16, 1814." in John Spencer Basset, ed., *Correspondence of Andrew Jackson.* Vol. II. 6 vols. Washington DC: Carnegie Institution, 1926-1935, pp. 2-3.

"Jackson, Andrew to Thomas Pinckney, February 17, 1814." in John Spencer Basset, ed., *Correspondence of Andrew Jackson.* Vol. II. 6 vols. Washington DC: Carnegie Institution, 1926-1935.

" Jackson, Andrew to Thomas Pinckney, May 18, 1814." in John Spencer Basset. ed., *Correspondence of Andrew Jackson,* Vol II. 6 vols. Washington DC: Carnegie Institution, 1926-1935.

Jacobs, Harriet A. *Incidents in the Life of a Slave Girl, Written by Herself.* 1861. Cambridge: Harvard University Press, 1987.

Jacobson, Matthew Frye. *Whiteness of a Different Color: European Immigrants and the Alchemy of Race.* Cambridge, MA: Harvard University, 2000.

Jefferson, Thomas. "Notes on the State of Virginia." in Ed. Adrienne Koch and William Peden, *The Life and Selected Writings of Thomas Jefferson.* New York: The Modern Library, 1944.

Jefferson, Thomas. *Notes on the State of Virginia.* Edited by William Peden. Chapel Hill, NC: University of North Carolina, 1955.

"Jefferson, Thomas to Andrew Jackson, February 16, 1803." in Andrew A. Lipscomb and Albert E. Bergh, eds., *Writings of Thomas Jefferson,* 20 vols. Washington DC: Thomas Jefferson Memorial Association of the United States, 1904-1905.

"Jefferson, Thomas to Senator Breckenridge, August 2, 1803." in Peter L. Ford, ed., *Writings of Thomas Jefferson,* 10 vols. New York: G. P. Putnam's Sons, 1892-1899, pp. 1136-1139.

Jencks, Christopher. et. al. *Inequality: A Reassessment of Family and Schooling in America.* New York: Harper Colophon, 1973.

Jenkins, William Sumner. *Pro-Slavery Thought in the Old South.* Chapel Hill: University of North Carolina, 1935.

Jenks, Jeremiah Whipple and W. Jett Lauck. *The Immigration Problem: A Study of American Conditions and Needs.* 1911 (1912). New York, London: Funk & Wagnalls Co. 1926.

Jennings, Francis. *The Invasion of America: Indian, Colonialism, and the Cant of Conquest.* New York: Norton, 1976.

Jensen, Arthur. "Social Class, Race and Genetics: Implications for Education." *American Educational Research Journal,* 5 (1968): 1-42.

Johanningmeier, Erwin V. *Americans and their Schools.* Dallas: Houghton Mifflin Co., 1980.

Johnson. James Weldon. *Black Manhattan.* 1930. New York: Atheneum, 1968.

Johnson, Michael K. *Black Masculinity and the Frontier Myth in American Literature.* Norman, OK, University of Oklahoma Press, 2002.

Johnson, Paul. *A History of the American People.* New York: Harper Collins, 1997.

Jordan, Winthrop D. *White Over Black: Attitudes Toward the Negro, 1550-1812*. Chapel Hill: University of North Carolina Press, 1968.

Katz, Michael B. ed. *School Reform: Past and Present*. Boston: Little Brown and Co., 1971.

Kay, Mary Katherine. *The Immigration Problem: A Bibliography*. Madison, WI: n.p. 1909.

Kincheloe, Joe. L. et al. eds. *White Reign: Deploying Whiteness in America*. New York: St. Martins, 1998.

King, Wilma. *Stolen Childhood: Slave Youth in Nineteenth Century America*. Bloomington, IN: Indiana University, 1995.

Kingsbury, Susan M. ed. *The Records of the Virginia Company*. Vol. II. Washington DC: U.S. Gov. Printing, 1933.

Kluger, Richard. *Simple Justice: The History of Brown v. Board of Education and Black America's Struggle for Equality*. New York: Vintage Books, 1977.

Koch, Adrienne and William Peden. eds. *The Life and Selected Writings of Thomas Jefferson*. New York: The Modern Library, 1944.

Knottnerus, J. David. "Status Structures and Ritualized Relations in the Slave Plantation System," in eds. Thomas J.Durant Jr. and J. David Knottnerus, *Plantation Society and Race Relations: The Origins of Inequality*. New York: Praeger, 1999, pp. 137-14.

Kopytoff, Igor. "Slavery." *Annual Review of Anthropology*, XI (1982): 207-230.

Kovacs, Martin L. ed. *Ethnic Canadians: Culture and Education*. Regina: University of Saskatchewan, 1978.

Kulikoff, Allan. "The Colonial Chesapeake: Seedbed of Antebellum Southern Culture?" *Journal of Southern History*, 45 (1975): 525-526.

Kulikoff, Allan. *Tobacco and Slaves: The Development of Southern Cultures in the Chesapeake, 1680-1800*. Chapel Hill: University of North Carolina, 1986.

LaFarge, Oliver. "Myths that Hide the American Indian." *American Heritage* (October 1956).

Larson, Edward J. *Sex Race and Science: Eugenics in the Deep South*. Baltimore, MD: Johns Hopkins University, 1995.

Lefebvre, George. *The Coming of the French Revolution, 1975*. Translated by R. R. Palmer. Princeton, NJ: Princeton University Press, 1975.

Levinson, Bradley A. U. *We Are All Equal: Student Culture and Identity at a Mexican Secondary School, 1988-1998*. Durham, NC: Duke University, 2001.

Levine, Erwin I. and Elizabeth M. Wexler, *PL 94-142: An Act of Congress*. New York: Macmillan, 1981.

Lewis, Edward Rieman. *America, Nation or Confusion: A Study of Our Immigration Problems*. New York and London: Harper and Brothers, 1928.

Lewis, S. J., M. Clifford and S. J. Loomis. ed. trans. *The Spanish Jesuit Mission in Virginia, 1570-1572*. Chapel Hill, NC: University of North Carolina, 1997.

Library of Congress, *The Records of the Virginia Company of London*, ed. Susan Myra Kingsbury, Vol. II. Washington DC: U.S. Government Printing, 1933.

Licht. Walter. *Industrializing America: The Nineteenth Century*. Baltimore, MD: Johns Hopkins University Press, 1995.

Lincoln, Abraham. "House Divided Speech, June 16, 1858." in Roy P. Basler and Christian O. Basler, eds., *Collected Works of Abraham Lincoln*, second supplement. New Brunswick, NJ: Rutgers University Press, 1990.

Lind, Michael. *The Next American Nation: The New Nationalism and the Fourth American Revolution.* New York: Free Press, 1995.

Link, Arthur S. *Woodrow Wilson and the Progressive Era, 1910-1917.* New York: Harper and Row, 1954.

Linnaeus, Carolus. *Systema Naturae.* 1758. Stockholm: Rediviva, 1977.

Litwack, Leon. *Been in the Storm So Long.* New York: Alfred A. Knopf, 1979.

Locke, John. *The Works of John Lock.* 10 vols. St. John's Square, Clerkenwell, England: J. Johnson, 1801.

López, Ian F. Haney. *White by Law: The Legal Construction of Race.* New York: New York University, 1996.

López, Ian F. Haney. "Then What is White?" in Richard Delgado, ed., *Critical Race Theory: The Cutting Edge.* 1997. Philadelphia: Temple University Press, 1999, pp. 542-550.

Lott, Eric. *Love and Theft: Blackface Minstrelsy and the American Working Class.* New York: Oxford, 1993.

Lurie, Edward. *Louis Agassiz: A Life in Science.* Chicago: University of Chicago, 1960.

Luther, Seth. *An Address delivered before the Mechanics and Working-men of the City of Brooklyn on the Celebration of the Sixtieth anniversary of American Independence.* Boston, MA: n. p. 1836.

MacConnell, Dean. *Empty Meeting Grounds: The Tourist Papers.* London: Routledge, 1992.

Mahan, Alfred T. *The Interest of America in Sea Power.* Providence, RI: Little Brown & Co., 1897.

Mahoney, Martha R. "The Social Construction of Whiteness," in Richard Delgado and Jean Stefancic, eds., *Critical White Studies: Looking Behind the Mirror.* Philadelphia: Temple University Press, 1977, pp. 330-333.

Main, Gloria. "Inequality and Early America: The Evidence from Probate Records of Massachusetts and Maryland." *Journal of Interdisciplinary History,* 7 (1976): 559-8.

Main, Jackson Turner. *The Social Structure of Revolutionary America.* Princeton, NJ: Princeton University Press, 1965.

Main, Jackson Turner. "The Distribution of Property in Post-Revolutionary Virginia. *Mississippi Valley Historical Review,* 41 (1954-5): 241-58.

Manyoni, Joseph R. *Ethnics and Non-Ethnics: Facts and Fads in the Study of Intergroup Relations* in Martin L. Kovacs, ed., *Ethnic Canadians: Culture and Education.* Regina, University of Saskatchewan, 1978.

Martin, James Kirby, Randy Roberts, Steven Mintz, Linda O. McMurry, and James H. Jones. "America and Its People: A Mosaic in the Making." in *The Challenge: Latinos in a Changing California.* Sacramento: [California] Senate Concurrent Resolution 43 Taskforce, October 17, 1995< http://clnet.ucr.edu/ challenge/ polim.htm>.

Martin, Jr.,Waldo E. *Brown v. Board of Education: A Brief History with Documents.* Boston: Beford/St.Martins, 1998.

Martinez, George A. "Mexican Americans and Whiteness," in Richard Delgado and Jean Stefancic, eds., *Critical White Studies: Looking Behind the Mirror.* Philadelphia: Temple University Press, 1997, pp. 210-213.

Massey, Douglas S. and Nancy A. Denton. *American Apartheid: Segregation and the Making of the Underclass.* Cambridge, MA: Harvard University Press, 1993.

McAfee, Ward M. *Religion, Race, and Reconstruction: The Public School in the Politics of the 1870s.* Albany: SUNY, 1998.

McCarthy, Martha M. "The Pennhurst and Rowley Decisions: Issues and Implications." *Exceptional Children,* 49 (April 1983): 520-521.

McCormack, Ross. *Cloth Caps and Jobs: The Ethnicity of English Immigrants in Canada 1900-1914.* In Jorgen Dahlie and Tissa Fernando, eds., *Ethnicity Power and Politics in Canada.* Toronto: Methuen Publications, 1981.

McCullough, David. *Truman.* New York: Simon & Schuster, 1992.

McIlwaine, Henry Read. ed. *Executive Journals of the Colonial Council of Colonial Virginia, 1695-1702* 6 vols. Richmond, VA: Richard D. Bottom, State Library of Virginia, 1925-1966.

McPherson, Edward. *The Political History of the United States During the Great Rebellion.* Washington: DC: n. p., 1865.

McPherson, James M. *The Negro's Civil War: How American Negroes Felt and Acted During the War for the Union.* 1965. New York: Vintage, 1967.

McPherson, James M., Laurence B. Holland, James M. Banner, Nancy Weiss, and Michael D. Bell. eds. *Blacks in America: Bibliographic Essays.* Garden City, NY: Prentice Hall, 1971.

McWilliams, Carey. *North From Mexico: The Spanish Speaking People of the United States.* New York: Greenwood, 1968.

Mead. Margaret. *Ethnicity and Anthropology in America* in Lola Romanucci-Ross and George De Vos, eds., *Ethnic Identity: Creation, Conflict, and Accommodation.* Palo Alto, CA: Mayfield Publishing Co, 1975.

Menard, Russell P. *Economy and Society in Early Colonial Maryland.* New York: Garland, 1985.

Mendez et. al. V. Westminister School District of Orange County et. al. United States District Court of the Southern District of California, Central Division, February 19, 1946.

Merton, Robert K. "The Self-Fulfilling Prophecy," in Lewis Coser, ed., *The Pleasures of Sociology.* New York: American Library, 1980, pp. 29-47.

Meyer, Adolphe E. *An Educational History of the American People.* 1957 2nd ed. New York: McGraw-Hill, 1967.

Meyer, Adolphe. *Development of Education in the Twentieth Century.* New York: Prentice-Hall, 1949.

Meyer, August, and John H. Bracey, Jr. "The NAACP as a Reform Movement, 1909-1965: To reach the Conscience of America." *The Journal of Southern History,* 59, 1 (February 1993): 4.

Miller, Kirby A., Bruce Boling, and David Doyle. "Emigrants and Exiles: Irish Cultures and Irish Emigration to North America, 1790-1922." *Irish Historical Studies,* 40, (1980): 99.

Montesquieu, Baron de. Translated by Thomas Nugent. Introduction by Franz Neumann, *The Spirit of the Laws,* Book XV. 1731. London: Collier MacMillan, 1949.

Moore, Opal. "A Happy Story," in Charles H. Rowell, ed., *Ancestral House: The Black Short Story in the Americas and Europe.* Boulder, CO: Westview, 1995, p. 419.

Moreland, Lois B. *White Racism and the Law.* Columbus, OH: Charles E. Merrill, 1970.

Moreno, José F. ed. *The Elusive Quest for Equality: 150 Years of Chicano/Chicana Education.* Cambridge, MA: Harvard Educational Review, 1999.

Morgan, Edmund. *American Slavery, American Freedom: The Ordeal of Colonial Virginia.* New York: Norton, 1975.

Morgan, Edmund. *Tobacco and Slaves: The Development of Southern Cultures in the Chesapeake,* 1680- 1800. Chapel Hill, NC: University of North Carolina, 1986.

Morgan, Edmund S. *Religion and Domestic Relations in 17th century New England.* New York: Harper, 1944.

Morgan, David Pierpont. "Executive Summary." *The Challenge: Latinos in a Changing California.* Sacramento, CA: Senate Concurrent Resolution (SCR) 43 Task Force. <http://clnet.ucr.edu/ challenge/polim.htm>.

Morgan, Philip D. *Slave Counterpoint: Black Culture in the Eighteenth Century Chesapeake and Low Country.* Chapel Hill: University of North Carolina, 1998.

Morison, Samuel Eliot. ed. *Journals and Other Documents on the Life and Voyages of Christopher Columbus.* New York, Heritage Press, 1963.

Morison, Samuel Eliot. *Admiral of the Ocean Sea: A Life of Christopher Columbus.* Boston: Little, Brown and Co., 1942.

Morrison, Toni. *Playing in the Dark: Whiteness and the Literary Imagination.* New York: Random House, 1992.

Morton, John. *Woodrow Wilson and the Politics of Morality.* Boston: Little, Brown and Company. 1956.

Morton, Samuel George. *Crania Americana; or A Comparative Views of the Skulls of Various Aboriginal Nations of North and South America.* Philadelphia: J. Dobson, 1839.

Morton, Samuel George. *Crania Aegyptiaca, or Observations on Egyptian Ethnography, Derived from Anatomy, History and the Monuments.* Philadelphia: J. Penington, 1844.

Mosteller, Frederick and Daniel P. Moynihan, eds. *On Equality of Educational Opportunity.* New York: Vintage Books, 1972.

Moynihan. Daniel P. "Equalizing Education: In Whose Benefit?" *The Public Interest.* 29 (Fall 1972): 70-80.

Muldoon, James. "The Indian as Irishman." *Essex Institute Historical Collections.* 111 (October), 1975, p. 269.

Myrdal, Gunnar. *An American Dilemma: The Negro Problem and American Democracy.* 1944. Twentieth Anniversary Edition New York: Harper & Row, 1962.

National Industrial Conference Board, *The Immigration Problem in the United States.* New York: National Industrial Conference, 1923.

Naturalization Act of March 26, 1790. ch. 1, 3, 1 stat 103.

Nevins, Allan. *American Social History as Recorded by British Travelers.* New York: Henry Holt and Co., 1929.

Newman, Joseph W. "Antebellum School Reform in the Port Cities of the Deep South," in Chap. 2 David N. Plank and Rick Ginsberg, eds., *Southern Cities, Southern Schools Public Education in the Urban South.* Westport, CN: Greenwood, 1990.

Nieto, Sonia. Language, *Culture and Teaching: Critical Perspectives for a New Century.* Mahwah, NY: Erlbaum, 2001.

Nieto, Sonia. *The Light in Their Eyes: Creating Multicultural Learning Communities.* New York: Teachers College Columbia Press, 1999.

Nieto, Sonia. *Affirming Diversity: The Sociopolitical Context of Multicultural Education.* 2nd ed. New York: Longman, 1996.

Nobles, Melissa. *Shades of Citizenship: Race and the Census in Modern Politics.* Stanford. California: Stanford University Press, 2000.

"Notice of Shipping Men and Provisions Sent to Virginia by the treasurer and Co.in the Yeare 1619." *The Records of the Virginia Company of London* XLIX, 1619.

Nott, Josiah C. *Two Lectures on the Connexion between the Biblical and Physical History of Man.* New York: J. B. Lippincott, 1849.

Nott, Josiah C. with Samual G. Morton, H.S. Patterson, George R. Gliddon. *Types of Mankind or Ethological Researches . . .* 1854. Miami, FL: Mnemosyne Publishing Co., 1969.

Novack, George. "The Rise and Fall of the Cotton Kingdom." in George Novack. *America's Revolutionary Heritage.* New York: Pathfinder, 1976, pp. 181-220.

Ogbu, John and Margaret A. Gibson. *Minority Status and Schooling: A Comparative Study of Immigrant and Involuntary Minorities.* New York: Garland, 1991.

Ogbu, John. *Minority Education and Caste: The American System in Cross Cultural Perspective.* New York: Academic Press, 1978.

Ogbu, John. *The Next Generation: An Ethnography of Education in an Urban Neighborhood.* New York: Academic Press, 1974.

Olneck, Michael. "The Recurring Dream: Symbolism and Ideology in Intercultural and Multicultural Education." *American Journal of Education* 98, 2 (1990): 147-174.

Orfield, Gary. et. al. *Dismantling Desegregation: The Quiet Reversal of Brown v the Board of Education.* New York: New Press, 1996.

Orfield, Gary and Carole Ashkinaze. *The Closing Door: Conservative Policy and Black Opportunity.* Chicago: University of Chicago, 1991.

Ottley, Roi, and William J. Weatherby, *The Negro in New York: An Informal Social History, 1626- 1940.* New York: Praeger, 1967.

Paley, William. *Principles of Mental and Moral Philosophy.* 1785. Bridgeport, CN: Sherman, 1827.

Paley, William. *Natural Theology.* 1802. Trenton, NJ: D. Fenton, 1824.

Patterson, James T. *Grand Expectations: The United States, 1945-1974.* New York: Oxford University Press, 1996.

Patterson, Orlando. *Rituals of Blood: Consequences of Slavery in Two American Centuries.* Washington: Civitas/Counterpoint, 1998.

Patterson, Orlando. *Slavery and Social Death: A Comparative Study.* Cambridge, MA: Harvard, 1982.

Park, Robert E. "Racial Assimilation in Secondary Groups with Particular Reference to the Negro, Publications of the American Sociological Society." Vol. VIII . 1913. in Everett Cherrington Hughes, et. al., eds., *Race and Culture: The Collected Papers of Robert Ezra Park,* Vol. I. Glencoe, Illinois: The Free Press, 1950.

Phillips, U. B. *Life and Labor in the Old South.* Boston: Little, Brown and Co., 1929.

"Proceedings of the Asiatic Exclusion League." San Francisco 1908 in Sol Cohen, ed., *Education in the United States: A Documentary History* Vol. V. New York: Random House. 1974, p. 2971.

Quinn, David B. *The Elizabethans and the Irish.* Ithaca: Cornell University Press, 1966.

Ravitch, Diane. *The Troubled Crusade: American Education 1945-1980.* New York: Basic Books, 1983.

Rawick, George P. gen ed. *The American Slave: A Composite Autobiography,* Vol. 18, Unwritten History of Slavery (Fisk University), Contributions in Afro-American and African Studies Number 11. 1941. Westport, CT: Greenwood Publishing Co. 1972.

Richardson, Genevieve. "Divided Societies: Northern Ireland's Religious Struggles and Racial Struggles in the United States." *International Journal of Educational Policy, Research & Practice,* 1, 4 (Winter 2000): 509-529.

Richardson, Theresa. *The Century of the Child: The Mental Hygiene Movement in the United States and Canada.* Albany, NY: State University of New York Press, 1989.

Richardson, Theresa and Donald Fisher. eds. *The Development of the Social Sciences: The Role of Philanthropy.* Stamford, CT: Ablex, 2000.

Richardson, Theresa and Erwin V. Johanningmeier, "Intelligence Testing: The Legitimation of A Meritocratic Educational Science," in Marc Depaepe, ed., *The Development of Empirical Research in Education: Contributions from the History of Science.* Oxford: Elsevier Science, 1998, pp. 699-714.

Riggs, Marlon. Directed by, *Ethnic Notions: Black People in White Minds.* Oakland, CA: California Newsreel Video, 1986.

Riordan, D. M. "What Shall We Do with the Indians?" in W. W. Catlin, ed., *Echoes of the Sunset Club, Comprising a Number of the Papers Read, and Addresses Delivered Before the Sunset Club of Chicago During the Past Two Years.* Chicago: Howard, Bartels & Co., 1891, pp. 234-235.

Roediger, David R. *The Wages of Whiteness: Race and the Making of the American Working Class.* 1991. rev. ed. New York, London: Verso, 1999.

Roediger, David. *Toward the Abolition of Whiteness, Essays on Race, Politics, and Working Class History.* New York: Verso, 1994.

Roediger, David. "White Looks: Hairy Apes, True Stories, and Limbaugh's Laughs." in ed. Mike Hill. *Whiteness: A Critical Reader.* New York: New York University, 1997, pp. 35-34.

Rogel, Juan. "Letter of Juan Rogel to Francis Borgia, From the Bay of the Mother of God, August 28, 1572," in *The Spanish Jesuit Mission in Virginia, 1570-1572.* Translated and Edited by Clifford M. Lewis and Albert J. Loomie. Chapel Hill: University of North Carolina, 1953, pp. 119-20.

Rosenberg, Emily S. *Spreading the American Dream: American Economic and Cultural Expansion, 1890-1945.* New York: Hill and Wang, 1982.

Ross, Dorothy. "Review of Carl N. Degler." *American Historical Review* (April 1992): 608-9.

Ross, Thomas. "The Rhetorical Tapestry of Race." in Richard Delgado and Jean Stefancic, eds., *Critical White Studies: Looking Behind the Mirror.* Philadelphia: Temple University Press, 1977, pp. 321-322.

Roundtree, Helen C. *Pocahontas's People: The Powhatan Indians of Virginia Through Four Centuries.* Norman, OK: University of Oklahoma, 1990.

Rowell, Charles H. ed. *Ancestral House: The Black Short Story in the America's and Europe.* Boulder CO: Westview, 1995.

Russell, Charles Marion. "Detail of an Oil Painting, original Montana Historical Society, Helena, Montana," in *The Worldbook Encyclopedia.* Vol 20 Chicago: Worldbook Inc., 1988, p. 150.

Sampson, Z. Sidney. *The Immigration Problem.* New York: D. Appleton & Co., 1892.

San Miguel Jr., Guadalupe. *Brown, Not White: School Integration and the Chicano Movement in Houston.* College Station, TX: Texas A & M University, 2001.

Saxton, Alexander. *The Rise and Fall of the White Republic: Class, Politics and Mass Culture in Nineteenth Century America.* New York: Verso, 1990.

Schlessinger Jr., Arthur. *The Disuniting of America.* New York: Norton, 1992.

Schlessinger Jr., Arthur. "The Disuniting of America: What We All Stand to Lose if Multicultural Education Takes a Wrong Approach." *American Educator* 15, 3 (1991): 14, 21-33.

Schermerhorn, R. A. "Ethnicity in the Perspective of the Sociology of Knowledge." *Ethnicity*, 1 (1974): 3.

Schweninger, Loren. *Black Property Owners in the South, 1790-1915*. Urbana, IL: University of Illinois, 1990.

Senate Concurrent Resolution (SCR) 43 Task Force. *The Challenge: Latinos in a Changing California*. Sacramento CA: California State, 17 October 1995. <http://clnet.ucr.edu/ challenge/polim.htm>.

Shockley, William. "Proposed Research to Reduce Racial Aspects of the Environment-Heredity Uncertainty." *Science*, 160 (April 26, 1968): 443.

Sleeter, Christine E. *Multicultural Education as Social Activism*. New York: State University of New York Press, 1996.

Smith, Henry Nash. *Virgin Land: The American West as Symbol and Myth*. New York: Vantage, 1950.

Smith, Samuel Stanhope. *An Essay on the Causes of the Variety of Complexion and Figure in the Human Species*, Edited by Winthrop D. Jordan. Cambridge: Belknap Press of Harvard University, 1965.

Solomos, John and Les Back. *Racism and Society*. New York: St. Martins, 1996.

Solow, Barbara Lewis and Stanley L. Engerman. eds. *British Capitalism and Caribbean Slavery: The Legacy of Eric Williams*. New York: Cambridge University, 1987.

"Southern Manifesto." *The Congressional Record*, 84th Congress, 2nd session, March 12, 1956, pp. 459-64, 220-221.

Spears, John R. *The American Slave Trade: The Facts About the Overcrowded Ships and Brutal Masters in the Odious Traffic in African Slaves*. New York: Ballantine, 1960.

Spencer, Herbert. *Social Statics*. 1865. New York: D. Appleton, 1892.

Spencer, Herbert. *Principles of Sociology*. 2 vols Introduction by Jonathan Turner. New Jersey: Transaction, 2002.

Spring, Joel. *Deculturalization and the Struggle for Equality: Brief History of the Education of Dominated Cultures in the United States*. 3rd ed. Boston: McGraw-Hill, 2001.

Stamp, Kenneth M. *The Peculiar Institution: Slavery in the Ante-Bellum South*. New York: Vintage Books, 1956.

Stanton, Lucia. "Those Who Labor for My Happiness: Thomas Jefferson and His Slaves." in Peter S Onuf, ed., *Jeffersonian Legacies*. Charlottesville, VA: University of Virginia, 1993.

Stuart, G. *A History of American Education*. New York: Rinehart and Company, Inc., 1954.

Sumner, William Graham. *Folkways: A Study of Sociological Importance* . . . 1907. Boston: Ginn & Co., 1940.

Sumner, William Graham. "Reply to a Socialist." in *The Challenge of Facts and Other Essays*. New Haven, CT: Yale University Press, 1914.

Sumner, William Graham with Albert Galloway Keller ed. *Science of Society*. 1874. New Haven, CT: Yale University Press, 1927.

Takaki, Ronald. *Iron Cages: Race and Culture in the Nineteenth Century*. New York: Knopf, 1990.

Takaki, Ronald. *A Different Mirror: A History of Multicultural America*. Boston: Little Brown and Co., 1993.

Tawney, Richard H. *The Agrarian Problem in the Sixteenth Century.* New York: B. Franklin, 1912.

Taylor, Yuval. ed. *I Was Born a Slave: An Anthology of Classic Slave Narratives, 1770-1849.* Vol I. Chicago: Lawrence Hill Books, 1999.

Tawney, R. H. *The Agrarian Problem in the Sixteenth Century.* 1912. New York: B. Franklin, 1961.

Thomas, Brook. ed. *Plessy v. Ferguson: A Brief History With Documents.* Boston: Beford Books, 1997.

Thomas, W. I. *The Child in America.* 1928. New York: Johnson Reprint, 1970.

Thompson, Edward P. "Rough Music: Le Charivari Anglais." *Annales: Economic; Societés; Civilization* XXVII (March-April, 1972): 286-87.

Thornbrough, Emma Lou. "The History of Black Women in Indiana." in Wilma Gibbs, ed., *Indiana's African American Heritage: Essays From Black History News and Notes.* Indianapolis: Indiana Historical Society, 1993, pp. 67-85.

Thorp, Willard, Merle Curti, Carlos Baker. eds. *American Issues: The Social Record.* Vol I New York: J. B. Lippincott, 1955.

Thurow, Lester C. "Education and Economic Equality, *The Public Interest.*" 289 (Summer 1972): 81.

Tocqueville, Alexis de. *Democracy in America.* Edited and Translated by Garvey C. Mansfield and Delba Winthrop. Chicago: University of Chicago, 2000.

"Top secret contingency plan–dated July 23, 1972—rejected" *The Star Press* [Muncie, Indiana]. Wednesday, January 1, 2003, p. 3A.

Trevelyan, George M. *A Shortened History of England.* New York: Longman, Green and Co., 1942.

Turner, Frederick Jackson. *The Frontier in American History.* 1920. New York: Holt, Rinehart & Winston, 1940.

Turner, Patricia A. *Ceramic Uncles and Celluloid Mammies: Black Images and their Influence on Culture.* New York: Anchor, 1994.

UNESCO. *The African Slave Trade From the Fifteenth to the Nineteenth Century: The General History of Africa Studies and Documents.* Paris: United Nations, 1979.

United States Department of Health. *Education and Welfare, Final Report: Bilingualism in the Barrio.* 2 vols. Washington DC: Office of Education, Bureau of Research, August 1968.

Van Deburg, William L. *Slavery and Race in American Popular Culture.* Madison: University of Wisconsin Press, 1984.

van den Berghe, Pierre L. *Race and Racism: A Comparative Perspective,* 1967. 2nd ed. New York: John Wiley & Sons, 1978.

Virey, Julien Joseph. *Historie Naturel du Genre Humane.* 1810. Paris: Crochard, 1824.

Wagoner, Jr., Jennings L. "The American Compromise: Charles W. Eliot, Black Education and the New South." in Ronald K. Goodenow and Arthur O. White, eds., *Education and the Rise of the New South.* Boston: G. K. Hall, 1981.

Wallace, Kendra R. *Relative Outsider: The Art and Politics of Identity Among Mixed Heritage Students.* Westport, CT: Ablex, 2001.

Ward, James Murphy. *The Immigration Problem.* Popular Bluff, MO: Republican Printing, 1917.

Ward, Robert De Courcey. *The Immigration Problem, Its Present Status and its Relation to the American Race of the Future.* New York: The Charity Organization Society, 1904.

Warner, W. Lloyd. "American Caste and Class." *American Journal of Sociology* XLII, 2 (September 1936): 234-237.

Warner, W. Lloyd, Marchia Meeker and Kenneth Eells. *Social Class in America: The Evaluation of Status.* 1949. New York: Harper, 1960.

Warren, Stanley. "The Evolution of Secondary Schooling for Blacks in Indianapolis, 1869-1930." in Wilma Gibbs, ed., *Indiana's African American Heritage: Essays From Black History News and Notes.* Indianapolis, IN: Indiana Historical Society, 1993, pp 29-50.

Washington, Booker T. *Up From Slavery* in Ed. Louis Harlan. *The Booker T. Washington Papers.* Urbana, IL: University of Illinois Press, 1972.

Watkins, William H. *The White Architects of Black Education: Ideology and Power in America, 1865-1954.* New York: Teachers College Columbia University, 2001.

Webster, Noah. *Dissertations of the English Language: With Notes, Historical and Critical.* Boston: Isaiah Thomas and Co., 1839.

Weider, Alan, *Race and Education: Narrative Essays, Oral Histories and Documentary Photography.* New York: Peter Lang. 1997.

Weisberger, Bernard A. "A Quartet to Remember: Since the Civil War the Nation has sent Just Four African American's to the Senate. Why?" *American Heritage* (April 1999): 16.

Weiss, Lois and Maxine Seller, eds., *Beyond Black and White: New Faces and New Voices in U.S. Schools.* Albany , NY: State University of New York Press, 1997.

Wertenbaker, T. J. *Patrician and Plebeian in Virginia, or, The Origin and Development of social classes in the Old Dominion.* 1910. New York: Russell and Russell, 1958.

West, Cornell. *Race Matters.* Boston: Beacon Press, 1990.

Westminister School District of Orange County et. al. v. Mendez et. al. United States Circuit Court of Appeals. Ninth Circuit, April 14, 1947.

Wiencek, Henry. *The Hairstons: An American Family in Black and White.* New York: St. Martin's Press, 1999.

White, Deborah Gray. *Ar'n't I a Woman? Female Slaves in the Plantation South.* New York: W. W. Norton, 1999.

Whitton, Charlotte. *The Immigration Problem for Canada.* Kinston: The Jackson Press, 1924.

Whitten, Jr., Norman E. and John F. Szwed. *Afro-American Anthropology: Contemporary Perspectives.* New York: Free Press, 1970.

William, R. *The Leopard's Spots: Scientific Attitudes Toward Race in America, 1815-1859.* Chicago: University of Chicago, 1960.

Williams, Eric. *The British West Indies at Westminister, 1789-1823.* 1954. Westport, CT: Negro Universities Press, 1970.

Williams, Eric. *Capitalism and Slavery.* 1944. New York: Russell and Russell, 1961.

Williams, Gregory, *Life on the Color Line: The True Story of a White Boy Who Discovered He was Black.* New York: A Plume Book, Penguin, 1993.

Williams, Jr., Robert. "Documents of Barbarism: The Contemporary Legacy of European Racism, Colonialism, Narrative Traditions of Federal Indian Law." in Richard Delgado, ed., *Critical Race Theory: The Cutting Edge.* Philadelphia: Temple University Press, 1995, pp. 98-109.

Willinsky, John. *Learning to Divide the World: Education At Empire's End.* Minneapolis, MN: University of Minnesota, 1998.

Wilson, William Julius. *When Work Disappears: The World of the Urban Power.* York: Knopf, 1996.

Wilson. Woodrow. *History of the American People*. Vol. V. New York: Harper and Brothers. 1901.

Wood, Gordon S. *The Radicalism of the American Revolution*. New York: Vintage Books, 1993.

Wood, Gordon S. "Founding a Nation," in Arthur M. Schlesinger, Jr., General Editor, *The Almanac of American History*. New York: Barnes & Noble, 1993, pp. 16-23.

Woodson, Carter G. *Free Negro Owners of Slaves in the United States in 1830*. 1924. New York: Negro Universities Press, 1968.

Wortham, Stanton, Enrique G.Murillo, Jr. and Edmund T. Hamann. *Education and the New Latino Diaspora: Policy and the Politics of Identity*. Westport, CT: Ablex, 2002.

Wray, Matt and Annalee Newitz, "Introduction." in Matt Wray and Annalee Newitz, eds., *White Trash: Race and Class in America*. New York: Routledge, 1997.

Wright, Jr., J. Leitch. *Creeks and Seminoles*. Lincoln: University of Nebraska, 1986.

Wright, Jr. Luther. "Race and Racial Classifications." pp. 321-322, in Richard Delgado and Jean Stefancic, eds., *Critical White Studies: Looking Behind the Mirror*. Philadelphia: Temple University Press, 1977, pp. 321-322.

Young, Pai and Susan A. Adler. *Cultural Foundations of Education*. 2nd ed. Upper Saddle River, New Jersey: Merrill, 1997.

Zuppan, Josephine. "The John Custis Letterbook, 1724 to 1734." Masters Diss. College of William and Mary, 1978.

INDEX

Race, Ethnicity, and Education: What is Taught in School, pages 301–327.
A Volume in: International Perspectives on Curriculum
Copyright © 2003 by Information Age Publishing, Inc.
All rights of reproduction in any form reserved.
ISBN: 1-59311-080-4 (paper), 1-59311-081-2 (cloth)

Printed in the United States
1474400002B/1-42

9 781593 110819